Redefining British Theatre History

General Editor: **Professor Peter Holland**

Redefining British Theatre History is a five-volume series under the general editorship of Professor Peter Holland. The series brings together major practitioners in theatre history in order to establish ways in which previous assumptions need fundamental questioning and to initiate new directions for the field. The series aims to establish a new future for theatre history, not least by making theatre historians aware of their own history, current practice and future.

Titles include:

Michael Cordner and Peter Holland (*editors*)
PLAYERS, PLAYWRIGHTS, PLAYHOUSES
Investigating Performance, 1660–1800

Tracy C. Davis and Peter Holland
THE PERFORMING CENTURY
Nineteenth-Century Theatre's History

Peter Holland and Stephen Orgel (*editors*)
FROM SCRIPT TO STAGE IN EARLY MODERN ENGLAND
From Performance to Print in Shakespeare's England

Peter Holland and Stephen Orgel (*editors*)
FROM PERFORMANCE TO PRINT IN SHAKESPEARE'S ENGLAND

W. B. Worthen and Peter Holland (*editors*)
THEORIZING PRACTICE
Redefining Theatre History

D1288047

Redefining British Theatre History
Series Standing Order ISBN 978–0–333–98219–8 (Hardback)
978–0–333–98220–4 (Paperback)
(*outside North America only*)

You can receive future titles in this series as they are published by placing a standing order. Please contact your bookseller or, in case of difficulty, write to us at the address below with your name and address, the title of the series and the ISBN quoted above.

Customer Services Department, Macmillan Distribution Ltd, Houndmills, Basingstoke, Hampshire RG21 6XS, England

---

263 1633

Players, Playwrights, Playhouses

Investigating Performance, 1660–1800

Edited by

Michael Cordner

and

Peter Holland

Redefining British Theatre History Series
General Editor: Peter Holland
In Association with the Huntington Library

792.0941
PLA

First published in hardback 2007
First published in paperback 2010 by
PALGRAVE MACMILLAN

Palgrave Macmillan in the UK is an imprint of Macmillan Publishers Limited,
registered in England, company number 785998, of Houndmills, Basingstoke,
Hampshire RG21 6XS.

Palgrave Macmillan in the US is a division of St Martin's Press LLC,
175 Fifth Avenue, New York, NY 10010.

Palgrave Macmillan is the global academic imprint of the above companies
and has companies and representatives throughout the world.

Palgrave® and Macmillan® are registered trademarks in the United States,
the United Kingdom, Europe and other countries.

ISBN: 978–0–230–52524–5 hardback
ISBN: 978–0–230–25057–4 paperback

This book is printed on paper suitable for recycling and made from fully
managed and sustained forest sources. Logging, pulping and manufacturing
processes are expected to conform to the environmental regulations of the
country of origin.

A catalogue record for this book is available from the British Library.

A catalog record for this book is available from the Library of Congress.

10   9   8   7   6   5   4   3   2   1
19   18   17   16   15   14   13   12   11   10

Printed and bound in Great Britain by
CPI Antony Rowe, Chippenham and Eastbourne

Contents

Part 4   Representations

List of Figures

List of Tables

Notes on the Contributors

Paula R. Backscheider is Stevens Eminent Scholar at Auburn University. She is the author of *Spectacular Politics: Theatrical Power and Mass Culture in Early Modern England* (1993) and has published in *PMLA, ELH, Theatre Journal*, and many other periodicals. A former president of the American Society for Eighteenth-Century Studies, she has held NEH and Guggenheim fellowships and is one of the few American members of the Institute for Advanced Studies, University of Edinburgh. Her most recent book is *Eighteenth-Century Women Poets and their Poetry: Inventing Agency, Inventing Genre* (2005).

Helen Burke is Professor of English at Florida State University and is the author of *Riotous Performances: the Struggle for Hegemony in the Irish Theater, 1712–1784* (2003). She has written numerous essays on eighteenth-century English drama and literature and is currently researching a book on the Irish diaspora and the eighteenth-century London stage.

Mita Choudhury is Assistant Professor of English at Purdue University Calumet. She is the author of *Interculturalism and Resistance in the London Theatre: Identity, Performance, Empire* (2000) and co-editor of *Monstrous Dreams of Reason: Body, Self and Other in the Enlightenment* (2002).

Michael Cordner is Ken Dixon Professor of Drama and Director of the Writing and Performance (Drama/Film/Television) development at the University of York. He is the founding General Editor of Oxford University Press's Oxford English Drama and has himself published five editions of plays by Restoration and eighteenth-century dramatists. He also regularly directs productions of early modern drama, most recently James Shirley's Caroline comedy *Hyde Park*.

Michael Dobson is Professor of Shakespeare Studies at Birkbeck College, University of London. His publications include *The Making of the National Poet: Shakespeare, Adaptation, and Authorship, 1660–1769* (1992), *The Oxford Companion to Shakespeare* (with Stanley Wells, 2001), *England's Elizabeth: an Afterlife in Fame and Fantasy* (with Nicola Watson, 2002), and *Performing Shakespeare's Tragedies Today: the Actor's Perspective* (2006). He has also published a number of articles on Renaissance and eighteenth-century drama, and reviews regularly for the BBC, for *Shakespeare Survey*, and for *The London Review of Books*.

Lisa A. Freeman is an Associate Professor of English at the University of Illinois at Chicago and the author of *Character's Theater: Genre and Identity on the Eighteenth-Century English Stage* (2002). She is currently working on a new book titled *Anti-theatricality and the Body Politic: From the Renaissance to the NEA*.

Susan Cannon Harris is Associate Professor of English at the University of Notre Dame and the author of *Gender and Modern Irish Drama* (2002). She is currently at work on a project on Ireland and eighteenth-century theatre, and articles deriving from it have appeared in *PMLA*, *Theatre Journal*, and (imminently) *Princeton University Library Quarterly*.

Peter Holland is the McMeel Family Professor in Shakespeare Studies at the University of Notre Dame. Among his books are *The Ornament of Action: Text and Performance in Restoration Comedy* (1979) and *English Shakespeares: Shakespeare on the English Stage in the 1990s* (1997). He is currently editing *Coriolanus* for the Arden Shakespeare. He is also editor of *Shakespeare Survey* and general editor (with Stanley Wells) of *Oxford Shakespeare Topics* for Oxford University Press.

Robert D. Hume is Evan Pugh Professor of English Literature at Penn State University. He is the author of numerous books and articles, including *The Development of English Drama in the Late Seventeenth Century* (1976), *Henry Fielding and the London Theatre, 1728–1737* (1988), *Reconstructing Contexts: the Aims and Principles of Archaeo-Historicism* (1999), and (with Judith Milhous and others) *Italian Opera in Late Eighteenth-Century London*, Vol. 1: *The King's Theatre Haymarket, 1778–1791* (1995), and Vol. II: *The Pantheon Opera and its Aftermath, 1789–1795* (2001).

Matthew J. Kinservik is Associate Professor of English at the University of Delaware. He is the author of *Disciplining Satire: the Censorship of Satiric Comedy on the Eighteenth-Century London Stage* (2002) and *'The Production of a Female Pen': Anna Larpent's Account of the Duchess of Kingston's Bigamy Trial of 1776* (2004).

Judith Milhous is Distinguished Professor of Theatre at the Graduate Center of the City University of New York. She has published on many aspects of eighteenth-century English theatrical production and financing, including *Thomas Betterton and the Management of Lincoln's Inn Fields, 1695–1708* (1979), and, most recently, the two volumes of *Italian Opera in Late Eighteenth-Century London* (1995 and 2001), with Robert D. Hume, Gabriella Dideriksen, and Curtis Price.

Shearer West is Professor of Art History and Head of the School of Historical Studies at the University of Birmingham. She is the author and editor of a number of books, including *The Image of the Actor: Verbal and Visual Representation in the Age of Garrick and Kemble* (1991), *Fin de Siècle: Art and Society in an Age of Uncertainty* (1993), *Portraiture* (2005), and (as editor) *Italian Culture in Northern Europe in the Eighteenth Century* (1999). She has also published many articles on the relationships between art and theatre in eighteenth- and nineteenth-century England.

Series Introduction: Redefining British Theatre History

Peter Holland

On the surface, it doesn't look like much of a problem: conjoining the two words 'theatre' and 'history' to define a particular practice of scholarship has a long and illustrious history. Nor does it appear to over-complicate matters to add the word 'British', for all that the word is so furiously questioned at different moments of history (and especially at the moment). Yet what kind of history theatre history is and what kind of theatre theatre history investigates, let alone what the Britishness is of its theatre history, is endlessly problematic. For all the availability of shelves full of the outcomes of its practices, theatre history is in need of a substantial reassessment. This series is an attempt to place some markers in that vital project.

It is hardly as if theatre history is a new area of scholarly enquiry and academic publication. Within a general, varyingly academic mode of publication, one could point, in the UK, to the longevity of *Theatre Notebook*, a journal founded in 1945 by the Society for Theatre Research; its subtitle *A Journal of the History and Technique of the British Theatre* neatly sets out its scope and the assumed scope of theatre history. A number of US journals have had similar concerns, including *Theatre Survey* (from the American Society for Theatre Research) and more narrowly defined examples like *Restoration and Eighteenth-Century Theatre Research* or *Nineteenth-Century Theatre Research*. Lying behind such work is the complex institutional history of the formation of university drama and theatre departments on both sides of the Atlantic and their vexed and often still unformulated connection both to theatre training (the university as feed to a profession) and to departments of English Literature.

For the early modern period theatre historians might chart the subject's early twentieth-century history as being encapsulated by the work of E. K. Chambers (especially *The Elizabethan Stage*, 4 vols [Oxford: Clarendon Press, 1923]) or G. E. Bentley in his continuation (*The Jacobean and Caroline Stage, 7* vols [Oxford: Clarendon Press, 1941–68]), phenomenal individual achievements of documenting theatrical events, theatre performers and theatrical contexts. Their work might be matched for a later period by, say, E. L. Avery et al., eds, *The London Stage 1660–1800*, 11 vols (Carbondale, Ill: Southern Illinois University Press, 1960–8) or Philip Highfill, Kalman Burnim and Edward Langhans, eds, *A Biographical Dictionary of Actors, Actresses, Musicians, Dancers, Managers and Other Stage Personnel in London, 1660–1800*, 16 vols (Carbondale, Ill: Southern Illinois University Press, 1973–93). Further back still comes the fundamental work of such people as Boaden (*Memoirs of Mrs Siddons*, 2 vols [London, 1827]) and Genest (*Some Account of the English Stage from the Restoration in 1660 to 1830*, 10 vols [Bath, 1832]), who saw themselves neither as scholars nor as academics and yet whose work implicitly defined the accumulative function of data collection as a primary purpose of theatre history. Behind them comes the achievement of the greatest of eighteenth-century editors of Shakespeare, Edmond Malone.

Yet, seeing that there is a practice of theatre history is not the same as understanding or theorizing such a project. While many academics are engaged in the practice of something they would unhesitatingly term 'Theatre History' and while they would differentiate it carefully from a variety of other contiguous fields (e.g. performance theory or history of drama), there has been remarkably little investigation of the methodological bases on which the shelves of accumulated scholarship have been based or the theoretical bases on which Theatre History has been or might be constructed. Even within organizations as aware of the need for theoretical sophistication as IFTR/FIRT (Fédération Internationale pour la recherche théâtrale) the emphasis has been placed more squarely on performance theory than on the historiographical problems of theatre. In part that can undoubtedly be traced to the disciplines or institutional structures out of which the work has evolved: one would need to examine its early and still troubled connection to literary studies, to the analysis of drama and, most visibly, to the study of the history of Shakespeare in performance or, on another tack, to consider the ways in which theatre departments have structured their courses in the US and UK.

By comparison with the traditionally positivist accumulation of data that marks, say, *Theatre Notebook*, one could, however, see signs of the emergence of a new concern with the processes of historiography as it affects the specific study of a massive cultural institution like theatre in, to take just one significant example, the collection of essays edited by Thomas Postlewait and Bruce McConachie, *Interpreting the Theatrical Past: Essays in the Historiography of Performance* (Iowa City: University of Iowa Press, 1989). But while individual theatre historians are demonstrating an expanding awareness of the specific areas of historiography relevant to their work (e.g. economic history) and while theorizing of performance including its historical traces has grown immensely over the past 15 years, there is little enough to set out on a large scale the parameters of something that might hope by now to see itself as a discipline. The shelves of libraries and bookshops and the reading lists of courses do not show major resources for understanding what theatre history is, while an unending stream of books offering to help students understand the history of theatre pours from presses. In part this may be connected to the absence of departments of theatre history and the further substantial absence, within theatre departments, of courses concerned to do more than teach theatre history as an assumed and shared methodology based on an acceptance of what constitutes evidence and of how that evidence generates the potential for meaning.

Redefining British Theatre History sets out, extremely ambitiously, to make a major statement by bringing together, in the course of its series of five volumes, some fifty major practitioners in theatre history in order to establish ways in which previous assumptions need fundamental questioning and in which a future for the field can be enunciated in modes as yet undervalued. It aims to be a significant review of where we are and what we think we are doing.

The project began from an unusual collaboration between research library and publisher. My gratitude goes first and foremost to Dr Roy Ritchie of the Huntington Library and Josie Dixon of Palgrave Macmillan for contacting me to see whether I would develop a proposal that would create a series of conferences and subsequent volumes based on a single theme. Their support, not least financial, has been crucial in bringing the project to a reality both in the pleasures of the conference and the creation of this book. If we succeed, *Redefining British Theatre History* should chart the beginnings of a new future for theatre history, not least by making theatre historians newly and self-consciously aware of their own history, their practice and their future.

Introduction: Expanding Horizons

Michael Cordner

Theatre historians who work on the long eighteenth century enjoy primary resources which colleagues who specialize in earlier periods can only envy. It is true that, as Robert D. Hume remarks in this volume, a scholar working on the 1780s–90s is faced with a plenitude of different kinds of documentary evidence unavailable to one whose research focuses on the theatre either side of the 1688 Revolution. But, from the perspective of pre-1642 theatre history, the 1660s onwards afford a richness of materials (including eye-witness reports) and information (about, for instance, performance dates and casting), for which the earlier period provides no equivalent. With this relative wealth, however, come challenges and snares. Possessing the diary, for example, of an ardent and opinionated theatregoer like Samuel Pepys for the first decade of the reopened playhouses is an extraordinary boon. But it can lure the unwary into treating the testimony of this most obsessively idiosyncratic of observers as if it offers us unmediated and infallible access to majority opinion among the variegated array of fellow spectators with whom he patronized the two, newly established monopoly theatres. Deriving maximum benefit from the invaluable record he has left us, while avoiding reifying the rest of the audience into his clones, demands delicate calculations.

Similarly, the resources made available by two magnificent achievements of theatre history in the last century, *The London Stage 1660–1800* and the *Biographical Dictionary*,[1] stand dauntingly on the shelves, often referred to, but rarely read with the care and attention they demand, assumed instead to offer positivist and transparent information about the day-to-day performance calendar and the careers of theatre workers across the period. We may have conspicuously more to deal with than our colleagues working on early modern theatre; but what have we done with what we have? And what should we be doing now?

Hume's contribution to this collection is much preoccupied with problems of this kind. He identifies opportunities galore for innovative contributions to scholarship, but is also critical of much contemporary scholarly practice in the field and laments what he sees as unadventurous or misguided use of those resources which previous tillers in the archives have already placed at our disposal. The theatre history for which he legislates is one where 'the ultimate objective is illumination of plays in their theatrical, social, and political contexts'; and, as he surveys the current fruits of research, he discovers relatively little which fulfils

1

his ideal vision of what this definition might/should in practice produce. His analysis is accordingly peppered with statements which begin with variations on the lament that 'no one has ever attempted' one of a dozen or more eminently accomplishable projects which he then proceeds to specify. The positive aspect of Hume's discontents is, therefore, his recurrent insistence on all that remains to be achieved, whether in the reinvestigation of terrain already provisionally but unsatisfactorily mapped or in the exploration of performance arenas – as, for instance, the theatre of the fairs – which have so far received very little systematic attention. Not every hare he starts is pursued in the subsequent essays in this volume, and most of our authors occupy methodological and theoretical positions radically disjunct from Hume's own;[2] but their essays are all characterized by a matching desire to expand the boundaries of theatre history's inquiries in the long eighteenth century.

My own contribution, which is the only one in the collection focused on Restoration theatre, seeks to do this by resituating one of Aphra Behn's Exclusion Crisis comedies, *The Roundheads*, in a longer history which includes Civil War and Protectorate polemic and vigorous and scurrilous traditions of sexual slander which reach further back still. In the process it seeks to override the barriers which have traditionally separated the pre-1642 and post-1660 theatres into firmly demarcated academic specialisms, with little constructive dialogue occurring between them. Behn constantly drew inspiration from other playwrights' work, including scripts from more than half a century earlier, but, in the process, she also imprinted what she adopted with her own concerns and distinctive invention. Charting how this general proposition works in the particular case of *The Roundheads* reveals a dramatist alert to the pressure of earlier crises upon the plays to which she was indebted for provocation and inspiration, and also canny and imaginative in remodelling the latter in response to the convulsive political crisis which was still unfolding as she put pen to paper, and which was itself deeply inflected by the mid-century upheavals from which her source-texts had themselves derived. One of the most productive ways forward for Restoration theatre history may be to look backwards with a renewed curiosity and vitality of purpose.

Paula Backscheider's essay extends our vision in a different direction – to the substantial, richly suggestive, yet largely unexplored, engagement of the eighteenth-century novel with the theatre. The scale and range of the material identified reaffirms, in her view, the extent to which drama was, in this period, 'the dominant genre' and how thoroughly knowledge of it informed other modes of writing. The instances Backscheider cites notate and interrogate audience behaviour, generic histories, and performance styles across the century. She discerns a clear evolution in the ways in which such in-set scenes can be interpreted as seeking to shape and refine theatregoers' taste and connoisseurship, and illustrates an increasingly detailed and sophisticated alertness in them to the contrasts between the techniques and accomplishments of leading players. Spectators of the 1670s doubtless debated the relative merits, for instance, of Thomas Betterton and Charles Hart in rake roles; but it is only in the new century that such aesthetic controversies leave textual records behind them. Backscheider's analysis opens up an enormously fertile area of investigation for future theatre historians.

Judith Milhous introduces us to even more uncharted territory. She modestly remarks that the documentary evidence with which she is dealing 'requires extensive processing'. The devoted care and technical agility with which she solves the interpretative challenges posed by the surviving playhouse account books and related financial documents are both exemplary and revelatory, an exciting rethinking of primary documentation, much of which she has been responsible for identifying. Her discussion documents clearly how little solid information we have previously possessed about 'the internal dynamics of each company' and how often conventional preconceptions about crucial issues have been mistaken – for instance, the belief that writers producing 'formula' product for the stage in the eighteenth century could earn a living wage from that source alone. Her pioneering research brings fresh definition to key moments – for instance, the astonishing initial success and extended opening run of *The Beggar's Opera* – but it also contributes crucially to establishing the secure foundations from which a radically innovatory history of eighteenth-century theatre must in future be constructed.

Lisa Freeman and Matthew Kinservik retraverse more familiar ground, but in ways which open up distinctive new perspectives upon it. Both are concerned with the period's campaigns for theatrical reform and focus, respectively, on the two key events on which histories of that subject have tended to concentrate – the Collier Controversy at the close of the seventeenth century and the 1737 Licensing Act. Analyses of the former have usually prioritized its moral and aesthetic dimensions and after-effects. In contrast, Freeman seeks to develop an understanding of the political quarrels which were also, in her reading, being fought out through the paper warfare and treats the individual pamphlet contributions as 'cultural performances in themselves that need to be read and interpreted', with each of them promulgating its 'own readings of history' and its 'own articulations of the body public'. Ardent polemicists espousing a common anti-theatricalism can thus be revealed as yet irretrievably opposed in the way they understand the legacy and implications of the Civil War, while one deft strategy for defending the theatre's indispensable value to society is shown to be inspired by 'a desire to leave behind' the 'legacy of violence and upheaval' repeatedly recycled by such obsessive retrospection.

Kinservik argues an equally revisionist case. With an abundance of evidence, he demonstrates an extensive, but until now completely neglected, 'tradition of philo-regulatory schemes' in the decades preceding the 1737 Act – that is, expansively argued theorizing by pro-theatre writers which regrets the contemporary state of the drama, attributes much of the blame for its imputed decadence to the playhouses' dependence upon the vagaries of audience taste and the market, and recommends the firm intervention of the state to impose higher expectations, stringently monitor theatrical output, and offer rewards to those playwrights who can meet the demanding standards thus set. A fundamental premise in such polemic is the credo that 'a commercial stage is incapable of producing quality drama' – a belief which, Kinservik argues, also underpinned the later campaigning for a British National Theatre. He identifies modern assumptions that freedom of expression is a primary value as anachronistic when applied to the eighteenth century and illustrates how easily government arguments in favour of the Licensing Act could draw sustenance from this widely disseminated 'philo-theatrical' tradition.

Michael Dobson's contribution shifts attention from the world of exclusively professional performance to that of amateur dramatics, a milieu to which recent – and indeed earlier – scholarship has paid disappointingly little attention. He underlines the contrast between the industriousness with which non-professional performance has been documented and analysed in the pre-Civil War period and the relative lack of interest shown in the much more voluminous evidence of such activity surviving from the eighteenth century. His discussion is throughout characterized by a keen pleasure in bringing back into public view an array of fascinating stories and events. He gives special prominence to 'the boom in non-professional drama in the 1770s and 1780s', maps the variety and complexity of the ways in which professionals and amateurs interacted, and sketches the arguments which contemporary critics of amateur drama deployed. His exploration climaxes with a detailed account of a double-bill, mounted in 1774 by an all-female cast in the Cathedral Close at Salisbury, and the waves it created. Like Backscheider's essay, Dobson's opens up fertile terrain which invites further inquiry.

His concerns are also with theatre outside London, what was once disdained as 'provincial'. With the chapters by Susan Cannon Harris and Helen Burke the spotlight moves to the Irish theatre and Irish playwrights, a challenge to the exclusivity of conventionally articulated British focuses on theatre in the period. Harris tracks in exhaustive and revelatory detail the intricate mutations which overtake the script of Thomas Sheridan's *The Brave Irishman* across sequential performances in Dublin and, subsequently, London. Already itself an adaptation of a French original, which had undergone earlier reinventions and re-domestications before Sheridan decided to annex it, *The Brave Irishman* proves, in Harris's analysis, subtly responsive to changing political and theatrical circumstances. Her analysis makes finely honed deductions about the fit which can be observed between its differing versions and the moment and location of their first performance, and in the process closely maps the shifting, multiple implications of its marriage plot and of its strategic manipulation of competing, contemporary stereotypes of the Irish male.

Helen Burke's essay also moves between Ireland and England, but she adds a second polarity by querying the way in which 'a town/country opposition' has 'served as a key structuring and delimiting concept' in the construction of 'eighteenth-century Irish and British theatrical archives' and, therefore, in the scholarship derived from them. Theatrical historiography has thus concentrated on urban locations, while non-urban performance practices have become the preserve of other kinds of experts. Burke's examination both of the behaviour of Dublin audiences in the eighteenth century, as heavy migration from the countryside took place, and of the provocations and influences which generated *She Stoops To Conquer*, calls such a separation emphatically into question. Goldsmith's masterpiece emerges in a decisively new light once it is returned, as it were, to the Irish countryside, to which, in this account, it owes its birth, and to which, in another sense, it was also fated to return, via John O'Keeffe's itinerant impersonations of Tony Lumpkin.

In her contribution Mita Choudhury draws on the theoretical writings of Judith Butler to challenge some of the conventional assumptions frequently encountered in narratives of the development of eighteenth-century acting, which claim to identify substantive transformations in contemporary representations of such figures as Shylock, Othello, and Oroonoko. Her argument ranges across the whole period, but also looks forwards to Biyi Bandele's 1999 dramatization of the Behn novella for the Royal Shakespeare Company. She seeks to anatomize the status (and consequences) of the 'theoretical principle' of 'universality . . . as a prescriptive rule in the theatre' and detects a consequent inveterate 'tendency toward the normative' in performance practice, which makes her regard with intense scepticism the claims which have been made about a novel realism or a paradigm shift in the theatrical representation of 'the other' via, for instance, the artistry of David Garrick.

Peter Holland's essay also focuses on this greatest of eighteenth-century actors, but asks very different questions of, and about, him. Observing with regret how preoccupied theatre history is with 'the visual rather than the aural', he seeks to begin to redress the balance by exploring how much, if any, evidence can be retrieved about how Garrick sounded. The answer turns out to be: a great deal. By deploying material from the Garrick bibliography to which previous investigators, including the actor's biographers, have granted scant, if any, attention, Holland lays before us a mass of detailed testimony – not all of it flattering – about his selection and deployment of inflection, phrasing, pause, timbre, and tempo in particular passages. From this he gradually educes a sense of the artistic priorities which inform the choices these witnesses record, but also leaves us with the conviction that we too 'start to hear' Garrick 'better, not yet clearly but no longer quite so inaudible'.

Where Holland's project rests on mobilizing and using to best advantage previously unidentified material, Shearer West concludes the volume by asking how best we might interpret and deploy a kind of evidence ubiquitous in the period (especially its later decades), the decoding of which, however, poses many problems – the 'healthy quantity of portraits of actors and representations of the stage' which the eighteenth century has bequeathed to us. She resists the naive impulse to read such 'images as documentary and revelatory', explores the 'enhancement of the visual sphere' from the mid-century onwards, and seeks to develop 'more nuanced ways' of conceiving the multiple forms of spectatorship this enhancement fostered, and on which it depended. She maps the differences between watching actors in performance and viewing static images of them, but is also alert to the ways in which the two experiences can overlap and interrelate. She then exemplifies, via a series of case-studies, the intricacy of signification discernible in, for instance, Reynolds's famous portrait of *Mrs Siddons as the Tragic Muse*. Here, as throughout the collection, there is evidence aplenty of rich, new possibilities opening up for the study of British and Irish theatre in the long eighteenth century, ways of thinking that are designed to provoke and question, challenge and reorient, so that those archival riches and their modern printed representations can start to show us the world of performance anew.

Notes and references

1. See E. L. Avery et al., eds, *The London Stage 1660–1800*, 11 vols (Carbondale: Southern Illinois University Press, 1960–68), and Philip H. Highfill et al., eds, *A Biographical Dictionary of Actors, Actresses, Musicians, Dancers, Managers and Other Stage Personnel in London, 1660–1800*, 16 vols (Carbondale: Southern Illinois University Press, 1973–93).
2. See, for instance, Robert D. Hume, *Reconstructing Contexts: the Aims and Principles of Archaeo-Historicism* (Oxford: Oxford University Press, 1999).

Part 1
Drama, Theatre, and History

1

Theatre History, 1660–1800: Aims, Materials, Methodology

Robert D. Hume

'Theatre history' is a discipline much practised but severely under-theorized. Astonishingly little has been written about what the theatre historian is to try to do, how it is to be done or why it is worth doing. Collecting evidence about the theatrical past has been done and can be done, but to what end? With what aims and according to what principles? We now work in a postpositivist world and we cannot simply assume that cheery antiquarianism is a thing good in itself. In this essay I want to address both some general questions about the discipline and some very specific ones about the problems and possibilities of working in the long eighteenth century. A great deal of scholarship has been published in this area during the last sixty years. Surveying what has been accomplished since 1945 from the vantage point of 2005, I am struck by how much of it is good, but also by how patchy and limited a lot of it is. Investigating what has been done in such realms as texts, performance records, performers, physical production circumstances, economics, socio-political contexts and audience responses, I find myself forced to admit that theatre history is a badly balkanized field. Scholars have mostly been unadventurous and unimaginative – one could say timid. Singularly poor use has been made of *The London Stage* and the *Biographical Dictionary*. Fundamental differences in the practice of theatre history between the late seventeenth century and the later eighteenth century have been little understood and have received almost no comment from either practising theatre historians or theoreticians of historiography. I shall argue that we need to get out of our ruts and make more imaginative use of the evidence available to us. Theatre history is wide open for transformational changes, both within this period and more broadly. Indeed, I shall make the claim that the objects of theatre history need to include kinds of interpretation rarely practised within this discipline.

I. Defining 'theatre history'

I must commence by attempting a bit of clarification and disentanglement. Scholars from many disciplines and with wildly varying interests make use of drama and theatre in their work. 'Theatre history', 'theatre studies', 'drama criticism', 'biography', 'literary history', 'cultural history', 'cultural studies' and 'performance studies' (among others) overlap in messy ways and sometimes seem radically contradictory in their aims, methods, rules and conclusions. My concern in the present essay is almost entirely with the study of scripted performances in public theatres (mostly in London) during the long eighteenth century. In a present-day world in which 'theatre historians' may deal with pantomime, music halls, vaudeville, minstrelsy, celebrity culture and the concept of 'performance' as applied to almost anything, my angle of vision is deliberately quite restrictive. I believe that there is plenty of room for all sorts of scholarship and criticism on an enormous diversity of subjects. Freely granting that other enterprises have their own aims and rules, I am trying to suggest that a lot of exciting work remains to be done in the historical investigation of English theatre and drama 1660–1800 – and to establish some basic ground rules for 'good practice' in this realm. This said, I want to address a very particular problem: how should we conceive the aims and subject of this sort of history?

We must address two fundamental questions: First, what is 'theatre history' a history *of*? And second, what exactly do we mean by 'history'? The problem of subject is by now a chestnut. Almost all practitioners concentrate either on *plays* or on *theatres, actors and production circumstances*. These focuses are understandable in practical terms, but unsatisfactory. Drama and theatre are not the same thing, but they cannot be readily separated. Plays can be studied in isolation by drama historians, though the results are sometimes more than a little peculiar, given that the success and impact of the plays depends heavily on performance. 'Drama history' normally consists of chronological consideration of *new* plays, which is methodologically ludicrous.[1] After the early 1660s the vast majority of perform-ances in London were of *old* plays (many of them very old plays), which often had far more influence than new ones (most of which quickly failed and disappeared). Plays were usually written with particular performers in mind, a circumstance that strongly affected their structure, design, and content. A play analysed as a play must be considered in light of its performance circumstances. One can treat play scripts as literature in purely verbal terms, but this takes us out of the realm of 'history' and into that of 'literary criticism'. The latter has its uses and virtues, but it is essentially a different discipline.

Drama historians often want to remove their subject from the grubby particu-larities of performance circumstances. Contrariwise, theatre historians have often tended to avoid the subject of plays, odd though that may seem. (An eminent historian of the theatre in this period once said to me, 'How can you bear to read those awful plays?') Important scholarship can admittedly be done without much reference to plays. Leslie Hotson's *The Commonwealth and Restoration Stage* (1928), for example, hardly mentions them at all, though it is an admirable and important book. Theatre historians are of course right to say that studying the plays without attention to the buildings in which they were performed and the physical circumstances of performance is misguided. Yet to study theatre archi-tecture, stages, machinery, scenery, lighting, and costumes purely as ends in themselves seems perverse. I grant that most plays in our period have relatively limited 'literary' value and even the best suffer in comparison with Shakespeare.

I would take the position, however, that if the plays are of no interest, then neither are the theatrical circumstances in which they were produced. We are dealing with commercial theatre scripts, which have their limitations but also their own performance pleasures and considerable value as cultural studies artifacts.

By way of a first principle, I will offer the thumping cliché that 'theatre' and 'drama' need to be studied together. Often said, seldom done. Of course one may legitimately work on lighting, just as one may legitimately study gender implications in play texts, but the conceptual split between text and performance is ultimately not admissible. For a literary critic, perhaps. For a theatre historian, no. Consequently we need to commit to an *integrative* rather than a *separatist* model of scholarship. Of what this means in practice, more in due course.

My second basic question about 'theatre history' concerns the nature of the enterprise. In my view, 'theatre history' can legitimately cover such matters as plays, production circumstances, and the socio-political contexts in which the plays were written and performed. These are appropriate subjects for 'theatre history' – things it can be *about* – always supposing that relevant evidence can be found. Well and good, but just what do we mean by 'history'? Do we mean any form of antiquarian investigation in which the scholar digs up such evidence as may be found about the past (i.e. 'historical scholarship')? Or does 'history' imply or require a sequential narrative? Theatre historians often eschew narrative; drama historians normally insist upon it – though new plays taken in chronological order have no necessary connection to one another. We can legitimately write the life of an actor (Garrick) or the story of a company (Drury Lane under the triumvirate management, 1710–32), but if our subject is drama, then what constitutes the basis of our narrative? 'Literary history' is often written as though plays, poems and novels are self-propagating animals obeying some sort of Darwinian rules, but this is a metaphor, not a fact.[2] Serious historiographers have generally concluded that history is best conceived as 'problem solving', not as 'story-telling'.[3] I agree. Narrative is by no means *verboten*, but narrative is not the point of our enterprise.

Having rejected the text/production dichotomy and a 'story' basis for theatre history, I want at this juncture to leave definitional generalities and turn to three more specific methodological issues. These are the implications of postpositivist principles, evidentiary constraints, and the haunting problem of 'enforced omission'.

(1) *Postpositivism*. The Bad Old Positivist Horse is long dead; it has been flogged to bloody mush; and no great virtue now attaches to one's pious declaration of loathing for the beast. Some left-over positivists (mostly of a closet variety) could still be found forty years ago and no doubt there are even now some innocents who simply pay no attention to the philosophical underpinnings of intellectual constructs. Basically, however, we all now know that objectivity is essentially delusory and that 'facts' do not have significance in themselves (etc. etc.). Fine. We are all postpositivists now. What are the practical and operational implications of this state of affairs for the theatre historian?

Collecting facts is now understood to be insufficient in itself. Contrariwise, however, we need to remember that collecting facts (or perhaps we should say 'data') is not a bad thing. One might with some justice argue that if someone does not gather factual information then we have no solid foundation on which to base any kind of historical investigation. If we do not possess data verifiable to some degree, then what we write is basically going to be fantasy fiction. This may be brilliant, amusing, and happy-making, but is it theatre history? Rejecting positivism is no ground for glorifying sloppiness, inaccuracy, and uncritical extrapolation of conclusions not subject to any form of proof. The inadequacies of positivism do not justify our using any ex-post-facto anecdote that happens to suit our prejudices.[4] By any logic I can find, postpositivism is a ground for demanding greater rigour in assembling and testing evidence, not for abandonment of all concern with its verification.[5]

Claims for a new, postpositivist theatre history were conspicuously mounted twenty years ago in an important essay by Bruce McConachie.[6] His biting analysis of Oscar G. Brockett's abominable *History of the Theatre* textbook (originally published in 1968 and still widely in use today in later editions) was admirable and overdue; his marxist demands for 'socio-criticism' made sense then and still do now. Viewed in retrospect, however, the essay does not get very far into the business of establishing a new set of principles for theatre history. The central thrust of the piece is actually a claim for the importance of scholarly attention to the social milieus in which plays were written, performed and received.

Tidy pigeonhole construction is not my ambition here, but McConachie's passionate and quite legitimate insistence on the importance of socio-political criticism invites some reconsideration of how we can most fruitfully conceive our enterprise(s). To define 'theatre history' as the collection of data and the reconstruction of performance conditions is excessively limiting and trivializing. At the other extreme, utilizing plays and performance as evidence for broader kinds of cultural studies analysis (which is where McConachie seems to be heading) takes us into markedly different kinds of projects. One of my fundamental points in this essay is to insist that *Interpretation of texts within their historical performance circumstances is an appropriate occupation for a theatre historian.* Where texts are being analysed for present-day literary meaning or dramaturgical potentialities, we are perhaps more in the realm of critical analysis than 'history'. There are no precise boundaries here and trying to impose them is misguided. We may usefully recognize, however, that different enterprises have different aims and rules.

I would suggest that one crucial function of the theatre historian is *To demonstrate how production and performance circumstances affected the writing and public impact of plays.* Depending on the availability of evidence, this may involve study of architecture, acting style, scenery, lighting, costume, the sociology of playwriting, company ownership and management, ticket prices, audience demographics, censorship, repertory, current events, and critical precepts of the time.[7] The theatre historian will always hope to be able to document the spectrum of public response to plays, performance and performers. He or she has the right – indeed, the obligation – to analyse plays and their performance in ways that help us comprehend why they were written, performed and received as they were. Textual analysis is an entirely legitimate part of theatre history and so is the kind of ideological and political analysis that treats the intellectual *content* and implications of the play as well as its genre and performance history. I would argue, however, that when we start to analyse a script towards present-day performance we are starting to undertake a different function. And when we use plays as evidence for cultural studies analysis (however historical in site), then we are definitely putting on a different hat and engaging in another kind of enterprise.

An essential difference among the three – theatre history, dramaturgical analysis and cultural studies – is that they have radically different claims to truth and different forms of verification. Theatre history, if it is anything but a self-indulgent game carried on for the self-aggrandizement of the historian, attempts to be *true*, to arrive at conclusions that will stand up under serious scrutiny and meet severe tests of evidentiary interpretation and challenge. Dramaturgical analysis makes no such claims: if an interpretation is effectively producible then it possesses a kind of legitimacy, even if the playwright never thought of it and the script has never yet been performed that way. Ernest Jones's Oedipal interpretation of *Hamlet* is a famous example. Cultural studies is another matter: such 'proofs' as can be offered of its conclusions are rarely of a sort even potentially susceptible of rigorous demonstration, so that two interpreters looking at the same body of evidence may arrive at radically incommensurable results with neither of them being 'wrong'. As an estimable illustration of such work I will offer James Grantham Turner's *Libertines and Radicals in Early Modern London: Sexuality, Politics and Literary Culture, 1630–1685* (2002). All three are valuable disciplines and the same person may at different times engage in all of them.[8] My point is merely that 'theatre history' (if seriously practised) makes a different kind of 'truth claim' and must be judged on that basis.

(2) *The limits of evidence.* What can be usefully investigated by the theatre historian necessarily depends on the evidence that can be found – something that changes enormously in the period at issue. If we look, for example, at Postlewait's excellent essay on historiographic practice, we will find that much of what he says is essentially irrelevant to anything that can be done in the eighteenth century.[9] His test case is the first London production of Ibsen's *A Doll's House* (1889). The kinds of evidence available at that date and for that particular event are simply not to be had for *any* theatrical performance before the nineteenth century. We have to accept the limits of our knowledge. We will probably never know much about the costumes worn in Shakespeare's day. We can only guess at what most of the scenery in Betterton's theatres looked like. The reception of *The Conquest of Granada* is essentially unreconstructable except by conjecture and will very likely always remain that way. If we insist upon speculating or fabricating 'evidence' about playwrights out of their plays or indulging in 'must have' claims, then the result is to destroy any real value that theatre history (or history of any kind) can have.[10]

Evidentiary issues are particularly tricky in the 1660–1800 period because the nature of what is available changes so drastically between those dates. Prior to

1705 we often know no more than five or ten per cent of what was performed night by night in a given season in London. After that, our performance records are close to 100 per cent complete, at least for theatres operated under a patent or royal licence. Our knowledge of late seventeenth-century theatre buildings is radically conjectural; of late eighteenth-century theatres, relatively detailed and precise. We do possess printed texts of a large majority of the plays professionally performed in London throughout the period, though extant promptbooks give us painfully little help in reconstructing production concepts and performance practices.[11] Not until late in the eighteenth century, however, do newspapers start to do detailed and systematic reviewing and even when they do we cannot build with much confidence on what they tell us. Because of evidentiary differences, working in the 1690s is a startlingly different enterprise from working in the 1790s (or even the 1730s) – a fact well known to practitioners who have attempted both, but little commented upon in print.

Whether the pertinent evidence is scanty or overwhelming, it needs to be known and used. Enormous amounts of new documentary material have been discovered in the last half century, long after pioneers like Hotson and Nicoll seemed to have exhausted the possibilities – or so a lot of people thought when I was a graduate student. I have no doubt (based on a lifetime of archival scholarship) that major discoveries are yet to come. Exciting as this is, we should not fail to make use of what is already known. One of the recurring themes of this essay is the frequency with which scholars under-use or ignore (or perhaps simply do not know about) major bibliographical and archival sources. I have counted seventeen separate occasions on which I have pointed to instances of such failure. I am sorry to seem monotonous, but this really is important.

(3) *Enforced omission.* Except where evidence is largely lacking or where the subject is extremely limited, almost all 'histories' are radically selective because they have to be. As an example, let me instance a chapter I wrote on 'Drama and Theatre in the Mid and Later Eighteenth Century.'[12] I was asked to cover the period 1730–1790 in thirty typescript pages. Some nine hundred professionally staged, attributed new plays from these years survive. Of necessity, I had basically to state and then ignore the fact that about 85 per cent of the performances at Covent Garden and Drury Lane were of *old* plays. I had no space to deal with adaptations, though there were a lot of important ones. The beginning and ending dates had virtually no logic in either drama history or theatre history: they were simply given to me by the publisher. I could not discuss parallels in the novel or influences from the novel. Gothicism and the picturesque had essentially to be ignored, as did the social and political issues that became so important in the 1790s. Dance was a conspicuous, important and expensive part of theatrical offerings, but I had no space to discuss it. I managed to name some eight-five plays *en passant* (and about twenty older ones for comparison), but the selection was a mish-mash of titles then popular and others now critically esteemed. Value judgements about dramatic genres had to be imposed: I could do no more than mention the enormous importance of pantomime and musicals, which conveys a badly distorted sense of theatregoers' experience at the time. The numerous and

important non-English sources and influences had to be ignored.[13] Discussion of the impact of staging was simply a lost cause. Make no mistake about it: 'History' is almost always a radically selective representation whose construction is heavily influenced by publication constraints and the objectives and prejudices of the history writer. This is essentially unavoidable, but an honest historian can at least bluntly disclose choices, prejudices and suppressions. Much can be said in favour of 'microhistory', but of course it cannot supply the big-picture overviews that even scholars seem to crave.

So where does this leave us? As I conceive our enterprise, the theatre historian needs to commit to the principle that the ultimate objective is illumination of plays in their theatrical, social and political contexts. He or she also needs to submit to the constraints of 'good practice'. Analysis of playscripts is very much a legitimate (indeed a vital) part of the overall undertaking. 'Narrative' history is appropriate in treating individuals and institutions – but not in drama history. Where the objectives and claims go beyond the realms of particularizable evidence, then one is practising something other than theatre history. Failure to respect the limits of available evidence produces shoddy scholarship at best. The often radical selectivity inevitable in all but the smallest-scale 'history' needs to be acknowledged bluntly by the historian and understood by the reader. Such are my assumptions about 'good practice' in principle. With these stipulations in mind, we are ready to consider the particularities of theatre history in the long eighteenth century.

II. Texts

Between 1660 and 1800 more than 2,400 'new' plays were professionally staged in London. This total includes both mainpieces and afterpieces and it includes quite a lot of translations and adaptations.[14] Consequently no exact definition of 'new' can be given. A very high proportion of the plays were published within weeks or months of their performance (in striking contrast to pre-1642 drama). Most were made available half a century ago on Readex Microcards and almost all are now even more accessible in electronic form via EEBO and ECCO.[15] Many post-1737 plays for the patent theatres also exist in the 'Larpent manuscripts' submitted to the censor (now in the Huntington Library). In the realm of texts, copious evidence survives.[16]

Of these hundreds of plays, only about twenty-five have received more than cursory critical analysis. The sole attempt at an overall critical survey is the first three volumes of Allardyce Nicoll's *History*, which contains valuable lists of known plays but which does little more than offer simplistic categorizations while delivering some offhand value judgements.[17] Two attempts have been made at comprehensive surveys of late seventeenth-century plays,[18] but large portions of eighteenth-century drama remain essentially unstudied since Nicoll issued his crude map in the 1920s and early 1930s. Book after book has been devoted to the plays of Etherege, Wycherley and Congreve – though most of them exhibit almost complete ignorance of other plays of their time. Quite a lot has been published on Dryden's 'heroic' plays (but singularly little about most of the rest of his output). Many studies have been made of *The Beggar's Opera*, though the only full-dress investigation of ballad opera came out in 1937 and ignores the music.[19] One will find a smattering of attention to the work of Farquhar, Fielding and Sheridan. Aphra Behn has enjoyed a boom in recent years. Overall, both the quantity and the quality of the modern criticism of this drama must be considered disappointing. The reason for this is simple. For the most part, these plays are highly effective theatrical vehicles, but they tend to possess little literary depth. They do not provide the complexities and ambiguities dear to teachers of English literature, to whom they offer little challenge. In explicative terms, these plays are usually unproblematical.

We have a huge number of playscripts for this period. What ought we to be doing with them? A good beginning is to try to understand the nature of the plays. Only towards the end of the seventeenth century did 'originality' become much of a desideratum and by the end of the eighteenth the theatres were more interested in the broad appeal that would fill increasingly huge theatres than in literary quality.[20] Writing for television or films today is a fair comparison. No play was advertised in London with its author's name attached until 1699 and even in the middle of the eighteenth century playbills for both old and new plays often omitted any mention of the author – even Shakespeare.[21] We need, however, to realize both that plays were only marginally regarded as 'literature' and that they were constructed for performance and must be understood in light of that context. By way of rough parallel I would observe that one can legitimately study song lyrics by themselves, but one misses a lot if one does not have (or chooses to ignore) the music.

In an essay in the first volume of this series, W. B. Worthen asks 'Is it possible to understand performance through the scripted form of dramatic texts?'[22] (My own answer is 'Only with great difficulty and in severely attenuated form.') Worthen goes on to point out that 'we are only beginning to understand the consequences of print as a delivery system for works of art in general and for dramatic writing in particular'. This is true: print delivers a *reading* experience and theatre offers a very different one. At various points throughout this essay I shall be endeavouring to address the problem of how one can attempt to translate text into performance analysis. Right now, let me say simply that the interpreter has to possess at least a good working knowledge of the physical theatre circumstances, the production norms of the time, the original performers (if known) and the generic conventions in force when the play was written.

Remarkably few attempts to analyse these plays in *theatrical* terms have ever been published. One good reason for this is that almost all editions have been produced by textual bibliographers who generally seem to be both ignorant of and uninterested in theatrical matters. One might, at a bare minimum, expect both student texts and standard editions (like those published by Oxford University Press) to provide (a) an explanation of changeable scenery theatres and demonstration of the scenic requirements of the play and (b) some analysis of the original cast for the light it sheds on the production concept at the time of première. I defy the reader to point to examples of such assistance to interpreters in any edition of 'Restoration and eighteenth-century plays' currently in print.[23] A theatre person devoting him or herself to analysis of scripts would not require such elementary assistance, but few theatre historians engage in such work and critics coming from literary backgrounds very definitely need all the help they can get. The continuing uselessness of modern scholarly editions for theatrical interpretation is difficult to understand. Even harder to see is why reviewers of editions of plays do not take the editors to task for failing to address the issue of theatrical context.[24] Much remains to be done with a large number of playscripts.

I should point out that almost all surviving texts were written for and performed in theatres operating under patents or royal licence. Plays performed there routinely got printed; other kinds of theatrical performances were less scripted, less elite and far more ephemeral. By no means, however, were they an insignificant part of the theatrical experience of the public in the 1660–1800 era. London had a fair amount of fringe theatre. Some of the things mounted, say, at the Little Haymarket in the 1720s and 1730s got printed (for example Fielding), but many did not. The drolls performed at Bartholomew and Southwark Fairs were hugely popular and made a fortune for an actor like Pinkethman, but we have only the sketchiest knowledge of what constituted most of them.[25] Like the chapbooks that sold in the tens and even hundreds of thousands (when plays usually sold only a few hundred copies), the theatre of the fairs was popular, not elite culture. *The London Stage* makes almost no effort to record puppet theatre (quite important in London *circa* 1710) or to report comic miscellanies and quasi-improvisations of the sort Tony Aston toured with for decades.[26] Lord Mayors' shows are very minimally recorded, though they have considerable socio-political significance.[27] We must also remember that most of the surviving evidence concerns theatre in *London*. We know of the existence of strolling companies and amateur groups in country houses and we sometimes know the titles of plays they performed, but theatrical conditions were certainly not those of Drury Lane and Covent Garden and one suspects that *Hamlet* as performed by Doggett's strollers had been 'mucked about with' a bit (and perhaps a lot).[28] The experience of theatre beyond the patent theatres in London remains profoundly murky and given lack of evidence seems likely to remain so. This is not, however, a reason for ignoring the subject or for failing to pursue such archival material as might be found.

III. Performance records

The publication of *The London Stage 1660–1800* in the 1960s provided a quite fantastic tool for the theatre historian.[29] Genest's ten-volume calendar (published as early as 1832) contained a good deal of the same information, but it reported the primary sources less fully and in a less helpful format. In *The London Stage* calendar one can see at a glance what each theatre was performing on any day. Casts and additional entertainments are reported; the standard of accuracy is very high indeed. What is there not to like? Several things, actually, though most of them are of relatively minor import. What is deplorable is the poor use made by scholars of one of the great reference works of our time. Of that, more shortly.

Most users have quickly discovered that the indexing varies greatly in quality from part to part. Avery's Part 2 (the first published) has a pathetic little index that omits performers. Hogan's Part 5 (the last published) has a very fine and detailed index. Anyone who has foolishly trusted the synoptic index published by Ben Ross Schneider, Jr. in 1979 has probably come to regret his or her folly. The Schneider index is quite accurate insofar as references are to be found on the pages specified, but the compiler accidentally conflates all sorts of people under single headings and his almost total failure to distinguish different versions of plays with the same title is simply a catastrophe.[30] Even after learning caution about the indexes, many users fall foul of what the editors called 'the ladder'. Wishing to save space, they did not repeat casts within a season. So after printing a cast in full once, they simply say 'As 5 November' (or whatever date) or 'As 5 November, but Ben – Doggett'.[31] Thus Garrick may have acted a part ten times in a season, but it will show up in the index only once. To get a complete role-performance count for an actor, you will have to go through every season play by play, paying close attention to each title in which your performer has been listed earlier and watching out for changes.[32]

A rather more treacherous drawback is that *The London Stage* editors saved space by using a standardized format to report playbill details and often summarized rather than reporting the original verbiage in full. Dance, song and music details often get squeezed and nontheatrical information is sometimes just dropped entirely. An instance is the reportage of command performances during the reign of George I. Only by going back to the original newspaper advertisements can one discover that the King was attending fully 50 per cent of the opera performances in London in some seasons, not just an occasional performance – a fact of some importance both financially and socially.[33] Anyone interested in more than title, date and cast will be well advised to do at least some spot checking in the primary sources rather than just assume that everything is to be found in *The London Stage*. Concerts, for example, get silently dropped out of the later parts; fringe performances get ruthlessly summarized or go unreported; citation of extant account books is accurate for what is given, but huge amounts of information are ignored and the editors are very erratic about what they choose to include even within a single season.

What is *The London Stage* good for? This would seem a stupid question if it had not been so little used and so badly used by most scholars. It gets cited to establish dates for plays and serves as the basis for performance counts.[34] Original casts were usually printed in the plays themselves, but *The London Stage* can be employed (and sometimes is) to trace cast changes – which can of course be an important clue to evolving production concepts. What scholars have largely failed to understand is that *The London Stage* puts under our noses a vivid story of ongoing competition, sometimes fierce, even destructive competition. (Genest failed to display the competition: he listed the plays at Drury Lane by date and then listed the plays at Covent Garden for the same season by date in a different chapter.) Night after night they go head-to-head trying to attract an audience (although at times they politely stayed dark on alternate nights, to cut costs while sharing a limited audience). If we choose to pay attention, the performance calendar shows us how each management responded to success at the other theatre or attempted to capitalize on its own. Entr'actes and special attractions get aggressively advertised. Puffs for playwrights and performers, special features and additions and song and dance are pushed for all they are worth. When John Rich starts to coin money with pantomimes at Lincoln's Inn Fields, Drury Lane grumpily tries to reply in kind. Amidst the innumerable old stock plays (which carry on decade after decade), fads appear, flourish and decline – the ballad opera boom triggered by the astounding success of *The Beggar's Opera*, for example. Periods of bitter competition alternate with periods of cartel cooperation. The daily records constitute a vivid, heavily documented shorthand history. Few drama or theatre historians have actually *read* the daily calendar. Many seem to have bought the paperback reprints of the introductions to the five parts – rich, important and helpful, but by no means the guts of the enterprise.

The performance calendar contains an implicit story of competition and innovation for every season – a story that really comes to life only when extracted and expounded by an expert interpreter. One of the few examples of such a venture is Judith Milhous's history of the 'second' Lincoln's Inn Fields at a time of hot competition after the actor rebellion of 1695.[35] This study bridges the exact period at which utterly scanty performance records give way to complete daily records, but even before the theatres realized that putting an advertisement in the *Daily Courant* every day was worth the cost, one can see the cut and thrust between two deeply hostile companies. They mount competing productions of old plays; they imitate new successes; they steal playwrights and performers; they look to Ireland for interesting new actors; they import entr'acte attractions. All this can readily be discovered in *The London Stage*, but only if one reads it as the history of an ongoing struggle rather than as a reference book in which dates and numbers of performances may be looked up. Some epic battles were fought in this period between managements operating on very different principles – as for example in the initial competition between the experienced actors of Killigrew's King's Company (who owned rights to almost all of English drama) and Davenant's beginners at the first Lincoln's Inn Fields (who competed successfully by resorting to new plays and innovation). This story is foundational for theatre in our period, but it has never yet been seriously told.

IV. Performers

If *The London Stage* is one pillar on which theatre history 1660–1800 rests, the Highfill–Burnim–Langhans *Biographical Dictionary of Actors* is the other.[36] Without the former, the latter could hardly have been attempted, but even with the great advantage of a performance calendar as complete as the records permit, the compilation of the sixteen-volume account of almost all known actors, musicians, dancers, managers and house servants by just three scholars working alone is amazing.[37] Published between 1973 and 1993, the *Biographical Dictionary* gives scholars an instantaneous capsule account with quite a lot of detail on almost every person (save playwrights and tradesmen) known to have been connected with the professional London theatre – a total of more than 8,500. Roles are extensively reported and the lists of known pictures of individuals (a rich selection of which are reproduced) are completely unprecedented. The only seriously regrettable feature of the editorial policy was the decision not to print at least *DNB*-style bibliographies, which leaves the user to hope the authors got everything right (which they generally do) and to wonder what evidence they were working from (which is sometimes unguessable even by a specialist). After the publication of the first four volumes, the authors significantly increased the number of parenthetical hints as to sources, but 'a document at Harvard' is not the same thing as an explicit citation in a footnote or even a list of references. The excellence of the many thousands of entries in the *Biographical Dictionary* must be saluted. That said, what is it good for? Quite a lot, in my opinion, though one would hardly guess that from the uses scholars have made of it in the decade since its completion.[38]

A very high proportion of the plays in this period were written with a particular company in mind. Roles were created for individual actors. Authors did not always get their plays accepted by the intended company or the parts filled by the desired performers, but they often did and in any case playwrights were routinely consulted about casting. Whether the cast was as envisioned or not, it can tell us a great deal about the original production concept and how the play probably came across in performance. Mr Sullen in Farquhar's *The Beaux' Stratagem* is now cast as a booby. Was this true in 1707? Far from it. The part was given not to one of the company's clowns (Jubilee Dicky Norris or Bullock) but rather to John Verbruggen, a heavyweight tragic actor who played Iago against Betterton's Othello. For Verbruggen to take the part makes the abuse of Mrs Sullen frightening, upsetting and unpleasant – and lends weight to the seriousness of the presentation of marital discord in the play. As another example, consider how radically different a play *The Provok'd Wife* inevitably must be if Garrick rather than James Quin takes the part of Sir John Brute.

Casts represent an enormously powerful tool for the analysis of original production concepts (and of evolving presentation of plays, decade by decade). To date, they have been singularly little employed by scholars for analytic purposes. There are exceptions. As early as the 1920s and 1930s the much-reviled Montague Summers studied the performers and their 'lines' and his commentaries are richly informed with his sense of the impact of performers, though he was not writing historical dramaturgic analysis of the sort we might now wish to see done. Back in 1979 Peter Holland analysed Congreve's use of performers in considerable detail, pointing out that he used the same people over and over and that he often cast against expectation.[39] The late Elizabeth Howe got excellent mileage out of her understanding of how playwrights came to use Elizabeth Barry and Anne Bracegirdle as contrasted heroines in plays around the end of the seventeenth century.[40] Exercising some critical license, one can illustrate production decisions by means of counterfactuals, as Judith Milhous and I did in *Producible Interpretation*. Congreve's *Love for Love* could have been produced either romantically or satirically by the Lincoln's Inn Fields Company in 1695, a point powerfully demonstrated by looking at what the casting choices would have been in order to present either of the concepts.[41]

Why have casts been so little used as a basis for dramaturgical interpretation? Literary scholars have often tended to see actual performance as a particularity that distracts from the ideal textuality of the play and those opposed to intentionalism have resisted the idea that casting is a strong indication of the authorial concept of a piece. Even where roles were very clearly written for particular performers with special skills and attractions, a literary slant can simply erase all considerations of performance. John Harrington Smith's useful and influential book on the 'gay couple' *never mentions the names of the performers who took these roles*, hard as that is to believe.[42] Even where an interpreter is ready and eager to make use of casting information, it is hard to employ effectively if one does not know the performers intimately – which, for a start, means that one needs to have read a very large number of old and new plays. Editors of plays in our period have done singularly little to help their users. Look at some very fine and highly respected editions (the Friedman *Wycherley*, the Kenny *Farquhar*, the Jordan-Love *Southerne*) and you will find virtually no annotation or apparatus of any kind to help the reader see how the roles got enacted.[43] Not all casts are especially useful. Some tell us merely that standard performer 'lines' were followed in a predictable way. Not much can be learned from the casting of a performer of great versatility – Betterton, for example, who took all sorts of roles, from heroic to villainous to contemptible. The fact remains that if we are trying to understand how a play was conceived by its author and how it probably came across in performance, the cast is usually the best evidence available – and in this period, it almost always *is* available.

Given theatre historians' failure to make full use of casting as an analytic tool, we can hardly be surprised at their not employing it in more complex ways. We need to remember that while the original cast is naturally of special interest (especially if chosen by or in consultation with the playwright), the casting history of revivals is virtually a book in which is written the production concept and impact of the play.[44] Much may be learned from comparisons. To contrast Garrick's Macbeth with John Philip Kemble's is an obvious thing to do and such comparisons have often been made. At least as interesting, however, are comparisons between the productions of competing companies – something rarely done. The original King's and Duke's companies had entirely distinct repertories, but this ceased to be true after the split of 1695. In the 1720s and the 1760s (for example), the two patent companies each mounted their own productions of a number of stock plays. Role-by-role comparison is instructive: some plays were apparently conceived much the same way by both troupes, but others were not. If George Powell is cast as the fine gentleman in any of a dozen comedies *circa* 1700 while Robert Wilks was on offer at the other house, one is not going to see the same thing either place. Just as interestingly, some plays were *not* mounted by a second company. In those cases, one company evidently felt that they could not match, let alone beat, the other's offering. Why did Lincoln's Inn Fields fail to offer *The Conscious Lovers* in the 1720s? In Garrick's time two years was considered a decent interval: evidently LIF did not believe it could put up a competitive production of an extremely popular play. Old plays were if anything more of an issue than new ones. A few famous collisions have been noticed by historians, as for example productions of *The Rehearsal* in 1742 and *Romeo and Juliet* in 1750, but mostly as a means of celebrating a particular star (in those instances, Garrick). One of the things one learns from studying multiple contrasting productions, however, is something about flavour and style. Elkanah Settle felt that bombastic heroic plays were better done by the King's than by the Duke's Company in the 1670s.[45] The reasons for such a difference need to be sought in their personnel – something not quick or easy to do and for which all shortcuts are welcome.

The greatest utility of the *Biographical Dictionary* is not as potted biography but as a highly efficient way of discovering what sorts of performers were used, what their 'lines' were and what plays they had been performing in. Highfill, Burnim and Langhans had of course not read all the plays and they can hardly be expected to have supplied prefabricated analyses of each performer's talents at each phase of his or her career. The critic still needs to read a lot of plays and to exercise serious judgement and analytic skill in seeing what use was made of each performer. Without the *Biographical Dictionary* this is an almost inconceivable task. With it, the job is merely daunting and time-consuming. A literary critic can choose to ignore performance; a theatre historian cannot.

This brings us up against a problem not only awkward but essentially insoluble: acting style. Until the twentieth century, when audio recording preserves line delivery and video recording preserves physical gesture, our grasp of the actor in performance is unavoidably tenuous at best. The eighteenth-century theatre historian can collect scraps of observational commentary from letters and diaries and late in the period can mine newspapers for reviews. This is good, but of limited assistance. Look, for example, at reviews of 1930s or even 1950s performances and then look at films of the production in question. The disconnect is jarring. What is 'natural' in dress, speech and gesture in one decade generally seems artificial, affected and awkward before many years have past. Garrick looked wonderfully natural to his audiences, but would probably seem wildly peculiar to us. When a reviewer says in 1770 that Garrick did something to the life, we must assume that this seemed true from that vantage point, but it tells us almost nothing about what the audience saw: quite inevitably, we impose our own assumptions and associations from whatever critical terminology is used.

The scholar can of course turn to treatises, textbooks and illustrated handbooks of various sorts. These have been wonderfully summarized in Dene Barnett's magisterial *The Art of Gesture: the Practices and Principles of 18th Century Acting*.[46] Some of the same sources had already been used in Joseph R. Roach's *The Player's Passion*.[47] Two very basic questions arise. First, most of the relevant books are continental in origin, not English. Did their precepts hold for England as well as for France, Germany and Italy? And second, almost all of the precepts concern serious acting in tragedy and opera. How well, if at all, do they apply to comedy? I see no way to supply a documented answer to either question. My best guess is that application to England is fairly sound, especially in the realm of opera, where the elaborately stylized language of gesture could go a long way towards rendering dramaturgy comprehensible to audiences most of whose members did not understand Italian. Contrariwise, I suspect that application of all this ponderous theory to comedy is essentially misguided. We do not know what the acting was like and we are not going to know. Then again, perhaps what we really need to understand is comparative. Garrick's style in Richard III was not Cibber's and we can to a considerable degree comprehend the difference. The historical construction of acting styles will always remain a dubious and contested matter. Some important sources remain largely unexplored: the mid-century interest in oratory (exemplified in the elder Sheridan's lectures, Macklin's coffee-house/lecture hall and Foote's *The Orators* for instance) all have much to tell us about prevailing ideals of grace, naturalism and persuasion in verbal address.[48]

V. Physical production circumstances

Under this heading fall theatre buildings, scenery, machinery, costumes and props. As with performance records, the difference between what we know in the late seventeenth century versus what we know a century later is truly drastic. One simply cannot work in the two areas in the same ways. A scholar who fails to realize this will either attempt the impossible or fail to make full use of available evidence.

More than thirty years ago, Richard Leacroft published his fabulously helpful scale reconstructions of English theatres.[49] A better aid to dramaturgical analysis would be hard to imagine, but I rarely see the book cited (let alone seriously employed) in accounts of plays. For the first half of our period, limited evidence does create problems. Leacroft offered no attempt at a reconstruction of the Dorset Garden Theatre because (so he told me) he found the evidence too scanty even to support guesswork.[50] His version of the 1674 Drury Lane gives us a stunningly effective and practical theatre and for all I know it could be very like the real thing. He did not stress the fact (and very few users seem to have realized) that this reconstruction rests almost entirely on the *supposition* that the so-called 'Wren section' at All Souls represents this theatre. It could just as easily be a discarded sketch unconnected to Drury Lane in any way. Vanbrugh's Haymarket remains doubtful and contested in a variety of important respects. Not until the 1732 Covent Garden could Leacroft build on something like satisfactory foundations. Alarming as this indeterminacy seems, I think it is not terribly important. What matters is less the precise particulars of the late seventeenth-century theatres than the *nature* of those theatres.

After 1663, all professional theatres in London employed changeable scenery. They came in different sizes, shapes, degrees of elegance and machine capacity. The extent of the thrust of the stage past the proscenium varied (and changed). What is crucial to understand, however, is (a) that unlike Elizabethan theatres, they represented particular locations in vivid pictorial ways; (b) that they could change those locations within seconds with an almost cinematographic freedom of motion; and (c) that by opening and closing shutters they could reveal and terminate action in process. The difference from the bare public stages of Shakespeare's day and from the fourth-wall-missing box-sets of the nineteenth century is truly drastic. A theatre person knows this and is annoyed by being told the obvious. Literature people need to understand it a lot better than most of them seem to. As I write, I have just seen a fine Cheek by Jowl production of *Othello* at Riverside Studios in London, done without setting and with audience on opposite sides of a long, bare rectangle. The production was staged at the Brooklyn Academy of Music last autumn. I guarantee that the impact on the audience was of necessity radically different in a proscenium arch theatre. I have also just seen *As You Like It* in the incomplete shell of the indoor reconstruction of the Rose Theatre being built at Kingston-upon-Thames. The difference in performance impact between this space and that of the Globe reconstruction in Southwark beggars description. Anyone who teaches English Renaissance plays needs to see some performances at the Rose of Kingston.

My point is simply that unless one has a feel for the size, the nature of the space, the scenic and machine arrangements and the lighting, one really cannot begin to imagine how a play would work in performance. Any performer understands that cubage, configuration and sightlines are critical. To write credibly about a 1660–1800 play except in purely literary terms, one has to start by coming to grips with the physical setting for which it was designed – no satisfactory account of which has yet been written. Richard Southern's *Changeable Scenery* remains foundational, but wrongly assumes the availability of complex late eighteenth-century arrangements in the seventeenth century.[51] What did the scenery look like? Few scene designs survive until well into the eighteenth century, so this is hard to say. Not until the era covered by Sybil Rosenfeld's *Georgian Scene Painters and Scene Painting* do we have more than a hazy and conjectural grasp of this subject.[52] This is frustrating, but does little real damage to criticism. What the critic needs to know is less what the scenery looked like than how it worked. The formulaic nature of most of the scenery is evident from extant inventories.

What of costume? Quite a lot of theatrical pictures survive (especially from the last three decades of the eighteenth century), but costume renderings are rare and we have little way to determine the historical accuracy of what is shown in most pictures of actors in costume. For contemporary costume one can work from the relatively copious documentation of seventeenth- and eighteenth-century dress and Diana de Marly's *Costume on the Stage, 1600–1940* gives a basic sense of what is known of theatrical costume as such.[53] Very occasionally, records survive that permit us to reconstruct costume designs for particular productions in considerable detail.[54] What these theatres regarded as 'historical' costume is more problematical, though Pepys's interest in the subject tells us that as early as the 1660s the nature of the costuming mattered to at least part of the audience.

Props, traps, machines, use of balconies, drops, cutaways, stage doors and other entrances represent a rich and understudied set of possibilities. By comparison with what Alan Dessen has accomplished in three books about the pre-1642 theatre,[55] scholarship in this realm seems meagre indeed. The standard treatment remains Montague Summers's *The Restoration Theatre*, a useful but badly dated book.[56] The best study of such matters yet done is Edward A. Langhans's 1955 Yale doctoral dissertation, 'Staging Practices in the Restoration Theatres, 1660–1682', which represents a major advance over Summers but contains more documentation than analysis and has never been published. The importance of these matters can be hard for literary readers to understand. Extant bills for 'incident charges', however, help us see that these theatres spent money on things like rented pistols, a doctor's case and real dirt for the gravediggers in *Hamlet* to shovel out of the gravetrap.[57] These theatres believed not only in visible settings painted on wing-and-shutter scenery, but in realistic supporting details of many kinds.

Reading the plays commonly taught to students and analysed by literary readers, one would not think that plays of this era demanded elaborate staging. Many of the shows that attracted huge audiences, however, were technically demanding. The spectacular semi-operas on which the Duke's and United companies spent so heavily (the 1674 *Tempest*, Purcell's *Prophetess*, *King Arthur* and *Fairy Queen*) swallowed quite fantastic portions of the annual budget and involved the most elaborate machine staging and technical effects the theatre was then capable of.[58] John Rich's wildly popular pantomimes (and Drury Lane's imitations of them) similarly stretched the machine capacities of the theatres, as did the 'English operas' that were the featured offerings of both companies towards the end of the eighteenth century (for example, Cobb's *The Haunted Tower* and *The Siege of Belgrade*). Huge sums went into the scenery, machinery and staging of such works. 'Restoration comedy' carries associations of elegant drawing rooms, but many audience favourites featured flashy technical display. They were, in a sense, the super-films of their day – 'FX movies' is the current term.

At this point we need to ask an unsettling question: to what extent do illustrations of various sorts help us visualize the actors, the costumes and the stage settings of these plays? This problem deserves far more systematic study than it has yet received. Huge numbers of popular illustrations began to appear in the 1770s in the Bell editions and others.[59] The faces and bodies of actors must be passably 'like' or the engravings would hardly have appealed to a public familiar with their looks. The degree to which costumes in such engravings were particular to actors or roles is seldom clear and neither is the plausibility of scenic settings when they are represented. Some of them are manifestly generic. Earlier in the century the illustrations are far fewer and the problems of assessment more severe. Artists tend to idealize (or at least to improve) their subjects; distortions can be imposed by page layout in books; the best picture is not necessarily the most faithful to stage reality.[60] Use of surviving pictorial representations as historical evidence remains a doubtful and contested subject. This is true both in particulars (e.g. how to interpret the two sets of illustrations for the Tonson editions of Shakespeare, 1709 and 1714) and in broader theoretical terms. Viewers tend to impose their own meanings on pictures and to see what they expect to see or want to see.[61]

VI. Economics

Of all the realms in which theatre historians have failed to make serious use of the evidence available to them, 'economics' is probably the most surprising. We are dealing, after all, with commercial theatres. The royal patents were granted in the 1660s to reward the loyalty of Davenant and Killigrew with a chance to make serious money. By the 1690s financial control of the London theatres had passed out of the hands of actors and playwrights and even when such people did share in ownership and management, they proved about as grasping as outside investors like Christopher Rich. Patent rights were sold and resold throughout the eighteenth century: the patent monopoly was worth huge sums. The growth of London's population in conjunction with the monopoly led to the construction of ever larger and more expensive theatres: the 1794 Drury Lane cost £150,000, which was supposed to be paid off out of operating profits.[62] London theatres were unsubsidized (with the exception of the opera house, which received a £1,000 annual grant in the time of Handel). They *had* to make their costs and people invested in them in the hope of making big money. The theatres' artistic policies, repertory and production norms were driven by financial considerations.

This was no doubt true for the pre-1642 theatres as well, but we have so little financial information about those theatres that the historian can do no more than guess in general terms at the impact of money on theatre operations. For the late seventeenth century, however, quite a lot of financial information survives and for the later eighteenth century the records are astonishingly full and detailed for many seasons. No daily account books survive prior to 1724–25 (and none for Drury Lane until 1745–46), but overall we possess about 100 complete sets of daily receipts for seasons at Lincoln's Inn Fields, Covent Garden and Drury Lane. They vary in what they contain, but all of them report daily receipts and most of them tell us quite a lot about outgo as well. Beyond account books, scholars have discovered upwards of 200 relevant Chancery and Exchequer lawsuits, many of them related specifically to money and some of them containing detailed reportage of costs. The survival of several hundred managerial documents for Drury Lane in the years 1713–16 (mentioned above) gives us a nitty-gritty picture of daily operations of a quite amazing sort. We must lament the fact that essentially no daily receipts are known prior to 1714 and individual salaries are rarely known until well into the eighteenth century, but overall our problem in this area is not lack of evidence but the sheer bulk and detail of it.

At the macro level, the knowledge of finances helps us answer broad questions. Why did opera in England collapse into more than half a century of utter mediocrity after the 1770s? The answer – only recently discovered – lies in Sheridan's deeply ill-advised leveraged buyout of the opera house and its company in 1778. In very short order, a solvent company found itself in debt that totalled more than five times its gross annual income, unable to cover its debt service, let alone repay the capital.[63] At a more particular level, money helps us understand the kinds of productions the audience saw and how they viewed them. The staging of Dryden's *Albion and Albanius* (1685) cost a reported £4,000, which amounted to something like 40 per cent of the total annual income for the United Company. Purcell's semi-operas cost little less. These were incredibly special productions on which the company lavished an astonishing proportion of its resources. Admission prices were initially doubled for such semi-operas, which clearly caused great excitement – and if the company were lucky, would serve for years as a treat and special attraction. When such a show bombed, the results were of course fairly dire, especially for actors whose income depended on a share of profits. Yet again, consider the newspaper advertisements that say 'New dressed' or mention new scenery. These were – as extant records prove – costly additions, even when only part of a cast was spruced up or a couple of scenes replaced. Most new plays were mounted with scenes and costumes drawn from stock, yet clearly the audience cared about seeing new ones.

What did the theatre spend its money on? What were its internal hierarchies? For example, theatrical dance rarely gets more than *pro forma* acknowledgement from scholars, yet the records say that throughout much of John Rich's long reign as owner-manager of Covent Garden (1714–61) the theatre often spent upwards of 25 per cent of its salary budget on dance – a fact that must have had a very substantial impact on what the audience experienced.[64] As for company hierarchies, I believe I am correct in asserting that no one has ever published an analysis of actor payscales in the eighteenth-century theatre. Salaries of individual performers are extensively but far from exhaustively reported in the *Biographical Dictionary*. Quite a lot of additional evidence is readily available in account books, although it has never been pulled together and studied. The character and dynamics of theatre companies changed quite a lot in the course of the eighteenth century and crucial evidence of the changes is to be found in changing salary structures. Why has this never been investigated?

A question that bears on both drama and theatre is glaringly obvious: What did playwrights earn from their plays? After 1660, playwrights received the net profits of the third night (and by the 1690s began to get the sixth and even the ninth night profits, if a play lasted that long). For the very large number of cases for which account books survive, a fairly exact calculation of the playwright's earnings from the theatre is easy to make. Most of the relevant figures were reported in *The London Stage* back in the 1960s, but until thirty years later no one bothered to collect the figures and analyse them.[65] Data on what the playwrights earned from sale of copyright to publishers is less easy to assemble, but in more than 150 cases it has been found. What do we learn from this material? Two clichés have been repeated for many decades: that staging first plays was a terrible risk because they often failed and that plays by women did not draw good audiences. The latter was true until the time of Elizabeth Inchbald; the former turns out to be quite untrue. Hard figures show that first plays were no more risky than new plays in general. How much of playwrights' earnings came from publication? Quite consistently as an average across the century the proportion amounted to about one-third, which is startlingly high and strong testimony to the importance of print culture. The most surprising and disconcerting conclusion, however, concerns the feasibility of earning a living by writing plays. The author of the standard and much-quoted study of professional writing in England says that by the mid-eighteenth century 'the theatre was prosperous enough to provide a living wage and more, for the writers who were prepared to write to formula'.[66] This is flat out wrong. The figures prove beyond reasonable argument that virtually no one actually earned a living from playwriting prior to Inchbald and a very few others in the 1780s. Fielding supported himself from playwriting for a few years in the 1730s and the improvident Isaac Bickerstaff did so after a fashion in the 1760s. Plays might provide a windfall (about £550 to Gay for *The Beggar's Opera*) and some owner-managers earned quite a lot from their playwriting (Cibber and Garrick) – but basically income from plays was not sufficient or regular enough to sustain middle-class life, let alone support a family. This significantly changes the way we understand the eighteenth-century London theatre.

Money drove theatrical offerings and careers, then as now. Enough evidence survives to tell us quite a lot about repertory choices, production norms and the internal sociology of the theatre companies. Here is a single example of a recent discovery. Painfully little is known about the amount of light supplied for eighteenth-century performances. Happily, a 'Schedule' appended to a Chancery lawsuit tells us exactly how much light was supplied at the King's Theatre, Haymarket, day by day for two seasons in the early 1780s – and also informs us that Sheridan increased the number of oil lamps at performances from 1,372 to more than 2,000 after he took over the theatre.[67] The same source tells us quite a lot about rehearsals of both opera and ballet, including the fact that the company sometimes premièred new operas without ever doing a technical rehearsal on the stage. Money is of course a grubby and degrading subject which no gentleman or lady would wish to stoop to investigate – but perhaps we should be prepared to demean ourselves in the service of scholarship.[68]

VII. Audience responses

Whatever we make of an eighteenth-century play, we would like to know what sort of audience attended it and what kinds of responses it elicited. Reception study is vital to our understanding of past theatre and drama, but it remains rudimentary because collection of the necessary evidence is difficult and its interpretation problematical. Except for some lists of opera subscribers dating from the 1780s and later (when they started to get published), we have no detailed records of who attended the theatre or the opera in London. Published letters and diaries have been duly searched; many of the more useful comments are reported in *The London Stage*. Pepys's somewhat eccentric opinions about plays and performers have naturally been quoted time and again. Quite a lot can be deduced from his diary about the broad range of people who attended in the 1660s, though of course the results are skewed by his naming famous persons and those in his own circle of acquaintance.[69] The old clichés about courtiers, wits and prostitutes in the time of Charles II are now thoroughly discredited, as are those about a bourgeois audience favouring sentimentalism in the eighteenth century.[70] Such drivel is, however, still repeated in textbooks, including the sainted Brockett's.[71]

We will never know exactly what sorts of people came to the theatres for different kinds of plays because no records were ever kept. Reactions to plays are not terribly common until newspapers and magazines began to devote space to reviewing in the 1770s and even then can be difficult to use with confidence.

Theatre proprietors bought shares in newspapers, had friends among journalists, fed press releases to their contacts, planted reviews, and seem sometimes to have paid off reviewers who invited contributions. Most reviews were more fan appreciations than critiques. The only serious study of reviewing across a broad period is ancient, limited and critically doctrinaire.[72] Theatrical scrapbooks of reviews at Harvard, the British Library and elsewhere can be very helpful, but often fail to identify the source newspapers (and sometimes omit dates). Quite a lot of scattered testimony in letters and diaries probably remains to be found, but locating it in dozens of libraries and local record offices is agonizingly slow and inefficient work of a sort few scholars are able or willing to undertake. Difficulties notwithstanding, the ongoing work of David Hunter (centred in the realm of Handel's audiences and based on comprehensive examination of the archives of individuals) suggests that paydirt exists and that important conclusions can be drawn from it.[73]

One very valuable way of getting at the eighteenth-century audience's understanding of the plays it saw is by way of genre – their notions of which were often quite different from ours. This is a tricky subject, in part because of the considerable discrepancies to be found between what critics proclaimed and what playwrights actually wrote – even when the playwrights themselves were the critics. If 'neoclassical critical doctrine' had expressed the tastes and preferences of the audience, we may assume that the offerings of the theatres would have been quite different from what they actually were. Add the complication of our own generic preconceptions and we may easily befuddle ourselves. Yet granting the treacherousness of the territory, exciting vistas can be opened up with a little imagination. As an example, I would instance the concept of dramatic satire. The modern satire theory that evolved among scholars in the 1950s and 1960s derived largely from Dryden, Pope and Swift. 'Augustan satire' as conceived by the school of Maynard Mack was punitive and seriously moral. This was not the only (or the dominant) mode of satire early in the eighteenth century, when both 'lampoon' of a nasty personal sort and more exemplary forms of instruction competed with what we now think of as the 'Tory' model. As Matthew J. Kinservik has tellingly argued, our presuppositions seriously distort our understanding of both the theory and practice of satire early in the eighteenth century.[74]

However difficult the audience itself is to reconstruct, we can often deduce its attitudes. Censorship, almost universally condemned with indignation by scholars during the last hundred years, was actually approved and supported by an overwhelming majority of educated eighteenth-century Englishmen. One can see the enactment of the Licensing Act and its effects in a wholly negative modern light. Alternatively, one can try to construct a more historically nuanced view – one which can help us understand that in Foucauldian terms censorship was productive (not merely restrictive) for the playwrights. Present-day critics tend not to like the plays that resulted, but if we wish to learn what the audience liked, wanted, approved and regarded as appropriate, then we need to see their point of view rather than merely imposing our own.[75]

Reception study in this realm will always suffer from serious limitations in available evidence. The difficulty is less the disappearance of evidence than its never having existed in durable form in the first place. Such problems notwith-standing, quite a lot remains to be done with audience composition, uncollected commentary, readership and the print culture dissemination of plays, the rise of reviewing and genre expectations. Two underworked sources seem wide open for exploitation. One is the full texts of newspapers: electronic search access should lead to the discovery of quite a lot of news items about the theatres and their audiences.[76] The other is pamphlet controversies, both critical and theatrical. Large numbers of ephemeral publications of this sort were catalogued a generation ago by Arnott and Robinson, but most of them have failed to attract the attention of scholars.[77] Many of these items survive in very few copies and they can be hard to find – but the existence of ECCO will make them immensely easier to get hold of. Exciting discoveries will be published from these sources in the next twenty years.

VIII. Socio-political contexts

Both directly and circuitously, plays reflect and present the events, issues and ideologies of their time. To understand them properly, a scholar must be familiar with their multifarious contexts. Conversely, the plays are themselves historical evidence, though by no means unproblematically so. The relationship between literature or drama and historical actuality is ever shifting, unstable and difficult to determine with any confidence. (What exactly is the connection between *The Man of Mode* and the real world of London society in 1676?) The importance of both explicit and non-explicit 'content' in drama is obvious: if plays are more than entertaining excursions to Cloudcuckooland, they need to have provocative rela-tionships to their socio-political contexts. 'Provocative' need not mean didactic. Neither does it imply overt propositions or clarity. Yet we must not forget that most of the eighteenth-century audience did not want a lot of substance and ideas in plays, a great many of which were written purely as entertainment. This does not, to be sure, mean that we cannot mine those works for what they tell us about the culture and society of the time.

For the critic anxious to take plays seriously, three obvious traps must be avoided. One is to fail to distinguish between 'commonplace' ideas – widely accepted and noncontroversial at the time the play was written – and ideological arguments made in support of a particular party or intellectual faction. As an instance of the latter, we might note that though royalist loyalism is a near-universal in Carolean serious drama, the proto-Tory ideas in Dryden's heroic plays reflect a controversial viewpoint. A second is the temptation to impose simplistic organizing constructs on more complex material (e.g. the Truewit–Witwoud–Witless hierarchy applies usefully to relatively few plays). A third is to ignore the diversity of the original audience. Not until the last twenty-five years have critics made any serious effort to come to grips with the problems posed by 'reader response' issues. The mix of reactions to the sex-comedies of the 1670s, for example, must have been incredibly chaotic. We simply cannot say that 'the audience of 1676 thought thus-and-so about Dorimant'. Quite aside from being unable to provide specific evidence on the point, we have every reason to believe that original responses were about as radically diverse as those of twentieth-century critics. These things said, a brief look at what has been done in socio-political realms is in order.

One area in which disconcertingly little has been attempted is 'character'. Between 1660 and the early nineteenth century quite astonishing changes occurred in the ways in which natural philosophers (or as we would now say, theorists of psychology) conceived human beings. That the conception of what makes and individuates people exerts a powerful influence on how playwrights conceive and present the persons in their plays should be beyond dispute. The rich possibilities of analysis in these realms are evident in studies as different in focus and method as Joseph W. Donohue, Jr.'s *Dramatic Character in the English Romantic Age* and Lisa A. Freeman's *Character's Theater: Genre and Identity on the Eighteenth-Century English Stage*.[78] The fact remains that no one has ever attempted a systematic investigation of how changing psychological theory affects play-writing and production.

Political analysis has come a long way from the superficial generalities of John Loftis's *The Politics of Drama in Augustan England* (1963) or the simplistic Hobbes – Filmer dichotomy employed as an organizing device in Anne Barbeau (Gardiner's) *The Intellectual Design of John Dryden's Heroic Plays* (1970). At its best, political analysis can supply major rethinking of how we should understand the content, effect and interchange of important plays in complex contexts. A good example is Susan J. Owen's *Restoration Theatre and Crisis*, which offers a detailed account of the numerous plays that were written during the various phases of the Popish Plot and the Exclusion Crisis.[79] The broader the subject, the more room for disagreement. Compare three solidly useful books, Bertrand A. Goldgar's *Walpole and the Wits: the Relation of Politics to Literature, 1722–1742*,[80] Christine Gerrard's *The Patriot Opposition to Walpole: Politics, Poetry and National Myth, 1725–1742*,[81] and Alexander Pettit's *Illusory Consensus: Bolingbroke and the Polemical Response to Walpole, 1730–1737*.[82] The complexity and subtlety required in such analysis are hard to overstate. The political categories were smudgy and ever-shifting at the time and are impossible to reconstruct with much accuracy now. Circumstances could change quickly, sometimes even between composition and performance. Extreme topicality is hard to allow for. The borderlines between partisan involvement, topical allusion for the sake of colour and patriotic commonplace are hard to establish. A play such as *Venice Preserv'd* can remain popular for many decades after it has lost all topical appeal and who is to say how much of the original appeal in 1682 was political and to whom? These problems notwithstanding, politics and political ideology are to be found in hundreds of plays throughout the period. Investigation of this phenomenon has barely begun.

Politics tend to be highly topical; sex and gender references are usually much less so. Less has been done in the latter realms than one would expect, which is disappointing. Examples of books worth reckoning with are Harold Weber's *The Restoration Rake-Hero: Transformations in Sexual Understanding in Seventeenth-Century England*[83] and Richard Braverman's *Plots and Counterplots: Sexual Politics and the Body Politic in English Literature, 1660–1730*.[84] Sex, marriage and gender-role issues are omnipresent in long eighteenth-century drama. For several reasons

they are extremely hard to study. They were highly controversial then and attitudes towards them changed rapidly throughout the period. Worse, our own
predispositions tend to be partisan. Critics can be for or against non-marital sex:
comedies long denounced as smut have of late been hailed for supporting sexual
freedom, but neither position is a sound basis from which to conduct historical analysis. Nonetheless, conceptions of gender and underlying socio-cultural
structures unquestionably help determine the content and values of these plays
and they need to be investigated, though the problems are formidable. Feminists
want to champion women's rights, but feminism of a modern sort is not a prominent feature of most plays written for eighteenth-century commercial theatres,
not even those written by women. Gay literature critics can find all sorts of relevance in these plays, but since the allusions are of necessity almost all indirect and
circumspect, they are easy to twist to almost any desired interpretation. Add the
problem of the wide spectrum of original audience response and the difficulties
seem truly daunting. Marriage and divorce issues are a little less slippery, but
have been much less investigated than one would hope. One reason for this is
no doubt the difficulty of disentangling commonplace from implicit ideological
argument. G. S. Alleman's classic *Matrimonial Law and the Materials of Restoration Comedy* remains largely unquestioned, unchallenged and unextended.[85] Lack
of any serious attempt to trace changing attitudes towards marriage in the mid-
eighteenth century comedies seems strange indeed.

Some readers of my draft of this essay objected at this point that I am wandering
away from theatre history and getting back into 'old-fashioned textual analysis of
drama as literature'. I would deny the charge (and I object to the terms in which
it is couched), but the expansion of 'theatre history' into realms its practitioners
have tended to ignore or shy away from is quite deliberate. In my own historicist,
non-marxist terms, I am endorsing and calling for a socio-political criticism of the
sort Bruce McConachie tried to promulgate twenty years ago. Both production
choices and the impact of performance are inextricably entangled with the explicit
and implicit socio-political values contained in every play. If 'theatre history' is to
deal with reception (and I think it must, where it can), then the theatre historian
cannot evade responsibility for correlating the contents of the plays with the
contexts in which they were written and produced. This is by no means merely
'literary' and out of bounds.

The particularities of class, gender and politics are hard enough to deal with,
but the underlying commonplaces and ideologies are an even tougher proposition. Until someone finds a means of describing and analysing the contested
ideologies contained in the drama of the long eighteenth century, we will have
only a very imperfect understanding of it. The one explicit attempt at a broad
ideological treatment of even a substantial part of this material has been a great
disappointment.[86] Canfield makes large claims and surveys many plays, but the
coverage consists of little more than plot summaries from a narrow and prede-
termined point of view. The results are tidy-box analysis, not the flexible, subtle,
nuanced response to complex material that we need. I frankly do not know how
to construct a methodology for the analysis of historical ideology in drama, but
someone needs to be laying the groundwork for this kind of investigation.

More limited and manageable opportunities are wide open. Why, for example, has no one yet written an analysis of *class* in Carolean comedy?[87] The plays are full of clichés (which still need to be catalogued), but they also question, challenge and subvert them. Look at Otway's *Friendship in Fashion* (1678) before making rash statements about libertinism. Look at Farquhar's *The Twin-Rivals* (1702), with its stolen inheritance and attempted rape, before assuming that playwrights have a comfortable view of social structure. The contemptibility of the country is one of the great clichés of Carolean comedy, but consider the suppressed Howard–Buckingham *Country Gentleman* (1669), which loudly champions country values in both social and political terms. Neither the sociology nor the values of these plays have yet been seriously analysed.[88]

IX. Some polemical conclusions

What can we usefully conclude as we contemplate the welter of generalities and particularities surveyed here? If theatre history is to be more than an antiquarian game played for the entertainment of the players, then I would suggest that the participants need to be clear on their aims and must accept some fairly strict rules. Our questions must be sharply defined. We hunt for evidence. We should employ that evidence with respect for its limits. Theatre historians look for scraps, bits, pieces, hints and try to build out of them – what? One legitimate objective is the reconstruction and documentation of theatrical circumstances. 'How did costume shops work?' is a good question. We definitely need to know that these theatres (a) supplied costumes to their performers and (b) pretty clearly had design-concepts for at least some of their productions. A different kind of question, but also a very useful one, is something like 'What was Thomas Harris's artistic policy as manager of Covent Garden?' If we have no sense of the managements that staged plays, then we will have little understanding of how playwrights saw their market or negotiated the sale of their products. Look at the comparative figures on what playwrights earned at Covent Garden and Drury Lane in the 1780s and 1790s and you will realize that Harris was a highly competent manager and Sheridan a disastrously incompetent one. Look at the figures for Garrick and you will discover that they strongly confirm his reputation for good management. Read his copious surviving correspondence (including the massive *Private Correspondence* volumes of 1831–32),[89] which few scholars seem to have done and you can see how patiently, tactfully and skilfully he prodded playwrights to sharpen and improve their scripts.

At this point the reader may want to raise an objection. Am I simply making 'theatre history' the handmaiden and drudge for 'drama history'? I think not. Theatre history is not a foundation on which drama history should be erected. Rather, drama history is merely one component of theatre history. As I have said in my *Cambridge History of English Literature chapter*:

> 'New plays' are a product of the theatre system in which they are produced and any attempt to treat them in glorious isolation must inevitably produce

fallacious and misleading results. New plays did not beget one another and neither were they necessarily a major influence on their immediate successors. . . . To write a meaningful narrative history of new plays is not feasible. We can, however, try to see how the dominant genres changed and how they were affected by theatrical circumstances. ('Drama and Theatre in the Mid- and Later Eighteenth Century', 316–17)

Drama history has more to learn from theatre history than vice-versa. Theatre history should deal with *both* texts and performance. The objects of theatre history are equally to reconstruct contexts and to provide historically grounded readings of plays with full attention to the contexts in which they were written and performed.

Looking towards some general principles of 'good practice', I want to offer two suggestions. First, any kind of historian needs to understand the fundamental differences between dearth and plenitude. The late seventeenth century supplies us with texts, documents, lawsuits and commentary on a scale far beyond what was available before 1642 (let alone before 1600), but it remains a realm in which we treasure every scrap of information. What we do not know is far greater than what we do know. Most playtexts survive, but 90 per cent of the performance calendar is a blank; receipts are unknown; we cannot get beyond cloudy generalities about the theatre buildings; details of scenery, costumes, props and staging are almost wholly conjectural; pictorial evidence is close to nonexistent. A great deal of what the theatre historian is forced to do amounts to extrapolation from extremely limited evidence. A century later our problem is not guessing how to generate a picture from scraps and hints and absences – but rather how to select the bits of evidence we will extract from great heaps of the stuff and choose to privilege. By the 1790s the London newspapers are increasingly numerous and inclined to provide extensive arts reportage (of admittedly dubious trustworthiness). Fat account books stuffed with operational detail exist for season after season. Letters survive in large numbers. The memoirs published in such a flood by the 1820s give us thousands of pages of material on the latter part of the eighteenth century (though trustworthiness is again a major issue). The bulk of material is minimal in comparison with the later nineteenth century, but for the Pantheon Opera, for example, we have many thousands of pages of documentation concerning just two seasons. The historian's problem is not how to tease possible meanings out of every scrap, but how to reduce bewildering floods of detail to compassable scale and intelligibility. I estimate that my collaborators and I actually presented the reader with no more than one per cent of the documentary evidence about the Pantheon at our disposal – and that figure omits librettos, music, memoirs and most of the numerous lawsuits. My point is simply that the methodological process by which one builds a picture from radically incomplete evidence is very different from the one by which one chooses to privilege some bits of evidence and summarizes or omits the rest. *Extrapolation* and *selection* are quite different scholarly universes.

My second proposition is that whether we are dealing with the minutiae of performance practice or the generalities of characterizing plays over a quarter century, a serious process of *verification* is a *sine qua non*. I say thus-and-so: can I *prove* it to the satisfaction of anyone but myself and any allies I happen to possess? This is not the place to enter into detailed arguments about standards of truth and the processes by which legitimation can be claimed.[90] Good history requires documentation and if another scholar, reviewing the same evidence, cannot replicate a predecessor's conclusions, then we have a problem. I shall not belabour this point here, but let me offer two examples of broad characterization that remained current for many decades even though the evidence that would demolish them was readily available to anyone who wanted to bother to use it. First case: 'Restoration comedy' consisted of smutty, immoral plays written to please an audience consisting of libertine courtiers, society floozies and prostitutes. This is wrong on every count. Only a tiny number of plays exhibit genuine libertinism and few of those that do so leave libertines unreformed or unpunished.[91] Simple math should have told early scholars that the court of Charles II did not contain enough courtiers to constitute a financially viable audience and reference to Pepys's widely-quoted diary would quickly have shown that all sorts of men and women of the 'middle sort' attended the theatre. The characterization of plays and audiences has usually been almost entirely a projection of the prejudices of the characterizers – a tendency against which we need to fight. Second case: 'sentimental comedy' dominated the eighteenth-century stage. This was repeated in book after book and taught as fact to students for many decades, but the truth is that there was no season in the eighteenth century in which 'sentimental' plays (by any ancient or modern definition) actually dominated the repertory. This was true even for new plays. Contrary evidence was readily available in Genest, but until the 1950s no one seems to have thought to appeal to it. To say that we must have evidence (and that we must test our conclusions against all available evidence) is a statement of the thumpingly obvious, but the history of scholarship in this field suggests that the adjuration is not pointless. One of the dangers of 'dearth' is that if there is little or no evidence we cannot easily be proved wrong. One of the dangers of 'plenitude' is that we can probably find and select evidence to prove whatever we want to claim. And almost inevitably, we are going to use evidence in ways never imagined or intended by those who generated the original documentation.[92]

Where does this leave us in more operational terms? On a very practical level, I have four points to make. (1) We have fabulous resources available in the realms of playtexts, performance records and information about theatrical personnel. We need to use them seriously. As Worthen has rightly said, playtexts are a less than satisfactory representation of plays, but this is no excuse for not making the best use of them we can. When we are talking about Dryden or Fielding or Sheridan we need to have read a whole lot of the plays that influenced them and competed with their work. And *The London Stage* and the *Biographical Dictionary* need to be seriously and imaginatively employed, not just used as a citation source for performance dates and lives of individuals.[93] (2) Interpreters of plays should make intensive use of what we know about the original performers. If we want to get beyond the limits of purely literary interpretation, then our first and best tool is those performers. Cast a play in two strongly contrasted ways and the result will be two radically different performance experiences. (3) We should exploit the materials available to us. Two examples: the Larpent manuscripts at the Huntington have been cited as examples of censorship but they have many other potential uses. Richard Bevis long ago pointed out that they demonstrate important differences between performance and reading texts: quite a lot of 'sentimental' matter got added to the printed versions of some of the plays.[94] The censor's copies sometimes show us versions prior to late revisions or contain important matter excised before print.[95] Dougald Macmillan's 1939 catalogue is very good, but discoveries and identifications can still be made in this material.[96] Second example: theatre music remains an underworked area. The Day and Murrie catalogue of song books is a magnificent piece of work, but they did not deal with the hundreds of single-song sheets – and their work stopped in 1702.[97] Music was a conspicuous and important part of the theatrical experience and huge amounts of material have yet to be explored and analysed.[98] Post-1700 theatre music is broadly treated in Roger Fiske's useful overview, but beyond that sketch the area remains almost unstudied.[99] More broadly, I would suggest that new electronic resources open up amazing possibilities for us. Scholars in this field have, however, been painfully slow to tackle obvious projects even before technology started to revolutionize the study of both texts and history. Almost twenty-five years ago I published a survey of resources and open questions in the 1660–1800 period. A surprising number of the possibilities I identified for further research and criticism remain untouched.[100] (4) Serious, systematic use of contexts is vital. We need to understand the finances that drove playwriting, acting and production. We need to investigate the socio-political issues that affected theatres and playwrights and that substantially influence the content of large numbers of plays. This is not work that can be done quickly or easily or tidily – but until we understand these things a lot better we have only a hazy grasp of how the theatres worked or what they presented to their audiences.

Let me end by returning to a fundamental conceptual point about our enterprise. *Theatre historians need to write criticism that uses performance history.* We cannot expect 'literary critics' to do this. Basically, they work from texts. Uncontextualized readings are not wonderful in the realms of poetry or fiction, but in drama they are basically a disaster. Theatre history can quite rightly concern itself with the recovery and analysis of performance conditions. In many realms this has been well done (and can be better done). Granted, there are both conceptual and evidentiary limits to what can be attempted in the reconstruction of historical performance. I want to suggest, however, that we have been timid or remiss in failing to claim the right to interpret plays as more than textual entities. Far too often, 'interpretation' has been left to literary critics. What is the 'use' of theatre history? At bottom, it supplies the contextual knowledge we need to carry out interpretation that is not limited to the words.[101]

Notes and references

1. For some of the objections, see Hume, 'Theatres and Repertory', *The Cambridge History of British Theatre*, Vol. 2: 1660–1895, ed. Joseph Donohue (Cambridge: Cambridge University Press, 2004), chap. 2.

2. I am passing lightly over this point here because I have written about it at length elsewhere. For my objections to 'story history' with causal explanations, see *Reconstructing Contexts: the Aims and Principles of Archaeo-Historicism* (Oxford: Oxford University Press, 1999), 102–16, and 'Construction and Legitimation in Literary History', *Review of English Studies*, n.s. 56 (2005): 632–61. For a broader assessment of 'literary history' as a discipline (with soberingly negative conclusions), see David Perkins, *Is Literary History Possible?* (Baltimore: Johns Hopkins University Press, 1992).

3. See David Hackett Fischer's comment on the point in *Historians' Fallacies: Toward a Logic of Historical Thought* (New York: Harper and Row, 1970), xii.

4. For a demonstration of the evils of such a procedure, see Thomas Postlewait's polite but devastating critique of Margreta de Grazia's *Shakespeare Verbatim* (1991) in 'The Criteria for Evidence: Anecdotes in Shakespearean Biography, 1709–2000', in *Theorizing Practice: Redefining Theatre History*, ed. W. B. Worthen with Peter Holland (Basingstoke: Palgrave Macmillan, 2003), 47–70.

5. A point well made by Thomas Postlewait in 'Theatre History and Historiography: a Disciplinary Mandate', *Theatre Survey*, 45 (2004): 181–8.

6. Bruce A. McConachie, 'Towards a Postpositivist Theatre History', *Theatre Journal*, 37 (1985): 465–86.

7. Little effort has ever been made to study the complex interrelationship of dramatic criticism and playwriting in this period – a tricky subject because playwrights tend not to do what critics say they should. The evolution of early dramatic criticism is a lot less tidy and linear than has been supposed. On this subject, see Paul D. Cannan, *The Emergence of Dramatic Criticism in England: From Jonson to Pope* (New York: Palgrave Macmillan, 2006).

8. For a systematic attempt to distinguish 'documentary reconstruction' from 'extrapolative analysis' and 'historical theorizing', see Hume, 'The Aims and Limits of Historical Scholarship', *Review of English Studies*, n.s. 53 (2002): 399–422. The fundamental difference between 'scholarship' and 'theory/criticism' may be illustrated by the handling of this essay by the editors of *RES*, who published it under the heading 'Opinion' and listed it that way in the Table of Contents as distinct from 'Articles'. I think they were right to do so: fact-based argument and methodological theory are different enterprises.

9. Thomas Postlewait, 'Historiography and the Theatrical Event: a Primer with Twelve Cruxes', *Theatre Journal*, 43 (1991): 157–78.

10. As a dismal example I offer Stephen Greenblatt's *Will in the World: How Shakespeare became Shakespeare* (New York: Norton, 2004), a book written by a smart and learned man, but which is essentially fiction, not scholarship. Compare David Lodge's *Author Author* (London: Secker & Warburg, 2004), which announces itself as a 'novel' based on the life of Henry James. Lodge is actually more conservative and responsible in his treatment of biographical fact, and he is far more honest in applying the term 'novel' to the results.

11. On this subject, see particularly Edward A. Langhans, *Restoration Promptbooks* (Carbondale: Southern Illinois University Press, 1981), and *Eighteenth Century British and Irish Promptbooks: a Descriptive Bibliography* (New York: Greenwood, 1987).

12. Published in *The Cambridge History of English Literature, 1660–1780*, ed. John Richetti (Cambridge: Cambridge University Press, 2005), 316–39.

13. I have discussed these omissions and distortions much more extensively in section II of 'Construction and Legitimation in Literary History', (see in note 2).

14. This total excludes operas, plays presented in a foreign language, and fair drolls.

15. EEBO is 'Early English Books On-line' (to 1700). ECCO (Eighteenth-Century Collections Online) is an electronic database made available by Thomson–Gale in 2004 that contains fully searchable texts in original format and pagination of approximately 300,000 volumes published in England or in English between 1701 and 1800.

16. A surprisingly small number of plays are 'lost', though some of these are merely ghosts. See Judith Milhous and Robert D. Hume, 'Lost English Plays, 1660–1700', *Harvard Library Bulletin*, 25 (1977): 5–33. No census of later lost plays seems to exist. Interesting lost plays do sometimes get discovered in manuscript. Instances are Howard and Buckingham's *The Country Gentleman* (1669) and Elizabeth Polwhele's *The Frolicks* (1671). Discovery of *The Contrast* (1731) – a work which sheds important light on Fielding – has just been reported by H. Diack Johnstone in 'Four Lost Plays Recovered: *The Contrast* and other dramatic works of John Hoadly (1711–76)', *Review of English Studies*, N. S. 57 (2006): 487–506. More will almost certainly be found.

17. *A History of English Drama, 1660–1900*, rev. edn, 6 vols (Cambridge: Cambridge University Press, 1952–59). On Nicoll's place in the sequence of attempts to write the 'history' of this drama, see Peter Holland, 'A History of Histories: From Flecknoe to Nicoll', *Theorizing Practice*, chap. 1.

18. Robert D. Hume, *The Development of English Drama in the Late Seventeenth Century* (Oxford: Clarendon Press, 1976) – a generic approach; Derek Hughes, *English Drama 1660–1700* (Oxford: Clarendon Press, 1996) – a reading more concerned with content.

19. Edmond McAdoo Gagey, *Ballad Opera* (New York: Columbia University Press, 1937).

20. On changing attitudes towards the writing of plays (until very recently a seriously neglected subject), see Paulina Kewes, *Authorship and Appropriation: Writing for the Stage in England, 1660–1710* (Oxford: Clarendon Press, 1998), and '[A] Play, which I presume to call ORIGINAL': Appropriation, Creative Genius, and Eighteenth-Century Playwriting', *Studies in the Literary Imagination*, 34 (2001): 17–47.

21. See *The Letters of John Dryden*, ed. Charles E. Ward (Durham, NC: Duke University Press, 1942), no. 59, and Robert D. Hume, 'Before the Bard: "Shakespeare" in Early Eighteenth-Century London', *ELH*, 64 (1997): 41–75. Only very recently have serious efforts been made to understand how radically views of Shakespeare evolved in the first half of the eighteenth century. On this still-hot subject, see particularly Michael Dobson, *The Making of the National Poet: Shakespeare, Adaptation, and Authorship, 1660–1769* (Oxford: Clarendon Press, 1992), Paulina Kewes, 'Shakespeare's Lives in Print, 1662–1821', *Lives in Print: Biography and the Book Trade from the Middle Ages to the 21st Century*, ed. Robin Myers, Michael Harris, and Giles Mandelbrote (New Castle, DE: Oak Knoll and British Library, 2002), 55–82, and Don-John Dugas, *Marketing the Bard: Shakespeare in Performance and Print, 1685–1740* (Columbia: University of Missouri Press, 2006).

22. W. B. Worthen, 'The Imprint of Performance', in *Theorizing Practice*, 213–34 at 213, 231.

23. I have developed this point at some length in 'The Aims and Uses of "Textual Studies"', *Papers of the Bibliographical Society of America*, 99 (2005): 197–230.

24. The situation is of course significantly different for pre-1642 drama, where editors and critics routinely pay at least lip-service to issues of the sceneryless stage, absence of female performers, and so forth. The changeable scenery theatre is far less familiar and harder to understand, which makes attention to it all the more necessary.

25. The standard study remains Sybil Rosenfeld's *The Theatre of the London Fairs in the 18th Century* (Cambridge: Cambridge University Press, 1960).

26. For an attempt to reconstruct his celebrated 'Medley', see Judith Milhous, 'An American Medley for New Haven? Or, Why Tony Aston Didn't Go to Yale', *Journal of American Drama and Theatre*, 16 (2004): 98–118.

27. For one of the few serious efforts to analyse them, see Paula R. Backscheider, *Spectacular Politics: Theatrical Power and Mass Culture in Early Modern England* (Baltimore: Johns Hopkins University Press, 1993).

28. For a rare bit of light on an early strolling company from an Exchequer lawsuit, see Judith Milhous and Robert D. Hume, 'Thomas Doggett at Cambridge in 1701', *Theatre Notebook*, 51 (1997): 147–65. The standard account of theatre outside London remains Sybil Rosenfeld, *Strolling Players and Drama in the Provinces, 1660–1765* (Cambridge: Cambridge University Press, 1939).

29. Ed. William Van Lennep, Emmett L. Avery, Arthur H. Scouten, George Winchester Stone, Jr., and Charles Beecher Hogan, 5 parts in 11 vols (Carbondale: Southern Illinois University Press, 1960–68).

30. Here is just one example. All performances of adapted plays given under the original title are indexed under the original author without warning of any kind. Thus all dates for the enormously popular operatic *Tempest* of 1674 (by Dryden, Davenant, and probably Shadwell) are listed under 'Shakespeare'.

31. This means that the cast for the day is the same as that for 5 November except that the actor playing Ben has been replaced by Thomas Doggett.

32. The new version of Part 2 by Milhous and Hume (in progress) does list all casts in full under date and indexes each performer for every date. Bound copies for the seasons 1700–1711 (fully indexed) are available in the British Library, the Bodleian, the Theatre Museum (London), the Folger, and the Harvard Theatre Collection. The material is available on the web at http://www.personal.psu.edu/faculty/h/b/hb1/ (the last element is h-b-arabic one).

33. See Donald Burrows and Robert D. Hume, 'George I, the Haymarket Opera Company and Handel's *Water Music*', *Early Music*, 19 (1991): 323–41.

34. Performance counts can of course be wildly misleading prior to about 1705 when the theatres start systematically to put an ad in the *Daily Courant* every day. Prior to that time a great many of the performances listed are for new plays, and many of the listings are merely estimates backdated from publication. Unfortunately, the standard estimate of time lapse between première and publication used by the editors of *The London Stage* is quite misleading. See Judith Milhous and Robert D. Hume, 'Dating Play Premières from Publication Data, 1660–1700', *Harvard Library Bulletin*, 22 (1974): 374–405, which offers significant redatings for nearly fifty plays. Between 1660 and 1705 the number of known performances of particular plays is almost meaningless: we have virtually no record of some popular stock plays. Failure to understand this basic fact about surviving records leads to terrible errors and misunderstandings: *The Country-Wife* did not enjoy a total of just three nights in the seventeenth century. Performance counts are not improved by the *London Stage* policy of listing all known reprints of plays as possible revivals up to 1700. Unwary scholars tend just to assume that the 'possible' revival did occur.

35. Judith Milhous, *Thomas Betterton and the Management of Lincoln's Inn Fields, 1695–1708* (Carbondale: Southern Illinois University Press, 1979).

36. Philip H. Highfill, Jr., Kalman A. Burnim, and Edward A. Langhans, *A Biographical Dictionary of Actors, Actresses, Musicians, Dancers, Managers, and Other Stage Personnel in London, 1660–1800*, 16 vols (Carbondale: Southern Illinois University Press, 1973–93).

37. The authors' excessive dependence on *The London Stage* becomes evident if one turns to the original account books, which list additional personnel and explain the company functions of many others. See Milhous, 'Reading Theatre History from Account Books', pp. 101–31.

38. Sometimes the *Biographical Dictionary* does not even get used for obvious identification purposes. See, for example, Kristina Straub's *Sexual Suspects: Eighteenth-Century Players and Sexual Ideology* (Princeton: Princeton University Press, 1992) – an intelligent and provocative book not improved by its author's failure to realize (for example) that Hester Santlow and Mrs Booth are the same person.

39. Peter Holland, *The Ornament of Action: Text and Performance in Restoration Comedy* (Cambridge: Cambridge University Press, 1979).

40. Elizabeth Howe, *The First English Actresses* (Cambridge: Cambridge University Press, 1992).

41. Judith Milhous and Robert D. Hume, *Producible Interpretation: Eight English Plays, 1675–1707* (Carbondale: Southern Illinois University Press, 1985), chap. 9.

42. John Harrington Smith, *The Gay Couple in Restoration Comedy* (Cambridge: Harvard University Press, 1948).

43. So far as I am aware, the first 'standard' edition of plays in this period to include such apparatus will be the forthcoming OUP edition of Congreve by the late D. F. McKenzie, who died without writing the 'Early Performers' section he put in his table of contents. Judith Milhous and I were asked to fill in the lacuna and supplied thirty pages of analysis of how Congreve chose to deploy the actors available to him.

44. As an instance I will offer the eighteenth-century history of Buckingham's 1664 adaptation of Fletcher's *The Chances* (*c*.1617?). The part of Don-John passed from Charles Hart to Robert Wilks to David Garrick (who twice further adapted the text) in what must have been radically different production concepts. For analysis, see the critical introduction in *Plays, Poems, and Miscellaneous Writings Associated with George Villiers, Second Duke of Buckingham*, ed. Robert D. Hume and Harold Love, 2 vols (Oxford: Oxford University Press, 2007).

45. Elkanah Settle, *A Narrative. Written by E. Settle* (London: Thomas Graves, 1683), Epistle Dedicatory, A2v.

46. Dene Barnett, *The Art of Gesture: the Practices and Principles of 18th Century Acting* (Heidelberg: Carl Winter Universitätsverlag, 1987).

47. Joseph R. Roach, *The Player's Passion* (1985; rpt. Ann Arbor: University of Michigan Press, 1993).

48. For this suggestion I am indebted to Matthew J. Kinservik.

49. Richard Leacroft, *The Development of the English Playhouse* (London: Eyre Methuen, 1973).

50. Dorset Garden was critical to the development of the elaborate machine staging so conspicuous in the eighteenth century. The only serious and plausible attempt at a reconstruction of it is Edward A. Langhans, 'A Conjectural Reconstruction of the Dorset Garden Theatre', *Theatre Survey*, 13 (1972): 74–93. For sharp debate over the nature of the theatre (and some new evidence about it), see John R. Spring, 'Platforms and Picture Frames: a Conjectural Reconstruction of the Duke of York's Theatre, Dorset Garden, 1669–1709', *Theatre Notebook*, 31 (1977): 6–19; Robert D. Hume, 'The Dorset Garden Theatre: a Review of Facts and Problems', *Theatre Notebook*, 33 (1979): 4–17; Spring, 'The Dorset Garden Theatre: Playhouse or Opera House?' *Theatre Notebook*, 34 (1980): 60–9; and Hume, 'The Nature of the Dorset Garden Theatre', *Theatre Notebook*, 36 (1982): 99–109.

51. London: Faber and Faber, 1952. For important correctives to Southern, see Colin Visser, 'The Anatomy of the Early Restoration Stage: *The Adventures of Five Hours* and John Dryden's "Spanish" Comedies', *Theatre Notebook*, 29 (1975): 56–69, 114–19; Edward A. Langhans, 'The Theatres' and Colin Visser, 'Scenery and Technical Design', in *The London Theatre World, 1660–1800*, ed. Robert D. Hume (Carbondale: Southern Illinois University Press 1980), chapters 2 and 3.

52. Sybil Rosenfeld, *Georgian Scene Painters and Scene Painting* (Cambridge: Cambridge University Press, 1981).

53. Diana de Marly, *Costume on the Stage, 1600–1940* (London: Batsford, 1982). For a more generalized sense of the 'public image' of the actor, see Shearer West, *The Image of the Actor: Verbal and Visual Representation in the Age of Garrick and Kemble* (New York: St. Martin's Press, 1991).

54. See, for example, Judith Milhous, 'The First Production of Rowe's *Jane Shore*', *Theatre Journal*, 38 (1986): 309–21, where evidence is used from the company's fabric purchases. Specific descriptions of all costumes for several operas and ballets survive for the Pantheon Opera in 1790–91. See Judith Milhous, Gabriella Dideriksen, and Robert D. Hume, *Italian Opera in Late Eighteenth-Century London*, Vol. II: *The Pantheon Opera and its Aftermath 1789–1795* (Oxford: Clarendon Press, 2001), Appendix IV ('The Wardrobe Book'), 702–28.

55. See Alan C. Dessen, *Elizabethan Stage Conventions and Modern Interpreters* (Cambridge: Cambridge University Press, 1984), *Recovering Shakespeare's Theatrical Vocabulary* (1995), and, in collaboration with Leslie Thomson, *A Dictionary of Stage Directions in English Drama, 1580–1642* (Cambridge: Cambridge University Press, 1999).

56. Montague Summers, *The Restoration Theatre* (London: Routledge, 1934).

57. See, for example, the extensive documentation of such practice contained in the hundreds of surviving daily bills from the Triumvirate management at Drury Lane, 1713–16, many of which are preserved in Folger W.b. 110–111 and Y.d. 95. These manuscripts were described and analysed by Leonard R. N. Ashley in 'The Theatre-Royal in Drury Lane, 1711–1716', unpub. diss. (Princeton, 1956). Little has ever been done with them in print, and far more can be dated and interpreted than Ashley realized. See Judith Milhous, 'Dates and Redatings for 141 Theatrical Bills from Drury Lane, 1713–1716', *Papers of the Bibliographical Society of America*, 79 (1985): 499–521. All known triumvirate bills are listed under date with brief descriptions in Judith Milhous and Robert D. Hume, *A Register of English Theatrical Documents, 1660–1737*, 2 vols (Carbondale: Southern Illinois University Press, 1991).

58. On these hugely expensive productions, see Judith Milhous, 'The Multimedia Spectacular on the Restoration Stage', in *British Theatre and the Other Arts, 1660–1800*, ed. Shirley Strum Kenny (Washington, DC: Folger Books, 1984), 41–66.

59. See Kalman A. Burnim and Philip H. Highfill, Jr., *John Bell, Patron of British Theatrical Portraiture: a Catalog of the Theatrical Portraits in His Editions of Bell's Shakespeare and Bell's British Theatre* (Carbondale: Southern Illinois University Press, 1998).

60. On representation of performers, particularly those outside the prevailing ideals of decorum, see Judith Milhous, 'The Ideal versus the Abnormal Body on the Eighteenth-Century English Stage', *Harvard Library Bulletin*, forthcoming. For a detailed assessment of the variant states of the quite extraordinary sets of illustrations for *Hob* (dating from the 1740s), see Milhous, 'Gravelot and Laguerre: Playing Hob on the Eighteenth-Century English Stage', *Theatre Survey*, 43.2 (2002): 148–75, who concludes that many details of costume and stage setting are quite accurate but that in some larger issues of scenery and stage picture the artists felt free to depart quite drastically (and inconsistently) from theatrical reality.

61. This is true even in present-day photographic evidence. See Barbara Hodgdon, 'Photography, Theater, Mnemonics; or, Thirteen Ways of Looking at a Still', in *Theorizing Practice*, chap. 5. On broader theoretical issues, see Thomas F. Heck (with contributions from others), *Picturing Performance: the Iconography of the Performing Arts in Concept and Practice* (Rochester: University of Rochester Press, 1999), and Peter Burke, *Eyewitnessing: the Uses of Images as Historical Evidence* (Ithaca: Cornell University Press, 2001).

62. The Economic History website (eh.net) calculates the 2002 value of this sum as more than £11,000,000 according to the retail price index (a fairly conservative indicator).

63. For this dismal tale, see Curtis Price, Judith Milhous, and Robert D. Hume, *Italian Opera in Late Eighteenth-Century London*, Vol. I: *The King's Theatre, Haymarket, 1778–1791* (Oxford: Clarendon Press, 1995).

64. See Judith Milhous, 'The Economics of Theatrical Dance in Eighteenth-Century London', *Theatre Journal*, 55 (2003): 481–508.

65. See Judith Milhous and Robert D. Hume, 'Playwrights' Remuneration in Eighteenth-Century London', *Harvard Library Bulletin*, n.s. 10 (1999): 3–90.

66. J. W. Saunders, *The Profession of English Letters* (London: Routlege and Kegan Paul, 1964), esp. pp. 68 and 113.

67. See Judith Milhous, 'Lighting at the King's Theatre, Haymarket, 1780–82', *Theatre Research International*, 16 (1991): 215–36.

68. I grant my own bias in favour of economic history. Judith Milhous and I are now at work on a book entitled *Theatre Finances in London, 1660–1800* covering both theatre and opera.

69. For an exemplary analysis, see Emmett L. Avery, 'The Restoration Audience', *Philological Quarterly*, 45 (1966): 54–61.

70. By far the best published account of the Carolean audience is Harold Love, 'Who were the Restoration Audience?' *Yearbook of English Studies*, 10 (1980): 21–44, though David Roberts, *The Ladies: Female Patronage of Restoration Drama, 1660–1700* (Oxford: Clarendon Press, 1989) is helpful in its realm. The fullest study remains Allan Richard Botica, 'Audience, Playhouse, and Play in Restoration Theatre, 1660–1710', D.Phil. thesis (Oxford University, 1986). The most useful accounts of the eighteenth-century audience are still Harry William Pedicord, *The Theatrical Public in the Time of Garrick* (New York: King's Crown Press, 1954) and Leo Hughes, *The Drama's Patrons* (Austin: University of Texas Press, 1971) – both of which are badly dated, impressionistic, and excessively influenced by the biases of their authors.

71. As a model for serious work of this sort in a realm where evidence is even more lacking, we might look to Andrew Gurr's *Playgoing in Shakespeare's London* (1987; 3rd edn., Cambridge: Cambridge University Press, 2004).

72. Charles Harold Gray, *Theatrical Criticism in London to 1795* (New York: Columbia University Press, 1931).

73. See David Hunter, 'Patronizing Handel, Inventing Audiences: the Intersections of Class, Money, Music and History', *Early Music*, 28 (2000): 32–49, and 'Who Heard Handel? A Preliminary Report', forthcoming. Hunter has identified more than 5,000 individuals who attended eighteenth-century performances and located material on some of them in more than two hundred and fifty archives. He expects to spend a decade or more investigating the archival material.

74. See Matthew J. Kinservik, 'Censorship and Generic Change: the Case of Satire on the Early Eighteenth-Century London Stage',*Philological Quarterly*, 78 (1999): 259–82.

75. On what one might flippantly call the Whig tradition of dramatic satire, see Matthew J. Kinservik, *Disciplining Satire: the Censorship of Satiric Comedy on the Eighteenth-Century London Stage* (Lewisburg, PA: Bucknell University Press, 2002).

76. The British Library hopes to make searchable text of its Burney newspaper collection available to the public in the near future.

77. *English Theatrical Literature 1559–1900: a Bibliography*, ed. James Fullarton Arnott and John William Robinson (London: Society for Theatre Research, 1970). Scholars' failure to make serious use of this magnificent bibliography continues to baffle me. Peter Holland's account of how Garrick 'sounded' is an excellent example of the kinds of discoveries that can be made by pursuing the material to be found in Arnott and Robinson (pages 248–70).

78. Joseph W. Donohue, Jr., *Dramatic Character in the English Romantic Age* (Princeton: Princeton University Press, 1970) and Lisa A. Freeman, *Character's Theater: Genre and Identity on the Eighteenth-Century English Stage* (Philadelphia: University of Pennsylvania Press, 2002).

79. Susan J. Owen, *Restoration Theatre and Crisis* (Oxford: Clarendon Press, 1996).

80. Bertrand A. Goldgar, *Walpole and the Wits: the Relation of Politics to Literature, 1722–1742* (Lincoln: University of Nebraska Press, 1976).

81. Christine Gerrard, *The Patriot Opposition to Walpole: Politics, Poetry and National Myth, 1725–1742* (Oxford: Clarendon Press, 1994).

82. Alexander Pettit, *Illusory Consensus: Bolingbroke and the Polemical Response to Walpole, 1730–1737* (Newark: University of Delaware Press, 1997).

83. Harold Weber, *The Restoration Rake-Hero: Transformations in Sexual Understanding in Seventeenth-Century England* (Madison: University of Wisconsin Press, 1986).

84. Richard Braverman, *Plots and Counterplots: Sexual Politics and the Body Politic in English Literature, 1660–1730* (Cambridge: Cambridge University Press, 1993).

85. G. S. Alleman, *Matrimonial Law and the Materials of Restoration Comedy* (Wallingford, PA: privately printed, 1942). For some important work relevant to these realms, see Susan Staves, *Married Women's Separate Property in England, 1660–1833* (Cambridge: Harvard

University Press, 1990), and Paula R. Backscheider, 'Endless Aversion Rooted in the Soul': Divorce in the 1690–1730 Theater', *Eighteenth Century: Theory and Interpretation*, 37 (1996): 99–135.

86. See J. Douglas Canfield, *Tricksters & Estates: On the Ideology of Restoration Comedy* (Lexington: University Press of Kentucky, 1997) and *Heroes & States: On the Ideology of Restoration Tragedy* (Lexington: University Press of Kentucky, 2000).

87. A useful beginning has recently been made by Mark S. Dawson in *Gentility and the Comic Theatre of Late Stuart London* (Cambridge: Cambridge University Press, 2005).

88. Religion is another subject that deserves far more attention than it has received. Non-Christian religion is more often presented than Christian, though Catholics often take a beating. The protests of Jeremy Collier and many others suggest that at least part of the potential audience objected on religious/moral grounds to what was said and shown in plays, and religious convictions must have had significant influence on the responses of many theatregoers. Providentiality is rife in serious drama. The rigidities and excesses of a book like Aubrey L. Williams's *An Approach to Congreve* (New Haven: Yale University Press, 1979) notwithstanding, all of these subjects are worth serious study.

89. *The Private Correspondence of David Garrick*, ed. James Boaden, 2 vols (London: Colburn and Bentley, 1831–2). These volumes include letters *to* Garrick, unlike *The Letters of David Garrick*, ed. David M. Little and George M. Kahrl, 3 vols (Cambridge: Harvard University Press, 1963) – an admirable edition, but sadly lopsided.

90. I have addressed such issues in detail in 'The Aims and Limits of Historical Scholarship' and 'Construction and Legitimation in Literary History', (see notes 8 and 2).

91. On which see Robert D. Hume, 'The Myth of the Rake in "Restoration" Comedy', *Studies in the Literary Imagination*, 10 (1977): 25–55.

92. This is a historiographic cliché, but for some particular theatrical applications, see Susan Bennett, 'Decomposing History (Why Are There So Few Women in Theater History?)', *Theorizing Practice*, chap. 4.

93. As an example from an earlier period of how records of theatre can be hugely beneficial to scholarship, I would point to the riches of the ongoing REED project and the way such material can be used in a book such as Scott McMillin and Sally-Beth MacLean's *The Queen's Men and their Plays* (Cambridge: Cambridge University Press, 1998).

94. See Richard Bevis, *The Laughing Tradition: Stage Comedy in Garrick's Day* (Athens: University of Georgia Press, 1980), chap. 2. Bevis originally made this important point in his Berkeley dissertation of 1965.

95. For examples of such discoveries, see Matthew J. Kinservik, 'New Light on the Censorship of Macklin's *The Man of the World*', *Huntington Library Quarterly*, 62 (1999): 43–66, and 'Satire, Censorship, and Sodomy in Samuel Foote's *The Capuchin* (1776)', *Review of English Studies*, n.s. 54 (2003): 639–60.

96. See Dougald MacMillan, *Catalogue of the Larpent Plays in the Huntington Library* (San Marino: Huntington Library, 1939) and Pierre Danchin, 'Unidentified Items in the Larpent Collection: Addresses, Prologues, and Epilogues', *Huntington Library Quarterly*, 64 (2001): 445–67.

97. Cyrus Lawrence Day and Eleanore Boswell Murrie, *English Song-Books, 1651–1702* (London: Bibliographical Society, 1940). For the next quarter century, see David Hunter's admirable *Opera and Song Books Published in England, 1703–1726: a Descriptive Bibliography* (London: Bibliographical Society, 1997).

98. As of the spring of 2005 a major new resource has just been made available in advanced draft form – Anthony W. Butler's 'Restoration Theatre Song Archive' http://www.arts.monash.edu.au/english/research/Archive/), which is an attempt to catalogue words and music for all known theatre songs from the period 1660–1710. I understand that Kathryn Lowerre is working on a similar project for the early eighteenth century.

99. Roger Fiske, *English Theatre Music in the Eighteenth Century* (1973; 2nd edn. Oxford: Oxford University Press, 1986).

100. 'English Drama and Theatre 1660–1800: New Directions in Research', *Theatre Survey*, 23 (1982): 71–100.
101. For advice, criticism, and help of various sorts I am much indebted to Paul D. Cannan, Don-John Dugas, Kathryn Hume, Paulina Kewes, Matthew J. Kinservik, Ashley Marshall, Judith Milhous, Thomas Postlewait, and David J. Twombly. This article was written during a sabbatical year during which I was a Visiting Research Fellow at the Institute of Historical Research (London), to whose library and staff I am much indebted.

2

Sleeping with the Enemy: Aphra Behn's *The Roundheads* and the Political Comedy of Adultery

Michael Cordner

The Restoration dramatic canon has been redesigned, and Aphra Behn's place in the firmament now appears assured. Some of her plays, however, are still treated as more equal than others. Re-explorations of the first part of *The Rover*, for instance, proliferate, while its sequel receives only intermittent attention. A paradoxical example of this process is provided by the fate of *The Roundheads Or, The Good Old Cause*, which still endures relative neglect, but also inspires radically contradictory opinions from those writers who do address it. To one scholar, it is a 'brilliant' achievement; to another, it reveals an author 'innocent of any historical sense'.[1] One dubs it 'blatant political propaganda', while others consider its partisan polemic 'a thin varnish to make old stuff shine'.[2] A script one authority considers a characteristic production of a committed Tory playwright leads another to try to explain its alleged dissimilarity from Behn's other contemporaneous comedies.[3] A play provoking this degree of disagreement should be worth reinvestigating.

One striking fact about *The Roundheads* gives us our starting point. Its premiere in midwinter 1681–82 represents the first recorded premiere, since 1660, of a new script whose cast-list includes an array of named historical figures, all of whom played significant roles in the 1650s republican regimes. Previous dramatists had masked behind (often slender) disguises allusions to players in the revolution.[4] *The Roundheads*, however, is the first post-1660 play to bring onstage, under their own names, the likes of John Lambert, Charles Fleetwood, John Desborough, and John Hewson – military commanders associated with the radical experiments of the Interregnum, which the restoration of the monarchy had finally aborted. The work's obvious kinship is, therefore, with the political pamphlet-plays of the 1640s and 1650s – a genre which was at first 'generally parliamentarian in sympathy', but which later gave derisory expression to various strains of opposition to republican rule, including (pre-eminently) royalist ones. The mode was a hybrid one, 'mixing elements of drama, reportage, satire, and prose polemic';[5] and its dramatis personae combined fictional characters with unflattering appearances by leading political and military figures, including Cromwell, Fairfax, and Ireton. Its tone was almost unrelentingly abrasive and contemptuous. Though indebted to pre-1642 theatre, the sexual explicitness and scatological relish in which it frequently specialized far exceeded anything that the peacetime stage would have contemplated.

Dedicating *The Roundheads* to the Duke of Grafton, Behn asserted that, since she wrote '*in an Age when Faction rages, and differing Parties disagree in all things*', embedded partisan allegiances would determine her play's reception. For Behn, the same battle-lines still divided the nation which separated royalists from their opponents during the civil war and its aftermath – a truth she claimed others were malignly conspiring to obscure. Her play's antagonists threw '*the* Act of Oblivion *in our Teeths, as if that (whose mercy can not make them forget their Old Rebellion) cou'd hinder honest truths from breaking out upon 'em in Edifying Plays*' (p. 361).[6]

The 1660 Act of Indemnity and Oblivion, a foundation-stone of the Restoration Settlement, promised that the actions, during the 1640s and 1650s, of all but a few excepted persons would not be held against their perpetrators by the restored regime. It also made it a crime to invoke recriminatingly the histories of particular individuals during those decades.[7] The Restoration was not a simple royalist victory, but the product of a freshly forged coalition between 'old and new cavaliers, ex-Presbyterian parliamentarians (survivors from the late 1640s) and some ex-Cromwellians (notably Monck, Montague, and the lesser men attached to them)'.[8] Erstwhile foes had suddenly become mutually indispensable allies, whose solidarity alone underpinned the new government's survival. It is therefore easy to perceive one reason why forgetfulness seemed so politically desirable, even if, in practice, unattainable.

Whatever the inhibitions governing new playscripts, rancorous recollection of individuals' mid-century deeds proceeded unimpeded by the 1660 Act in many other areas of Restoration life. The Popish Plot and Exclusion Crises in the late 1670s/early 1680s further aggravated this situation. The renewed convulsions were interpreted on all sides as a disastrous reliving of the mid-century catastrophe. This in turn prompted 'a full-scale resurrection of the political literature of the earlier crisis'[9] and inspired, for example, a journal retelling, incident by incident, the events of 1641.[10] All such recountings were inflected by partisan editorializing and could prove perilous. *The Roundheads* includes a minor character modelled on Stephen College,[11] evidence against whom, at the 1681 trial which resulted in his execution, included his provocative 'justifying of the late Long Parliament's actions in '40'.[12] Those with Behn's Tory loyalties read things differently. As one rhymester phrased it, 'Remember ye wiggs, what was formerly done, / remember your mischeifs in forty and one'.[13]

Comedy *c*.1680 often displays the imprint of this long view, as, for instance, when Otway's Beaugard and Courtine in *The Soldiers' Fortune*, self-professed heirs of the 'old Cavaliers', denounce contemporary England as a place where such as they starve for their loyalty, while the descendants of those who brought Charles I to the block still plot and undermine, and are rewarded for their treachery with prosperity. In a way characteristic of the post-1660 drama, however, Otway's soldiers direct their fury at type figures, not real people.[14] Whatever liberties in narrating the histories of historical individuals might be indulged elsewhere, a severer decorum reigned in the playhouses – until, that is, *The Roundheads* decisively breached this twenty-year-old tradition.

According to Behn, Whig conspirators fostered a co-operative forgetfulness to achieve their nefarious ends and deliberately exploited Charles II's '*Vast and God-like Clemency*' in the Act of Indemnity and Oblivion to ensure that the evidence of their forebears' pre-1660 outrages could not be freely deployed to unmask their present sedition. In this account, regal magnanimity risked mutating into tactical naivety, while disobeying the king's command manifested true loyalty. The Tory dramatist accordingly had a duty to follow the example of non-dramatic polemicists and portray, under their own names, some of the '*Meane, (and till then obscure) Villains*' who '*Rul'd, and Tyraniz'd*' the country in the 1650s (p. 362). Otherwise, a nation rendered oblivious of history's testimony would be condemned to relive its horrors.

Behn's insistence on the urgent political implications of communal memory leads me to distrust those modern readings of the play which treat its 1659–1660 setting as a matter of relative insignificance – as, in effect, a thin veil behind which immediately contemporary preoccupations could be negotiated more safely.[15] I am similarly sceptical about a growing tendency to regard *The Roundheads* as the product of a moment of unadulterated Tory triumphalism. In this account, Charles II irreversibly outmanoeuvred his opponents in spring 1681 by his switch of tactics at the Oxford Parliament – a political transformation which, it is claimed, was swiftly registered at the time, inspiring a wave of royalist plays in the succeeding months. *The Roundheads*, therefore, contributes to a 'prevailing trend in comedy . . . to celebrate the defeat of Exclusion and to portray the Tory victory as a re-enactment of the King's restoration in 1660'.[16]

The wisdom of hindsight is, I believe, at work here. New comedy in the winter of 1681–82 certainly flew Tory colours; and, while a strenuous propaganda war was still being fought, production of loyalist polemic now began to outstrip 'that of opposition material'. From this point on, 'loyalists were pushing at a door that was at least ajar, if not half open'.[17] Yet 'pushing' still seemed urgently required. During the extended crisis opposed factions had recurrently won and lost the initiative only to regain and lose it again. Who could be certain that the final turn of fortune's wheel had now occurred? In spring 1682, Charles II still thought it necessary to order meticulous preparations to ensure that the Catholic Duke of York's long delayed return to London encountered no resistance from hostile mobs – a plan only partly successful, since on the day 'Whig crowds armed with long canes paraded through the streets shouting "a Monmouth, a Monmouth, no York, no York" and tried to extinguish all the bonfires lit in honour of the duke', with 'violent clashes' erupting 'between Whig and Tory groups at a number of places'.[18] Had the time really yet come when playwrights could convincingly assert irreversible Tory victory?

In any case, Behn's decision to analogize the events of 1678–82 with the final days of the mid-century revolution was potentially a provocative one, since it could be read as implicitly conceding the failure of the ecstatic hopes of May 1660. She might lay the blame for the continuing mayhem on the irreconcilables whose machinations undermined the nation's stability; but the tacit admission was that the restored monarchy had, to date, proved inadequate to resisting its enemies' scheming. Linking the two convulsions thus raised the question of why the heady excitements of 1660 had bred the renewed confrontations of 1678–82. Edgier thoughts may be in play here than a simple celebration of assured political victory.

This is not the only way in which *The Roundheads'* modern interpreters arguably simplify its historical positioning. The intricate interplay it develops between the sexual and political realms has inspired some interesting commentary, but also some bizarre claims. Robert Markley, for instance, asserts that 'What distinguishes this comedy from other Royalist plays of the period – and what may account, in part, for the violent reaction the play elicited from Shaftesbury's followers – is that her political satire is cast in sexual as well as socioideological terms' – a statement falsified by its accompanying footnote, which cites, without acknowledging the fact, several contemporary plays which adopt identical tactics, and which contribute to the wave of Tory cuckolding comedies generated by the Exclusion Crisis.[19] This kind of playwriting, however, is also part of a longer history of the interweaving of the political and the erotic. Susan J. Owen, for instance, has noted the widespread use of 'rape as a trope of monstrosity' in Restoration political debate, including playhouse scripts.[20] But *The Roundheads* ultimately feeds off, and derives from, traditions of public insult which substantially predate the events of 1660.

Historians have only recently begun to explore the fertile inventiveness with which early modern culture used sexual innuendo and accusation to discredit those exposed to public gaze.[21] The target might be a reforming cleric in 1630s Dorchester or a Jacobean Secretary of State; but one preferred mode of attack in both cases was to undermine the victim's public status, not by a reasoned attack on his philosophy or his discharge of his office, but by scandalous revelations about his personal life. Thus, the Dorchester cleric was alleged to seduce his female parishioners, while the court grandee imputedly suffered from terminal syphilis.[22] Political position and doctrinal allegiance were therefore 'discredited by association with sexual license'.[23] This tactic was part of the common arsenal of the culture, open to energetic exploitation from all positions on the political and ideological spectrum. It was also deployed, and relished, at 'all levels of society',[24] though especially effective as a tool for wounding one's betters.

Before the civil war, this primarily remained an oral and manuscript phenomenon; but the collapse of the censorship, and the propaganda needs of both sides, led to its eruption into print in the 1640s–1650s, with the most lurid practices being attributed to political opponents. Cromwell, for example, was credited with being, from the first stirrings of puberty, the 'town bull of Ely'.[25] But sexual incapacity could also readily be exploited. Here, the history of the Earl of Essex, commander-in-chief of Parliament's forces, who had been divorced from his first wife on grounds of impotence, and 'whose second had run off to [royalist] Oxford with a lover at the beginning of the Civil War', played into his enemies' hands, who remorselessly invoked it to assert that his military incapacity matched his sexual inadequacy.[26] Parliament's polemicists were equally happy to deploy this tactic. The interception and publication of some of Charles I's personal correspondence with Henrietta Maria provided the occasion for lubricious glee in claiming to unmask a monarch indecorously subservient to his spouse's imperious will – a 'Sonnetting' monarch, content to be 'wholly managed by the Queen; though she be of the weaker sexe, borne an Alien, bred up in a contrary Religion'. This provoked royalist retaliation in kind, in the form, for instance, of sneers that one of parliament's journalistic hacks who had jeered the king and queen had been reduced, via infection from his whore, 'to Salivation, Sweat and dryed Racke of Mutton'.[27]

The despoliation of majesty, it was claimed, even extended to the attempted examination of Charles I's body, after the regicide, in the hope of finding 'evidence of the pox or impotence'.[28] Proof of either lewdness or incapacity would serve the propagandists' purposes equally well. Each side in this conflict 'claimed to represent legitimate masculine authority'[29] and would use whatever weapon came to hand to denude its opponents of sexual dignity. Those who allegedly explored the king's corpse were only atypical in attempting to establish the facts. The satiric polemic of the war years and after often feeds off 'absurd accusations',[30] which primarily give extravagant vent to radical hostility and agonized contempt. Truth-telling is not the issue here; rather, a communal language of rhetorical denunciation is liberally deployed to deride those whose claims to political authority it is the purpose to undermine.

Royalist counter-assertions of masculine potency sometimes took extreme forms. Painting one's enemies as impotent could, for example, engender, as a logical extrapolation, boastful tales about how famished parliamentarian wives had gratefully found solace with cavalier lovers,[31] while 'licentiousness ... became a kind of political badge' in some schools of royalist poetry.[32] Even on the battlefield the lines could be similarly drawn. Essex's sexual ignominy led to his being confronted there by banners proclaiming 'cuckold we come' – a flamboyance outdone in turn by another royalist standard which flaunted 'a naked soldier with an unsheathed sword and an erect penis', with the accompanying boast, 'Ready to use both'.[33] Many supporters of Charles I found such sexual braggadocio discreditable; but it is one strain in the variegated inheritance which the multiple royalisms of the 1640s and 1650s bestowed on the Restoration.

In the swooning response of Lady Lambert in *The Roundheads* to the amplitude of cavalier charms we can discern a clear echo of such machismo. Exploring the implications of Behn's play repeatedly leads us back to the mid-century and earlier, as indeed befits her comedy's declared agenda, in ways which defy the periodization which bedevils the study of early modern theatre. Experts in the post-1660 and pre-1642 drama respectively tend to be incurious about what falls outside the chronological limits of their own specialisms. Behn's persistent rewriting of earlier scripts to 1670s/1680s agendas is just one of the important subjects which consequently lack an authoritative modern study. *The Roundheads* is the work of a writer who carefully studied playwriting from two decades earlier about the mid-century conflicts and drew sustaining inspiration, in particular, from two strongly contrasted scripts from that period by John Tatham and Sir Robert Howard.

Behn was old enough to have personal memories of the Interregnum; and Jane Jones has claimed that *The Roundheads* shows 'considerable knowledge of events and the people involved' in the crises of 1659–60.[34] Behn may have possessed such knowledge; but Jones offers no evidence to justify her assertion, and for the historical part of her action Behn depends almost entirely on a comedy from two decades earlier, Tatham's *The Rump; or, The Mirror of the Late Times*. She frequently re-orders the material she adopts; but I have identified no addition by her which draws on independently derived information. For her narrative of the successive pre-Restoration crises, she therefore relies on a writer who lived in the capital throughout those months, and whose own political alignment we cannot simply assume to be identical with her own. From one angle, this might be viewed as Behn performing what she preaches and absorbing into her own work eye-witness testimony of the anarchy which she fears may once again overtake the nation. But *The Rump* has its own priorities. To what extent do those carry over into *The Roundheads*? Or does Behn, in the light of subsequent experiences of which Tatham was necessarily innocent, successfully refashion what she annexes to serve her own 1680s agendas? And what attracted Behn to this source in the first place? Characteristically, she did not acknowledge her indebtedness to Tatham. That should not discourage us, however, from exploring his play closely in its own right.

Different scholars adopt different positions about when *The Rump* was written. One assigns its premiere to June 1659, which makes it predate the events it chronicles and awards Tatham prophetic powers.[35] Others assume that it dates from after Charles II's return in May and treat it as one of the first fruits of Cavalier reaction. Yet its action chronicles no event later than Lambert's imprisonment in the Tower in early March 1660. It makes no reference, for example, to his subsequent escape and attempt to mount a serious challenge to General Monck's control of events. *The Rump* also lacks the chorus of concluding hosannas in celebration of the Restoration, which became politically obligatory from the Declaration of Breda onwards – no ecstatic prophecies of the 'Golden Age' Charles II will inaugurate, for example, or breathless 'amazement' at the providential suddenness of his 'aenigmatical Return',[36] none of that 'exalted sense of wonder' duly inculcated by Tatham himself in his first post-Restoration Lord Mayor's pageant.[37] The evidence is necessarily circumstantial; but the signs are, therefore, that the play was most likely written in *c.* March 1660, as part of the euphoric anti-Rump celebrations which followed Monck's seizure of the initiative on February 11.[38] Since we know of companies of players intermittently operating in London at this time, we may reasonably surmise that it was also staged at that time – probably 'the first regular play' to be premiered in London 'for eighteen years'.[39]

Who was John Tatham? He is first glimpsed as an aspirant playwright associated with the Red Bull Playhouse in the late 1630s, in circles led by established dramatists like Richard Brome and Thomas Heywood.[40] His stage ambitions were thwarted by political catastrophe, and the closure of the theatres this brought with it. His was a generation 'T'whom Civill War' was fated to become 'a nursery'.[41] When he re-emerged as a writer for performance, it was as scriptwriter for the

Lord Mayor's shows in the City of London from 1657 to 1664.[42] He therefore played a key role in the ceremonial mediation between metropolitan and national government in a period when the latter was, initially, a republican regime under Oliver Cromwell and, later, a resurgent monarchy under Charles II. Crafting shows which served the City's interests and were acceptable – or, at least, inoffensive – to those who in turn decreed state policy demanded delicate judgement. Their entrusting him with this responsibility across a period of profound political transformation suggests that the London authorities considered Tatham to be a writer closely attuned to their interests and equally alert to the changing imperatives of national politics.

Commentary has often homogenized Tatham's script with post-May 1660 comedies on Civil War and Interregnum themes.[43] Harold Love more helpfully associates *The Rump* with earlier non-dramatic satires on Puritans, which 'followed well-established models'.[44] Its sketches of overparted commanders fumbling with responsibilities to which they are wholly inadequate reiterate tropes long familiar from conservative caricatures of lowly-born Puritan – and, more recently, parliamentarian – leaders who betray their humble origins as they misperform disastrously in roles for which neither birth nor education qualifies them.[45] Tatham's satire indeed awards his principal historical figures the identical attributes for which other widely disseminated attacks had already made them individually notorious.[46] His script therefore restores to the public stage caricatures constantly rehearsed in print across the previous two decades.

The satirical techniques deployed in a specific work can, however, derive from a lengthy genealogy of similar mockery *and* be idiosyncratically inflected because of the particular circumstances from which it is generated, and to which it responds. For Richard W. Bevis, *The Rump* 'exists to spew venom on the Cromwellians, who are seen as grave threats to social order'.[47] This elides a distinction on which the play insists, since it depicts a rooted enmity between the legatees of the Cromwellian tradition and the military men who, in the winter of 1659–60, had the country's future in their hands. The latter never use Oliver's name without sneering at it, and Lambert, the leading figure in the new junta, proclaims as a key priority the achievement of 'my revenge upon that family' (I ii 69).[48] The acrimony provoked by this schism energizes scene after scene. What exactly is happening here?

The Rump sets its action at a pivotal moment. It opens with soldiers elated at the Rump Parliament's eviction by the army commanders, which means that London and its wealth are now at their mercy:

> 1 *Soul* . . . The town's our own, boys.
> 2 *Soul*. And all the wealth in't.
> 3 *Soul*. And wenches to boot, boys.
>
> (I i 3–6)

They are confident that Lambert, whom they adore, can now be 'our protector, our king, our emperor, our Caesar, our Kaiser, our – even what he pleaseth himself'

(51–3). In this new world 'the soldier's dialect' – which is to say, the 'searching language of the sword' (76–7) – rules all, and he who commands that can fashion the nation to his will.

Their hero, Lambert, is similarly obsessed with the opportunity within his grasp; but, for him, the moment when it can be finally realized is never quite yet, though it is always 'drawing near' (I ii 37). Tatham's derisory portrait of Lambert imputes to him an enfeebling incapacity to seize the chance fortune offers him. He is surrounded by self-interested fellow travellers, who supinely ask him 'what government must we have' (III i 41). But he comprehensively lacks the resolution required, and the comedy repeatedly notates his bathetic inaction. By the play's later stages the political initiative has as a consequence irretrievably passed into others' hands. As one of his dependents glumly remarks, 'Hereafter comes not yet, then, it seems' (III i 50). *The Rump* retrospectively evokes 'one of the defining moments of the English polity', when 'the future was to play for', and when those best placed to take the initiative faltered and fell.[49]

The historical Lambert was one of the outstanding figures of the mid-century, a supremely gifted commander, who could lay claim to joint credit with Cromwell for some key parliamentarian victories,[50] and who was the 'architect, and heir apparent, of the early Protectorate'.[51] No trace of this man of 'subtle and working brain'[52] is to be perceived in *The Rump*'s image of Lambert, which instead derives from a lengthy satiric tradition which depicted him as abjectly Cromwell's creature and creation – a legend reinforced, in popular rumour and comic burlesque, by awarding him cuckold's horns and crediting his master with bestowing them on him.[53] Early in the play, one of the delights of supreme command proposed to Lambert is the prospect that 'Princes have power o'er the persons of both sexes' – a privilege explicitly associated with Cromwell's reign: 'Oliver had it; his time is past, and your time's coming on' (I iii 114–15). But Lambert, publicly unmanned by Oliver during the latter's lifetime, can never, after his death, succeed in redressing the balance by exercising a matching control over the lives and rights of others. He will always remain the humiliated also-ran his conquering rival has made of him. His 'revenge upon that family' will never be fulfilled.

Salt is rubbed in his wound by the frantic gyrations of his wife. If he habitually procrastinates, she repeatedly telescopes the desired future into the present. Thus, at her first appearance, she insists on being called 'your Highness' (II i 41) in anticipation of the title she will gain as a result of his (she assumes) imminent elevation. Their abrasive encounters turn on her accelerating demands that her desires 'be put off no longer' (III i 271) by his failure to deliver. The domineering wife, tongue-lashing the inadequate husband, is a stereotype of early modern political satire, as imputed failure on the national stage is echoed, and confirmed, by an individual's display of similar inadequacy in maintaining hierarchy within the family.[54] The charge-sheet in such indictments often includes sexual incapacity. When Lady Lambert tells her maid that her husband 'is gone to be made a man' (i.e. seize supreme power), the latter inevitably misconstrues her and commiserates with the 'ill time' her mistress has had in bed (II i 29–32). But the error points us in the right direction. The play measures Lambert's insufficiency on a variety of fronts against the superabundant potency of his dead master.

Cromwell's presence in the play is Janus-faced.[55] From one perspective, the portrait of him as a sexual marauder brands him as a man who overrode moral and legal inhibitions in search of pleasure and the exercise of his will. From another, it identifies him as an antitype to Lambert's derided impotence. Placed in identical circumstances, Cromwell seized the moment without hesitation. The play insistently recollects the extraordinary sovereignty he so recently enjoyed. His widow, the principal custodian of his flame, scorns the pretensions of the current military leaders and stresses the annihilating contrast between their puny talents and the unique abilities of 'Oliver the First' (II ii 25). Their flagrant inadequacies indeed offer the ultimate evidence of his miracle-working powers:

> He that outdid all histories of kings or kaisers; was his own herald and could give titles of honor to the meanest peasants; made brewers, draymen, cobblers, tinkers, or anybody lords. Such was his power; no prince ever did the like. Amongst the rest, that precious piece thy husband [i.e. Lambert] was one of his making. (V i 16–23)

Once death removes him, those he transformed appear in their original baseness. *The Rump* chronicles with relish their pained realization that they have been 'but princes in disguise all this while' (IV vii 162–3). One key component in its tormenting of them is, therefore, the reiterated charge that they are grotesquely inadequate to the challenge of being Oliver's inheritors.

Cromwell's widow is not, in the main, a dignified figure in *The Rump*, which punitively reduces her at last to plebeian labour on the streets. The claim that the mid-century upheavals had seen the natural governing class displaced by rule by the lowest of the low is commonplace in contemporary satire, and *The Rump* reaffirms that vision in its final scene consigning the junta members and their hangers-on to trades – cobbling, selling turnips and oranges, etc. – it sneeringly deems more apt to their native gifts and humble origins. Only Mrs Cromwell is accorded the vision to foresee their inevitable fate. Her defence of her husband's pre-eminence in the face of denigration alerts her to how changed times rewrite reputations. Panegyrists – whether in poetic encomia or staged celebrations – are attuned to present realities and, with altered political circumstances, swiftly adopt fresh agendas. In the process, they may be required to deride those they had previously lauded. Accordingly, as Mrs Cromwell laments, 'the very names of the Cromwells will become far more odious then ever Needham could make the Heroicks [i.e. royalists]' (II i 99–102);[56] and, by hastening this process, Lambert and the rest blindly sow the seeds of their own downfall, since their only claim to power derives from their erstwhile Cromwellian loyalties and dependence.

Mrs Cromwell's scepticism speaks to Tatham's challenge in composing *The Rump*. How, at a moment of rapid, and as yet unconcluded, political change, can a dramatist, who had himself penned words in Cromwell's praise, safely negotiate such sensitive recent events? How, for example, should he evoke recollections of Cromwellian rule? In *The Rump* those who denigrate Cromwell are themselves systematically derided, which suggests that the play's view of him may be more complex. Many of those appalled by the anarchy to which they feared military rule was consigning the nation had previously accommodated themselves – with varying degrees of facility or reluctance – to the Protectorate government because, among other reasons, it seemed to offer the best prospect of lasting settlement. Their alarm at what was now happening in turn helped fashion the coalition which made the king's return possible. Charles II was thus the beneficiary of the contrast many perceived between the relatively stable rule of Cromwell and the chaotic uncertainties associated with the present military regime. Many of *The Rump*'s invocations of Cromwell's memory are indisputably negative. But other passages invite different responses, as, for instance, the bitter, trembling recollection from a Scottish republican – relishable, one surmises, to many in a London audience in early 1660 – that 'Cromwell was the veriest limmer loon that e'er cam intol our country' (III i 101–2). At the same time, some of its satiric jibes – for instance, Lambert's grumble that 'bribes, you know, are not now so frequent as they were in Noll's time' (III i 213–5) – implicitly acknowledge the self-fashioned dominance the Lord Protector had indisputably possessed. Whatever the ends to which he employed his gifts, Cromwell was, as Lady Lambert's personal experience enables her to testify, 'a man every inch of him' (II i 71).

If his direct political legatees are represented, in the same mode of punning, as men of 'no long standing' (II ii 19), what alternative models of male potency does the play celebrate? As street fighting between soldiers and civilians erupts, one such emerges in the bravura defiance of an unnamed apprentice, who leads his fellows against Colonel Hewson's troops. The notorious incident in which the latter fired on apprentices demonstrating against the current regime, and killed several of them, was an iconic moment in the disintegration of military rule, and one which Tatham elaborately stages. The apprentices' leader's pretensions to manhood are mocked by one of his peers – 'Thou a man! a meer pigmy!' (IV i 4) – and then justified by his offstage action, in overt retaliation for Hewson's outrages, in maiming (and possibly killing) 'a very fine fellow, some officer no doubt' (IV i 69–70). In the heavily gendered world of *The Rump* true male authority is reasserting itself.

The apprentices are, however, aware that they prepare the way for one greater than themselves – not Charles II, but General Monck, a hero whose credentials, like Cromwell's, are partly forged by his proven capacity to hold Scotland in a strong grasp. Monck's descent on London with his army prompts the evacuation from the capital of 'the fanatics' (IV viii 13),[57] whose supremacy he will end. His first major action, however, provokes alarm. Obeying the orders of the restored Rump, he forcibly dismantles the city's defences.[58] Tatham's apprentices record this event in the language of phallic aggression which is the play's recurrent idiom for notating political/military authority (or the lack of it). In the words of the apprentice hero,

> I know not what to think on't. Was ever such a rape committed upon a poor she city before? Lay her legs open to the wide world, for every rogue to peep in her breech. (V ii 3–6)

Having demonstrated his masculine credentials, however, Monck reveals his true political priorities and uses his undisputed supremacy to side with the City, promise 'a free Parliament' (V iii 21–2), and thus determine the Rump's final fall. The jubilant lead apprentice celebrates this outcome as the final resolution of a crisis begun two decades earlier and scornfully asks his fellows whether they are finally liberated from their 'fears and jealousies' (V iii 31). That phrase had been the watchword of parliamentary distrust of Charles I in 1640–2.[59] Now the time has come for such 'dirty suspicion' (V iii 32) to be abandoned in favour of faith in a military leader who, unlike Lambert, promises the City security from others' rapacity and a calm restoration of its, and the nation's, customary rights.

The play's concluding scenes enact the Rump-burning celebrations of February 1660 and record the humiliating fates of the would-be grandees who have now been irretrievably evicted from power. As the bonfires flame, the lead apprentice proclaims that 'we are beginning the world again' (V iv 73–4), while Desborough confesses that he and his cronies now possess 'No remedy against the king's evil' (V v 15). So these closing moments do embrace as inevitable Charles II's imminent return. The primary dramatic emphasis, however, rests on what is being ended, not on an extended envisioning of the brave new world which may lie ahead. This comedy by the City's favoured scriptwriter gives precedence to the capital's escape from the horrific threat to its prosperity and property represented by continued republican rule rather than to outright celebration of the triumphant justice of the restoration of monarchy. For examples of the latter, we must look elsewhere in the voluminous writings of spring and early summer 1660.

In tune with these priorities, *The Rump*'s epilogue informs its spectators that they have been offered '*here in a* MIRROUR *the Crimes / Of the late Pageantry Changeling Times*', but also interrogates their response to this spectacle and claims to judge from its inspection of their '*Brows*' (p. 68)[60] that they have contrived to pass the crucial test. The watchful performers have detected no symptoms of guilt at past actions or traces of residual loyalty to vanquished causes in their reactions to the comedy's satire. The epilogue's tone is difficult to pin down. How straight-faced is it? Might its delivery have allowed some glancing acknowledgement that the sudden political transformations overtaking the nation imposed on at least some of those present a need to refashion their public behaviour and reinvent their political credentials? The immediately preceding final speech of the play proper is a soliloquy from Bulstrode Whitelocke, working out his own tactics for survival in a potentially hostile environment. The real Whitelocke, because of his conspicuous involvement with successive 1650s regimes, ran the risk of being one of those excluded from the mercy offered by the Act of Indemnity and Oblivion, and only gained security after circuitous negotiations.[61] Audiences for *The Rump* – before and after Charles II's return – must have contained many whose 1640s and 1650s histories would not sustain close inspection in the new dawn of 1660. Behn's decision to adopt for her own play material from a script like Tatham's, so intimately inflected by the political experience of a highly specific moment of complex transition, represents an intriguing move.[62]

Behn's indebtedness to texts from twenty years earlier does not end with *The Rump*. *The Roundheads* is also profoundly influenced by another earlier comedy about the Interregnum, Sir Robert Howard's *The Committee* (1662), which had earned itself a regular place in the post-1660s repertoire. In this case, however, the effect is more on structure and design than on particular passages of dialogue. Tatham's and Howard's portraits of life under republican control diverge emphatically. Here too, it will be helpful to explore *The Committee* in its own right before finally re-examining Behn's deployment of this intricate and contradictory inheritance in her own work. Contextualizing *The Committee*, however, can best begin by invoking another play which in its turn influenced Howard's own tactics. This is the first 'new' comedy on Interregnum experiences to be performed post-May 1660: Abraham Cowley's *Cutter of Coleman Street* – a work, which, like *The Rump*, bears witness to the strain of living in times of rapid political flux. Cowley's controversial play introduced to the Restoration stage key issues which would, two decades later, be of fundamental importance to *The Roundheads*.

Cutter is a provocative rewriting of *The Guardian*, a play Cowley had improvised at high speed two decades earlier. In March 1642, the worsening crisis prompted the removal of the Prince of Wales, the future Charles II, from an increasingly unsafe London. He stayed at Trinity College, Cambridge, on his way north; and, despite having only one week's notice, the college prompted Cowley to devise a five-act comedy to entertain its guest. *The Guardian*'s author later recorded that it was 'neither *made* nor *acted*, but *rough-drawn* onely, nor *learnt without-Book* by the *Actors*', though the prince reportedly 'gave all signs of a great acceptance which he could, and more than the University dared expect'.[63]

The Guardian's action is identified as occurring on the day on which it was premiered in Cambridge, 12 March 1642. The prologue insists that the metropolis is now unsafe for the loyal: '*by the rout | We perish if the Roundheads be about*' (p. 161).[64] But the London *The Guardian* itself portrays is a peacetime one, familiar from numerous city comedies of the 1630s and earlier. The dialogue lovingly evokes its famous sights, assembly points, and pleasure places – 'the Queens Cake-House' in Moorfields (p. 163), and trips 'to Mortlake in the Easter-holy-days' (p. 196). Its playhouses and other performance sites inspire resonant evocations, whether it be seeing '*Tamerlain* at the Bull' (p. 195) or the street theatre of 'the dancing o' the ropes, and the Puppet-play of Nineve' (p. 217). The prologue stresses the inveterate hostility of the king's enemies to plays, but within the fiction the capital's favourite entertainments proceed unmolested. Similarly, the play's dialogue gives no hint of any serious challenge to the authority of the Court, which remains in *The Guardian* securely ensconced at Whitehall.

In his 1663 preface to *Cutter*, Cowley insisted that '*Comedy is humble of her Nature, and has alwayes been bred low, so that she knows not how to behave her self with the great or the accomplisht*' (p. 263). *The Guardian* reflects that principle by focusing on figures struggling to evade the irreversible descent into absolute penury and social oblivion which constantly threatens them. Cowley here reveals his Jonsonian loyalties. Numerous passages of invective echo, in particular, the mutual excoriation of Face and Subtle in *The Alchemist*'s opening scene, where Face pictures Subtle 'Taking your meale of steeme in, from cookes stalls, / Where, like the father of hunger, you did walke / Piteously costiue', and Subtle retaliates by proclaiming that he rescued Face 'out of dung, / So poore, so wretched, when no liuing thing / Would keep thee companie, but a spider, or worse' (I i 26–8, 64–6).[65] Cowley's Dogrel similarly indicts Cutter: 'Those breeches he wears, and his hat, I gave him: till then, he went like a Paper-mill all in rags' (p. 171), while Cutter returns the compliment woundingly: 'I'll tell you how I found him; marry walking in Moorfields cross arm'd: he could not pluck his hat over his eyes, there were so many holes in it: he had not so much linen about him as would make a cuff for a Bartlemew-fayr-baby' (p. 170).

Such disdainful narratives of shameful origins are matched, as in *The Alchemist*, by repeated prophecies of these characters' imminent, enforced return to their native condition, as in the contemptuous prediction that Dogrel will soon 'Be abandon'd by all men above a Tapster; and not dare to looke a gentleman i'the face; unless perhaps you sneak into a Play-house, at the fifth Act' – i.e. when admission was free. Even worse is the prospect of becoming the butt of others' derision. Thus, another character shivers at the prospect of being 'sung in Smithfield' and the fear that 'not a blinde Ale-house, but *the life and miserable death of captain Blade* shall be pasted up' (pp. 181–2). It is not only in the lowliest taverns, however, that such spectacles are relished. This is a comedy about an undignified struggle for survival, fashioned for the delectation of spectators who can observe these figures' humiliations from a comfortable distance.

The road to eventual thriving here, as in most city comedy, is trickery, and the potential targets a Puritan widow and her daughter. The conmen's ruse is a (temporary) pretended conversion to the women's separatist beliefs, and their ultimate goal ensnaring the latter, and their wealth, in marriage. In the *Cutter* preface, Cowley reminded his readers of the derivation of their denigrators' favourite abusive epithet for Puritans – '*Hypocrites (that is, by interpretation Actors with a Vizard)*' (p. 263). This hostile stereotype insisted that the Puritan espousal of extreme austerity was mere masquerade, and that their lives evinced a total contradiction between professed belief and reality of practice. Thus, in a familiar sneer, they were represented as opposing stage playing, not because they genuinely judged it impermissible, but because they intended to have no professional rivals to their own real life histrionics.[66] Accordingly, *The Guardian* proposes an apt nemesis for its two '*Hypocrites*' – i.e. that they should be ensnared by a pair of low-grade tricksters who insolently mimic the women's own performances and pretences. The victory is easily secured, and puritan resistance melts swiftly away, not even to be revived when the imposture is revealed. Outside the fiction, these may be times when, as the prologue asserts, the loyal must be prepared to defend their cause with their lives. Within it, the enemy's representatives can be swiftly neutralized by play-acting so transparent it derides those who are taken in by it. *The Guardian* effectively denies the political schism which brought it into existence.

According to Cowley, the play's stage history was sustained after its single Cambridge performance by several private stagings '*during the troubles*'. He also continued to work on it himself, revising '*many things in it which I disliked*'. Its final reinvention as *Cutter of Coleman Street* involved, he claimed, '*the changing of it almost wholly*' (p. 261). That is an exaggeration; but some aspects of its updating were indeed radical. *Cutter* is explicitly – and very unusually for a seventeenth-century comedy – set three years before the date of its first performance, in the final summer of Oliver Cromwell's regime; and some of its leading characters are royalists, confronting the dilemma of how to accommodate themselves to rule by their former enemies. If *The Guardian* elides the political conflagration engulfing the nation, *Cutter* confronts directly some painful consequences of the mid-century crisis for the king's supporters.

This proved to be a tender subject for audiences in 1661, and Cowley found himself faced with accusations that he had written '*a piece intended for abuse and Satyre against the Kings party*'. His immediate reaction was to assert that '*After having served it twenty years during all the time of their misfortunes and afflictions, I must be a very rash and imprudent person if I chose out that of their Restitution to begin a Quarrel with them*' (p. 261). This could itself be construed as a '*rash and imprudent*' response, since it leaves out of account Cowley's notorious preface to his 1656 *Poems*. There he had conceded the permanent defeat of the royalist cause and argued that 'we must' therefore 'lay down our *Pens* as well as *Arms*'. The gracious victor has allowed 'a *General Amnestie*, as a *favor*', and in reciprocation the defeated must avoid cultivating 'a kind of *Artificial Memory* of those things wherein we are all bound to desire, like Themistocles, the Art of Oblivion'. Party names 'should be extinguished', and it should be 'accounted no less unlawful to *rip up old wounds*, then to *give new ones*', to which end Cowley records that this 1656 collection reprints none of his partisan pieces.[67]

The explicitness of this statement earned Cowley many enemies, and after the Restoration he never enjoyed the favour from Charles II he anticipated. A regime which passed its own Act of Indemnity and Oblivion was not in this instance inclined to forgetfulness.[68] In such circumstances Cowley's revision of *The Guardian* as *Cutter of Coleman Street* must have seemed to some indiscreetly provocative. In *The Guardian* Captain Blade has, through his own indiscretion, lost his estate to a now dead usurer. By wooing the latter's widow, Blade succeeds in repossessing what had once been his own. In *Cutter* Colonel Jolly, formerly a commander in royalist service, has had his estate confiscated by one of the sequestration committees, which punished in this way those who had borne arms against Parliament. His land was then immediately purchased by 'My good Neighboor, . . . Collonel *Fear-the-Lord-Barebottle*, a Saint and a Sope-boyler', who is 'dead, and boiling now himself' (p. 273). So the same means of revitalizing his fortunes presents itself to Jolly as to Blade, but the stakes are higher for Jolly.

Cowley's portrayal of him projects his audience back to a recent time of edgy uncertainty, when the road to a restored monarchy seemed perilously uncertain, and when simple survival was the primary goal for many who had steadfastly served the royalist cause, and who now could only gaze in horror at the flamboyant prosperity of their triumphant enemies. Desperate times breed undignified alliances. Thus, in his alcoholic depression, Jolly tolerates as his drinking companions the seedy conmen Cutter and Worm, whom he also intensely despises and recurrently arraigns. These *Alchemist*-inflected diatribes echo those in *The Guardian*, but now give their targets a distinctively post-1642 history, as spivs who eke out a living by claiming fraudulent royalist war records, with which they gull and pillage the impressionable – 'young Foremen of the Shop, or little beardless Blades of the Inns of Court' (p. 276). In his most furious eruption, Jolly banishes both from his house on threat of having 'my Scullions batter you with Bones and Turneps, and the Maids drown you with Pisspots' (p. 317).

Such a proud insistence on traditional lines of social demarcation is not always practicable for Jolly. Marrying Mistress Barebottle, in particular, requires that he overcome intense revulsion. As his niece points out, if 'the King should come in again, ... you'd be very proud of a Soap-boyler's Widow then in *Hide-park*, Sir' (p. 297). *The Guardian* had not insisted in this way on the hierarchical divide between its equivalent figures. In contrast, *Cutter* takes as read the conservative 1640s/1650s propaganda polarization which pitted royalist gentry against revolutionary upstarts, who bizarrely defied their abject origins to strut forcefully, if undignifiedly, on the national stage. Adjusting himself to the practical exigencies of his dire situation means that Jolly must, in effect, commit a form of miscegenation, so complete is the gap between his and the widow's blood-lines conceived as being. But need dictates, and the alliance is finally achieved. *Cutter's* dialogue recurrently generates wishes for Charles II's eventual return, but it never bestows prophetic powers upon its characters. Thus, a drunken wish that the king may return 'In Triumph' is yoked with the hope that he may 'live till he see, / Old *Noll* upon a Tree' (p. 295). After the Restoration, Cromwell's corpse was dug up and his butchered limbs displayed; but his sudden death, later in that same summer in which Cowley chose to set *Cutter*, rendered unrealizable the hope that Charles would one day personally witness his hanging. Retrospection acquainted audiences in 1661 with knowledge unavailable to the play's characters. In the meantime, the latter must take, with their limited knowledge, the urgent decisions the struggle for survival demands of them.

In one other crucial respect, *Cutter* plays on information unavailable to its characters. Why did Cowley change the play's title for its Restoration restaging? Coleman Street and the surrounding area had long been known as a part of London in which separatist congregations clustered. So it provides an apt location for the Barebottle family. But January 1661 had made the place newly infamous. During the night of 6–7 January a group of Fifth Monarchists, led by Thomas Venner, completed worship in their meeting-house off Coleman Street and then took to the streets, armed, to bring in the reign of Christ by violence. The uprising cost numerous lives, took three days to put down, and prompted unnerving rumours throughout an alarmed city that it heralded a more widespread insurrection. The fears it generated played into the hands of the architects of the Cavalier Reaction, which resulted, over the next few years, in the passing of an extraordinary sequence of repressive legislation.[69]

Including Coleman Street in the title unavoidably recalls these recent events – an effect compounded by the conjoined use in it of Cutter's name, since the latter's contemporary meanings included a 'person overready to use a weapon', 'a cutthroat' (*OED*, *n*., 3). Cowley emends the language of the scenes of Cutter's mock conversion in ways which prompt further memories of the January outrages.

Accordingly, Cutter now anticipates declaring 'to the Congregation of the Lovely in *Coleman-Street'* his vision that 'Venner shall march up to us from the West in the figure of a Wave of the Sea, holding in his hand a Ship that shall be call'd the Ark of the Reform'd'. Cutter also foretells his own 'return upon a Purple Dromadory, which signifies Magistracy, with an Ax in my hand that is called Reformation' (p. 308) and protests that he who is 'zealous even to slaying' cannot 'walk in the streets without a Sword' (p. 329). The equivalent passages in *The Guardian* take no such risks. In both plays, the premise is that the language Cutter spouts is nonsense; but in *Cutter* it is nonsense which recently brought bloodshed to London's streets. In his preface to *Cutter*, Cowley confesses that comedy is '*an Edg'd Tool'* (p. 261), while in his epilogue for a Court performance he asserts the need to see '*Tragique Follies brought to Comedy'* (p. 341). *Cutter* was premiered in December 1661. On 19 January of the same year Pepys had witnessed Venner 'upon a sledge' on his way to be hanged, drawn and quartered.[70] Was Cowley accurate in judging that those events could already be safely deployed to update a conman's patter in a plot invented two decades earlier in decisively different circumstances? The fact that revivals of *Cutter* later in the 1660s appear to have been advertised under the title of *The Guardian* may suggest that he had miscalculated.[71]

The objections to *Cutter* Cowley himself recorded, however, hinge on its representation of royalism. He replied that human imperfection has always provided '*the Principal Subjects of all Comedy'* (p. 262), and that charting the fallibilities of a man like Jolly in no way involved slandering the honourable cause he had served. But such abstract arguments were beside the point. *Cutter* vividly reminded its audiences of a recent time when compromise with the current regime had been indispensable to many. To some at least among them, that was an indiscreet and unwelcome move on Cowley's part. The following year saw the premiere of a comedy much more to the taste of such spectators – one which would earn, half a century later, the accolade, as reported by *The Spectator'*s Sir Roger de Coverly, of 'a good Church of *England* Comedy'.[72]

Sir Robert Howard's *The Committee* centres on the confrontation between defeated royalists and the sequestration committee which aims to plunder their estates. So, what figured as backstory in *Cutter* now provides the primary focus for conflict. Characterization of the two sides is rigidly polarized on lines indebted to 1640s and 1650s satires on these agents of parliamentarian rule.[73] The committee officials are lowly born, greedily self-interested, craven, and hypocritical, while the royalists are intensely principled, mutually supportive, courageous, and insistent on the purity of their bloodstock. Social disdain, provoked by irksome experience of a world turned upside down where 'The great ones obey, / While the rascals do sway' (IV ii 99–100),[74] inflects exchange after exchange. Thus, a royalist colonel, arrested for debt by bailiffs, finds the situation intolerably indecorous: 'Must I wait your leisures?' (III.iii.3). When later instructed by the same oppressors that 'Blood is dear', he sneers back: 'Not yours, is it?' (IV i 12).[75] It is, therefore, characteristic of Howard's tactics that the committee chairman's domineering wife, Mrs Day, is soon unmasked as formerly a 'kitchen maid and in time of yore called Gillian' (III i 18–19).

The play establishes a double perspective upon this situation. When its plot requires, the peril with which parliament's supremacy confronts its heroes is emphasized, and the occasion provided for bravura demonstrations of defiance and resolve. In the process, *The Committee* distinguishes itself absolutely from *Cutter*. Where Jolly devoted himself to reclaiming his property by any means available, Howard's colonels abjure compromise with the present regime, even if that means losing their estates. Their composure in the face of adversity is sustained by hopes, however tentative, of another reversal of fortune's wheel:

COLONEL BLUNT The day may come when those that suffer for their consciences and honor may be rewarded.
MR DAY Aye, aye, you make an idol of that honor.
COLONEL BLUNT Our worships, then, are different. You make that your idol which brings your interest. We can obey that which bids us lose it.

(II iv 202–7)

Such rhetoric is alien to the spirit of Cowley's comedy, but here it wins the rapt applause of two heiresses whose estates the Days also aim to absorb. One of them, Ruth, is already passed off by them as if she were their daughter, while they have targeted the other, Arbella, as a potential wife for their hapless son Abel. Much plot energy is consumed in preventing this happening. In the world of *The Committee* miscegenation must be avoided at all costs. A myth of blood purity is being reaffirmed, disregarding the reality of a conflict in which members of the same gentry family had often espoused different loyalties. Even Howard's own kin had 'not been unanimous in' their 'allegiance to the Crown'.[76]

From another perspective the play's events offer a different kind of experience to its royalist leads, especially the women. Mrs Day's Amazonian dominance of her husband derives from the same satiric tradition which fed *The Rump*'s portrait of Lady Lambert. But the gender power balance on the royalist side also favours the women. Colonels Blunt and Careless are assigned numerous admirable qualities, but in wit and initiative Ruth, in particular, definitively outplays them, and for her the experience of the action in which she participates is mainly a comic one. In her encounters with the Days she often turns aside to share with the audience the laughter to which their gyrations provoke her. At other moments she is agog with anticipation for the next 'sport' (I ii 159) their actions will generate for her to savour. She is also often the active orchestrator of the scenes she relishes, as when she instructs Abel how to slow down yet further his already ponderous demeanour. His lethargic pomposity is conceived as a dismissive caricature of puritan pretensions, and Ruth in effect functions here as the playwright's surrogate, intensifying (at his behest) his existing effects and weaving enhanced climaxes out of the role's basic joke.

She also takes the lead in advocating humour as a key royalist weapon in times of adversity, as when she advises Arbella that 'Cheerful spirits are the best bladders to swim with; if thou art sad, the weight will sink thee' (I ii 236–8), to which Arbella gladly responds that 'they cannot bring us to compound for our humours; they shall be free still' (242–3). Careless too picks up the same theme, as when he asserts, before the sequestration committee, that 'clear souls make light hearts' (II iv 221). In this play, parliamentarians are by definition incapable of genuine humour, and can only be its butts; while the royalist penchant to relish the absurdity of the world around them allows them to defy its ability to subdue them to the time's imperatives. Thus, Howard reaffirms that central pretension of royalist war-time propaganda: that wit was 'the natural inheritance of men "Borne to rule"'.[77]

Ruth's comic gifts are not only exercised on parliamentarians. Careless is also made to feel their force. Unlike his friend Blunt, Careless, as his name indicates, has libertine inclinations. He is attracted to Ruth, but believes her to be the Days' offspring and thus beneath him as a potential wife. When Blunt asks if he could 'love any of the other breed', his punning reply is: 'Not honestly' (III i 101–2) – i.e. not virtuously or chastely, though he would be happy to bed her 'dishonestly' outside marriage; but also, he could not marry her and remain faithful to his royalist principles, a contemporary meaning of 'honest' Howard keeps in play throughout, but which he also at one point glosses for us:

> MUSICIAN . . . You seem honest gentlemen.
> COLONEL CARELESS   Cavaliers, thou mean'st.
> (IV ii 88–90)

In his wooing of Ruth, Careless fulfils one stereotype of the arrogant Cavalier seducer, proposing nonchalantly that, while it would be against his conscience 'by the way of matrimony honestly to increase your generation', he would happily create bastards with her, since ' 'tis not fit a Committeeman's daughter should be too honest, to the reproach of her father and mother' (III iv 189–90, 195–7). Ruth's response to this is double – delight that he will not contemplate marrying into the Days, mingled with disapproval of his loose sexual habits. So, a bewildered Careless finds himself receiving sermons in morality from someone he still believes to be a Day – including an insistence that, because he is 'honest' in his refusal to compromise with his political enemies, he should also be undeviatingly 'honest' in all aspects of his behaviour, including eschewing all 'dishonest love' (V ii 57). In their climactic encounter she finally reveals that she also loves him 'honestly', since her genealogy and politics are irreproachably gentry and royalist. As Careless accepts re-education in what it is to be a self-consistent royalist, Day's extra-marital imbroglios are humiliatingly unmasked. Another firm antithesis between cavalier and rebel has therefore been constructed; and, in the process, Careless has been fashioned into an antitype to Cowley's louche, drink-loving, compromising Colonel Jolly. *The Committee* is designed as a brisk purification of royalism's self-image, which seeks to open the eyes of those who mistakenly believe that sleeping with the enemy can be reconciled with true loyalism.

One final contrast with *Cutter* invites noting. In its concluding stages, *The Committee*'s royalists turn the tables on their persecutors and blackmail them into relinquishing the confiscated estates they control. In effect, their initiative secures for them, under the republic, the consummation devoutly wished for, and often not obtained, by the similarly dispossessed after the king's return. Complaints about the unfair nature of the land settlement post-1660 were legion, and Howard was himself closely involved in the process, both as supplicant and office holder.[78] The 'mythmaking ability' Susan Staves observes in him is at work here.[79] Whereas *Cutter* permits its characters the limited freedom of manoeuvre plausible for its 1658 setting, *The Committee* credits its royalists with the skill to cheat history and achieve a personal victory under the very gaze of the republic, and tops its insouciance off by concluding on a couplet which instructs the Days that 'If you will have good luck in everything, / Turn Cavalier and cry, "God bless the King"' (V vii 232–3). It is almost as if the Restoration were already an accomplished fact.

In devising her own play about living under republican rule it was natural for Behn to look for inspiration to this group of plays written on the cusp of the Restoration itself. In Howard and Buckingham's *The Country Gentleman* (1669), a loquacious landlady's attempt to recount her father's death (doubtless, in royalist service) is halted by another character's brusquely instructing her, 'No history now I beseech you'.[80] That neatly captures the priorities of stage comedy in the late 1660s and throughout most of the 1670s. Life in the 1640s/50s was now, in comedy, effectively a closed book, and allusions to mid-century turmoils became infrequent, and usually a matter of only glancing reference. The Popish Plot and Exclusion Crisis transformed this situation once again; but, even then, before *The Roundheads* no author chose to make the kinds of situation Tatham, Cowley, and Howard had addressed central to the design of a new comedy.

From *The Rump* Behn took her line-up of historical figures and numerous satiric encounters between them, including domestic spats between Lambert and his wife and feckless assemblies of would-be grandees grossly inadequate to the challenges with which their Cromwellian inheritance burdens them. She emended and elaborated what she borrowed, but a great deal of Tatham's script survived essentially unaltered. She departed from it, however, in three decisive ways. Firstly, her action continues to the moment of the Restoration itself. Secondly, her comedy displays none of the affection for London, its citizens, and its government which was fundamental to Tatham's writing. She retains, for instance, the description of Monck's dismantling of the city's defences as an act of rape; but what in Tatham causes alarm is here inflected with anti-Puritan relish (pp. 419–40). A rebellious city is getting its just deserts. And, finally, the prologue to *The Rump* boasts that its action indulges '*No Amorous Puling passions*' (sig. A2v), a precedent *The Roundheads* disregards.

It is here that the influence of *The Committee* shows itself most clearly. Behn followed Howard in making central to her plot two cavaliers' vexatious dealings with the sequestration committee which holds their patrimony in its grip. She also echoed him in complicating this action by giving each cavalier a love-interest. In *The Committee*, one of these caused her wooer discomfort because she appeared to belong to his enemies' bloodline. *The Roundheads* weaves a provocative variation on this, by selecting as its principal female characters women married to the leading military commanders Lambert and Desborough, each, of course, a key player in the republic's final days. So, courtships which might/will lead to marriage are replaced by potentially adulterous entanglements. This identifies *The Round-heads'* kinship with the rich sequence of adultery comedies premiered during the Exclusion Crisis, which pit Tory lover/seducer against Whig citizen for possession of the latter's wife.[81] None of Behn's fellows had, however, devised such a complex situation as the one on which the most striking scenes in *The Roundheads* hinge.

One of the partnerships is founded in long-established affection. Whereas Howard's Arbella can only ineffectually wish that she could do something to rescue Blunt's property and simultaneously struggle to avoid marriage into the Day tribe, Behn's Maria has demonstrated her devotion to Freeman by marrying Desbor-ough, an action undertaken to secure Freeman's estate, of which her husband's chicanery has made him master. Her self-sacrifice is rewarded by Behn's decreeing Desborough's unhistorical death at the very moment of the Restoration, which enables her finally to reunite Freeman with his lost acres.

Their encounters, however, also shadow *The Committee*'s other key partnership. In a co-operatively candle-lit chamber, Freeman tries to woo Maria into bed with him, arguing that 'you've only lent your Body out to one whom you call Husband, and whom Heav'n has mark'd for Cuckoldom', and that the adultery would there-fore be 'an Act of honest Loyalty, so to revenge our Cause' (p. 397). But, just as Careless's decadent brand of royalism was chastened by Ruth's purer defini-tion of the meaning of 'honest', so Maria rebukes Freeman's facile opportunism by insisting that complying with his desires would prove that she was 'so much debauch'd by Conventickling to turn a Sainted Sinner'. As Ruth affirmed that her absorption into the Day tribe was only apparent and temporary, so Maria claims that her willingness to give herself in marriage to a man she detests does not subdue her to the nature of those with whom she must now associate. Freeman cannot produce coherent sense from what she says. For him, making 'a League and Covenant with such Villains' and then keeping 'the sinful Contract' is simply bizarre, and he counsels the virtue of 'a little harmless Lying and Dissimulation'. Her response is a resounding reaffirmation of her brand of royalism:

> I'm true to my Allegiance still, true to my King and Honour. Suspect my Loyalty when I lose my Virtue; a little Time, I'm sure, will give me honestly into thy Arms, if thou hast Bravery show it in thy Love.

Like Careless before him, Freeman yields before this evocation of true faith: 'You will o'recome, and shame me every way' (p. 398). Recent commentators have often echoed his sentiments and accepted Maria's rhetoric at face value.[82] But this disregards the gulf which separates the clarity of the instructions in cavalier honesty Ruth bestows on Careless from the problematic selectivity of Maria's conception of 'Virtue'. The marriage-vow here dwindles to a promise of bodily fidelity, while in every other way the wife is licensed to scheme against the partner she willingly embraced. This esoteric definition of 'Virtue' works to justify the fact that the other promises made in wedlock were taken by Maria with fully premeditated deceitfulness. Extreme times produce extreme responses, and the play clearly applauds her self-sacrifice; but her unstable attempt to bestow ethical coherence on her actions exposes how radically the world of *The Roundheads* diverges from that of *The Committee.*

This plot's intricacies look pallid, however, beside Behn's flamboyant development of the relationship between Lady Lambert and Loveless. From one perspective, their story reruns the stereotypical narrative of the sexually dissatisfied parliamentarian wife magnetically drawn by the spectacle of cavalier manhood in its prime. But that core situation is relentlessly complicated by Behn. For a start, this is no ordinary parliamentarian wife. Behn aggravates the overweening aspirations of Lady Lambert as portrayed in *The Rump* to the point where her domination over her husband now makes her the real architect of their joint ascent to power. One scholar has claimed that Behn absolves her of responsibility 'for the political corruption of England', because as a woman she is 'disempowered' and has 'been bartered or coerced into marriage', and represents 'a figure of resistance within the Roundheads' debased political order'.[83] This denies what the text clearly asserts and reasserts. Behn's Lady Lambert is a zealous participant in the revolutionary project, which for her coincides totally with her own self-advancement. She energetically incarnates the propaganda trope which deploys the image of the 'woman-on-top' as emblematic of a political world-turned-upside-down. Behn renders her apostasy undeniable by larding her dialogue with incriminating titbits. After the regicide in 1649, for instance, a royalist newsbook indignantly credited Cromwell with a humiliating plan to apprentice Charles I's youngest son to the trade of brewing[84] – a scheme which Behn's Lady Lambert explicitly regrets was not carried out. Hearing her say this provokes Loveless to thoughts of violence; but, in the same speech, he acknowledges 'the Joy she gave me but now' (p. 386). Howard's Careless struggled with the mistaken belief that Ruth carried polluted blood; but Loveless's dilemma is a far more convulsive one. He is ardently and hypnotically attracted to a woman who represents everything he politically detests.

In the civil war stereotype the potent cavalier invaded the roundhead bed in order to perform the offices an inadequate husband left unperformed and then went carefreely on his way. Parliamentarian sexual inadequacy polarized against royalist erotic prowess is one inherited antithesis Behn imports wholesale into *The Roundheads.* But sleeping with the enemy here causes turmoil in the cavalier breast. The encounters between Lady Lambert and Loveless are persistently unstable in mood. Space does not permit a detailed examination of all of them; so I intend to concentrate on an extraordinary sequence from Act 4, where the political and the amorous intertwine in ways unprecedented in Restoration comedy.

Behn's cuckolding plot is complicated by two facts: the husband is already a cuckold, and the cuckold-maker was no less a person than Oliver Cromwell. Memories of the Lord Protector are as ubiquitous and resonant in *The Roundheads* as in *The Rump*, and prove as humiliating in their implications for his political legatees. His shadow also haunted Restoration England. Demonization mingled with compelled respect. Clarendon, for instance, stressed the wickedness Cromwell had committed, but also recorded that:

he must have had a wonderful understanding in the natures and humours of men, and as great a dexterity in the applying them, who from a private and obscure birth, (though of a good family,) without interest of estate, alliance or friendships, could raise himself to such a height, and compound and knead such opposite and contradictory tempers, humours, and interests, into a consistence that contributed to his designs and to their own destruction; whilst himself grew insensibly powerful enough to cut off those by whom he had climbed, in the instant that they projected to demolish their own building.[85]

Even in the year of the king's return, a biography appeared which treated Cromwell 'with intelligent sympathy'; and, at moments of crisis or despair in the succeeding years, his record was always liable to be cited in unfavourable comparison with present governmental shortcomings, since 'the reality of success' was his. He 'had led victorious armies', 'united the three kingdoms', 'brought order where chaos had formerly prevailed' and 'asserted the nation's international position in forceful ways'.[86] He had also never been ousted. Royalism's victory had been made possible only by the void left by his untimely death. His defenceless body could be insulted and mutilated, but he remained forever undefeated.

The liaison into which Loveless is being drawn therefore includes not two, but three, other parties – a wife, a husband, and a previous, now dead, lover. So, that neat, familiar antithesis of potent cavalier and impotent parliamentarian is here disrupted by memories of a libertine Cromwell, whose sexual mastery matched his political dominance, and who cannot therefore, on either account, be convincingly subdued by the casual contempt the play casts on its other abject representatives of republican rule. If he too becomes Lady Lambert's lover, Loveless will not only be displacing the woebegone Lambert, but also competing against the ghost presence of her omni-potent original seducer.

An early exchange between Behn's cavalier heroes foreshadows the complexities to follow:

FREEMAN   But suppose now, dear *Loveless*, that one of the Wives of these Pageant Lords should fall in love with thee, and get thy Estate again, or pay thee double for't?
LOVELESS   I wou'd refuse it.
FREEMAN   And this for a little dissembled Love, a little Drudgery —
LOVELESS   Not a night by Heav'n – not an hour – no not a single kiss, I'd rather make love to an *Incubus*.
FREEMAN   But suppose 'twere the new Protectoress her self, the fine Lady *Lambert*?
LOVELESS   The greatest Devil of all; Damn her, dost think I'll Cuckold the Ghost of old *Oliver*?
FREEMAN   The better; there's some Revenge in't; do'st know her?
LOVELESS   Never saw her, nor care to do.

(p. 370)

Cowley's Jolly sought to retrieve his estate by marriage with his enemy's widow – in 1661, for some, a controversial premise around which to shape a comic plot.

Twenty years later, Freeman calmly recommends that his friend achieve the same outcome by serving as gigolo to a junta wife and then dresses this action up as revenge upon her previous lover. The real triumph would, of course, have been to displace Cromwell as Lady Lambert's paramour during the former's lifetime. That would have implied extraordinary daring, but would have replicated the strategy of numerous *c.*1680 cuckolding plays, in which Whig husbands are humiliated by being sexually displaced by Tory rakes. Nothing in *The Roundheads*, however, renders this a conceivable scenario. Like Lambert, Desborough, and their fellows, Loveless's opportunity comes only *because* Cromwell is dead. It is revealing that Loveless slips into treating him as Lady Lambert's authentic spouse, when he describes the proposed adultery as a matter of cuckolding 'the Ghost of old *Oliver*'. The lover's authority is so total that he has become her *de facto* husband, just as Cromwell had also become *de facto* ruler of the nation; and that authority persists even after his death, so that it is he, not Lambert, who would be cuckolded if Loveless deigned to follow Freeman's advice.

Behn's Lady Lambert, like Tatham's, eloquently celebrates Cromwell's peerless supremacy, but outgoes her predecessor in the expansive frankness with which she spells out his phallic dominance. Her forlorn husband is, for instance, the target of this onslaught:

> You'll warrant? you're a Fool and a Coxcomb; I see I must go my self, there will be no bus'ness done 'till I thunder 'em together: They want *Old Oliver* amongst 'em, his arbitrary Nod cou'd make ye all tremble; when he wanted Power or Money, he need but Cock in Parliament, and lay his hand upon his Sword, and cry, I must have Money, and had it, or kick'd ye all out a doors: And you are so mealy mouth'd, you cannot Cock for a Kingdom. (p. 387)

By the time of their climactic encounter in Act IV, however, she is awarding Loveless the kind of praise she previously reserved for the Lord Protector. Giving him a diamond bracelet, she narrates its history:

> This the great Monarch of the World once ty'd about my Arm, and bade me
> wear it, till some greater man shou'd chance to win my Heart:
> Thou art that man whom Love hath rais'd above him;
> Whom every Grace and every Charm thou hast
> Conspire to make thee mightier to my Soul;
> And *Oliver*, Illustrious *Oliver!*
> Was yet far short of thee.
>
> (p. 405)

In her eulogies of Cromwell, his ability to 'Cock' was exemplified in the political arena as persuasively as in the boudoir. Her praise of Loveless, in comparison, risks depending principally on penis comparisons ('yet far short of thee'), as she eyes the charms of the man she wants to bed. From a royalist/Tory perspective, Loveless may evince the political virtue of passive loyalty – a man secure in his allegiance to Stuart kingship, but waiting patiently for events, and the actions of others, to procure the restoration of the monarch he serves, and on whose fortunes he depends. At this point, however, Lady Lambert remains devoted to her own advancement and does not treat Loveless's political loyalties seriously. For her, their burgeoning relationship demonstrates and confirms her own pre-eminence, and, even as she lauds him, she vainly portrays the generosity she displays towards him as the kind of action 'Persons like me ... must do ... for their Glory' (p. 404). Her path to supreme power via her manipulation of her husband and his cronies remains her central fixation; and her control over fortune is merely further validated for her by her ability to commit adultery with Loveless with impunity.

Her imperial fantasies are further enhanced by the presence in the chamber with them of those ultimate symbols of royalty, a crown and sceptre resting on '*a Velvet Cushion*' (p. 404). To Lady Lambert they intensify her erotic excitement, but, for Loveless, they have a quite contrary effect. He is appalled that he had failed to sense the proximity of these 'Sacred Reliques' before she revealed them and devoutly abases himself before this 'Emblem of great Majesty' (p. 405). Markley asserts that, in this scene, the relics 'are sanctified to the extent that they are depoliticized' and 'represent Cavalier nostalgia for a golden age that transcends – and represses the knowledge of – the political circumstances that led to the Civil War'.[87] Once again, I can only disagree. Sanctification of the royal martyr and of the symbols associated with him was itself a profoundly and deliberately political tactic with a long mid-century history[88] – and one which played a crucial role not only in preparing the ground for the Restoration itself, but also in strengthening Charles II's hand during the Exclusion Crisis.[89] The polarization of Cromwell against Charles I which underpins Behn's scene also had its roots in 1640s–1650s polemic and propaganda, whether it was a matter of representing 'Cromwell the brewer' as 'a comic inversion of Charles the tragic martyr-king and of the high aesthetics of the courtly beautiful'[90] or of weighing Cromwell the transformative performer on history's stage against Charles 'the royal actor born', only able to imprint himself on history by the perfected art of his death-scene.[91] Here too, *The Roundheads* participates in a dialogue which long predates 1660. Indeed, Loveless's awed response to that 'Emblem of great Majesty', the crown and sceptre, gains added resonance when we recollect that 1630s Caroline iconography had, with a distinctive emphasis, repeatedly associated Charles I with these symbols of his authority.[92]

How might we now expect this encounter to develop? In Behn's version, Loveless's prostrate reverence provokes Lady Lambert to a reassertion of her ambitions. She imagines herself as, in effect, already a queen and regrets that she cannot permanently bestow the crown on him as her publicly avowed consort. He rebuffs her attempt to place it on his head. His following speech may, however, surprise us:

> Forbear, and do not play with holy things,
> Let us retire, and love as Mortals shou'd,
> Not imitate the Gods, and spoil our Joyes.
>
> (p. 405)

In an alternative scenario, the sight of the icons of a martyred king might still all thoughts of a sexual relationship between them, at least until she has abandoned her current allegiances and overreaching fantasies. Behn's Loveless lectures her about the unreality of her hopes and is allowed a prophetic glimpse of the evanescence of republican supremacy. But his instinctive assumption remains that their affair can still proceed unimpeded. His only request is:

> for Heav'ns sake, Madam,
> Let us not be profane in our Delights,
> Either withdraw, or hide that Glorious Object.
> (p.405)

Fornication in the presence of the martyr's insignia would be insupportable; but obscuring them with a curtain, or removing themselves to another room, would transform the situation. Oblivion can here be easily inflicted – at least temporarily – on the royal martyr, while adulterous desire urgently holds sway. The effect is rendered more piquant by the insistent association of Charles I and Henrietta Maria with the virtues of marriage – an iconographical emphasis which had sometimes generated rueful and/or invidious comparisons with the sexual conduct of their son, Charles II.[93] Loveless, while professing reverence for all that the royal martyr represented, yet seems able to contemplate with equanimity sleeping with, as this play represents her, one of the most inveterate enemies of that martyr's son.

Behn then presses this astonishing scene one step further. They are warned that Lambert and his drunken cronies are approaching. Domestic exigencies take over, since Lady Lambert must prevent her husband finding out about their embryonic affair. So Loveless is reduced to the indignity of lying on her couch, concealed under a carpet. The set-up is a familiar one from farce[94] and is played out as we might expect, when Lambert eventually sits unsuspectingly on Loveless:

> LAMBERT   My only dear, be patient; hah!
>   Something moves under me! Treason, Treason.   *He rises*
>   *Loveless rouls off, and turns Lambert over, the rest of the men run out crying*
>   *Treason, Treason, overthrowing the Lights, putting 'em out*
> LADY LAMBERT   Treason, Treason! my Lord, my Lord!
> (p. 407)

The scene may have many precedents and analogues, but for Lady Lambert it is a novel experience, a feeling Behn allows her to express in a marvellous aside:

> I'm ill at these Intrigues, being us'd to Lovers that still came with such Authority, that modestly my Husband wou'd withdraw ... (p.406)

Even without Cromwell's 'Authority' to make life easy for her, however, she takes confident control of the situation and prevents Loveless's discovery. Left alone with her, he expresses delighted awe at her skill in deceitful improvisation, which prompts a triumphant response from her, on which the Act closes:

> That's the first Lesson Women learn in Conventicles; Religion teaches those Maxims to our Sex, by this!
> Kings are depos'd, and Commonwealths are rul'd;
> By Jilting all the Universe is fool'd.

(p. 409)

So, the arts to which he gratefully owes his escape are those which have undone monarchy and created republican rule. Her mastery of them distinguishes her from the muster-roll of idiots, among whom her husband takes his place, and whom she has just duped – those legatees of the Cromwellian tradition, who are haplessly incapable of sustaining it. And to whom does she owe this mastery? The play has already answered that question in her earlier boast that Cromwell 'first infus'd Politiques into me' (p. 380) – a pun which blends a characteristic Puritan idiom often mocked by satirists – of infusing (or imparting) religious illumination or spirit to another – with another sense in which spirit – i.e. semen – can be infused. So, the scene and act end with a flamboyant demonstration of Cromwell's posthumous potency – and one in which its cavalier hero rejoices. He lives to serve again because of the long shadow cast by the not quite departed Lord Protector.

In Behn's last act the political landscape is rapidly transformed by the sudden onrush of events on the streets of the capital ushering in the Restoration, and with it comes a complete reversal of the power balance between Loveless and Lady Lambert. In this new dawn, his royalist credentials are her only insurance against the violence that might be inflicted on her, and which many contemporaries might have thought was the due reward for her earlier flagrant espousal of self-interest. So she becomes an extreme exemplification of the indemnity and oblivion the new regime proffered. Gratitude for Loveless's magnanimity woos her to revise her political opinions and renounce 'the Lies and Cheats of Conventicles, / That taught me first to think Heroics Divels' (p. 418). Yet, what she had learned in 'Conventicles' was also what had enabled her to rescue Loveless and herself from imminent disaster in Act IV. The change overtaking her seems to be more a vivid conviction of the charms of this particular 'Heroic' than, as yet, a principled renunciation of her past ambitions and convinced embracing of royalist principles. Her last words in the play are a plaintive farewell to 'all my hopes of Royalty' (p. 421), as she moves onward into the new world of Stuart monarchy in the embrace of a man who is not her husband.

When *The Roundheads* was premiered, Lambert indeed still survived, languishing in the imprisonment which had been his fate since spring 1660. A moment before, Maria has announced her husband's unhistorical, but convenient, exit and triumphantly proclaimed him 'Dead as old *Oliver*' (p. 421). The juxtaposition is provocative. Desborough's removal licenses the consummation between Freeman and Maria she had earlier outlawed. So, that story is accorded a closure which at least satisfies the terms she had set. The contrast with the play's other principal amorous duet is, however, striking. Behn does not revise history a second time and consign Lambert to a convenient death as well. So, an adulterous future awaits Loveless and Lady Lambert. We have moved far from the simple clarities of *The Committee*'s ending.

And, finally, though Cromwell may indeed be dead, there are clearly important senses in which he can also be thought to live on. As in *The Rump*, he provides a measure of masculine potency against which all others who tread the stage in this play are found wanting. In addition, the commanding knowledge he so intimately imparted to Lady Lambert proves invaluable at a moment of critical need and provokes from Loveless an intensity of admiration for her he has not earlier expressed. Above all, the play's constant, and intricate, reinvocations of his memory affirm that, for Behn too, he weighs powerfully in the imagination – a key presence in that recent past which remains a present, unconcluded, story.

In a celebrated definition Richard Schechner has described performance as 'Restored' or 'twice-behaved' behaviour, which he defines as 'not empty but loaded behavior multivocally broadcasting significances'.[95] For Herbert Blau, 'one of the universals of performance, both East and West, is its ghostliness, its sense of return, the uncanny but inescapable impression imposed upon its spectators that '*we are seeing what we saw before*' – a thought Marvin Carlson subsequently echoed in his exploration of theatre as 'the repository of cultural memory', where the 'present experience is always ghosted by previous experiences and associations while these ghosts are simultaneously shifted and modified by the processes of recycling and recollection'.[96] As my argument will have made clear, I regard *The Roundheads* as a multiply haunted script – both in its adventurous revisiting and reinvention of dramatic models offered by the work of Behn's predecessors in the early 1660s and by its parallel and overlapping engagement with crises and figures from the mid-century, whose ghosts still haunted, shaped, and threatened to overwhelm her contemporary world. Tracking some of the complexity of the ways in which these dialogues with the past inform her play's design has repeatedly led us to traverse the boundaries erected by academic specialisms and reinvestigate her pre-1660s inheritances. It has also, I hope, suggested a less monochromatic view of her theatrical Toryism than some previous accounts of the play have favoured. Intense as her partisan loyalties often were, we must take care not to stereotype her thinking by our preconceptions. Her engagement with the ghosts that haunted her culture frequently yielded results which may surprise us.

Notes and references

1. Robert Markley, ' "Be Impudent, Be Saucy, Forward, Bold, Touzing, and Leud": The Politics of Masculine Sexuality and Feminine Desire in Behn's Tory Comedies', in J. Douglas Canfield and Deborah C. Payne (eds), *Cultural Readings of Restoration and Eighteenth-Century English Theater* (Athens and London: University of Georgia Press, 1995), 125; Edward Burns, *Restoration Comedy: Crises of Desire and Identity* (Basingstoke: Macmillan, 1987), 136.

2. Elaine Hobby, *Virtue of Necessity: English Women's Writing 1646–1688* (London: Virago Press, 1988), 116; Eric Rothstein and Frances M. Kavenik, *The Designs of Carolean Comedy* (Carbondale and Edwardsville: Southern Illinois University Press, 1988), 250.

3. Deborah C. Payne, ' "And Poets Shall by Patron-Princes Live": Aphra Behn and Patronage', in Mary Anne Schofield and Cecilia Machecki (eds), *Curtain Calls: British and American Women and the Theater, 1660–1820* (Athens: Ohio University Press, 1991), 113–18; Susan J. Owen, ' "Suspect my loyalty when I lose my virtue": Sexual Politics and Party in Aphra Behn's Plays of the Exclusion Crisis, 1678–83', *Restoration: Studies in Literary Culture, 1660–1700*, 18 (1994): 41–4.

4. On 2 December 1668, for example, Samuel Pepys recorded his distaste for one instance of this, when he judged Edward Howard's *The Usurper* 'a pretty good play in all but what is designed to resemble Cromwell and Hugh Peters, which is mighty silly' (Samuel Pepys, *Diary*, ed. Robert Lathan and William Matthews (London: G. Bell and Sons Ltd, 1970–83), Volume 9, p. 381.

5. Joad Raymond, *The Invention of the Newspaper: English Newsbooks 1641–1649* (Oxford: Clarendon Press, 1996), 203 and 205.

6. Quotations, and the accompanying page references, for *The Roundheads* are taken from Aphra Behn, *Works*, ed. Janet Todd (London: William Pickering, 1996), Volume 6.

7. J. P. Kenyon, *The Stuart Constitution: Documents and Commentary* (Cambridge: Cambridge University Press, 1969), 365–71.

8. G. E. Aylmer, 'Crisis and Regrouping in the Political Elites: England from the 1630s to the 1660s', in J. G. A. Pocock (ed.), *Three British Revolutions: 1641, 1688, 1776* (Princeton, NJ: Princeton University Press, 1980), 156.

9. Jonathan Scott, 'Radicalism and Restoration: the Shape of the Stuart Experience', *The Historical Journal*, 31 (1988): 459.

10. Odai Johnson, *Rehearsing the Revolution: Radical Performance, Radical Politics in the English Restoration* (Newark: University of Delaware Press, 2001), 16–17.

11. Melinda Zook, 'Contextualizing Aphra Behn: Plays, Politics, and Party, 1679–1689', in Hilda L. Smith (ed.), *Women Writers and the Early Modern British Political Tradition* (Cambridge: Cambridge University Press, 1998), 80–1.

12. Mark Goldie, 'Danby, the Bishops and the Whigs', in Tim Harris, Paul Seaward and Mark Goldie (eds), *The Politics of Religion in Restoration England* (Oxford: Basil Blackwell, 1990), 100.

13. *Advice to the City* (London, 1682), [p. 1].

14. See, on this, Michael Cordner, 'Introduction', in Michael Cordner, with Ronald Clayton (eds), *Four Restoration Marriage Plays* (Oxford: Oxford University Press, 1995), viii–xxii.

15. Frances M. Kavenik, 'Aphra Behn: the Playwright as "Breeches Part" ', in Schofield and Machecki (eds), *Curtain Calls*, p. 187.

16. Derek Hughes, *The Theatre of Aphra Behn* (Basingstoke: Palgrave, 2001), 139. Cf. Anita Pacheco, 'Reading Toryism, in Aphra Behn's Cit-Cuckolding Comedies', *Review of English Studies*, New Series, 55 (2004): 697–99.

17. Mark Knights, *Politics and Opinion in Crisis, 1678–81* (Cambridge: Cambridge University Press, 1994), 347.

18. Tim Harris, 'Understanding Popular Politics in Restoration Britain', in Alan Houston and Steve Pincus (eds), *A Nation Transformed: England after the Restoration* (Cambridge: Cambridge University Press, 2001), 148–9.

19. Markley, 'Be Impudent', pp. 125 and 139.

20. Owen, 'Suspect my loyalty', p. 37.

21. See, for instance, Adam Fox, 'Ballads, Libels and Popular Ridicule in Jacobean England', *Past and Present*, 145 (November 1994): 47–83; Thomas Cogswell, 'Underground Verse and the Transformation of Early Stuart Political Culture', in Susan D. Amussen and Mark A. Kishlansky (eds), *Political Culture and Cultural Politics in Early Modern England: Essays presented to David Underdown* (Manchester and New York: 1995), 277–300; Andrew McRae, 'The Verse Libel: Popular Satire in Early Modern England', in Dermot Cavanagh

and Tim Kirk (eds), *Subversion and Scurrility: Popular Discourse in Europe from 1500 to the Present* (Aldershot: Ashgate, 2000), 58–73. One dimension of the story has recently been valuably extended into the Restoration by Harold Love, *English Clandestine Satire 1660–1702* (Oxford: Oxford University Press, 2004).

22. David Underdown, *Fire from Heaven: Life in an English Town in the Seventeenth Century* (London: HarperCollins, 1993), 27–8; Pauline Croft, 'The Reputation of Robert Cecil: Libels, Political Opinion and Popular Awareness in the Early Seventeenth Century', *Transactions of the Royal Historical Society*, 6th Series, 1 (1991), 58–62.

23. Susan Wiseman, ' "Adam, the Father of all Flesh," Porno-Political Rhetoric and Political Theory in and after the English Civil War', in James Holstun (ed.), *Pamphlet Wars: Prose in the English Revolution* (London: Frank Cass, 1992), 140.

24. Alastair Bellany, *The Politics of Court Scandal in Early Modern England: News Culture and the Overbury Affair, 1603–1660* (Cambridge: Cambridge University Press, 2002), 101.

25. Roger Howell, Jr., ' "That Imp of Satan": the Restoration Image of Cromwell', in R. C. Richardson (ed.), *Images of Oliver Cromwell: Essays for and by Roger Howell, Jr.* (Manchester and London: Manchester University Press, 1993), 34. This tradition carries on into Restoration biographies of Cromwell. See, for instance, the claim that as a teenager he was so completely a '*young Tarquin*' that his shamed Fenland family sent him to London, because such behaviour would be less noticed there ([James Heath], *Flagellum: Or The Life and Death, Birth and Burial of Oliver Cromwell* (London, 1663), 9–10.)

26. Ian Gentles, 'The Iconography of Revolution in England 1642–1649', in Ian Gentles, John Morrill, and Blair Worden (eds), *Soldiers, Writers and Statesmen of the English Revolution* (Cambridge: Cambridge University Press, 1998), 101. Cf. Jason McElligott, 'The Politics of Sexual Libel: Royalist Propaganda in the 1640s', *Huntington Library Quarterly*, 76 (2004), 75–100.

27. Derek Hirst, 'Reading the Royal Romance: Or, Intimacy in a King's Cabinet', *The Seventeenth Century*, 18 (2003): 214, 216, and 219.

28. Lois Potter, 'The Royal Martyr in the Restoration: National Grief and National Sin', in Thomas N. Corns (ed.), *The Royal Image: Representations of Charles I* (Cambridge: Cambridge University Press, 1999), 251.

29. David Underdown, *A Freeborn People: Politics and the Nation in Seventeenth-Century England* (Oxford: Clarendon Press, 1996), 87.

30. Lois Potter, *Secret Rites and Secret Writing: Royalist Literature 1641–1660* (Cambridge: Cambridge University Press, 1989), 22.

31. See, for instance, Diane Purkiss, 'Dismembering and Remembering: the English Civil War and Male Identity', in Claude J. Summers and Ted-Larry Pebworth (eds), *The English Civil Wars in the Literary Imagination* (Columbia and London: University of Missouri Press, 1999), 233.

32. Arthur F. Marotti, *Manuscript, Print, and the English Renaissance Lyric* (Ithaca and London: Cornell University Press, 1995), 80 and 82.

33. Ian Gentles, 'Iconography of Revolution', p. 101.

34. Jane Jones, 'New Light on the Background and Early Life of Aphra Behn', in Janet Todd (ed.), *Aphra Behn Studies* (Cambridge: Cambridge University Press, 1996), 316. For another unsubstantiated claim of the same kind, see Kate Aughterson, *Aphra Behn: the Comedies* (Basingstoke: Palgrave Macmillan, 2003), 218.

35. Paula R. Backscheider, *Spectacular Politics: Theatrical Power and Mass Culture in Early Modern England* (Baltimore and London: Johns Hopkins University Press, 1993), 25.

36. John Collop, *Itur Satyricum: In Loyall Stanzas* (London, 1660), 5; Martin Lluelyn, *To The Kings Most Excellent Majesty* (London, 1660), 6.

37. Nicholas Jose, *Ideas of the Restoration in English Literature, 1660–71* (London and Basingstoke: Macmillan, 1984), 120.

38. Mark Jenner, 'The Roasting of the Rump: Scatology and the Body Politic in Restoration England', *Past and Present*, 177 (November 2002): 84–120.

39. John Freehafer, 'The Formation of the London Patent Companies in 1660', *Theatre Notebook*, 20 (1965): 9. Some aspects of Freehafer's argument in favour of a specific venue for the first performance of *The Rump* were challenged by Gunnar Sorelius, 'The Early History of the Restoration Theatre: Some Problems Reconsidered', *Theatre Notebook*, 33 (1979): 52–61. In my view, however, Sorelius misreads the changing imperatives of public panegyric in spring–summer 1660 when he claims that, 'even if the King had not been mentioned at all in Tatham's script' (p. 55), this fact would have had no implications for dating its moment of origin. The case for a February/March date had earlier been made by Virgil Joseph Scott, 'A Reinterpretation of John Tatham's *The Rump: Or The Mirrour of the Late Times'*, *Philological Quarterly*, 24 (1945): 118–144.

40. Martin Butler, *Theatre and Crisis 1632–1642* (Cambridge: Cambridge University Press, 1984), 185 and 190–1.

41. I. R., 'TO *My dear Friend* Mr John Tatham, *On his Excellent Play*, The Distracted State', in John Tatham, *The Distracted State, A Tragedy* (London, 1651), sig. A3r.

42. Kenneth Richards, 'The Restoration Pageants of John Tatham', in David Mayer and Kenneth Richards (eds), *Western Popular Theatre: the Proceedings of a Symposium sponsored by the Manchester University Department of Drama* (London: Methuen, 1977), 49–73; Susan Wiseman, *Drama and Politics in the English Civil War* (Cambridge: Cambridge University Press, 1998), 165–89.

43. See, for example, Susan J. Owen, 'Restoration Drama and Politics: an Overview', in Susan J. Owen (ed.), *A Companion to Restoration Drama* (Oxford: Basil Blackwell, 2001), 126.

44. Harold Love, 'State Affairs on the Restoration Stage, 1660–1675', *Restoration and 18th Century Theatre Research*, 14 (May 1975): 1.

45. For two illuminating investigations by Patrick Collinson of the early history of these stereotypes, see 'The Theatre Constructs Puritanism', in David L. Smith, Richard Strier, and David Bevington (eds), *The Theatrical City: Culture, Theatre and Politics in London, 1576–1649* (Cambridge: Cambridge University Press, 1995), 157–69, and 'Elizabethan and Jacobean Puritanism as Forms of Popular Religious Culture', in Christopher Durston and Jacqueline Eales (eds), *The Culture of English Puritanism, 1560–1700* (Basingstoke: Macmillan, 1996), 32–57.

46. See, for instance, Neil Durkin, 'His Praeludiary Weapons: Mocking Colonel Hewson Before and After the Restoration', in Cavanagh and Kirk (eds), *Subversion and Scurrility*, pp. 106–24, which identifies a host of tropes common to the play's portrait of Hewson and to his satiric representation in other contemporary texts.

47. Richard W. Bevis, *English Drama: Restoration and Eighteenth Century, 1660–1789* (London and New York: Longman, 1988), 72.

48. Quotations from, and act/scene/line references for *The Rump* are to the text of the play edited by Judith Bailer Slagle in J. Douglas Canfield (ed.), *The Broadview Anthology of Restoration & Early Eighteenth-Century Drama* (Peterborough, Ontario: Broadview Press), 1596–641. When the play was first published, the names of the historical figures were partially masked by the inversion of syllables, so that Lambert became Bertlam, Fleetwood Woodfleet, and so on. I have used the real historical names throughout in the forms Slagle adopts, except for the figure she calls Huson, where I have adopted the standard modern form, Hewson.

49. Derek Hirst, *England in Conflict 1603–1660: Kingdom, Community, Commonwealth* (London: Arnold, 1999), 316.

50. Austin Woolrych, *Britain in Revolution 1625–1660* (Oxford: Oxford University Press, 2002), 278, 418, 486, and 521; David Farr, *John Lambert, Parliamentary Soldier and Cromwellian Major-General, 1619–1684* (Woodbridge, Suffolk: Boydell Press, 2003), 3, 44, and passim.

51. Ronald Hutton, *The Restoration: a Political and Religious History of England and Wales 1658–1667* (Oxford: Clarendon Press, 1985), 44.

52. Bulstrode Whitelocke, as quoted by Farr, *John Lambert*, p. 56.

53. These allegations originated in the late 1640s (cf. Farr, *John Lambert*, p. 151) and swiftly became the common material of political satire, as, for instance, in *The Famous Tragedie of King Charles I* (London, 1649), which juxtaposes the regicide with Cromwell's energetic dalliance with Frances Lambert. (For an extended description, see Dale B. J. Randall, *Winter Fruit: English Drama 1642–1660* (Lexington, Kentucky: University Press of Kentucky, 1995), 103–11.) *The Famous Tragedie* was republished during the Exclusion Crisis; so Behn may well have known it.

54. One recent book-length treatment of the subject can be found in Underdown, *Freeborn People*.

55. Laura Lunger Knoppers, *Constructing Cromwell: Ceremony, Portrait, and Print, 1645–1661* (Cambridge: Cambridge University Press, 2000), provides relevant observations on recurrent complexities and ambiguities in the contemporary representation of Cromwell in both panegyric and satire. For Aphra Behn's own disinclination to mock his memory, see Janet Todd, *The Secret Life of Aphra Behn* (London: Andre Deutsch, 1996), 278–9.

56. The invocation of Marchamont Nedham here is weighted, since his extreme changes of allegiance had made him notorious. To one satirist he was 'a Mercury with a winged conscience, the Skip-Jack of all fortunes, that like a Shittle-cock drive him which way you will, falls still with the Cork end forwards' (*The Character of the Rump* (London, 1660), 3). Cf. Blair Worden, ' "Wit in a Roundhead": the Dilemma of Marchamont Nedham', in Amussen and Kishlansky (eds), *Political Culture and Cultural Politics*, pp. 301–37.

57. This meaning of 'fanatics' – i.e. Protestant religious extremists – was a coinage of these early months of 1660. See Thomas Fuller, *Mixt Contemplations in Better Times* (London, 1660), 1.

58. For an account of the complex tensions of this moment, see Godfrey Davies, *The Restoration of Charles II 1658–1660* (London: Oxford University Press, 1955), 276–82.

59. Cf. Edward Hyde, Earl of Clarendon, *The History of the Rebellion and Civil Wars in England Begun in the Year 1641*, ed. W. Dunn Macray (Oxford: Clarendon Press, 1888), Volume 1, p. 493; Samuel Butler, *Hudibras*, ed. John Wilders (Oxford: Clarendon Press, 1967), 1.

60. Slagle inexplicably fails to reproduce the prologue and epilogue for *The Rump* in her edition; so they are quoted here, with accompanying page references, from John Tatham, *The Rump: Or The Mirrour Of The Late Times. A New Comedy* (London, 1660).

61. Ruth Spalding, *The Improbable Puritan: a Life of Bulstrode Whitelocke 1605–1675* (London: Faber and Faber, 1975), 221–52.

62. For a parallel exploration of another early 1660s comedy with similar preoccupations, John Wilson's *The Cheats*, see Michael Cordner, 'Zeal-of-the-Land Busy Restored', in Martin Butler (ed.), *Re-Presenting Ben Jonson* (Basingstoke: Macmillan, 1999), 174–92.

63. Abraham Cowley, *Poems* (London, 1656), sig. a1v; Arthur H. Nethercot, *Abraham Cowley: the Muse's Hannibal* (London: Oxford University Press, 1931), 73–4.

64. Quotations from *The Guardian* and *Cutter of Coleman-Street*, and accompanying page references, are taken from: Abraham Cowley, *Essays, Plays and Sundry Verses*, ed. A. R. Waller (Cambridge: Cambridge University Press, 1906). The text of the prologue reproduced when *The Guardian* was first printed in 1650 post-dates the Cambridge performance, since it contains an allusion to the destruction of Cheapside Cross, an event which did not occur until May 1643. The prologue, however, directly addresses Prince Charles; so my working hypothesis is that Cowley (?) has interpolated into the original script a reference to a striking instance of later iconoclasm and perhaps made other changes, but that the prologue still derives from, and to some extent reflects, the welcome actually performed in 1642.

65. Ben Jonson, *Works*, ed. C. H. Herford and Percy Simpson, Volume 5 (Oxford: Clarendon Press, 1937), 296–7.

66. John Cleveland's sneer is typical: 'since the *Stages* were voted down, the onely *Play-house* is at *Westminster*' (*Poems. With Additions, never before Printed* (n.p., 1653), p. 89.) Cf. Rick Bowers, 'Players, Puritans, and "Theatrical" Propaganda, 1642–1660', *Dalhousie Review*, 67 (1987): 464–8; Randall, *Winter Fruit*, p. 374.

67. Cowley, *Poems*, sig. a4r-a4v.
68. Cowley's fate is rendered the more piquant by his own long-term engagement with ideas of mercy, oblivion, and amnesty. See Andrew Shifflett, 'Kings, Poets, and the Power of Forgiveness, 1642–1660', *English Literary Renaissance*, 33 (2003): 88–109.
69. B. S. Capp, *The Fifth Monarchy Men: a Study in Seventeenth-Century English Millenarianism* (London: Faber and Faber, 1972), 198–201.
70. Pepys, *Diary*, Vol. 2, p. 18.
71. See, for instance, Pepys, *Diary*, Vol. 9, p. 272. For a different, but not mutually exclusive, explanation of the reversion to the original title, see Robert D. Hume, 'Securing a Repertory: Plays on the London Stage 1660–5', in Antony Coleman and Antony Hammond (eds), *Poetry and Drama 1570–1700: Essays in Honour of Harold F. Brooks* (London and New York: Methuen, 1981), 164.
72. *The Spectator*, ed. Donald F. Bond (Oxford: Clarendon Press, 1965), Volume 3, p. 239.
73. For examples of the latter, see Nigel Smith, *Literature & Revolution in England, 1640–1660* (New Haven and London: Yale University Press, 1994), 79; Randall, *Winter Fruit*, pp. 295–6.
74. Quotations from, and act/scene/line references for *The Committee* are taken from the text of the play edited by Cheryl L. Nixon in Canfield (ed.), *The Broadview Anthology*, pp. 472–525.
75. Nixon here follows the reading of the early texts, which attributes the following continuous block of text, in Nixon's modernizsed version, to the First Bailiff: 'Very well, surly sir. We will carry you where you shall not be troubled what pace to walk. You'll find a large bell. Blood is dear. Not yours is it? A farthing a pint were very dear for the best urine you have.' This is seriously incoherent as it stands, but can easily be rendered cogent by the hypothesis that a speech prefix has dropped out, and that the First Bailiff's speech should end with 'Blood is dear', which then provokes a sarcastic retort from Blunt. This is the reading followed by the eighteenth-century editions, which also sensibly emend 'large bell' to 'large bill' and, more debatably perhaps, 'urine' to 'blood' (see Carryl Nelson Thurber's edition of the play (Urbana, Illinois: University of Illinois Press, 1921), 47, 88, and 123).
76. H. J. Oliver, *Sir Robert Howard (1626–1698): a Critical Biography* (Durham, NC: Duke University Press, 1963), 3.
77. P. W. Thomas, *Sir John Berkenhead 1617–1679: a Royalist Career in Politics and Polemics* (Oxford: Clarendon Press, 1969), 121.
78. Oliver, *Sir Robert Howard*, pp. 39ff.
79. Susan Staves, *Players' Scepters: Fictions of Authority in the Restoration* (Lincoln and Nebraska: University of Nebraska Press, 1979), 203.
80. Sir Robert Howard and George Villiers, Duke of Buckingham, *The Country Gentleman*, ed. Arthur H. Scouten and Robert D. Hume (London: J. M. Dent, 1976), 52.
81. See, for example, J. Douglas Canfield, *Tricksters & Estates: On The Ideology of Restoration Comedy* (Lexington, Ky: University Press of Kentucky, 1997), 75–96.
82. See, for instance, Owen, 'Suspect my loyalty', p. 42: 'This bizarre yoking of cavalier mores and the virtue of chastity somehow succeeds, so thoroughly does Behn link lust and secret sex with canting, hypocritical puritans'. A more sceptical view is supplied by Hero Chalmers, *Royalist Women Writers 1650–1689* (Oxford: Clarendon Press, 2004), 171–6.
83. Markley, 'Be Impudent', p. 127.
84. Laura Lunger Knoppers, ' "Sing old Noll the Brewer": Royalist Satire and Social Inversion, 1648–64', *The Seventeenth Century*, 15 (2000): 32.
85. Clarendon, *History*, Vol. 6, p. 91.
86. Howell, 'That Imp of Satan', pp. 34–5.
87. Markley, 'Be Impudent', p. 129.
88. See, for example, Joad Raymond, 'Popular Representations of Charles I', in Corns (ed.), *The Royal Image*, pp. 47–73.

89. Kevin Sharpe, ' "So Hard a Text"? Images of Charles I, 1612–1700', *The Historical Journal*, 43 (2000): 391–400.
90. Knoppers, 'Sing old Noll', p. 33.
91. Andrew Marvell, 'An Horatian Ode upon Cromwell's Return from Ireland', *The Complete Poems*, ed. Elizabeth Story Donno (Harmondsworth: Penguin Books, Ltd., 1972), 56.
92. David Starkey, 'The Real Image of Regal Power', *The Times Literary Supplement*, 12 March 1999, pp. 18–19.
93. Ann Baynes Coiro, ' "A ball of strife": Caroline Poetry and Royal Marriage', in Corns (ed.), *The Royal Image*, pp. 26–46.
94. Leo Hughes, *A Century of English Farce* (London: Oxford University Press, 1956), 41.
95. Richard Schechner, *Between Theater & Anthropology* (Philadelphia: University of Pennsylvania Press, 1985), 36.
96. Marvin Carlson, *The Haunted Stage: the Theatre as Memory Machine* (Ann Arbor: University of Michigan Press, 2003), 1–2.

3
Shadowing Theatrical Change

Paula R. Backscheider

Eighteenth-century novels are filled with what became a set piece: a young heroine sits among her friends absorbed in a play.[1] She is beautiful in profile, gentle in demeanour, intelligent, and marked by ideal sensibility. Her acquaintances chatter, flirt, call out, and make rude observations not only about the play but also about the heroine and her unfashionable behaviour in the theatre.

For scholars of the theatre, a few of these scenes give useful information about access to production. Often written in fits of spleen by would-be playwrights, they are usually edited out of second editions of novels and, therefore, sometimes hard to find. Examples are in Charles Johnstone's *Chrysal: or the Adventures of a Guinea* (1760–65), Tobias Smollett's *Adventures of Peregrine Pickle* (1751), and Frances Brooke's *The Excursion* (1777). Primarily, however, for drama critics, these scenes are examples of the familiar noises of the audience. Perhaps less annoying than hisses, cat-calls, banging with sticks on anything wooden, calls for 'God Save the King', demands for the manager to appear and answer to them, and shouts to individual performers because the chattering was a constant din, the gossipy talking of audiences seems nearly continuous. The theatre was a place that allowed cross-gender, cross-class conversation difficult to hold anywhere else, and many took advantage of that freedom.

For novel critics, these scenes are usually rather uninteresting moments when the heroine demonstrates qualities we already know she has or when novelists pay brief tributes to a favourite play, playwright, or actor. Intriguingly, novel specialists who work with 'the figure of theatre' and the uses of theatricality in eighteenth-century novels seldom work with these scenes.[2] The 'threat of the theatrical position' as described by David Marshall, for instance, could be productively theorized in these scenes. Feminist critics easily find evidence that women are spectacles to be tested. In Sarah Fielding's *The History of Ophelia* (1760), for instance, the heroine is set up to be the entertainment: 'Lord *Dorchester* and Lady *Palestine* were . . . taken up in observing the Passions imprest on my Countenance. They told me, I might more properly be said to act the Play, than some of the Persons on the Stage.'[3] Although the slow growth of ensemble acting can be marked in this passage by its mention of shifting moods rather than individual actors, the centre of attention is the heroine of the novel and her predictable behaviour.[4]

I want to argue, however, that these scenes should be examined as part of the century's project of teaching correct cultural consumption and studied as over-looked, significant participations in theatrical controversies – alternative histories, if you will, of a number of things with which we as theatre critics are presently engaged. Incidentally, they almost completely overlooked eyewitness descriptions of performances. Critics have established that novels are obsessed with teaching their readers to read aright, but the novel also became a site for educating their readers in how to enjoy, understand, and benefit from attending plays. It is as parti-cipants in contemporary debates, however, that these scenes are most important. As contributions to performance theory and history they are sometimes illumin-ating versions of familiar debates and occasionally have the potential to add detail to and modify accepted understandings of controversies and changing perform-ance practices. In the first part of my paper, I will trace the evolution of novel scenes as sites for educating theatregoers, and in the second part analyse some episodes that participate in cultural negotiations about representative theatrical issues. Because of the focus of this book, I have privileged scenes written by novel-ists who were also playwrights.

*   *   *

I have become persuaded that my hypothesis regarding the function of these scenes can be extended to locate the time – the decade of the 1750s – when these scenes changed and the project of teaching readers to consume perform-ances became obvious. For instance, when Eliza Haywood, although an actress and playwright, sends characters in her early fictions to plays, the plays are not identi-fied. We do not learn what play the heroine attended in *Fantomina* (1725) as she watches 'a great Number of celebrated Toasts' and several gentlemen 'extremely pleased' by 'entertaining a Woman who sat in a Corner of the Pit'.[5] Nor do we learn the plays performed on the next nights when Fantomina returns disguised as a lady of the town. By 1751 when *The History of Miss Betsy Thoughtless* was published, Haywood had had plays produced and had written both volumes of *The Companion to the Theatre*. As texts such as *The Invisible Spy* demonstrate, she was especially aware of the functions literature performs in society, the claims made for literature, and the volatile possibilities of publication. *Betsy Thought-less*, published twenty-six years after *Fantomina*, can be read as another kind of mid-century 'dilated' novel, a fiction starring Colley Cibber's Lady Betty Modish (*The Careless Husband*, 1704) and an extended illustration of how to benefit from plays.[6] It certainly joins other mid-century novels in assuming that readers will have great familiarity with plays, characters, and even specific interpretations of characters.

Some texts written by dramatists, such as Samuel Foote's 1747 *Treatise on the Passions*, record a rising sense of the need for educating playgoers. He begins,

'It seems strange to me, that in a Country where Theatrical Representations are so much admired, and both Kinds of the Drama carried to so great a Perfection, the Business of the Stage should be so little understood.' Out of an estimated 12,000 regular 'Play-Followers', he says that fewer than one-fifth have 'a Capacity of determining on the Excellence, or Imperfections of a Performance'.[7] He, other theatrical writers – and a large group of novelists – seem determined to increase this number.[8] In 1770, Francis Gentleman observed 'that three-fourths of every audience are more capable of enjoying sound and shew, than solid sense and poetical imagination'.[9] Depressing as he surely felt this figure to be, it is a larger percentage than Foote's. These and other writers are reacting to the growing heterogeneity of the audience. John Dennis had recognized the implications when he wrote in 1702 that 'in the reign of King *Charles* the Second, a considerable part of an Audience had such an Education as qualified them to judge of Comedy. . . . Poetry and Eloquence were then their Studies . . . In their Closets they cultivated at once their Imaginations and Judgements . . . The discourse, which now every where turns upon Interest, rolled then upon the Manners and Humours of Men.'[10]

In the 1740s, the decade when Foote recognized the need for educating audiences, novelists' criticism of the theatre and of specific plays becomes more frequent and more extensive.[11] At this time, much of it repeats conventional, accepted truisms about literature in general. Sarah Fielding, author of a play and sister of a great playwright, has several theatrical episodes in *The Adventures of David Simple* (1744). She constructs a satiric, cacophonous conversation in which a surprised and disapproving David hears race and class prejudices that have determined the participants' judgements of *Othello* and *The London Merchant*. Like a moral tacked to the end of a fable, however, Sarah Fielding's David Simple observes that characters should be judged by whether they were 'drawn from Nature', and whether the audience was moved to compassion at the distresses of the good, was incited to imitate their good actions, and felt indignation at the vices of the bad and avoided their conduct.[12] Here Fielding imposes these standards by which the century was encouraged to judge all literature, and she conflates acting with the written part. More interesting are the portraits of characters who are terrible consumers of theatrical culture. For instance, Cynthia in *David Simple* recalls a woman who became perpetually miserable by applying to herself a line from William Congreve's *Double Dealer*: 'If Happiness in Self-content is plac'd,/ The Wise are wretched' (198). Characters laugh in the wrong places and ridicule those who are moved at appropriate moments in plays, such as during the reconciliation scene between Don Sebastian and Dorax in John Dryden's *Don Sebastian*.

Novelist-playwrights quickly show a decided impatience with theatre audiences. In Tobias Smollett's *Peregrine Pickle* and the anonymous *History of Betty Barnes* (1753), characters are satirized for knowing which playwrights and players to praise but not why. Part of the essential education of the daughter of the beggar woman whom Peregrine transforms into a fashionable lady is to learn to repeat 'choice sentences' from William Shakespeare and Thomas Otway and to drop the 'names and epithets of the most celebrated players'.[13] Mrs Miller in *Tom Jones* rebukes Partridge with 'all the Town's' opinion of Garrick, and the young woman buys acceptance with similar pronouncements. Sarah Fielding's fashionable gathering of women sound like 'the Cackling of Geese' and punctuate their babble with '*Otway, Congreve, Dryden, Pope, Shakespeare, Tom Durfey*, &c. &c. &c. . . . tho' no one could tell who spoke them, or whether they were mention'd with Approbation or Dislike' (66).

In the sustained discussion of acting in *Peregrine Pickle*, Smollett takes a shot at the audience by having the knowledgeable knight of Malta remark that the London audiences 'relish' 'low characters of humour' (274). These scenes are gentle satires of audience taste and fashionable conduct but do not often contribute to the project of creating discriminating theatregoers. A decade later, Oliver Goldsmith, who would become an excellent playwright, has the Vicar and a strolling player in *The Vicar of Wakefield* (1766) discuss the public's taste in plays, and the player grumbles, 'The public think nothing about dialect, or humour, or character . . . they only go to be amused. . . . It is not the composition of the piece, but the number of starts and attitudes, that may be introduced into it, that elicits applause.'[14] As well as notice of these writerly elements that are actuated (or not) by performance and provide the most popular moments in the rhetorical style of acting, the playwright-novelists of this decade began to include more specific instruction in judging acting and even on its contribution to a play's meaning and success. The manager of the strolling company in *The Vicar*, for instance, singles out George's 'voice, his figure, and attitudes',[15] and these are the elements that David Garrick and other authors of handbooks on acting highlighted.

At this point, I want to use examples from Frances Burney's *Evelina* (1778) to illustrate how such episodes educate theatre audiences and participate in artistic controversies. That this aspect of her texts has been largely overlooked in spite of the fact that she has long been recognized for her didacticism suggests the promise of the application of performance history and theory methods to her novels. In the theatrical scenes, Burney compliments Garrick, teaches her readers to be connoisseurs of his acting in one of his now-neglected types of roles, joins other novelists in modernizing the instructional uses of the theatre, and, most significantly of all, launches a multi-faceted examination of the nearly overwhelming tide of sentimental plays and novels.

Almost immediately upon arriving in London, Evelina exults that Garrick will perform, and the part Burney chooses to portray is Ranger, the role in Benjamin Hoadly's *The Suspicious Husband* that Garrick created in the play's first run in 1747 and selected for two performances in his farewell season of 1776. Evelina exclaims, 'How fortunate, that he should happen to play!'[16] The *London Magazine* called Ranger one of Garrick's most celebrated parts, Garrick played it more than any other part, and the play is exceptionally well written and filled with excellent stage business. So famous was Garrick in the part that Edward Kimber titled his *roman-à-clef* about Garrick *The Juvenile Adventures of David Ranger, Esq.* Burney moves Evelina rapidly from star-struck to connoisseur, and she lists the strengths for which Garrick was known and that had, incidentally, set the standards for other actors.

Today's author of a historical novel or general theatrical history would probably pick Garrick's performance as Hamlet, Lear, or Richard III, all parts that are in more familiar plays and that he selected to play for his retirement season. For Burney to immortalize him in his most famous role as a debauchee underscores the importance of recognizing the act of recovery in doing performance history. From early in his career, Garrick has been recognized as supreme in his ability to play 'complicated passions', as the retirement eulogist for the *Universal Magazine* called them, parts in which he used his mobile face and flexible body and voice to represent a character simultaneously feeling 'grief and anger, fear and rage'.[17] For specialists today and in his time, he is also seen as supreme in his performance of a rake who is at heart virtuous, too intelligent to approve of his lifestyle, but drunk every night and ready for any adventure.[18] Ranger, for instance, sees a ladder propped to the window of a strange house and, without a thought, climbs it. Reviews from the time of his first performance of the part responded as this viewer did: 'I lost the entertainment of the stage, and imagin'd myself all the while upon the *Look-out* with him for midnight adventures.'[19] He was, as in the other parts, 'nature' displayed. Connoisseurs awarded him first prize for representing the drunken man, here Sir John Brute in *The Provok'd Wife*:

> In all playhouses there is generally one or another of the actors who can represent a drunken man very tolerably. The reason for this is not far to seek. There is no lack of opportunity for observation, and, whatever may be the main motive of the play, such a part must, in the nature of things, have no narrow or sharply defined limits. In spite of this Mr. Garrick plays the [drunk] in such a way that I should certainly have known him to be a most remarkable man, even if I had never heard anything of him and had seen him in one scene only . . . [20]

One reviewer compared all other performers of the part as 'copper' beside Garrick's 'gold',[21] and Burney gives us a bit of forgotten theatrical history, a reminder that virtuoso performances that we should study come from now-forgotten, 'minor' plays as often as from the monuments of English theatre.

The role of Ranger is small in comparison to that of Mr Strickland, the suspicious husband, and to those of Jacintha, Bellamy, and Frankly. Garrick's contemporaries recognized that he often selected smaller parts when those parts offered his gifts more opportunity for display or when they were, in fact, more challenging and complex than larger parts in the same play. Moreover, from the beginning of his career, the strength of Garrick's voice was in question. Charles Macklin once said that Garrick in his great tragic parts was almost always hoarse by the fourth act,[22] and reviewers of his performances in his last years consistently mentioned his weakening voice. Especially in his retirement year, Ranger allowed Garrick to play masterfully and rest his voice for the rigours of the next performance – perhaps of Lear. When given its due, Burney's scene contributes to a more balanced, nuanced understanding of Garrick's selection and performance of parts and develops our understanding of a working actor's methods of coping with the rigours of repertory theatre.

Novelists like Burney also transformed the classical, satiric reject/emulate instructional paradigm based on 'universal' standards of moral conduct into more modern socializing purposes, including gendering. As is well-known, Frances Burney's *Evelina* provides an example, but one that I think has been consistently under-interpreted. The major characters attend William Congreve's *Love for Love* (1695) and use its characters as weapons against each other. Captain Mirvan rather surprisingly represents a point of view coming to the fore and expressed in Oliver Goldsmith's *Essay on the Theatre: Or, A Comparison between Sentimental and Laughing Comedy* (1773), in which he attacked empty sentimentality and 'weeping' comedies.[23] In response to Orville's observation that it is not a play ladies can approve, the Captain says, 'What, I suppose it is not sentimental enough! . . . or else it's too good for them; for I'll maintain it's one of the best comedies in the language, and has more wit in one scene, than there is in all the new plays put together' (126). As the scene unfolds, it becomes clear that Burney and Capt. Mirvan agree, and this episode needs to be given due weight when the character of Mirvan is interpreted.

The admirable Lord Orville gives a powerful endorsement to the afterpiece, George Colman the Elder's *The Deuce is in Him* (1763), which Burney critics seem to have neglected. Lord Orville describes it as 'the most finished and elegant *petite piece* that was ever written in English' (129). Popular from its first production, this farce has important parallels to *Love for Love*, and Burney uses it, too, as a means of attacking the rise of sentimental literature. Col. Tamper returns from battle pretending to have lost a leg and an eye in order to test whether his fiancée Emily loves him, not for his handsome exterior but 'for his own sake'. She, like Angelica, discovers the trick, turns it back on him and marries the chastened hero.[24] As shocking as *Love for Love* with its *double entendres* is,[25] *The Deuce is in Him* is as shocking because of its outrageous jokes about war injuries in a time of war when the injured were all around the playgoers. Emily violates all of the standards of good taste and feminine compassion with lines like these about Col. Tamper's maimed body: 'I could never conquer my disgust' (38).

The fact that the audience knows that Emily knows the trick excuses her, but Tamper's hearty cheerfulness demands an even greater disassociation of art and life. He, for instance, corrects Emily who calls his injuries 'misfortunes': 'no misfortunes at all – none at all to a soldier – nothing but the ordinary incidents and common casualities of his life – marks of honour'. And when she asks if his sight is 'quite lost', he responds, 'Blind as a mill-horse'.[26] Colman's play is a powerful attack on stock sentimental situations; in fact, Tamper's fault is identified as excess sensibility, which has led him into making this cruel test, and sensibility seems to be inseparable in Colman's play from arrogance. Burney's novel, like this afterpiece, is a departure from the sentimental novels being written by many women – and men – of her time and includes tough-minded satire. In *Evelina*, she even approves of Samuel Foote's raucous, satirical comedies as Evelina sees *The Minor* (1760) and *The Commissary* (1765). Although it is Mr Smith who casts his vote for an evening of entertainment at Foote's Haymarket Theatre, Evelina was 'extremely entertained'.[27]

The scene in *Evelina* is part of Burney's socializing project, including lessons in gendering, some conservative (familiar) and some revisionary (less so). Angelica,

Emily and Evelina are scrutinized and tested by the male sex. The men, including the more sensitive Orville, can enjoy Congreve to the fullest, but the women appear to be expected to keep their opinions to themselves and even to look away at times. That Burney makes Captain Mirvan's observation so emphatic and depicts Mrs Mirvan and Orville recommending Angelica for study leads into the juxtaposition of Lovel's pretence of not watching the play. The more mature and experienced, exemplary people matter-of-factly expect the young women to watch the play and learn.

Novel scenes written in the last third of the century move from connoisseurship of stars to integrating stars' performances into evaluations of the success of productions and the quality of plays. Frances Brooke, who had three plays produced and a hit in *Rosina*, a comic opera performed over 200 times between 1782 and 1800, includes a scene in *The Excursion* that offers to teach this as-yet somewhat unusual lesson in a novel. It is also, incidentally, the second incident of personal protests against the vagaries of access to production in this novel and the one not edited out of the second edition.[28] Maria, although she 'eagerly listens' to Robert Jephson's *Braganza* (1775) while her companions laugh, talk, whisper and look 'round with their glasses to reconnoitre their acquaintances in the boxes', is dismissive of the play. She is deeply moved by Mary Ann Yates's performance in the last scene, where she becomes 'the indignant queen, the tender wife, the steady heroine, the generous victim to the happiness of her people. Her voice, her look, her attitude – the whole *tableau* was striking beyond description. But you must have heard her'.[29] Yates must have done a superb job, because the part as written is hardly moving. The reviewer for the *London Magazine* remarked tartly: 'It is but barely doing justice to Mrs Yates's admirable performance, to say the author had no small obligations to her.'[30] Louisa, Yates's character, has been waiting in great anxiety for the outcome of a battle, when the usurping villain, Velasquez, comes disguised and begs sanctuary. She lets him in, and, when Braganza enters, Velasquez seizes Louisa as a hostage and means to revenge. He threatens to stab, slash, gore, and mangle her. After just a moment of suspense and emoting, he is captured as Braganza's men arrive. Louisa has a few good lines, such as her defiant one to Velasquez, who is holding her as a body shield: 'feel, do I shrink or tremble?' (72). There is not even a romantic conclusion, for the emphasis is on the mob ripping Velasquez to pieces. Significantly, this virtuoso performance is not the delivery of a speech or speeches but in the kind of voice-face-body-gesture method of Garrick.

Brooke's scene also pushes the audience toward a recognition of an accelerating emphasis on print in literary culture, one that encouraged the writing of closet dramas in the Romantic period. Earlier Bookweight, the bookseller in Henry Fielding's *The Author's Farce* (1730), had said,

> There are your acting plays and your reading plays. . . . your acting play is entirely supported by the merit of the actor, without any regard to the author at all. In this case, it signifies very little whether there be any sense in it or no. Now your reading play is of a different stamp and must have wit and meaning in it. (1.6.21–2, 24–8)

The anonymous author of *An Examen of the New Comedy, call'd 'The Suspicious Husband'* is typical in his demand that plays stand up to the test of being both when he writes, 'The Town, tho' greatly pleas'd by the Representation of this new Comedy, was doubtful whether it wou'd answer Expectation in the Reading; but I believe the Point is now settled, and it is agreed by all, that it is not only an *acting* but a *reading* Play.'[31] For theatrical people, as the large number of closet dramas in the nineteenth century indicate, the differences became greater in the last quarter of the century and were even institutionalized. Part of the successful publicity campaign for *Braganza* had been Jephson's friends reading the play 'in most of the great Families in London',[32] as Addison had *Cato* years earlier. *The Excursion* offers an early, somewhat covert lesson on theatrical discourse. Maria notes that *Braganza* is filled with 'fine writing', 'but only' fine writing. She admires it, but is unmoved by it.[33] The stylistic flourishes, some of which fall into the category of 'sentiments', were often written into plays but unperformed[34] and, of course, actors could easily rephrase sentences they deemed more characteristic of other genres. In Jephson's play, however, the substance of the play is 'fine writing', that category that Brooke's contemporaries ridiculed as 'Affectedly ornate or elegant' (*OED*, 'fine', adj., 18a). In the third speech a simple officer says, 'We have not mines of unexhausted gold/ To feed rapacious Spain and stern Velasquez'. In a typical line, the hero himself says, 'My nimble thoughts shoot thro' their whirling round'.[35] Superfluous metaphors that would fit in Fielding's *Tom Thumb* abound. The increasing emphasis on recognizing that an excellent play might not read like fine literature accompanies what I would call the movement by dramatists away from novelistic emphases to the more theatrical and even spectacular effects of the late century stage. The *Morning Chronicle* for May 1771, for instance, noted that 'A fine poem may be a very bad play; a fine play may be a very bad poem' (262).

Maria has written a tragedy, and she leaves *Braganza* 'satisfied' that Mrs Yates is 'capable of filling the character of her poetic heroine' – in other words, she has been auditioning the actress and her company. Again, the reader can learn something – to assess casting and to consider how well a company is equipped to actualize the potential of a play, even a decidedly mediocre play like *Braganza*. Educating readers in assessing acting skillfully became increasingly important in these scenes. At the height of Sarah Siddons's reign, for instance, while Julia in Helen Maria Williams's novel has appreciated her in *Douglas*, the ridiculous and gauche Mrs Chartres is 'disappointed' by *Macbeth*, which, we are told by the somewhat didactic narrator, is 'an unforgivable crime against taste' (2:44). Siddons, of course, is one of the greatest players of the part of Lady Macbeth and had notably reinterpreted the part. Williams writes that *Douglas* 'had not ... its full effect upon the heart' until Siddons played Lady Randolph, 'whose power over the human passions' is supreme (1:34). Like the pathetic tragedies by Ambrose Philips, Nathaniel Lee, Nicholas Rowe, and Otway, it provided a vehicle for an actress to perform a variety of powerful, contrasting emotions including despair, rage, and ecstasy that led to madness or suicide or both. As Elizabeth Inchbald said in comparing Siddons's and Ann Barry's performances of Lady Randolph, Siddons added 'matronal beauty of person, and dignity of action' to Barry's 'bursts of pathetic tenderness' and, therefore, brought out the full power of the part. While Inchbald is more specific, Williams makes the same point and leads the reader to Inchbald's conclusion: 'perhaps few classical plays have been more indebted . . . to the art of acting' (4).

*   *   *

Two of the most interesting debates recorded in the novels are over the effects of reading plays and of having an opinion of the playwright before seeing performances. One of the first examples of these is in a section of Samuel Richardson's *Pamela . . . in Her Exalted Condition*, better known as *Pamela II*. This 1741 novel provided an important new paradigm for novelistic scenes, one endlessly repeated, that of the innocent, rural young woman (or man) arriving in London and partaking of a series of city pastimes and entertainments. Significantly, Pamela has read Ambrose Philips's *The Distressed Mother* before seeing it but has not read *The Tender Husband*, although she admires its author, Richard Steele, and remarks that 'the authors of the *Spectator* cannot possibly produce a faulty scene' (255). Thus, perhaps inadvertently, Richardson raises two fascinating questions: (1) does reading prior to performance aid or hinder play watching? (2) to what extent does knowing the playwright, or his or her other works and reputation, impact reception?[36] David Roberts has argued that, in the Restoration, reading the play, knowing the reputation of the playwright, and gathering information from reliable friends played an important part in women's decisions to attend,[37] and Richardson and others are depicting and testing the effects of such prior knowledge in the later period. These scenes are quite rich, containing layers of his sifting of fashionable opinion and its influence on interpretation of plays. As he did with so many other novel conventions, he extended the didactic and especially the socializing potential of the novel greatly with this soon-to-be-formulaic trip to the theatre by a naive provincial.

Ambrose Philips's *The Distressed Mother* (1712) was a stock play, 'a Standard of Entertainment at both Theatres, being generally repeated several Times in every Season', by the time Richardson wrote his novel.[38] As a reader, Pamela says that she has 'wept [at] the distresses of the injured Hermione . . . been moved by the murder of the brave Pyrrhus, and shocked by the madness of Orestes'. Gradually Richardson depicts her response as that of the average audience member and as almost as naive as Partridge's at *Hamlet* in *Tom Jones*; yet after seeing it Pamela describes it aright: 'half of it is a tempestuous, cruel, ungoverned rant of passion, and ends in cruelty, bloodshed, and desolation' (253). These characters and Andromache, the 'distressed mother', have plotted to kill each other, themselves, and Andromache's little son. Their shifting loyalties, violent outbursts, and drives for power would seem likely to make them all reprehensible to a person like Pamela. The 'injured Hermione', for instance, lingers around the court enraged at her unfaithful betrothed, Pyrrhus, and attempts to persuade the lovesick Orestes to dishonour himself and his country by assassinating Pyrrhus. Upon seeing the play, in contrast to her response as a reader, Pamela complains of 'rant and fury' and that love 'sweeps down reason, religion, and decency; and carries every laudable duty away before it'.[39]

It is the epilogue, however, that determines Pamela's overall judgement of the performance.[40] She is shocked and outraged at Ann Oldfield's metamorphosis from 'the widow of Hector' to the speaker of a suggestive epilogue, one that alludes to Hector's and Pyrrhus's virility. This epilogue was very famous and much requested. *Spectator* no. 341, which discusses it, invokes Dryden's example and asserts, 'The Moment the Play ends, Mrs. *Oldfield* is no more *Andromache*, but Mrs. *Oldfield*'.[41] This knowledgeable essay calls attention to the understanding of a separation between play and epilogue and to the tradition of the saucy, sexy She-Prologues begun by Anne Bracegirdle, Mary Betterton, Elizabeth Barry, and especially Nell Gwynn, in which Oldfield excelled.[42] These epilogues, especially when the audience called for repetitions of them as they did the one for *The Distressed Mother*, were part of the entertainment, more akin to the inter-act rope and Irish dances than to the kind of epilogue that identified and emphasized a moral taught by the play.

As Pamela says, this one insults modern women. 'I Hope you'll own, that with becoming art,/ I've play'd my game, and topp'd the widow's part', Oldfield begins; 'Which of you all would not on marriage venture,/ Might she so soon upon her jointure enter?' The epilogue forces Pamela to detach from her reading of the play, and she is disappointed because it differs from what she imagined as she read what she conceived to be a 'true', historical account of great classical personages. Elizabeth Inchbald, who consistently compares the experiences of reading and of witnessing performance in her 'Remarks' prefacing the 125 plays in *The British Theatre* (1806–1809), observes that the play will always 'gain more favour with a reader than a spectator', because the imagination gives 'graces, charms, and majesty ... which their representatives cannot always so completely bestow'. She also observes that more is described to the audience than happens on stage and that it is 'chiefly narrative' (as opposed to dramatic).[43] The Epilogue attacks the 'graces' and especially the 'majesty' of the characters and forces the contemporary into the consciousnesses of playgoers in at least two ways. First, it suggests that Andromache is like the scheming widows of mid-century England, and, second, it reminds the audience of Ann Oldfield's personal life. B—— is the exemplary playgoer, of course, not Pamela. He observes, 'I never saw this play, rake as I was, but the impropriety of the epilogue sent me away dissatisfied with it, *and with human nature, too*' (2:254).[44]

B—— lectures Pamela on how able actors are 'to personate any thing for a sorry subsistence' (2:254) but finds a contemporary application. He comments on women's unwillingness to marry because of a desire to protect their children's inheritances, and Andromache is doing exactly that. Years earlier, Joseph Addison had emphasized this point by having Sir Roger attend a performance of the play and remark twice on the perverse recalcitrance of widows. He returns her to the fact that plays are representations, not history lessons, and Richardson may be commenting on Ann Oldfield specifically. Two contemporary biographies of Oldfield point to parallels between her and Andromache, as Oldfield refused to remarry after bearing two illegitimate sons. Pamela concludes by saying that the 'extravagant scenes and characters' should be enough to condemn the play and observes that the epilogue assured that the audience would not be 'improved by the representation' (2:254).

There are numerous episodes in novels in which characters have read the plays that they see. In contrast to Richardson's portrayal and Pamela's response, for instance, Sarah Fielding depicts Ophelia as having read *Macbeth* before seeing it, and even having 'heard many of the Speeches much more to Advantage' when read by Lord Dorchester, but she was delighted 'extremely' and found the play 'so much more lively' in performance. It is notable that the production is *Macbeth*, one of Garrick's successes and a play he moved away from the performance of individual speeches toward ensemble acting.

Richard Steele's *The Tender Husband* (1705), whose author but not text Pamela knows, leaves Pamela 'grievously disappointed' in its morality and its 'probability'. She concludes, '[I] am forced to disapprove of every character in it, and the views of every one' (253–4). Again, morality and probability are the standards, and this comedy, one of the weaker examples of the provoked wife/husband comedies done so well by John Vanbrugh, Colley Cibber, and Thomas Southerne, is improbable in its premises and episodes. Richardson has Pamela observe that Steele seems to have been 'carried away by the luxuriancy of a genius' and by 'custom'. Although dressing the country bumpkin in his father's wedding suit was good comedy, the father and son are complete stock characters by this time and, in fact, do not stand up very well to Richardson's own Darnford family in *Pamela II*.[45]

This time the author and his non-dramatic writings have determined Pamela's expectations. Significantly, the only episode she truly enjoys is the one in which Capt. Clerimont pretends to be a portrait painter and does an extended comic riff on the 'airs' and excuses of female subjects; this knowing satire is very much like the best of the *Spectator* papers. In a time when the playwright's name was almost never listed on playbills or in newspaper advertisements and managers and the company had significant power to revise a play, Steele's name proves to be misleading information for theatregoers like Pamela. Both prior reading and knowledge of authorship, then, prove to be dubious guides to comprehending a play and even obstruct benefiting from its 'lessons'. Richardson, however, indirectly attacks the morality of both players and playwrights, portraying them as willing to do anything for 'a sorry subsistence'. Pamela learns more about Oldfield and Steele and what Richardson suggests is their true character than she does from the actual plays. In the rising competition between the novel and drama, Richardson may be illustrating how much better – more probably and moralistically – the novel could represent experiences and feelings. Pamela would, of course, be slighted as Hermione was, fear the loss of her child as Andromache did, and be estranged by markedly different sensibilities from her husband as the Clerimonts were. Richardson is certainly on the forefront of using allusions to plays to activate greater emotional force.[46] He is also among the first to use fleeting allusions to plays, characters, or very familiar lines as a kind of shorthand to convey situation, emotion, or personality to readers. Important as these things are for students of the novel, they are equally significant for us as evidence of the fact that drama was the dominant genre, that it penetrated into the everyday life and the thinking of almost all classes, and that a repertory of novelistic techniques developed that relied upon knowledge of plays even as the novel took up the project of educating playgoers.

Incidentally, in the scenes in *Pamela II*, Richardson is tacitly arguing against absorption in the play and identification with the characters. His novel is, then, one of the places where we can find explicit comment on consumer position and the choice between absorption/identification and analysis/judgement, a major debate about the consumer's relation to art. Most early novelists attempted to keep readers analytical, and the epilogue to *The Distressed Mother* might be considered a parallel technique. Such playgoers might have been like a character in *The Correspondents* (1775), who says, 'I have *laughed* at the sorrows of [Nathaniel Lee's] *Theodosius* and the ravings of *Roxana*' (in his *Rival Queens*).[47] In spite of grumbling about these old repertory plays, characters often attend, enjoy, and learn from them – and they *absorb* the audience. In the first half of the century, consumers learned by analysing and judging characters and their actions, while in the second half absorption led to identification with the characters. The disguised Charlotte Seymount in *Memoirs of Lady Woodford, Written by Herself* (1771) is completely absorbed in *Jane Shore*; she describes herself as feeling 'the force of every line almost as keen as if real scenes had been presented to my view'. She sees herself in Jane and applies Jane's actions to what she had escaped, and 'shudders' at her near fall; the author, thus, endorses the admonitory power of the stage.[48]

At midcentury, plays and novels repeatedly raise the question of the extent to which consumers of art should give themselves over to illusion, an issue of great significance for literary history. Increasingly novelists and dramatists were encouraging consumers to be consumers, not thinkers, to pay far less attention to how something came about and to give themselves over to identification with characters. This controversy is another that we have studied longer with prose fiction than with the drama but is equally present in theatre history. John Home's *Douglas*, a play with many similarities to *The Distressed Mother*, is both frequently read and watched in novels in the last decades of the century. Frances Sheridan's *Memoirs of Miss Sidney Biddulph*, for instance, begins with the characters reading and discussing the play. The effect of this play is quite different from Philips's, in that audiences and readers were absorbed in it, and intended to be so. Scene after scene in novels, as in the attendance at *Douglas* in Helen Maria Williams's *Julia*, depicted characters, male and female, lost in the play and the hopes and distresses of the characters. The people who gave themselves over to Siddons's powerful effects were the readers of the gothic page turners, and novel scenes of play-going appear to record the acceptance of art as a leisure activity, one that privileges enjoyment over instruction and also assumes a more experienced and initiated audience for theatre.

*   *   *

These scenes from novels sometimes allow us to add detail and nuance to major theatrical events. My example is David Garrick's introduction to the London audience. We know that Garrick's style did not immediately triumph in spite of statements such as this one by Thomas Davies in his *Memoirs of the Life of David Garrick* (1780): 'Mr. Garrick shone forth like a theatrical Newton; he threw new light on elocution and action; he banished ranting, bombast, and grimace; and restored nature, ease, simplicity, and genuine humour.'[49] Writing even later (1807), Richard Cumberland recalled a performance of *The Fair Penitent* in which James Quin, Lacy Ryan, and Garrick played together: 'But when after long and eager expectation I first beheld little Garrick, then young and light and alive in every muscle ... it seemed as if a whole century had been stept over in the transition of a single scene.'[50]

These retrospective assessments underscore the significance of his arrival on the stage and have been influential in shaping our histories of acting, but the sheer number of letters Garrick received and of descriptions of Garrick's acting in his first three years on the London stage argue how intrigued and reflective audience members actually were.[51] Garrick's performance of Richard III at Goodman's Fields in 1741 had created a sensation, and his performances of Bayes and other parts in 1742 had been no less sensational. The fact that he performed an astonishing eighteen roles in 169 performances by spring 1742 contributed to the impression that audiences were witnessing an attempt at revolution.

London audiences were attracted to novelty – sword swallowers, contortionists, freaks of nature – as consistently as to quality, and Garrick's performances were novel. Although evaluative quotations from actors, who had the most at stake, abound, novels record his reception, too. What raised the controversy, it seems to me, is Garrick's use of his body and voice.[52] Georg Christoph Lichtenberg observed that he moved 'to and fro among other players like a man among marionettes'.[53] Male actors at the time were relatively immobile, striking the poses of orators. Some contemporary writers suggest that they even avoided lifting their arms above their eyes, as Quintilian prescribed for orators. The knight in Smollett's *Peregrine Pickle* describes Garrick's 'whole art' as asthmatic and identifiable with spasmatics and bedlamites (274), a reaction common in Garrick's early years. Theophilus Cibber complains of 'frequently affected Starts, convulsive Twitchings, Jerkings of the Body, ... slapping the Breast and Pockets ... the Caricatures of gesture suggested by pert vivacity – his pantomimical Manner of acting every Word in a Sentence'.[54] Horace Walpole mentioned 'mimicry and burlesque'.[55] Macklin described Garrick's method as 'all was bustle-bustle-bustle'.[56] In the age of declamation, Garrick used his voice like a virtuoso violin soloist. Fielding's *Champion* summarized his natural advantages: 'His Voice is clear and piercing, perfectly sweet and harmonious, without Monotony, Drawling, or Affectation ... neither ... whining, bellowing, or grumbling ... perfectly easy in its Transitions, natural in its Cadence and beautiful in its Elocution.'[57] Part of the secret of Garrick's consummate ability to depict rapidly-changing passions and moods in characters is explained here. A contemporary account of his playing a single scene as Hastings in Rowe's *Jane Shore* includes these descriptions of his speaking: 'in a deep affecting tone that was truly heart rending', 'contrived by a little pause', 'the address to heaven ... with great energy and firmness', 'comparatively in a whisper', 'swelled his cadence but immediately subsiding ... into a whisper'.[58] When he completed the speech with the famous 'Remember this' passage, according to all accounts, even the actress was hypnotized.

At first, descriptions of Garrick's performances in various scenes in novels can be divided into evaluative vs. partisan. Later such episodes attempt to allow someone unfortunate enough never to have seen him act a scene imagine it, and they record the acceptance of his method. For instance, Geoffrey Wildgoose, the hero of Richard Graves's *The Spiritual Quixote* (1773), who describes himself as 'an enemy to all theatrical Entertainments', professes his admiration for Garrick for bringing Nature 'back upon the stage'.[59] The mid-century novels' episodes can be profitably set beside performances by Garrick and treatises written by working playwrights. In 1742, for instance, Garrick had reinterpreted Bayes in George Villiers, Duke of Buckingham's *The Rehearsal* (1671), and his parodies of Dennis Delane, Sacheverel Hale and Ryan (not Quin) included bellowing, strutting, and their signature rhetorical quirkiness. In training a young actor, he later described the older style of speaking as 'Yaw, waw-waw, waw'.[60] Foote's 1747 *Treatise* has as part of its title, '*with a critical inquiry into the Theatrical Merit of Mr. G——k, Mr. Q——pt-n, and Mr. B——y*'.

Two years later and eight years after Richardson composed the model of the young country protagonist attending London entertainments, Henry Fielding published the conventional compliment to an actor scene, which everyone knows as his tribute to Garrick and the model for many, many episodes in which a painfully naive character reacts to a performance. The scene ridicules absorption and giving in to illusion, and it is an early, important example of the movement toward teaching playgoers to take acting into account and evaluate it. I want to look at it, however, as one of the many examples of the ways novels joined in the controversy over David Garrick's acting style that marked, at least, his first few years on the London stage.

As you recall, although Partridge keeps reminding himself that it 'is but a Play' and 'nothing at all in it',[61] he judges all the actors by a naive standard of realism, as when he comments that he once had a sexton who could have dug three graves while the actors dug one. With some attention to the historical time period covered by the novel, Fielding recalls David Garrick's appearances in 1746 at

Covent Garden. Partridge chooses the king as the finest actor in the performance. He praises him for speaking distinctly and much louder than the 'little Man', Garrick. Fielding was probably thinking of Roger Bridgwater.[62] Claudius had been one of Bridgwater's parts since 1738, and at his peak he was known for his thundering voice. He had played to Garrick's Hamlet in the fall of 1746 at Covent Garden. In that year, discussion of styles was at its peak, and there had been no easy victory for 'natural' acting. Aaron Hill praises it, and rightly gives Macklin credit for his part in its rise in *The Actor* (pt. 1, 1746), but Roger Pickering's *Reflections upon Theatrical Expression in Tragedy*, published in the same year, insisted upon the rhetorical tradition.[63]

Aaron Hill in a 1735 *Prompter* had blamed the audience for awarding the '*loudest, and most general Applause* to the *highest-stretch'd Elevations* of the *Voice*', and later Garrick cautioned William Powell against '*Splitting the Ears of the Groundlings*' for the sake of 'the Applause of [the] Multitude'.[64] Thomas Davies noted that 'Barry, not having middle tones in his voice, could not give the requisite grave energy to sentiment; he was therefore obliged, in some situations of character, to raise his powers of speech above their ordinary tone. Garrick, by an expressive countenance and flexible voice, gave full force to profound ... reflections'.[65]

The fact that Fielding does not identify the theatre or include details that point to a specific ensemble suggests that he wanted to take a strong stand on acting styles and extend his emphasis in *Tom Jones* on teaching his readers to be discriminating. In fact, along with the most refined viewers of the brief period when Garrick, Barry, and Quin were acting, Fielding in other texts helps lead readers to appreciate different styles and to see that each can be effective and sometimes enhance different parts. In *The Jacobite's Journal* for 6 February 1748, for instance, he wrote that Garrick, Quin, Susannah Cibber, Kitty Clive, and Peg Woffington were 'in their several Capacities' examples of the ability to 'copy Nature'.[66] Two years later connoisseurs reportedly watched Barry in the first three acts of *Romeo and Juliet* and then dashed to Drury Lane to see Garrick in the last two acts.[67]

Tobias Smollett's novels participate more substantively than Fielding's in the debate over competing acting styles, and we can discern the same spirit as Fielding displayed in *The Jacobite's Journal*. In *Roderick Random* (1748), Smollett had satirized Quin as Bellower, but in *Peregrine Pickle* (1751), published in the year of Quin's retirement, he integrates two balanced, evaluative, extended conversations about Quin and the rising Garrick.[68] These passages, actually eye-witness accounts, splenetic and personal as some remarks in them are, testify to the fact that Garrick's performances were strikingly new and that they aroused in these first audiences reflection, confusion, and, to varying degrees, resistance.[69] In the first conversation, the knight of Malta criticizes Garrick in the part of Hamlet for, among other things, acting 'the part of a youthful prince, in the habit of an undertaker' and 'shak[ing] his fist with all the demonstrations of wrath at his mistress, for no evident cause, and behav[ing] like a ruffian to his own mother' (274, 273). What Smollett is identifying can be ascribed to faulty interpretation – the knight's in not recognizing that Garrick's Hamlet was still wearing mourning and Garrick's in some gestures resulting from his still uneven skills.[70] In fact, even late in his career, Garrick would adjust a gesture or the delivery of a line, continually striving to improve.[71]

Foote's *Treatise* and the fact that in the 1746–47 season Garrick and Quin played some of the same roles (*Richard III* notably) and appeared together in *The Fair Penitent*, *I Henry IV*, and *Jane Shore* to sell-out audiences attest to widespread, unprecedented active engagement with performance styles. Quin, Ryan, and Garrick performing together made comparison easy and enriched John Rich, who surely saw the possibilities of commodifying the controversy. Audiences enjoyed this comparison in life and described it in novels and essays. When Quin played Horatio, Garrick Lothario, and Ryan Altamont in *The Fair Penitent* at Covent Garden, audiences flocked to the ten nearly consecutive performances, and sometimes embarrassed the actors with their exuberant applause. One of Smollett's lengthy theatrical conversations in *Peregrine Pickle* is a report from the College of Authors on one of these performances.

Quin was a large man praised for 'statuesque dignity', gravity, and pathos. John Hill observed, 'No man every [*sic*] arriv'd at an equal perfection in speaking the sublime with Mr. Quin'.[72] In the knight's opinion, Quin is 'inferior to him in personal agility, sprightliness and voice', and every sentence highlights the differences between him and Garrick. Quin's utterance is 'a continual sing song, like the chanting of vespers, and his action resembles that of heaving ballast into the hold of a ship' (274). In memorably biting words, he excoriates Quin's acting of some of his most famous parts, and his attack is on the declamatory style: 'beating his own forehead, and bellowing like a bull'. The knight is fair enough to give Quin his due when he plays Falstaff, Henry VIII, the Plain Dealer, and Sir John Brute even as his criticisms of his 'loud, shallow, blustering' performances of other characters convey the monotony of the conventional declamatory method.[73] These performances brought many kinds of contrasts among the men to the audiences' attention; for instance, Quin as Falstaff had no trouble lifting Garrick as Hotspur on his back, where, according to Thomas Davies, Garrick 'looked like a dwarf on the back of a giant' while Quin 'tugged and toiled to raise Barry [when he played the part] from the ground'.[74] Because the novelists were more numerous and represented a larger variety of backgrounds, social classes and opinions about commercial art, their accounts of the ways the styles of the older Spranger Barry and especially James Quin were thrown into sharp relief by Garrick add new detail and open new, revisionary lines of inquiry. For example, I believe that widespread discussion of performance styles played a significant part in laying the foundation for acceptance of Garrick's and John Kemble's vigorous and intellectual engagement with Shakespeare's plays and for an openness to new interpretations of parts that characterized the careers of actors in the next generation.

Conclusion

In the early novels, the theatre was, as it was in *Pamela II*, one of a series of obligatory amusements to be experienced by every visitor to London. The playhouse also functioned almost like a masquerade – it was a public space where the sexes and various classes mingled for a predictable London experience. In fact, a few days after seeing the plays, Pamela went to a masquerade. Novelists felt free to have unidentifiable performances (as Richardson did with *The Tender Husband*) or to treat plays with considerable freedom, as Fielding did in *Tom Jones* in which he even reversed major scenes from Act 3 in *Hamlet*.[75] As the significance of taste and the project of educating consumers of art grew, these scenes, although still an obligatory part of the journey through London amusements, become very different. Striking is the rise of the centrality of the emotional impact of the play. Not only is the playgoers' response a gauge of their character but whether or not the actor had the power to move the audience a measure of player, company, and playwright.

Incidentally, these scenes remind us that theatregoers of the eighteenth century saw far more mediocre or even bad plays than they did excellent ones, just as moviegoers today do. Critics have said that novelists usually wrote, in Gale Noyes' words, about 'the most famous dramas of earlier times',[76] but, in fact, they engaged with the most popular plays of their time, as likely to be repertory as new plays. These plays were at the crux of a contemporary discussion or controversy, such as those regarding absorption, sentimental literature, she-tragedies, or whether an actor represents or actually feels the emotion being performed.[77] The episodes offer especially important evidence about what a drama-mad nation England was. More and more characters in plays become quick reference points, allusions that are clearly intended to be immediately recognized by readers. For instance, Ophelia in Sarah Fielding's *The History of Ophelia* – note the name – who has been mesmerized by a performance of *Macbeth*, is tricked into getting in the wrong carriage and kidnapped, and says of the coachmen that 'my Imagination . . . clothed them like the Murderers in *Macbeth*'.[78] The vocabulary of theories of acting is also integrated into novels. When the heroine of Burney's *The Wanderer* disqualifies herself from acting as a profession, she does it by finding herself too weak – uncertain she can resist the 'dangers and improprieties' but primarily lacking 'nerves'. A twentieth-century novel critic would hardly recognize here the theory of acting drama specialists like Joseph Roach have identified with Garrick: his ability to express physically the Idea he imagines, setting in motion a current through the nerves from the brain to the muscles.[79] Not only are numerous country house performances described, but scenes with strolling players and performances in barns, school rooms, livery company halls, and warehouses seem even more numerous than attendance at London theatres. Famous scenes, such as the one in Burney's *Camilla* (1796), and entire novels, now forgotten, are about these itinerants. Among them are *Young Scarron* (1752) by Thomas Mozeen – and *Alwyn: or, The Gentleman Comedian* (1780) by Thomas Holcroft, one of the most successful dramatists of the century.

Writers at the end of the century are intolerant of behaviours taken for granted earlier, and theatre-attendance episodes take on new formulaic elements. Even in small ways, this is apparent. Intelligent, admirable characters remark that among the emotions experienced in the theatre is anger – 'I could not bear with Patience the Noises that were sometimes made', Ophelia Lennox says in *The History of Ophelia*.[80] A specific kind of satiric scene becomes as common as the beautiful heroine displaying sensibility. Harriet Denby, for example, in Sophia Briscoe's *The Fine Lady* (1772) plans her 'performance' at the play she will attend, announcing that 'I will assume a delicate languor': 'My features shall to-night correspond with my habit (of first mourning): besides it is to the tragedy of Zara we are going.' Another character describes her success: she 'never yet appeared to so much advantage ... She attracted the eyes of the whole house.'[81] Henry Man uses such a moment at a play as a turning point in his plot in *Mr. Bentley: or, the Rural Philosopher* (1777). Miss Melbourne, to whom Fairfield is attracted, arrives late to draw the most attention to herself and then is 'fashionably indifferent to the play', although she uses her glass to examine the most striking dresses worn by the audience members. When she makes Fairfield and others notice her by dropping her gloves, whispering, and snapping her fan, she pretends absorption in the play, and at the exactly correct moment, 'when the superior tenderness of *Belvidera* disarms the impetuous fury of her husband, she condescended to take out a fine cambrick handkerchief to enjoy the luxury of her triumph unperceived'.

The end of this sentence comes as something of a shock, as Miss Melbourne does not even fake tears but hides a smile of victory. Fairfield is taken in, attributes sensibility to her, and is 'uncommonly infatuated'. Melbourne, however, cannot sustain her performance and begins to flirt and ogle the audience, and he rejects her.[82] This scene demonstrates the author's appreciation of good acting and inserts telling criteria for judging it. Moreover, the scene satirizes both the novelists who use such scenes to prove the heroine's sensibility and women who use the theatre, as prostitutes once did, to ensnare men. Perhaps they even record something of an advance for women – rather than the unwilling spectacles at plays,[83] they become performers who, to various degrees, control their reception.

Notes and references

1. I would like to thank Heather Hicks, the Defoe Graduate Research Fellow, and Lacey Williams, my research assistant, for their many contributions to this essay.
2. I am thinking of important studies such as David Marshall's *The Figure of the Theater* (New York: Columbia University Press, 1986) and Joseph Litvak's *Caught in the Act* (Berkeley: University of California Press, 1992). Emily Allen in 'Staging Identity: Frances Burney's Allegory of Genre' discusses briefly Evelina's first trip to the theatre; *Eighteenth-Century Studies*, 31 (1998): 438. Sarah Bilston's 'Authentic Performance in Theatrical Women's Fiction of the 1870s' examines women's portrayals of actresses and offers a model for critics of earlier literature; *Women's Writing*, 11 (2004): 39–53.
3. Sarah Fielding, *The History of Ophelia* (1760; New York: Garland, 1974), 1:161.
4. Kitty Clive was famous for flirting with members of the audience while the other actors spoke their lines. In the trial scene of *The Merchant of Venice* she often did a series of imitations of famous, living lawyers; Jean Benedetti, *David Garrick and the Birth of Modern Theatre* (London: Methuen, 2001), 55–6. Occasionally newspaper reviews mentioned especially distracting conduct by actors waiting their turn to speak. Fielding commented on how Garrick 'is attentive to whatever is spoke and never drops his character when he has finished a speech, by either looking contemptibly on an inferior performer ... or suffering his eyes to wander through the whole circle of spectators'; *The Champion*, reprinted in *Gentleman's Magazine* 12 (October 1742), 527.

5. Eliza Haywood, *Fantomina* in *Popular Fiction by Women, 1660–1730*, ed. Paula R. Backscheider and John J. Richetti (Oxford: Oxford University Press, 1996), 227.

6. See my 'Literature as Immediate Reality', *Blackwell's Companion to the Eighteenth-Century Novel and Culture*, ed. Paula R. Backscheider and Catherine Ingrassia (Oxford: Blackwell, 2005), 504–38, especially 515–16.

7. [Samuel Foote], *A Treatise on the Passions with a critical inquiry into the Theatrical Merit of Mr. G——k, Mr. Q——n, and Mr. B——y.* (1747; New York: Blom, 1971), 3. Calculations by Arthur H. Scouten in *The London Stage, 1729–1747* support this figure (Carbondale: Southern Illinois University Press, 1968), clxi–clxii.

8. Other tracts with this educational mission written in the 1740s include David Garrick, *An Essay on Acting* (1744); Aaron Hill, *The Art of Acting, Part I* (1746); James Eyre Weeks, *A Rhapsody on the Stage: or, the art of playing in imitation of Horace's Art of Poetry* (Dublin, 1746); Eliza Haywood's second volume of *Companion to the Theatre* (1747); and Theophilus Cibber, *Two Dissertations on the Theatre* (1750).

9. Francis Gentleman, *Dramatick Censor*, quoted in James Lynch, *Box, Pit, and Gallery* (Berkeley: University of California Press, 1953), 233.

10. Quoted in *The Revels History of Drama in English, 1660–1750*, ed. Richard Southern, John C. Loftis, Marion Jones, and Arthur H. Scouten (London: Methuen, 1975), 5:14.

11. In his still useful study, *The Neglected Muse: Restoration and Eighteenth-Century Tragedy in the Novel (1740–1780)*, Robert Gale Noyes describes the criticism in novels as 'abundant', 'voluminous', and even 'comprehensive' (1740–1780) (Providence: Brown University Press, 1958), 3–4. He quotes generously from the hundreds of novels mentioned; I disagree with some of his conclusions, especially that the 'bulk of "fictional", criticism of repertory is concerned . . . with the most famous dramas of earlier times' (5).

12. Sarah Fielding, *The Adventures of David Simple*, ed. Peter Sabor (Lexington: University Press of Kentucky, 1998), 65–8.

13. Tobias Smollett, *The Adventures of Peregrine Pickle*, ed. James L. Clifford (London: Oxford University Press, 1964), 600. There are, of course, many other allusions to plays and actors in this novel; cf., discussion of *The Fair Penitent*, James Quin, other plays and players, 651–9. Allusions to and quotations from Shakespeare's history plays are especially numerous. Joyce Grossman identifies Mary Collyer as the author of *Betty Barnes*, 'Social Protest and the Mid-Century Novel: Mary Collyer's *The History of Miss Betty Barnes*', *Eighteenth-Century Women*, 1 (2001): 165.

14. Oliver Goldsmith, *The Vicar of Wakefield* (Oxford: Oxford University Press, 1971), 102.

15. Goldsmith, *Vicar*, 111.

16. Frances Burney, *Evelina*, ed. Kristina Straub (Boston: Bedford Books, 1997), 70 and see 70n. 1. Edward Kimber's strange *roman-á-clef* about Garrick, *The Juvenile Adventures of David Ranger, Esq.* (1757), capitalizes on the part of Ranger and has 'Ranger' begin his acting career in a barn playing Hamlet; for a brief discussion of this novel, see Robert Gale Noyes, 'Shakespeare in the Eighteenth-Century Novel', *ELH*, 11 (1944), 224–5. In Garrick's later years, he performed only 20–30 times a year, while in his early years he would sometimes perform five different characters in a week; Jane Freeman, 'Beyond Bombast: David Garrick's Performances of Benedick and King Lear', *RECTR*, 14 (1999): 1–2. Burney's characters were fortunate to get in the theatre to see him; on the crowding and difficulties of seeing Garrick see Lynch, *Box, Pit*, 200–2.

17. 'A Review of the Theatrical Character of the English Roscius', *Universal Magazine*, 59 (July 1776): 23, and John Genest, *Some Account of the English Stage from the Restoration in 1660 to 1830* (1832; New York: Franklin, 1965), 5:499, respectively.

18. *Cf.* Arthur Murphy, *The Life of David Garrick*, 2 vols (1801; New York: Benjamin Blom, 1969), 1:37–9, 119–44, and George Winchester Stone and George M. Kahrl, *David Garrick: a Critical Biography* (Carbondale: Southern Illinois University Press, 1979), 313–53, 473–5.

19. This review is comically written from the perspective of 'the Fool' in the pit and was reprinted in *The Gentleman's Magazine* 17 (February 1747), 80.

20. Georg Lichtenberg is describing Garrick as Sir John Brute, *Lichtenberg's Visits to England*, trans. Margaret L. Mare and W. H. Quarrell (New York: Benjamin Blom, 1969), 18.
21. Cited from an unidentified source by Harry W. Pedicord, 'On-Stage with David Garrick: Garrick's Acting Companies in Performance', *Theatre Survey*, 28 (1987), 69.
22. Quoted in Genest, *Some Account of the English Stage*, 5:499.
23. I am aware that numerous critics believe that Garrick's portrayals of heroes, including Shakespeare's, were sentimental; see, for example Jean I. Marsden's summarizing essay, 'Improving Shakespeare: From the Restoration to Garrick' in *The Cambridge Companion to Shakespeare on Stage*, ed. Stanley Wells and Sarah Stanton (Cambridge: Cambridge University Press, 2002), especially 30–5.
24. For more complex reasons, Congreve's Valentine has pretended madness, and Angelica brings about the happy ending.
25. It is likely that the version Evelina would have attended had removed lines such as the exchange between Tattle and Miss Prue in which she says he will have to push her down to force his way into her room, and he replies that he will 'come in first, and push you down afterwards' (2.1.651–8) and Valentine's observation that his child's nurse, had she known her business, would have 'overlaid the Child a fortnight ago' (1.1.211–13). These and other suggestive lines are cut in the 1776 edition 'As performed at the Theatre-Royal in Drury-Lane, Regulated from the Prompt-Book, By Permission of the Managers, By Mr. Hopkins, Prompter' reproduced in the Bell edition.
26. George Colman the Elder, *The Deuce is in Him*, in *The Plays of George Colman the Elder*, ed. Kalman A. Burnim, 6 Vols (New York: Garland, 1983), 1:16.
27. Burney, *Evelina*, 229–30. Margaret Doody, one of the few critics to take these trips to plays seriously, gives a good reading of Burney's enjoyment of farcical plays and their relationship to Madame Duval; *Frances Burney: the Life in the Works* (New Brunswick, NJ: Rutgers University Press, 1988), 49–54. Although the plays were not performed on a single night, they were often done in succession, as they were on 18, 19, and 20 June and 24, 25, and 26 June 1767, and very close together as they were 28 and 30 June 1775.
28. See also Charles Johnstone, *Chrysal: or the Adventures of a Guinea*, ed. E. A. Baker (London: Routledge & Sons, 1907), 373–8 (also on Garrick).
29. Frances Brooke, *The Excursion*, ed. Paula Backscheider and Hope D. Cotton (Lexington: University Press of Kentucky, 1997), 56–7.
30. 'The British Theatre', *London Magazine*, 44 (March, 1775), 106.
31. *An Examen of the New Comedy* (London, 1747), 7.
32. Quoted in Noyes, *Neglected Muse*, 174. Although not a common practice, private readings and rehearsals were employed by canny managers, authors, and friends to help plays succeed throughout the century, see Lynch, *Box, Pit* for other examples, 210.
33. Brooke, *The Excursion*, ed. Backscheider and Cotton, 56. In fact, *Braganza* was critically acclaimed and ran for 19 nights when first performed at Drury Lane in 1775.
34. Numerous editions of plays published after 1770 announce on the title page, 'Marked with the Variations in the Manager's Book, at the Theatre Royal', and a hand with a pointing finger below the cast list or on the page opposite the prologue reads, 'The Reader is desired to observe, that the passages omitted in the Representations at the Theatres are here preserved, and marked with Inverted Commas'. These editions are important evidence about the growing recognition of different audiences for printed plays. Especially in comedies, many of the omitted speeches resemble moral discourses commonly found in novels and show an awareness of readers' practices of art consumption.
35. Robert Jephson, *Braganza. A Tragedy* in *The Plays of Robert Jephson*, ed. Temple James Maynard (New York: Garland, 1980), 1 and 17 respectively.
36. Samuel Richardson's novel was styled 'The Third and Fourth Volumes' of *Pamela*, usually identified as '*Pamela II*', and had the ungainly title, *Pamela, or Virtue Rewarded. In a Series of Familiar Letters from a Beautiful Young Damsel, to Her Parents: And Afterwards, in Her Exalted Condition, between Her, and Persons of Figure and Quality, on the Most Important and Entertaining Subjects*. All quotations are from *Pamela. Volume Two* (1914; London: J. M. Dent, 1950).

37. David Roberts, *The Ladies: Female Patronage of Restoration Drama, 1660–1700* (Oxford: Clarendon, 1989), 73. The exemplary teacher in Sarah Fielding's *The Governess* cautions her students to avoid plays not recommended to them 'by those who have the care of your Education'; ed. Candace Ward (Peterborough, ON: Broadview, 2005), 156.

38. Quoted from *The Companion to the Playhouse* (1764) by Noyes, *Neglected Muse*, 115, and see his discussion of the play in novels, 114–22. The play was among the most popular of the century; it was performed almost every season, at least 186 times before 1776. Fielding refers to a performance of the play in *Tom Jones*, Bk. 4.1.

39. Richardson, *Pamela II*, 253.

40. See *Spectator* no. 338 (28 March 1712) and Donald Bond's notes (1965; Oxford: Oxford University Press, 1987), 3:250–4. The notes discuss the authorship of the epilogue.

41. *Spectator* no. 335 for 25 March 1712, Bond 3:241; Richardson and Fielding may have learned from this scene. Joseph Addison says Sir Roger gives 'a piece of Natural Criticism', 241. See also 3:250–4, 3:265–9, and 251n.2 on authorship. Eustace Budgell's quotation is 3:266.

42. Autrey Nell Wiley points out that 'coquetry' explains their popularity; 'Female Prologues and Epilogues in English Plays', *PMLA*, 48 (1933): 1060–79; for 'coquetry', see 1065. This *Spectator* essay listed as by Budgell was probably written or substantially revised by Addison.

43. Elizabeth Inchbald's *Remarks* in the collected edition are not sequentially paginated but numbered individually; they are arranged alphabetically by play; these are for *The Distressed Mother*, *Remarks for The British Theatre (1806–1809)*, introduction by Cecilia Macheski (Delmar, NY: Scholars' Facsimiles & Reprints, 1990), 4–5.

44. In fact, the epilogue calls attention to 'human nature', both in the person of Ann Oldfield and in the public's reaction to her and Andromache. Thomas Davies in *Dramatic Miscellanies* wrote, 'Notwithstanding [that Oldfield's connections with Arthur Maynwaring and Charles Churchill] were publicly known, she was invited to the houses of women ... as much distinguished for unblemished character as elevated rank' (London, 1784), 2:434. Edmund Curll under the pseudonym of William Egerton writes in *Faithful Memoirs of ... Mrs. Anne Oldfield* (1731): 'The *Distresst Mother* seemed now to be the case of Mrs. Oldfield both on, and off the Stage', quoted in Kristina Straub, *Sexual Suspects* (Princeton: Princeton University Press, 1992), 93. She also quotes Davies. See also F. W. Bateson, 'The Stage (1713)', *Modern Language Notes*, 45 (1930): 27–9.

45. The date of the composition of *Pamela* means that Richardson would have seen even more successful, excellent comedies in this genre, including Cibber's *The Provoked Husband* (1728). On Richardson's friendship with Cibber, see Ira Konigsberg, *Samuel Richardson and the Dramatic Novel* (Lexington: University of Kentucky Press, 1968), 12–13, 59, 70.

46. As Margaret Doody points out, Pamela quotes Andromache's speech on 'A Mother's Sorrow for an only Son' and, in contrast to Philips's characters, represents ideal restraint and 'exemplary generosity'. She calls Richardson's use of these comparisons 'audacious', see *A Natural Passion* (Oxford: Clarendon Press, 1974), 84–6; quotation, 85, and on *Clarissa* and pathetic and heroic tragedy, see 107–28 *et passim*. She also compares Sir Roland in *Grandison* to Richard Steele's Sir Harry Gubbin, 285; see also 289.

47. Quoted in Noyes, *Neglected Muse*, 43; see also 73–5. *The Correspondents* is sometimes described as based on actual letters between Thomas, Lord Lyttleton, and Mrs Peach, a widow he married, see ESTC.

48. *Memoirs of Lady Woodford* (London, 1771), 2:44–50. This book is treated as a novel in Richard Sheridan's *The Rivals* (1775) and in the *Monthly Review*, 44 (June 1771), 498, but the *Critical Review* treats it as an actual memoir, 31 (31 January 1771), 482. The obituary of a Lady Woodford, wife of Sir Ralph, is recorded in the *London Times* (19 June 1794), 3. I am grateful to my assistant Lacey Williams for her research on this text.

49. Thomas Davies, *Memoirs of the Life of David Garrick* (London, 1780), 43.

50. Richard Cumberland, *Memoirs* (London, 1807), 80–2. See also Murphy's *Life of Garrick*, in which he describes Garrick's performance as Bayes as 'a keen and powerful criticism of the absurd style of acting that prevailed on the stage', 1:32.

51. Stone and Kahrl characterize the letters as approving some actions, criticizing others, and expressing surprise at others, *David Garrick*, 541.

52. I accept that Garrick was the living exemplum of the 'science of acting' that Joseph Roach and others have demonstrated was his theory. Garrick, for instance, once wrote that, 'when Macbeth kills Duncan, "his faculties are intensely riveted to the murder alone". This concentration of awed and terrified attention reacts on the entire body ... "He should at that time be a moving statue, or indeed a petrified man".' Roach is paraphrasing and quoting Garrick's *An Essay on Acting*, 'Garrick, the Ghost and the Machine', *Theatre Journal*, 34 (1982): 440. This Cartesian physiology has been identified in acting manuals from the late 1720s but it was Garrick who represented it and made it controversial. Aaron Hill gives a clear schematic in his periodical *The Prompter*: 'The imagination assumes the idea'. 'Its marks and characteristical impressions appear first in the face'. 'Thence, impelled by the will, a commissioned detachment of *animal spirits* descending into ... the muscles ... bends and stimulates their elastic powers into a position ... to express the ... idea', quoted in Roach, 'Garrick, the Ghost', 436. See also Denise S. Sechelski, 'Garrick's Body and the Labor of Art in Eighteenth-Century Theater', *Eighteenth-Century Studies*, 29 (1996): 378–9, and Christine Gerrard, *Aaron Hill: the Muses' Projector, 1685–1750* (Oxford: Oxford University Press, 2003), 167–71.

53. Lichtenberg, *Lichtenberg's Visits to England*, 6.

54. Quoted from *Two Dissertations on the Theatre* (1750) in Sechelski, 'The Labor of Art', 380.

55. Quoted in Sechelski, 'The Labor of Art', 380.

56. Quoted in Genest, *Some Account*, 5:499.

57. *The Champion*, 1741, reprinted in *Gentleman's Magazine* 12 (October 1742), 527.

58. Quoted in Leigh Woods, *Garrick Claims the Stage: Acting as Social Emblem in Eighteenth-Century England* (Westport, CT: Greenwood, 1984), 43.

59. Quoted in Noyes, 'Shakespeare in the Eighteenth-Century Novel', 217.

60. Benedetti, *David Garrick*, 65–6 and 196.

61. Henry Fielding, *The History of Tom Jones*, introduction and commentary by Martin Battestin, ed. Fredson Bowers (Oxford: Oxford University Press, 1975), 2:852–7.

62. The standard edition of *Tom Jones* says that Fielding is thinking of 'Billy' Mills. Mills played Claudius as early as the 1720s and throughout the early 1740s. Mills played many parts and was a safe journeyman; his voice was once described, however, as 'unequal to the Swellings and Throws of the Sublime'. By 1742 he played to Garrick's Hamlet at Drury Lane, but his last performance as the king seems to have been in March 1744. Garrick also played Hamlet with William Bridges as Claudius (Drury Lane, 1744–45). Although Bridgwater is the most likely actor, Fielding may not have had anyone in particular in mind. On Fielding alluding to Billy Mills, who played Claudius at Drury Lane in the season of 1741–42, and to whom Fielding had compared Garrick in *The Jacobite's Journal* (23 April 1748), see *Tom Jones*, 2:855n. 2 and 856n. 2. Garrick played Hamlet in a performance with Mills as the king on 16 November 1742.

63. See Fredson Bowers' summary in *The History of Tom Jones*, ed. Bowers, 853n. 2 and 854nn. 1, 2. For contextualizing information, see Gerrard, *Aaron Hill*, 144–71.

64. Quoted in Gerrard, *Aaron Hill*, 167–71, and Garrick quoting *Hamlet* 3.2.12f in Letter no. 345, 12 December 1764, *Letters of Garrick*, ed. David M. Little and George M. Kahrl (Cambridge: Belknap Press of Harvard University Press, 1963), 2:436.

65. Thomas Davies, *Dramatic Miscellanies*, 3:78.

66. Quoted in Fielding, *Tom Jones*, 1:493n. 2.

67. Frederick and Lise-Lone Marker, 'Actors and Their Repertory' in *The Revels History of Drama in English, 1750–1880*, ed. Michael Booth, et al. (London: Methuen, 1975), 101. Francis Gentleman's *Dramatic Censor* (London, 1770) is filled with eye-witness comparisons of these actors and more, cf., 1:107–13, 150–5.

68. Peregrine remarks that 'It was not to be supposed that one actor could shine equally in all characters', *Peregrine Pickle*, 275. For a good account of reactions to Garrick's first season, see Benedetti, *David Garrick*, 42–67.
69. I agree with Howard Buck that the passages vary in judiciousness but give unusually vivid accounts of, for instance, Garrick's 'force, daring, and intelligence' and even the exchanged delivery of lines by Quin and Garrick, *A Study in Smollett, Chiefly 'Peregrine Pickle', With a Complete Collation of the First and Second Editions* (Mamaroneck, NY: Paul P. Appel, 1973), especially 91–2 and 651–5. Buck also gives detailed information about Smollett's relationships with Quin and Garrick. For a good account of reactions to Garrick's first season, see Benedetti, *David Garrick*, 42–67.
70. The novels and theatre sources remind us that Garrick worked continuously on his parts, cf. Thomas Davies, *Dramatic Miscellanies* in which he remarks that 'After [Garrick] had fully satisfied his fancy, and ripened his judgment by the experience of two or three years, he was pronounced to be perfect [as Sir John Brute] as in any of his most approved parts', 3:428–9.
71. Eye-witness accounts of Garrick confirm this, especially regarding Lear. Cf. Aaron Hill, *London Daily Advertiser* (27 February 1752), 48–9; Davies, *Memoirs of the Life of David Garrick*, 2:97–8.
72. Frederick and Lise-Lone Marker, 'Actors and Their Repertory', *Revels History*, 6:96.
73. In the second, more specific episode, members of the College of Authors report on *The Fair Penitent* and Edward Young's very popular *The Revenge* (1721).
74. Davies, *Dramatic Miscellanies*, 1:273–5.
75. A. J. Hassall, 'Garrick's "Hamlet" and "Tom Jones",' *Notes and Queries*, 24 (1977): 247–9.
76. Noyes, *Neglected Muse*, 5.
77. An important contribution to this discussion is in Frances Burney's *The Wanderer*, ed. Margaret Doody, Robert Mack, and Peter Sabor (Oxford: Oxford University Press, 1991). Burney's scene leads to a sense of balance, suggested by something that Garrick once wrote, 'I have Hamlet in my head, & can say & think of Nothing Else', letter no. 727, 18 December 1772, *Letters of David Garrick*, ed. Little and Kahrl, 2:838.
78. Fielding, *Ophelia*, 1:261.
79. The group of auditors raise the question 'Whether this excellence were the result of practice and instruction, or a sudden emanation of general genius'. Her best effect is assigned to 'deep research into the latent subjects of uneasiness belonging to the situation of Lady Townly. This, however, was *nature*, which would not be repressed; not art, that strove to be displayed' (emphasis mine), *Wanderer*, 94–9, 398–400. And see note 48.
80. Fielding, *Ophelia*, 1:161–2.
81. Quoted in Noyes, *Neglected Muse*, 146.
82. Henry Man, *Mr. Bentley: or, The Rural Philosopher* (Dublin, 1777), 2:209–13.
83. David Roberts argues a different situation for women in the Restoration, concluding 'There is, furthermore, no indication that the unexceptional, inconspicuous majority needed to attend with a male escort any more than they had to worry about the damaging effects of a new play on their reputations', *The Ladies*, 94.

4
Reading Theatre History from Account Books

Judith Milhous

A surprisingly large number of account books and related financial documents survive for the patent theatres of eighteenth-century London, but they remain largely unused by theatre historians. Daily receipts now known from ninety-plus books covering more than sixty seasons were printed in *The London Stage* a generation ago.[1] However, the sources of this information, which range from prompters' diaries to full-length daybooks, often contain further, unused particulars, chiefly about companies at Drury Lane and Covent Garden theatres. Some opera sources also exist. Access to these volumes is not difficult: most of the records are preserved in the Folger and the British Library, where the MSS have been available for many decades. They vary greatly in what they were originally designed to do and what they provide, which can make comparisons between companies or across seasons or genres problematic. Scholars have occasionally traced the success or failure of a single play, followed a playwright's earnings, or calculated a performer's benefit gains. To date, however, the accounts have almost never been used systematically, perhaps because the sheer bulk of financial material and the amount of detail are intimidating. I believe that many of the utilization problems can be solved, and that these books have much to tell us.

My objects in this essay are twofold. I want both to survey the extant material, explaining it in general terms, and briefly to illustrate some of the questions we can ask of it. I shall begin by describing the basic layout of account books and then demonstrate the rather limited use made of these resources in *The London Stage* and the *Biographical Dictionary*.[2] I shall try to explain briefly how budgets and financial records worked in the eighteenth-century London theatres. After sketching some of the potential uses a theatre historian might make of salary and benefit information, I shall conclude by reviewing some questions these financial resources have already helped to answer. Eighteenth-century London theatres were set up as profit-making businesses: their accounts can help us understand the size, shape, and managerial operation of those businesses better than we do at present.

I. Surviving account books and related materials

What exactly is an 'account book'? They differ quite a lot in what they include, but most have some basic features in common, which Table 4.1 illustrates. It shows the opening for Saturday, 8 November 1746 from BL Egerton MS 2268, for Covent Garden. Let us follow the layout. Each opening usually records income and outgo for a single day, which is almost always a performance day. The date, play title, and afterpiece, if any, are recorded at the top of the entry. (Authors' names are almost never mentioned. Since they were owed no royalties, they were irrelevant.) Ordinarily, total cash receipts appear on the left, details of outgo on the right, though in this case the left-hand page also includes an actors' paylist. In the top corner of that page is an additional, unexplained calculation: the minimal constant charge of £34 1*s*., recorded in another book, has been silently deducted from the receipts, and the remaining £9 16*s*. of cash added to the balance. On the right-hand page appear the servants' salaries and other expenses, to which is added the performers' salary total (£109 3*s*. for men, £56 10*s*. for women). The resulting £203 16*s*.' worth of expenses for the day is subtracted from the cash on the left hand page, to show a balance of just £65 4*s*. 6*d*. Each actor on the left and each staff member on the right is assigned an index number, which refers to that individual's page in a ledger (now lost). The check marks show that every entry has been verified against the same figure recorded in that other book. Back on the right, below the staff list, we find unanticipated items approved for payment that day: the hiring of two new employees, a costume purchase, and a loan to the assistant prompter. Table 4.1 shows an unusually full page. On many days, no more than the receipts and one or two specially-approved items appear in such a book. Most performers and house servants were paid once a week; tradesmen's bills came in irregularly and were often settled at long intervals; taxes and payments to shareholders and bondholders were paid erratically when they fell due or as payment was demanded.

Income appears in standard forms, but the detail in which outgo is recorded varies drastically from book to book. Treasurers normally kept a running total of cash in hand, but because any book is part of a system now incomplete, that figure may have little to do with the actual profitability of the theatre. Some treacherous quirks exist. For example, clerks seldom mark negative balances, or shifts from negative to positive and vice versa. Thus the figures can be quite disconcerting at first sight. In many books, no relationship is calculated between income and outgo. The 'aftermoney' received for late admission can be recorded that night or not until the next day. The few pounds at issue made no difference to the theatre's total income, but might matter to historians who wish to chart the drawing power of different plays.

Most surviving account books are *ex post facto* constructions. Their contents were fair-copied from bills, receipts, and loose papers, normally within a few days of the face date. From wide variation in form and content, we can deduce that managements had distinctly different policies as to the level of detail they wanted preserved in what amounts to a daily ledger-of-record. Our knowledge of the

Table 4.1: Transcription of Egerton MS 2268, fols. 23v–24r. Covent Garden Theatre, Saturday 8 November 1746

Fol. 23v:

Rece' 43:17:0

		Salary	✓
2	Mr Quin	21-00-00	✓
4	Ryan	12-00-00	✓
4	Hippisley	7-00-00	✓
6	Chapman	5-00-00	✓
7	Morris	5-00-00	✓
7	Rosco	5-00-00	✓
9	Woodward	4-00-00	✓
9	Cashell	4-00-00	✓
10	Havard	4-00-00	✓
11	Leveridge	4-00-00	✓
10	Lalauze	4-00-00	✓
12	Bridgwater	3-00-00	✓
13	Gibson	2-00-00	✓
13	Bencraft	2-00-00	✓
14	Arthur	2-00-00	✓
14	Marten	2-00-00	✓
15	James	2-00-00	✓
15	Ridout	2-00-00	✓
16	Villenueve	2-00-00	✓
19	Harrington	1-13-00	✓
19	Stede	1-10-00	✓
21	Dunstall	1-10-00	✓
20	Morgan	1-10-00	✓
20	Davies	1-10-00	✓
23	Carr	1-05-00	✓
24	Stoppelaer	1-00-00	✓
24	Anderson	1-00-00	✓
25	Thompson	1-00-00	✓
25	Vaughan	1-00-00	✓
26	Hayman	1-00-00	✓
26	Paddick	1-00-00	✓
27	Kennedy	1-00-00	✓
34	Smith	0-15-00	✓
35	Connor	0-10-00	✓
		109-3-0	

Ballance Brot over	259-00-06
Reced by balance of the Recet	9-16-00
	269-00-06
	203-16-00
	£65-04-06

Name		✓	Amount
Mrs Pritchard	5	✓	10-00-00
Horton	6	✓	6-00-00
Vincent	8	✓	3-00-00
[blank]¹	11	✓	3-00-00
Lampe	8	✓	5-00-00
Hippisley	16	✓	2-10-00
Hale	17	✓	2-00-00
Havard	10	✓	2-00-00
James	15	✓	2-00-00
Younge	17	✓	2-00-00
Norris	18	✓	2-00-00
S Vincent	18	✓	2-00-00
Martin	21	✓	1-10-00
Dunstall	21	✓	1-10-00
Bland	22	✓	1-10-00
Lebrun	22	✓	1-05-00
Rowley	29	✓	1-00-00
Vaughan	25	✓	1-00-00
Villenueve	16	✓	1-00-00
Gordon	30	✓	1-00-00
Haughton	29	✓	1-00-00
Ferguson	31	✓	0-15-00
Allen	32	✓	0-15-00
Morrison	31	✓	0-15-00
Daniel	32	✓	0-15-00
Valois	33	✓	0-15-00
Stevens	34	✓	0-10-00
			56-10-00
			109-03-00
			165-13-00

Fol. 24r:

1746 Saturday Nov' 8 Provok'd Wife and King &c

			✓
41	Mr Page a weeks Sallary	1-00-00	
40	Mr Perry 6 Days	1-10-00	
41	White D°	1-00-00	✓
40	Hamersley D°	1-04-00	✓
43	Cundell D°	0-12-00	✓
42	Jarvis D°	0-12-00	✓
42	Osborne D°	0-12-00	✓
44	Potter D°	0-12-00	✓
46	Carny D°	0-10-00	✓
44	Rabbitt D°	0-09-00	✓
45	Bethune D°	0-09-00	✓
51	Women Dressers D°	04-13-00	✓
54	Chairwomen D°	3-14-00	✓
46	Lucas a Week's Sallary	0-10-00	✓
64	Meares (Taylor) on acct.	4-04-00	✓
33	Miss Mullart Enter'd from Saturday last at $5 pr Week	0-5-00	✓
5	Mr. Pritchard enter'd from D° at $40 pr Week	2-00-00	✓
61	Mr. Hamersley for a Black Velvet Suit of Women's Cloaths For M⁵ Cibber	8-01-00	✓
19	Mr. Stede as p' Note of hand	6-06-00	✓
		38-03-00	✓
		165-13-00	
		203-16-00	

¹ This unnamed salary is entered consistently throughout this season and the two nearest seasons with surviving account books (1757–58 and 1760–61). I conjecture that it represents money paid to Mrs Priscilla Rich, a former actress, no longer appearing on the stage.

underlying paperwork is largely supposititious, with two exceptions, which I will take up below, when I discuss the 'process' reflected in these bills.

Seventeenth- and eighteenth-century theatres actually kept several kinds of account books, though exemplars of most of them do not survive.[3] Some may have been generated by different departments; at the least, they were based on information provided from throughout the theatre. We may deduce something like the following series. (1) What we now call the box office kept a day book in which total ticket sales and attendance figures were logged.[4] This office sometimes kept another day book in which to list total receipts, deduct a specified minimal constant charge, and record the transfer of all other cash to the treasurer. As part of the operation of this office, sales of particular tickets for the night's perform-ances were recorded, but that was not its principal job, because most tickets were bought at the door. (2) The treasurer's office was often a separate, more private location. One or more clerks there kept several ledgers in which they recorded transactions with different groups – e.g., fabric merchants and clothing purchases; dealings with oil, wax, and tallow chandlers; the various tax authorities. The treas-urer's office also made up separate weekly performer and house servant paylists, for practical purposes of distribution. At a guess, the treasurer kept his own master list of payments and verified them against departmental records. One can easily see how sub-account books might have totalled between six and a dozen for a season. (3) Some treasurers – probably most – kept a paginated general ledger in which they recorded all payments to individuals. This book provided an instant payment history and prevented duplicate reimbursements. No such ledgers for Covent Garden have survived in their entirety, but their existence is proved by the index numbers that appear to the left of many entries, as shown in Table 4.1:.[5] The pattern of the numbers shows rough divisions allotted to performers, servants, tradespeople, and miscellaneous entries. An example of such a ledger does survive for Drury Lane.[6] (4) The heads of several department around the theatre kept note-books, or at least loose files of papers, for recording workers' attendance, according to which they distributed the lump sums they collected from the treasurer – e.g., the tailor for his shop staff, the wardrobe keeper for dressers, the painter for his assistants, someone in the band (not always the leader) for musicians.[7] Prompters' diaries would also fit into this category. The extent to which such accounts were compiled into separate books no doubt varied from management to management. I know of no trace of a distribution book for scene men, for example, though the head of crew who paid them must have kept notes on which to base the bills he submitted to the treasurer. Some of the lowliest daily servants at the Pantheon Opera were actually required to sign an official paylist ledger when they collected their money.[8]

Most of these contributory materials have vanished without trace, and what we see in the summary accounts is a selective representation of much fuller original documentation. The nature of the summary record varies drastically. British Library Egerton MS 2267, for example, is a daybook for Covent Garden in 1735–36 in which a clerk recorded the night's income and then deducted from it set components of the constant nightly charge and the very few other bills he was authorized to pay that night without further consultation. The treasurer then took possession of the cash that remained and signed a statement saying, 'Rec'd the above Balance of [sum] For Mr John Rich.'[9] The point here was the bottom line, not where the money would eventually go, which was recorded elsewhere. A daybook of this sort records income but is comparatively uninformative about expenditure. Unlike departmental accounts, most books that survive are composite overviews, many of them taken home by the owner/manager, where they were safer from fire than at the theatre.[10] Failure to recognize the particular function of an account book has led some scholars astray, a problem to which I shall return.

Small variations in bookkeeping practice, even within comprehensive account books, can make a huge difference in the amount and kinds of information available to historians. Some clerks describe each piece of second-hand clothing the company bought, with details of colour, fabric, and decoration, as well as price paid; others just note a total figure for the purchase and move on: 'Paid Mr Price for Men's Cloaths, as pr Bill 150-00-00' (Egerton MS 2280, 5 December 1777). In such a case, the full description was probably entered in an inventory book maintained by the wardrobe keeper. Some companies record monthly or quarterly bills from wax and tallow chandlers and oil merchants; others merely note a pre-determined weekly allowance for light, or for any given commodity. These differences arise less from theories of bookkeeping than from practical decisions about what management thought was useful to record in a particular book. When we have lump sums for salaries but no paylists, that means they were recorded elsewhere, not that paylists were not kept. A huge practical problem for the historian is the tendency of office staff to enter names without functions. Entries that say 'To Mr Shepard per bill £4 16 5' and 'To Mr Leach £13 5 0' tell us almost nothing unless we know that Shepard was the tallow chandler and Leach the handbill printer.[11] Only by piecing together information from stray references within the account books, with occasional reference to a *London Directory*, can we figure out what a theatre was spending its money on.

Account books were kept, alas, for the convenience of theatre owners and managers, not that of historians. Accounting procedures were primitive. Double-entry bookkeeping, although known, was not practised in many English businesses.[12] Tax-audits were a thing of the future, and treasurers often did not follow procedures we would expect. For example, John Rich's books for Covent Garden rarely show any attempt to reach a final balance with a statement of profit or loss. The incompleteness of what is entered is sometimes obvious. Even when Rich's running balances appear to be negative, large cash payouts get made. Obviously Rich – or the theatre – had cash that was not showing in the book that survives. For example, despite a cash balance technically below nil, the accounts for 1749–50 (Egerton MS 2269), record numerous payments of a weekly salary list that usually ran well over £150. Can Rich have been digging into his own pocket to pay critical bills? More likely, the money was available, just not carried in this book. On 1 March 1750, the clerk records, 'Advanc'd towards purchasing Mr Smollet's Copy of Alceste £100.' This sizeable investment turned out to be a waste, as the opera was never done – but the theatre had the money. Thus we can deduce that Egerton MS 2269 was a daybook rather than a comprehensive account book; it was probably never intended to include all transactions. That ought to affect how we read it.[13] Across the century, shifts in management did not always produce instant changes in accounting. The books continue in much the same pattern through the regime of John Beard, Rich's successor, and only gradually during that of the Colman-Powell-Harris-Rutherford group do modifications appear. Not until after the businessman Thomas Harris became sole manager in May 1774 do we begin to see some concern to balance and close the books each season and to arrive at a definite bottom line.

In the extant account books we see the results, incompletely and inconsistently reported, of managerial processes that must remain largely opaque to us, with two exceptions. The working papers for Drury Lane, 1713–1716, help us to comprehend the underlying process.[14] Bills flowed into the treasurer's office daily, both from departments inside the theatre and from suppliers outside. Payday was Saturday. On that day Wilks, Cibber, and Booth reviewed accumulated bills and authorized partial or full payment.[15] People inside the theatre responsible for properties, maintenance, housekeeping, and other functions, aware of the schedule, often arranged to turn in their bills close at the end of the week. Bills from outside, or bills passed on by staff who dealt with outside suppliers, might come in any day. All three managers were supposed to sign a bill to authorize payment, and their annotations and deletions show that they mercilessly scrutinized even tiny charges. Cibber in particular regularly knocked off half-pence, pennies, and occasionally shillings. Wilks once stopped 5*s.* of the printer's charges, 'for ffalse Spelling in ffryday's Bills'.[16] Math was occasionally erroneous, though as often to the disadvantage of the biller as to the theatre.[17] Duplicates were sometimes submitted but usually caught.[18] Extra charges were regularly disallowed. Oliver Purville, the properties master, lost a 'Stage Ring', for which he had to pay 7*s.* 6*d.* out of his own pocket.[19] This was not a trivial sum of money: it certainly represented more than twice his day's wages. Most of the material in these bills would disappear into lump sum totals in an account book. How other theatre companies handled managerial oversight of finances we seldom have any documentation, but the processes used by the Pantheon management at the end of the century were similar in many ways.[20]

Table 4.2 gives a complete list of known sources for day-by-day season receipts up to 1800. The vast majority are post-1750, and from 1771–72 the records are complete for Drury Lane and almost so for Covent Garden, lacking only four seasons. In a few instances (not marked in bold), we possess daily receipts for full seasons from documents that are not part of any sort of account book. Some are clearly drawn from such books now lost (e.g., Drury Lane 1742–43); others are approximations of the daily gross jotted in prompter's notes (e.g., Drury Lane 1746–47). The accuracy of the latter estimates, to judge from seasons where we have both account books and prompter's estimates, is less than wonderful.[21] In the few instances in which we can check accounts, however, the books proper seem to be reliable. Although we must learn their limitations, extant sources unquestionably contain a vast amount of under-utilized material. At this point, let us turn to a

Table 4.2: Extant daily receipt records and account books

This list identifies all known seasons for which we have daily receipts for a theatre in eighteenth-century London. Actual account books are indicated in **bold**. RR refers to 'Rich's Register', performance records in the Folger Shakespeare Library and the Garrick Club. 'Cross' refers to the prompter's diaries of Richard Cross, continued by William Hopkins, in the Folger Shakespeare Library.

Season	LIF/Covent Garden	Drury Lane
1714–15	RR	
1715–16	RR	
1716–17	RR	
1717–18		
1718–19		
1719–20		
1720–21	RR	
1721–22	RR	
1722–23	RR	
1723–24	RR	
1724–25	**BL Eg. 2265**	
1725–26		
1726–27	**BL Eg. 2266**	
1727–28	**Harvard MS**[1]	
1728–29	RR	
1729–30	RR	
1730–31	RR	
1731–32	RR	
1732–33	RR	
1733–34		
1734–35		
1735–36	**BL Eg. 2267**[2]	
1736–37		
1738–39		
1739–40		
1740–41	Folger W.a. 94	
1741–42		Rylands 1111
1742–43		PRO[3]
1743–44		
1744–45		
1745–46		**Aberystwyth**[4]
1746–47	**BL Eg. 2268**	Yale[5]
1747–48		Cross
1748–49		Cross
1749–50	**BL Eg. 2269**	
1750–51		Cross
1751–52		Cross
1752–53		Cross
1753–54		Cross
1754–55		Cross
1755–56		Cross
1756–57		
1757–58	**BL Eg. 2270**	Cross
1758–59		
1759–60	**Folger W.a. 95**	Cross
1760–61	**BL Eg. 2271**	

Table 4.2: (Continued)

Season	LIF/Covent Garden	Drury Lane
1761–62		
1762–63		
1763–64		Cross
1764–65		
1765–66		
1766–67	BL Eg. 2272	Folg. W.b. 273
1767–68	BL Eg. 2273	
1768–69	BL Eg. 2274	
1769–70	BL Eg. 2275	
1770–71		
1771–72	BL Eg. 2276	Folg. W.b. 274
1772–73	BL Eg. 2277	Folg. W.b. 275
1773–74	BL Eg. 2278	Folg. W.b. 276
1774–75		Folg. W.b. 277
1775–76		Folg. W.b. 278
1776–77	BL Eg. 2279	Folg. W.b. 279
1777–78	BL Eg. 2280	Folg. W.b. 280
1778–79		Folg. W.b. 281
1779–80	BL Eg. 2281	Folg. W.b. 282
1780–81	BL Eg. 2282	Folg. W.b. 283
1781–82	BL Eg. 2283	Folg. W.b. 284
1782–83	BL Eg. 2284	Folg. W.b. 285
1783–84	BL Eg. 2285	Folg. W.b. 286
1784–85		Folg. W.b. 287
1785–86	BL Eg. 2286	Folg. W.b. 288
1786–87	BL Eg. 2287	Folg. W.b. 289
1787–88	BL Eg. 2288	Folg. W.b. 290
1788–89	BL Eg. 2289	Folg. W.b. 291
1789–90	BL Eg. 2290	Folg. W.b. 292
1790–91	BL Eg. 2291	Folg. W.b. 293
1791–92	BL Eg. 2292	Folg. W.b. 294
1792–93		Folg. W.b. 295
1793–94	Folg. W.b. 436	Folg. W.b. 296
1794–95	BL Eg. 2293	Folg. W.b. 297
1795–96	BL Eg. 2294	Folg. W.b. 298
1796–97	BL Eg. 2295	Folg. W.b. 299
1797–98	BL Eg. 2296	Folg. W.b. 300
1798–99	BL Eg. 2297	Folg. W.b. 301
1799–1800	BL Eg. 2298	Folg. W.b. 303

[1] Harvard fMS Thr 22 covers the period 24 October 1726 through 22 February 1728[/9].

[2] Most of another kind of account book is preserved in nineteenth-century transcriptions in BL Add MS 32,251 and 11791.dd.18 vol. 3 fols. 177–89. Published in Milhous and Hume, 'John Rich's Covent Garden Account Books for 1735–36', *Theatre Survey*, 31 (1990): 200–241.

[3] Daily receipts are listed in The National Archives, LC 5/204, pp. 62–98 and have been published by Judith Milhous and Robert D. Hume in 'David Garrick and Box-Office Receipts at Drury Lane in 1742–43', *Philological Quarterly*, 67 (1988): 323–344.

[4] Account book in the Library of the University of Wales, Aberystwyth. Transcription published by Milhous and Hume in 'A Drury Lane Account Book for 1745–46', *Theatre History Studies*, 10 (1990): 67–104.

[5] Manuscript in the Osborn Collection, Beinecke Library, purchased at the Phillips sale of 19 March 1992. Transcription published by Milhous and Hume, 'Receipts at Drury Lane: Richard Cross's Diary for 1746–47', *Theatre Notebook*, 49 (1995): 12–26, 69–90.

consideration of how it has been represented and employed to date, and what the deficiencies of such uses may be.

II. Utilization in *The London Stage* and the *Biographical Dictionary*

The only serious and systematic use of eighteenth-century account books for the London theatre has been by the editors of the last four parts of *The London Stage*. As a primary source, the books seem never to have been studied at all. I am aware of only two articles that deal with the subject in its own right. Back in 1926 E. Beresford Chancellor published a descriptive appreciation of Drury Lane accounts for 1746–48, summarizing some of the figures the book contains, rather than analysing the whole.[22] Emmett L. Avery reconstructed the shape of the budget for Lincoln's Inn Fields in 1724–25, chiefly from Egerton MS 2265 – but this solid essay concerns a single company during a single season.[23] The introductions to each part of *The London Stage* include a brief section on theatrical finances, tendering an overview of financial operations for the period at issue. Probably because each part of the performance calendar was separately edited, no attempt was made at broad comparisons, and neither was any analysis offered of account books more generally as a source.

The *London Stage* editors were primarily concerned with daily receipts and only very secondarily with anything else. Their reports of the gross each night are extremely accurate, and if either account books or newspapers indicate that a performance was a benefit for a playwright, a performer, or anyone else, they faithfully record that fact. Unfortunately, until Part 5, they did not usually bother to report the source of the figures they supplied. The season headnotes often do not identify the pertinent account book or state where it is to be found, and the general bibliographic lists in the fronts of volumes do not connect books to particular seasons. A few scattered references in the text sometimes permit an eagle-eyed and expert user to deduce the book at issue, but this is the exception, not the rule. Nowhere in *The London Stage* is there a list of extant sources such as I have supplied in Table 4.2. One result of this virtual suppression of bibliographic information has been lack of attention to account books.

To get daily receipt totals the editors had to look at every opening in the account books, and when they saw items that interested them, they sometimes quoted or summarized them under relevant dates, or occasionally in a season introduction. The results are unquestionably valuable, and much may be gleaned by scanning the full text of the performance calendar, though this is something very few scholars appear to have done (most having bought the paperback editions of the introductions to each part).

Unfortunately, the excerpts as printed are also misleading. All sorts of information got dropped, because the editors did not understand it, were not interested in it, or had no space for it. Their own prejudices governed their choices. In Part 4 (1747–1776), for example, G. W. Stone recorded at least a summary of all references to Garrick and a lot of other Drury Lane material, but almost completely ignored Covent Garden, except for the season of 1746–47, when Garrick was a member of that company. I will offer one example of the sort of thing omitted. At the start of the Covent Garden book for 1757–58, the clerk set out to record an elaborate outline of the 'nightly charge'. He laid out the standard categories and began to list names and salaries for music, men's dressers, and billstickers. Disappointingly, he did not finish his outline, but *none* of the information he did put down is reported in *The London Stage*. Now, mark what follows. The authors of the *Biographical Dictionary* sometimes returned to the primary source account books, but, quite understandably, they relied to a great extent on the performance calendar. Since none of the musicians is included in the *London Stage* roster for 1757–58, none is reported in the *Biographical Dictionary* as being there, though they manifestly were. The rare and important salary information is also missing, and the same is true for the men dressers and billstickers.[24] Thus our principal reference books misrepresent the continuity of forty careers.[25]

Like the authors of the *Biographical Dictionary*, all scholars depend on the company rosters for each season in *The London Stage*. For significant actors and actresses, the rosters are reasonably complete and accurate. They come from first edition cast lists and newspaper ads. For lesser actors, musicians, dancers, and servants of all kinds, the rosters are far from complete and satisfactory. Large numbers of names appear in the account books, very often without function explicitly identified. Many people are described in the *Biographical Dictionary* by imprecise or inaccurate terms that systematic reference to the account books would correct or modify.[26] Even if the rosters were corrected, for most seasons our knowledge would still be incomplete and imperfect. This assertion arises from the example of the Pantheon Opera, for which documentation survives on a scale completely unparalleled for any other eighteenth-century British theatre. The *London Stage* roster for the Pantheon in 1790–91 is exceptionally full, containing 111 names (including six ghosts and one error), but from the Bedford Opera Papers we can document fully 242 company employees, more than 100 of whom are entirely unknown to the authors of the *Biographical Dictionary*. For 1791–92, the *London Stage* roster lists only twenty-seven names, whereas the Bedford Papers give us 216, ninety-nine of whom are not in the *Biographical Dictionary* (only twenty-five of them overlapping with addenda for 1790–91).[27] These are sobering figures. Account books can tell us much more than our principal reference books do, but their picture is by no means exhaustive. *The London Stage* and the *Biographical Dictionary* often eliminate or seriously misrepresent a lot of house servants. Worse, in many respects, they often do not reflect significant information about both major and minor performers. Numerous loans to performers, for example, are almost totally ignored (a subject to which I will return).

The *London Stage* editors adopted an entirely comprehensible policy of excluding information about tradesmen and their bills, as originating outside the theatre. They chose to privilege information concerning plays and their performers, with summary reportage on entr'acte and other supplementary entertainments. All the editors were, to be sure, literary scholars. If, however, our objective is the reconstruction of performance conditions and impact, then we urgently need to know how each company spent its money, at least to the extent that the surviving records will allow us to calculate the allocation of resources. This project demands a return to the line-by-line reportage of outgo. Eighteenth-century treasurers seem unlikely ever to have calculated the kinds of budget figures a present-day theatre would routinely demand.[28] Our inability to identify all items in the account books makes *ex-post-facto* calculations less than perfect, yet for many seasons the account books give us enough particulars to let us see how much went to light, how much to taxes, how much to new and refurbished costumes, how much of the performer salary total to music and dance. Only when we know such things do we start to have a real grasp of what kind of company we are dealing with and how it operated.

Scholars have never carried out detailed financial comparisons of companies from season to season, or from decade to decade. Neither have they systematically investigated the subject of what actors earned and what company payscales tell us about the internal dynamics of each company. Knowing what an individual earned per night or per season tells us little unless we know where that salary falls in the broader scheme of things – and what such an income would buy in terms of standard of living. Account books do not tell us everything we would like to know, but they contain a huge amount of salary information not to be found in our reference books. One of the most obvious kinds of broader comparison concerns a company's total income, outgo, and profitability. This is not as easy to determine as it might seem, even where we have account books. Lacking a cut-off date for the end of a season, many of them mix old and new bills promiscuously in ways that make tidy divisions extremely arbitrary. Some managements (John Rich's prominent among them) seem to have been quite content to take large sums out of the business and meander along from season to season with no particular concern about precise calculation of profitability. If they were solvent, they were happy. Rich collected £5 5s. per acting day as owner in 1757–58, but he also dipped into the till for £3 here and £10 there every week, and sometimes several times a week. It was *his* theatre, and it was an ongoing business with no particular need for closed-out balances dictated by the calendar. The Harris management at Covent Garden in the last quarter of the century functioned very differently, so comparing their finances is tricky at best, but ways can be found to do it.

My point is that we have to return to the primary sources if we want to go beyond the selective figures to be found in *The London Stage* and the *Biographical Dictionary*. Should we wish, for example, to know what plays appealed to the gentry and how important box-occupancy was to profitability, then we must study the few account books that report attendance broken down by each segment of the auditorium. By looking at the Harvard accounts for Lincoln's Inn Fields in spring 1728, one gets a surprisingly exact sense of where the theatre was full (or less than full) throughout the amazing first run of *The Beggar's Opera*.[29] If one is concerned with profitability, or salary scales, or budget allocation, then one is going to have to do a lot of reconstruction and analysis. One cannot simply pluck the figures off the page. The scholar must also understand how these theatres operated. Benefits, for example, could in rare instances be free, but most people had to pay 'house charges', which could vary quite a lot even within a single season.[30] Failure to allow for deduction of charges can only produce gruesomely distorted results.[31] To understand the particulars recorded in account books, we must have some grasp of the financial assumptions and practices of the theatres whose money they record, the subject to which we now turn.

III. The shape of the budget

A theatre historian might want to know how much money passed through the theatre and where it went. So, presumably, did eighteenth-century owners and managers, but their categories and budget theory were rather different from what we would expect, so their thinking requires some adjustments on our part. All account books are set up in terms of the season, which normally opened in September and concluded in May or June. In the previous century, intermittent summer seasons were carried on by the actors for their own benefit, but by 1714 such arrangements were more closely supervised and gradually died out. Theatres at mid-century kept a few hundred pounds on hand over the summer, to pay maintenance workers and late bills, but usually had no income to show until well into October. Little but salaries got paid until late November, when some cash had accumulated. A lot of bills were paid off in December. There was a slow-down over Lent (when the tailor's shop, for example, might cease to function), and a push after Easter to pay off outstanding obligations. Nowhere in this seasonal rhythm does one find any attempt to categorize outgo or any overall sense of a season, either in prospect or in retrospect.[32]

These books represent the business in terms of the night, not the season, which usually ran between 160 and 180 nights. The fundamental budgetary concept was the notion of the nightly constant charge.[33] The only major source of income was nightly receipts. Ticket prices were stable at 4s. in a box, 3s. in the pit, 1s. 6d. in the first gallery, and 1s. in the second, except that box seats inched up a shilling in the 1740s. Relatively little inflation occurred between the mid-seventeenth century and the Napoleonic era, and theatre capacity increased from roughly 800 in the 1670s to 3,000 or more in the 1790s. That should have meant more money coming in, even if houses were rarely anything like full at the end of the eighteenth century. However, companies had begun to expand when afterpieces became the norm in the 1720s, and specialization pushed management towards maintaining semi-distinct troupes for comedy and tragedy. Top salaries kept going up; scenery and machinery became vastly more elaborate. Theatres brought in fortunes, but spent them too.

A manager's sense of how the company was doing and what he could afford rested on a silent comparison with what opening the doors cost, on average. Few contemporaneous break-outs of the constant charge survive, but the relevant figure must have been graven in the mind of every manager. As companies grew in size, the charge included a larger and larger salary component, and further incidental costs were added on. The constant charge represented the break-even point, and if receipts fell markedly under it, the prudent thing to do was cancel the performance.[34] The charge appears to have been about £20–25 in the Carolean era; about £35 around 1700, but already £50 by the 1730s; and it rose to £167 and up by the early 1790s. Management and employees regularly disagreed over whether charges should reflect the break-even point or include a margin of profit for the theatre.[35] Benefit performances allowed management to offer the prospect of remuneration without much risk to itself, giving up the possibility of profit but covering the possibility of loss for a given night. Like other aspects of this hierarchical business, benefit costs could be negotiated, so the historian cannot simply assume that a standard fee applies to all.

Moreover, since components of the nightly charge were sometimes standardized, even when the charge is itemized, it may not reflect actual expenses. Experienced managers often settled on seasonal allowances, known as 'stoppage accounts', designed to cover expenses such as light, incidental charges, and salaries for music, dressers, barbers, scene changers, as well as rent, without which no performance could take place. Such allowances could have been figured for regular salaries, but were not. I have already mentioned the 1757–58 'Estimate of A constant Nightly Charge' (Egerton 2270, folio 1r), with forty overlooked names and salaries. This calculation is worth reproducing, both for its figures and as an illustration of the difficulties of making sense of account books (see Table 4.3.)

Table 4.3: Treasurer's estimate of the 'Constant Nightly Charge' at Covent Garden for 1757–58, from Egerton MS 2270

Per annum	Category	Per day	Category	Per day
	Renters 54 Shares @ 2s.	5-08-00	Rents &c	11-07-00
£100	Ground Rent of the Theatre		Guards	0-14-00
30	Ditto Buildings in Hart Street		Barbers	0-05-04
25	Mrs Thurmonds House in Bow Street Passage	1-00-08	Scenemen	2-10-00
155	[Total]	6-08-08	Musick	5-03-04
			Candles & Additional Lamps	4-04-00
	Taxes Viz		Lamps as Charg'd last season	0-13-06
85-02-00	Land & Window Taxes for the Theatre		Coales	0-10-00
5-15-06	Ditto for Thurmonds		1 Days Bills	1-07-00
20-00-00	Poors Rate		Advertisement	0-05-00
1-05-00	Ditto Thurmonds		Billsetters	0-11-06
8-06-08	Watch Rate		Wardrobe pr List	1-00-00
0-10-06	Ditto Thurmonds		Ditto for Extras pr Estimate	0-15-00
6-13-04	Rectors Rate		Property mans Sallery	002-00
0-08-04	Ditto Thurmond		Mr J. Rich	5-05-00
5-00-00	Scavenger		Mr C. Rich	1-00-00
0-06-04	Ditto Thurmond		Incidents as pr estimate	0-02-00
4-00-00	Water		[Total]	35-19-08
137-07-08	[Total]	0-18-04		
600	Hutchinson Mure Esqr	4-00-00		
	[Total of] Rents &c	11-07-00		

A few explanations are in order. (1) The 54 'renters' shares' are in essence payments to bondholders; debt service that often cost upwards of 10 per cent of income. The patent theatres continued to raise capital this way, despite the expense: for the 163 nights of this season, the 'renters' collected over £880. Each of them was entitled to free admission to all performances, a perquisite buyers continued to value. In simple monetary terms, management would have done far better to retire the bonds and use a savings scheme to amass the working capital the bonds represented, but these investors provided contacts that could be useful, both personally and professionally. (2) Although the theatre building was owned outright, the Duke of Bedford owned the site, so 'ground rent' had to be paid. Taxes of various sorts, always rising, amounted to nearly £130 per annum. Trash collection and water added another £9. (3) The startling £4 *daily* payment to Hutchinson Mure concerns a mortgage of some £10,000 loaned 'On the Patant, Cloaths and Scenes'.[36] (4) 'Guards' were private police employed to maintain order. (5) The stoppage accounts allowed 10*s*. per diem for heat and over £5 for lamps and candles. They ran close to average costs, but sometimes had to be topped up.[37] (6) Newspaper advertisements and the printing and posting of playbills came to £1 5*s*. 6*d*. each day. (7) In this season, John Rich paid himself 5 guineas per acting day as principal proprietor; his brother Christopher Mosyer, who owned a small share, got just £1.

Adding debt service, ground rent, utilities, and taxes to light, heat, selected house servants' salaries, advertising, and the proprietors' cut yielded a sum close to £36 per night. The treasurer did not complete the salary section of the outline he started, but from figures in Egerton MS 2270 we can compute the average daily cost of performers and the rest of the house servants this season at close to £46 per diem, for an expanded total of close to £82 per diem or nearly £500 in a six-day week.[38] Receipts fluctuated wildly from day to day. In the week of 7–12 November 1757, for example, they varied from £55 to £118, and averaged £80. As the expense figures show, if the average was not running at or above £82 per night, then the theatre was functioning in the red.

The treasurer's calculation for 1757–58 also includes an estimate for 'incidents', expenditures required by particular performances. When a portrait had to be rented for Angelica Bianca in *The Rover* or dirt acquired for the gravediggers in *Hamlet* to shovel out of the gravetrap, those were incidental expenses. A very common extra is 5*s*. to a French horn player if the music for a play demanded one. Some productions – pantomimes and English 'operas' especially – required additional personnel, such as dancers, chorus singers, and musicians. By the 1760s, managements were adding the incident charge to the sum deducted at many benefits.

Beyond constant and incident charges, management had to allow for supplies and maintenance of various sorts (mostly not very expensive) and the cost of scenery and costumes. The books do not show whether individual departments had set budgets or new productions were allotted a fixed sum of money to get them up, but I am inclined to doubt it in both cases. Most new plays were mounted with stock scenery and costumes, and if new ones were created for a première, the scenes or clothes were usually generic rather than particular and could thereafter be used for any show. Close scrutiny of the account books indicates a low level of investment in specific productions. One can find evidence of upgrading the scenery and wardrobe in the course of most seasons, though some managements do this much more than others. The amounts George Colman spent at Covent Garden in the early 1770s resulted from a decision to upgrade the stock the Beard and Rich managements had left. In the eighties and nineties, one can see Harris starting to invest more money in particular productions, especially blockbuster musicals. In general, management could get by for a while with stock costumes and scenery, although if there was surplus money in the till, it was often invested in improvement of that stock.

In the late seventeenth century staggering sums of money – as much as 30 and 40 per cent of the theatre's annual income – were lavished on fabulous semi-opera productions, and Cibber remarks that they were gambles meant to 'bring home the *Indies*'.[39] Later managements decided that such extravagant investment was unnecessarily risky. In the realm of ordinary plays, many new ones were never revived after their first few nights. Of those, an even smaller number reappeared after their first season. A sensible manager therefore risked little cash on them, as the account books demonstrate season after season. Exceptions can be found in pantomimes, which were explosively popular from their introduction in the 1720s and for decades after, and in the large-scale English musicals or operas that began to loom so large in the repertories of the 1780s and 1790s. Garrick's long management at Drury Lane (1747–1776) is interesting in this respect. His preference seems to have been for high-quality daily offerings (that is, careful script selection and doctoring, sterling principal performers), and risk management. Probably he learned a lesson from the *Chinese Festival* fiasco of 1755, which cost management about £4,000 to fix riot damage.

One of the things clearly evident in most of the extant account books is the stability of these long-term, ongoing enterprises. The companies employed the same performers, support staff, and house servants year after year after year. They mounted a stable repertory of stock favourites, varied with a few revivals of proven scripts and a smattering of new plays to pique audience interest. Only a very badly managed company, lumbered with the costs of unmanageable debt service, could not meet its payroll and also provide the owner(s) with a very comfortable income. The Charles Fleetwood management at Drury Lane in the 1730s and 1740s stands out as an example of insolvency, but receipt figures for 1742–43 discovered after publication of *The London Stage* prove conclusively that in operational terms the theatre was making about £3,000. Its problem was close to £5,000 in debt service.[40] The magnitude of Richard Brinsley Sheridan's incompetence as managing owner at Drury Lane did not become fully evident until the later 1790s, but he also succeeded in turning a fabulous cash cow into a financial basket case.

The account books manifest stability in another, almost totally neglected area, that of tradespeople. At all levels, managements preferred to deal repeatedly with the same people, whether shopkeepers, craftsmen, or providers of services. The theatres' business might be worth hundreds of pounds a year to dealers in fabrics or oil, tallow, and candles. But even when the sum was under £50, theatre personnel repeatedly went back to the same shoemaker, the same drycleaner, the same purveyor of brushes. These connections might extend across generations and through changes in the organization of the dealership.[41] In some instances, we can document the fact that tradespeople bought company shares or loaned managers money.[42] Theatre people were in and out of some shops many times during a season, buying more hardware, delivering cut fabric to be embroidered, picking up an extra dozen wax candles in anticipation of a royal visit. Gossip and publicity got passed along in both directions. Some merchandise, such as second-hand clothes and coals, had to be delivered, so there was a constant stream of outsiders coming to the stage door. When the *London Stage* editors eliminated the names of such outsiders, they cut out the dimension of how the theatres related to the business community.

In the 1990s, both theatre professionals and the public were shocked when insiders reported that at the National Theatre and the Royal Opera House, there were no set budgets for various departments or even for particular productions. Very eighteenth century! There is, however, more excuse for so cavalier an operating policy in the eighteenth-century theatres. They normally had good cash flow, and an experienced manager knew without a lot of accounting fol-de-rol what things should cost, how much money he had to spend, and what would please the public. After 1737 Covent Garden and Drury Lane usually enjoyed a monopoly in legitimate theatre, at a time when the population of London was expanding rapidly. Experience and a clear knowledge of normal costs was vital but, in a sense, sufficient. Inexperienced managers could produce insolvency in a hurry, as Sheridan and his successor William Taylor found at the King's Theatre in the early 1780s. Yet Giovanni Andrea Gallini managed to run the same opera company quite profitably from 1785 to 1789. Robert Bray O'Reilly produced horrendous deficits in his one season at the Pantheon in 1790–91, but in 1791–92 the vastly experienced Antoine Trancart restored financial order almost overnight. What we see in the account books in less tumultuous times, such as the 1760s, is traditional, conservative management by knowledgeable insiders.

IV. Salaries and benefits

As an illustration of the kinds of things account books might help a theatre historian do, I want now to turn to the subject of salaries, salary scales, and benefits. Surprising as it may seem, no one has ever published a study of actors' pay in the eighteenth-century London theatres (though Robert D. Hume and I are now at work on one). To have any real grasp of a company as a whole, one must know its salary totals and scale. By far the largest expense for any eighteenth-century theatre was salaries of performers and staff. Despite management's strenuous efforts to control the total, it kept growing. House servants were paid very little, and through the period rates for most of them rose not at all, though their numbers multiplied. Many salary figures were omitted from *The London Stage*, and while the *Biographical Dictionary* includes samples, the figures are too scattered and too random in dates to permit systematic comparisons or the construction of all-important salary scales. Consequently one must return to the primary sources. A practical difficulty is non-uniform reportage of figures. Most account books give weekly payments, but the totals vary with the number of the days the company performed and so might represent four, five, or six nights. The highest-paid actors usually had annual lump-sum contracts, and many of them collected varying amounts as they needed the money. To make the figures comparable, the only sensible procedure is to calculate per-diem rates of pay. This does not, of course, address the issue of additional income from a benefit, which could constitute half an actor's annual income.

First question: what sort of range is there from top to bottom? Table 4.4 illustrates the salary spread in selected companies over the span of a full century. In the United Company, the difference amounted to a factor of 20. In the fringe company of 1732–33 for which some figures exist, the difference is drastically less: the top is only 4.2 times the bottom figure, so everyone starved together (or held other jobs). To make Rich's scale for 1735–36 comparable, we must omit the proprietor/performer himself, who collected £3 6s. 8d. per diem, or 40 times the bottom salary. Without him, the top salary was 29.4 times the bottom one.

Table 4.4: Performer salary ranges for selected companies from *c*.1690–1790

United Co. c. 1694[1]	Fringe Co. 1732–33[2]			Covent Garden 1735–36[3]	Drury Lane 1775[4]	Covent Garden 1789–90[5]	Drury Lane 1789–90[6]
	Operas	Plays	Opera of Operas				
					£4 8s 4d / £2 10s 0d ↑	super scale / £3 0s 0d ↑	super scale / £2 16s 8d ↑
				£2 9s 0d ↑			
	21s ↑						
16s 8d		10s 6d ↑	10s 6d ↑				
↑							
10s							
8s 4d							
6s 8d			5s				
|			|				
4s 2d		2s 6d	2s 6d				
|					2s 6d	2s 6d	2s 6d
1s 8d	1s			1s 8d			

[1] *Source*: Judith Milhous, 'United Company Finances, 1682–1692', *Theatre Research International*, 7 (1981–82): 37–53, at 42–3.
[2] *Source*: Judith Milhous and Robert D. Hume, 'J. F. Lampe and English Opera at the Little Haymarket in 1732–3', *Music & Letters*, 78 (1997): 502–31, at 514, 520, 528.
[3] *Source*: Judith Milhous and Robert D. Hume, 'John Rich's Covent Garden Account Books for 1735–36,' *Theatre Survey*, 31 (1990): 200–241, at 231.
[4] *Source*: Judith Milhous, 'The Economics of Theatrical Dance in Eighteenth-Century London', *Theatre Journal*, 55 (2003): 481–508, at 493.
[5] *Source*: Ibid., 498.
[6] *Source*: Ibid.

At Drury Lane in 1775 the difference was a multiplier of 35.3, but the trend was not always upward. At both patent theatres in 1789–90, the 'normal' top was only 22 times the bottom; but the multiplier for superscale levels was far higher – one 176 times, the other 216 times the bottom. These are hardly surprising figures if one thinks in terms of present-day movie-star salaries, but they do clarify the great and growing divide between the ends of the scale. We must also remember that the chance of making serious money from benefits was largely restricted to the upper end of the hierarchy. Lower-end performers could choose to participate in shared benefits, if allowed, but they seldom cleared much from the effort. In terms of normal annual income from salary (and ignoring work at fairs or with strolling companies in the summer), what do these figures imply? Over a 180-night season, a low actor's or middle servant's rate of 1s. 8d. per diem would yield £15. The high end of the daily servants' scale, 2s. 6d., translates to £22 10s.; 5s. per diem, a rate where many actors clustered, comes to only £45; 10s. to £90; twice that, or £180, starts to be a noticeable income; £3 per diem yields £540.

These samples bring us up against the problem of what the figures might mean. No simple multiplier will give us a present-day equivalency, and I must flatly refuse to offer one, but here are some contemporaneous estimates that may help with context. Writing in 1734, Jacob Vanderlint tells us that seven-eighths of the population belonged to families that on average had no more than £55 per annum to support husband, wife, and four children.[43] By that gauge, a £45 season take for an actor was not a bad living. Vanderlint reckoned that the minimum income on which one could set up as a 'gentleman' was £500, which only actors at the top of normal scale might achieve. Peter Earle's modern reconstruction of the lifestyle and income of the 'middling sort' in this period arrives at £200 as a more than decent income for what would now be thought of as a middle-class family.[44] One could live nearer the margins on a lot less: Samuel Johnson claimed to have got by on £30 a year in his first decade in London.[45] Or to take a more material instance, consider the price of books. Plays usually cost 1s. or 1.s 6d. Is this a small price or a large one? When Tonson published the six-volume Rowe *Shakespeare* in 1709, the *Term Catalogues* advertised over 150 titles, more than half of which sold for 1s. or less. Only seven of them cost more than 6s. One of these was the Tonson *Shakespeare*, which went for a dizzying 30s. – a price equivalent to a multi-volume Oxford University Press scholarly edition today.[46] Could an actor making £45 for the season afford to buy Rowe's edition? Only if he were unmarried and childless.

A second question, given that the salary range is quite broad: how do salaries spread out across that spectrum? By way of an answer, I offer Table 4.5, which displays the salary spread in a passably typical late eighteenth-century company, Covent Garden in 1777–78. One feature this table cannot display proportionally is the superscale stars, Macklin and Mrs Barry, who earned respectively thirty and sixty times the bottom performer salary, 2s. per diem, and twelve and twenty-four times the most common one, 5s. The status of house servants is painfully clear: thirty-five of them made less than all but one of the eighty-nine

Table 4.5: A proportional representation of the pay scale for Covent Garden in 1777–78

The increments are by shillings, with actual pay rates in **bold face**. Where there is more than one rate within the span of a shilling, the range is shown, and the employees in that range have been combined. Approximately eight servants paid annual salaries are also absent from this list. To display the salary disparity between the superscale cases (Macklin and Barry) and the next highest salary would require three pages of blank lines. The source is British Library Egerton MS 2280.

Per diem salary **superscale**	*Male performers* Macklin[1]	*Female performers* Mrs Barry[2]	*Servants*
2-04-04	1		
2-03-00			
2-02-00			
2-01-00			
2-00-00			
1-19-00			
1-18-00			
1-17-00			
1-16-00			
1-15-00			
1-14-00			
1-13-04	1		
1-12-00			
1-11-00			
1-10-00			
1-09-00			
1-08-04	1	2	
1-07-00			
1-06-08	4	1	
1-05-00			
1-04-00			
1-03-04	1	3	
1-02-00			
1-01-00 to 1-01-08	1	1	
1-00-00	4	3	
0-19-00			
0-18-00			
0-17-00			
0-16-08	1		
0-15-06	1		
0-14-00			
0-13-04	1	1	
0-12-00			
0-11-01	1		
0-10-00	5	2	
0-09-00			
0-08-04	3	1	
0-07-00			
0-06-08	6	8	1
0-05-00-0 to 05-10[3]	14	2	1 + barbers

Table 4.5: (Continued)

Per diem salary	Male performers	Female performers	Servants
0-04-02	1	6	
0-03-04 to 0-03-06	5	7	1
0-02-00 to 0-02-06	1		35

[1] Macklin earned £500 in salary, or nearly £3 per diem.
[2] Mrs Barry earned £1057 in salary, or nearly £6 per diem.
[3] Twelve men and one woman earned only 5s. per diem.

performers – roughly £20 per annum. Many of the servants probably had second jobs or working spouses, but they were clearly at the bottom of the pecking order. The highest paid among them was the prompter, an official of some importance and power within the company, but he earned no more than 6s. 8d. per diem. On average, women earned less than men. Twenty-five performers made £1 a day or more, but sixty-one of them made no more than half a pound. Thirty performers earned between 5s. and 6s. 8d., which translates into an annual income on the order of £50. Thirty-six performers, and all servants but the prompter, made 5s. or less per diem.

The salary scale constructed in Table 4.5 demonstrates a brutally clear hierarchy, with some very big steps on the ladder. This seems to be an eighteenth-century phenomenon. Late seventeenth-century companies cannot be described as democratic – the old distinction between 'sharers' and 'hirelings' remained in force – and even the Lincoln's Inn Fields actor-cooperative was far from egalitarian. Incomplete knowledge of salaries and 'share' earnings in the King's, Duke's, and United Companies makes detailed comparison impossible, but the figures that survive strongly imply that the gap between bottom of scale and top of scale was far less drastic. In the extremely closed theatrical system after 1737, market forces kept the distribution of salaries and the top of normal scale under constant downward pressure.

The 'big steps' issue raises a third question. What hope did a person of lowly status and salary have of improving his or her income? Instances of spectacular rises exist. In 1685 Elizabeth Barry was already a very major star and a principal attraction for the United Company, but she was earning 8s. 4d. per diem – just half the top of scale.[47] She improved her finances through the privilege, for some years unique to her, of an actor benefit. When Colley Cibber was promoted from unpaid probationer to salaried peon (so that the salary could be docked because he had botched a scene), he received a less than munificent 1s. 8d. per diem.[48] Both performers were to become decidedly prosperous, as much through positions in which they advised management as through their acting. In general, however, the evidence of the account books suggests that dazzling improvements in salary were exceptional. Managements, never enthusiastic about raises, took various measures to control them, some quite harsh. The written cartel agreement between Lincoln's Inn Fields and Drury Lane in the 1720s and the essentially open collusion between

Table 4.6: The salary trajectories of selected Covent Garden performers over a twenty-year period

Name	Salary, 1757–58	Salary 1767–68	Salary, 1777–78
David Ross	1-00-00 (7th)	not there	2-04-04 (top of normal)
Matthew Clarke	0-12-00 (15th)	1-00-00 (6th)	1-06-08 (4th)
George Mattocks	0-10-00 (16th)	1-03-04 (5th)	1-03-04 (5th)
John Dunstall	0-13-04, with wife (15th)	1-00-00 (6th)	1-00-00 (8th)
John Cushing	0-06-08 (20th)	0-06-08 (12th)	0-06-08 (15th)
Dumay (dancer)	0-05-00 (25th)	0-05-00 (13th)	0-05-00 (19th)
Rotchford (dancer)	0-05-00 (25th)	not there	0-05-00 (19th)
Jane Green	0-10-00 (16th)	0-10-00 (10th)	0-03-04 (22nd)

Note: Numbers in parentheses indicate the place in the salary scale of that rate in that season; that is, when David Ross was paid £1 a week in 1757–58, there were six rates higher that season.
Source: British Library Egerton MSS 2270, 2273, and 2280.

Sheridan and Harris in the later 1770s made serious negotiation of salaries almost impossible except near the top.[49] Even in times of greater competition and fairer labour practices, however, raises were hard to come by. Consider, for example, Table 4.6, which displays the career trajectories of eight people who performed at Covent Garden in most or all seasons between 1757 and 1778. This cross-section shows that Ross, Clarke, and Dunstall improved their circumstances, though only Ross got beyond the point of a 'middling' class income, earning some £392 in 1778. Cushing, Dumay, and Rotchford never got above their 1757 salaries. Mrs Green's position in the company rose, even though her salary did not; then both came down badly. (No other woman lasted long enough to make this comparison.) Mattocks is a special case. He was a singer and low comedian who got raises for ten years before he hit a ceiling. He was married to an actress of some importance, who consistently out-earned him and who appears to have worked harder than he did. Perhaps the theatre continued to pay him well to keep them both happy. My best guess is that further compilations will show great stability in salaries and relatively firm ceilings for various ranks of performers, with flexibility only at the top.

The impact of benefits on performers' income has yet to be seriously investigated. Beyond the generalities in the *London Stage* introductions, the only broad study is St Vincent Troubridge's pamphlet, which is limited at best.[50] No one has yet calculated for whole companies and over time what proportion of performers' income came from benefits, or how much the results varied, or what repertory was used and why.[51] Much can be deduced about the actor–audience relationship. Some account books record distribution of tickets by part of theatre. Though much of this information is reported in *The London Stage*, it is not analysed there. What can be learned? For example, in the late-1760s at Covent Garden, some upper-end actors apparently ceased bothering to peddle tickets for pit and galleries, choosing to approach only people who might buy box seats. Their complacency suggests that they felt they earned enough to dispense with the effort of reaching the whole audience. However, lower-level actors who conscientiously worked all three levels of the theatre sometimes outdrew better-paid colleagues who had ignored pit and gallery.[52]

One area in which account book evidence has been almost totally ignored by scholars is loans to theatre personnel. From at least as early as 1746–47, the Covent Garden books record a few loans each season, mostly to actors and seldom to more than ten people. The amounts were often trivial – a few guineas – but occasionally amounts were larger, and the total might run as high as £400 or £500.[53] Repayment was expected, but is not always recorded in the books that survive. Where it is traceable, I have found only one mention of interest, on the comparatively large sum of £300; nor were loans ever deducted from salary payments.[54] The availability of these loans fluctuated, and the question of who was eligible for one is complex.[55] However, the mere possibility that the theatre might provide a financial stopgap, let alone a major injection of cash, should enter into assessments of company morale.

The importance of salary analysis seems obvious. The figures that can be found in account books tell us about company structure, about individual status and prestige, about career trajectory, and about the economic/cultural status of actors. Such analysis is fundamental to any serious grasp of the economics of the theatre and to an understanding of how management thought it could best appeal to the ticket-buying public. Especially as the eighteenth century wore on, the theatres became more centred on their performers and less on their repertory. As many have observed, 'the theatre of Georgian London was an actors' theatre',[56] and one of our best sources of hard information about those actors is the account books, which tell us what they earned, how their careers progressed, what they borrowed, and what favour their benefits found with the public.

V. Some examples of account book utilization

In the previous section I sketched some possibilities in a realm that I have only started to explore. By way of a conclusion to this essay I want to offer six brief 'case studies' in which account books and ancillary financial records have helped answer important questions in theatre history. The first cases centre on individuals; the others take up general problems.

(1) *How did the salary of the reigning European castrato Farinelli compare to theatrical salaries in the early 1730s?* Farinelli met with hysterical adulation and extravagant rewards when he came to London in 1734 and attracted equally hysterical condemnation after he left three years later. He made a convenient symbol of foreign

corruption, first for those concerned to whip up patriotic sentiment in the War of Jenkins' Ear and later in the face of invasion threats.[57] Gauging his income is difficult because of gifts, stipends for arranging concerts, and a sell-out benefit, but his base salary cannot have been less that £1,500, which averages about £30 per night in the standard 50-night opera season. Quite apart from political concerns, theatre people were bound to resent Farinelli's earning power. Figures from Covent Garden for 1735–36 show that, before adding on supplements, Farinelli took home in one night the same pay that a theatre company of more than ninety staff and performers divided among themselves, £30.[58]

(2) *How much impact did Garrick have when he joined the Drury Lane company in 1742–43?* Garrick's explosive effect on the London theatre scene when he appeared at Goodman's Fields in 1741–42 is one of the legends of eighteenth-century theatre history. The prodigy then moved to Drury Lane, where he continued to command attention. However, the sceptical theatre historian prefers more substantive evidence than anecdote, and the discovery twenty years ago of a list of daily receipts at Drury Lane for 1742–43 made a quantitative investigation possible.[59] The financial figures are, if anything, even more astonishing than the rhapsodic stories. The current break-even point, ignoring abnormal and non-theatrical debt service, appears to have been no more than £60 per night. On 78 nights when Garrick performed, sometimes in minor roles, income averaged £117. On 59 nights when he did not appear, the average fell to £55. He literally doubled average income (though that effect did not last throughout his career). Given these figures, we can see how Garrick was able to turn a 500-guinea salary with one benefit the previous season into a 600-guinea salary with three benefits in 1742–43. His earnings from Drury Lane totalled £1,135 in his first full season at a patent theatre. Anecdote is often inflated or unprovable, but in this case the figures more than bear out rumour.

(3) Still, we may ask, *How even the unparalleled Garrick got to buy into Drury Lane almost immediately and for no money down?* So dominant was he in the second half of the eighteenth century and so dominant in later recitals about the period, that his taking control of a patent theatre has seemed somehow natural and inevitable. In fact, this turning point in English theatre history was far from predictable. The duopoly conditions reinforced by the Licensing Act of 1737 had made the patents valuable far beyond even Garrick's buying power. Only in highly peculiar circumstances could someone in his position have acquired a half-interest in one of them. In 1744 James Lacy and partners bought the financially wrecked Drury Lane from Charles Fleetwood. The new owners haggled over salary and let Garrick go to Ireland the next season and to Covent Garden in 1746–47. Comparison shows that Covent Garden outdrew their rivals by an average of more than £50 on non-benefit nights that season.[60] When Lacy's partners declared bankruptcy, the only way for him to keep his collapsing venture in business was to invite Garrick to become co-owner, manager, and star attraction. Drury Lane made over £15,000 in profits in just two seasons, and Garrick paid off the whole purchase price within three. He capitalized brilliantly on the opportunity – but only total incompetence on the part of first Fleetwood and then Lacy gave him the chance

to do so. Far from being right and inevitable, Garrick's becoming co-owner and manager was the result of an improbable fluke. Garrick remains an extraordinary individual. What of larger concerns?

(4) *How important was dance in the offerings of eighteenth-century London theatres?* Anyone who has dipped into the *London Stage* calendar knows that dance was conspicuously advertised at a very large number of performances throughout the century, though scenarios and detailed reportage are almost entirely lacking. The importance of dance is even clearer if one goes to playbills or newspaper advertisements, on which *The London Stage* skimped to save space. Account books can help us construct a clearer – even a quantified – picture of how various companies used dance. Some books are much more helpful than others, and different managements prove to have had quite different advertising policies. To a surprising degree, though, we can tease out a sense of how dance figured in a company's operations.[61] At the beginning of the century, John Vanbrugh's plan for a troupe of actors, singers, and dancers allotted 14 per cent of the performer budget to dance, but half that sum is for night-by-night payments, not contractual salaries (evidence of low status and incidental importance). Vanbrugh clearly expected to use dance as a minor attraction within plays and in entr'actes. At Covent Garden in 1735–36 John Rich devoted some 25 per cent of his performer budget to dancers: he used them many ways, but they were crucial to his popular pantomimes. Later Covent Garden account books show that the one-quarter proportion was not a temporary aberration: it was identical in Rich's last season, 1760–61. The next management was less dance oriented: in 1767–68 the dance percentage was down to about 19 per cent. Account books are less helpful with Drury Lane, which in general used dance less centrally – though in 1775–76, Garrick's last season as manager, they too spent a quarter of the performer budget on dancers. Their allocation of pay among dancers is also radically different: stars were emphasized, rather than teamwork. The cutbacks continued: by 1789–90 Covent Garden's dance budget was a mere 9.5 per cent of the performer total. What explains this precipitous decline in emphasis? Vestris and Noverre had brought large-scale *ballet d'action* to the opera house in London in the early 1780s, and the patent theatres could not compete with the expensive foreign performers hired to astonish audiences, who were suddenly conscious of a whole new level of sophistication in the world of dance. This was a very big shift in one of the offerings companies had featured for decades. To the text-oriented literary critic, dance is merely an irrelevancy – but eighteenth-century theatres would hardly have spent what they did on dancers, decade in and decade out, if their performances had not been a crucial part of what attracted audiences.

(5) *What did playwrights earn from their plays?* Standard wisdom long said that playwriting became highly profitable in the later seventeenth century, and that writers prepared to write to 'formula' could earn 'a living wage, and more' by writing for the patent theatres during the eighteenth century.[62] Is this true? What did playwrights actually earn, and did the figures change during the century? Were first plays and plays by women terrible risks (as was then believed)? Secure financial figures are available for 246 of 580 patent company mainpieces between

1714 and 1800, and for 118 of 788 afterpieces.[63] Systematic analysis of the data tells us that while individual results varied wildly, the average earnings from mainpieces rose from about £97 before the Licensing Act to some £267 in the 1790s. Afterpieces tended to be very scantily compensated. Plays by women were indeed a poor bet until the time of Elizabeth Inchbald late in the century, but the riskiness of first plays turns out to be purely mythical: they drew slightly above the average for all new plays. Perhaps most startling is the discovery that with very few exceptions (e.g., Henry Fielding and Isaac Bickerstaff), hardly anyone actually earned a living by playwriting until the 1780s, and only a few people did then. Big sums were made from particular plays, and actor-managers like Cibber and Garrick found playwriting highly profitable, but basically not enough new plays were regularly and successfully staged to provide writers an income on which to live. This considerably changes our picture of the sources of script supply. From account books we also learn that by the 1780s managers were buying copyright from playwrights so as to be able to withhold successful plays from print, at least for a while, and that some kinds of script-doctoring were compensated with flat payments rather than benefits. The abandonment of the author-benefit system in 1793 made a huge difference to playwriting as a profit-making activity, but though the details of the change are writ large in account books, they have gone almost unnoticed by scholars.

(6) *Why did the King's Theatre opera company collapse into chaos and mediocrity after 1778?* London's opera had always been a financially shaky venture, but from 1720 into the 1770s it had often been artistically distinguished, and it was a social centre for the rich and powerful. It charged high prices; it often had a lot of subscribers and a huge cash flow, and these sums increased dramatically in the 1790s and the early 1800s. Why did it then become artistically mediocre and stay that way for more than half a century? The answer is essentially economic. In 1778 Sheridan engineered what we would now call a leveraged buyout, vastly overpaying for a financially marginal operation. He and his partner Harris put up none of the £22,000 purchase price, assuming that they could pay £10,000 out of operating profits in just four years while covering costs on a £14,000 mortgage.[64] Unfortunately, they ran up no profits, just enormous losses. Within seven years the company was lumbered with unpayable debts of about £100,000, on which a series of managements could not even cover the debt service. The theatre burned in 1789 and was rebuilt at huge expense on yet more borrowed money. Although the Pantheon was set up as a fresh-start alternative, it was not properly financed or managed and ran up another £40,000 debt in just two seasons; it also burned down, having been torched by its unhappy backers. The Lord Chancellor then ruled that the right to perform opera could not be removed from the King's Theatre, because to do so would deprive its innumerable creditors of any chance of being paid. Never mind the fact that the old obligations were totally unpayable even before the King's Theatre was forced to accept responsibility for the Pantheon's debts: the situation was in fact unfixable by 1785. The details of the mess could not be disentangled and fully understood until the discovery of the Bedford Opera Papers two hundred years later, but the crux is simple: the opera

company was crippled by debts it could never pay. Its immense cash flow at the beginning of the nineteenth century should have made it at least solvent, but under the circumstances it was doomed to a dismal mediocrity.

*   *   *

This six-item survey has been offered as a demonstration of the kinds of theatre history problems that may be effectively addressed via financial records in general and account books in particular. Why has relatively little ever been done in this realm? I think the answer lies partly in prejudice against suggesting that grubby issues of money may control the production of art (a fact, but not a palatable one to many scholars). Another major contributory cause, however, is the nature of the evidence that can be derived from account books. We mine them for information, but much of what we can pick up are not gold nuggets that can be placed intact and unprocessed in our books and articles. The daily gross and particular salaries can indeed be plucked and used that way. Most of the material, however, requires extensive processing. We get our gold not as nuggets but as tons of rock that must be elaborately sifted and refined. To do so requires both expertise and considerable expense of time and effort. We can calculate all sorts of things, but the process is decidedly laborious. Even so obvious a matter as playwrights' earnings remained untotalled for thirty years after most of the necessary figures were printed in *The London Stage*.

Looking beyond the examples of account book utilization that I have given, I should point out that no one has yet made any systematic effort to use finances as a key to repertory in eighteenth-century London. This is surely one of the most obvious and exciting subjects on which financial evidence can be employed. No management could afford to defy the taste of the public, and the record of that taste is clearly inscribed in what people would pay to see. The kinds of work literary critics (then and now) demanded and praised were often quite different from what the public chose to attend. Much work remains to be done to correlate repertory choices with box-office results. I grant that the correlation is rendered difficult by the prevalence of afterpieces. Scholars have enthused, for example, over average receipts for Shakespeare plays in the 1720s. If, however, one separates out Shakespeare mainpieces performed without wildly popular afterpieces, then a very striking contrast emerges. One discovers that not many people tended to turn out for Shakespeare unadorned, but that plenty were willing to see some Shakespeare if it was packaged with one of Rich's pantomimes. Another problem is time of year: attendance varied quite a lot with the calendar. Such difficulties notwithstanding, I am convinced that much may yet be learned about audience taste if we analyse repertory in terms of its bottom-line results.

Literary historians, and even some theatre historians, often scorn money-minded managements. This remains true today: the last director of the National

Theatre in London, a heavily subsidized operation, was often belaboured for 'safe' repertory choices and innumerable performances of middle-brow musicals in the Olivier, its biggest space. Yet bills must be paid, even by nonprofit organizations – and the commercial theatres of the eighteenth century made no pretence of lack of interest in profits. The floods of pantomimes and farces which occupied that stage, and the rising tide of big-bang musicals that are so prominent a feature of the late-century repertory, tell us a lot about the cultural milieu we are studying. We may not like what they tell us, but they are an intractable truth. Let me end, therefore, by stating a principle that no responsible historian of the theatre can ignore: money does not *determine* art, but money very definitely *conditions* art. We are vastly fortunate in possessing a great deal of account book evidence about the eighteenth-century English theatre. We need to use it.

Notes and references

1. *The London Stage, 1660–1800*, ed. William Van Lennep, Emmett L. Avery, Arthur H. Scouten, George Winchester Stone, Jr., and Charles Beecher Hogan, 5 parts in 11 vols (Carbondale: Southern Illinois University Press, 1960–1968).
2. Philip H. Highfill, Jr., Kalman A. Burnim, and Edward A. Langhans, *A Biographical Dictionary of Actors, Actresses, Musicians, Dancers, Managers, and Other Stage Personnel in London, 1660–1800*, 16 vols (Carbondale: Southern Illinois University Press, 1973–1993).
3. Lawsuits in the first decade of the century always speak of the (plural) 'books of accounts', even when references concern a single season, and BL Egerton MS 2265 states that approval of the treasurer's accounts for the 1724–25 season was based upon entries in 'nine severall Books'. See Emmett L. Avery, 'The Finances of an Eighteenth-Century Theatre', *Theatre Annual*, 13 (1955): 49–59, at n. 1.
4. Ticket takers in 'offices' at each level of the theatre made out nightly reports, which were compiled in the box office. In addition, some companies employed 'numberers' to count the audience and separate functionaries to act as 'cheque[s] on the Office' for both the King's Side and the Prince's Side (Egerton MS 2272, 3r-v, 1766–67).
5. Incomplete transcriptions of a lost book for 1735–36 suggest that it was of this sort (BL Add. MS 32,251, pp. 299–308, and BL 11791.dd.18, vol. 3, fols. 177–89). See Judith Milhous and Robert D. Hume, 'John Rich's Covent Garden Account Books for 1735–36', *Theatre Survey*, 31 (1990): 200–41. Separate leaves survive from others later in the century.
6. See E. Beresford Chancellor, 'A Manuscript Account Book of Drury Lane Theatre for 1746–48', *Connoisseur*, 75 and 76 (August and October 1926): 217–21, 90–4. This MS, which was in private hands, was microfilmed for Part 4 of *The London Stage*. Its present whereabouts are unknown.
7. See, for example, Bedford Opera Papers (Woburn Abbey), Box 3, Vol. XI: Taylors and Mantua-Makers Attendance Book, Nov. 1791–Jan. 1792, listed in Judith Milhous, Gabriella Dideriksen, and Robert D. Hume, *Italian Opera in Late Eighteenth-Century London*, Vol. II: *The Pantheon Opera and its Aftermath, 1789–1795* (Oxford: Clarendon Press, 2001), Appendix VIII.
8. See the Bedford Opera Papers, Vol. II not in Boxes: 'Nightly Servants', a ledger that records servants' attendance night by night, with total salary paid and holograph signatures acknowledging payment. Also Vol. III not in Boxes, which records payments to 'weekly' house servants in 1790–91.

9. The sum is repeated in figures at the level of treasurer Richard Ford's signature. The date at which he acknowledged a turnover is often several days after the face date of the page, and he often collected several days' remainders at once.

10. A statement at the back of various Covent Garden books late in the century shows that towards the end of the season, all the contributory books and bills were taken by the treasurer to Thomas Harris's house, where they were audited and accepted by Harris as the true and official account of the season's finances. Some of the auditing checkmarks that appear in the books may have been made then. Others may have been made as information was transferred from contributory books to the main book. Most of the books that survive for that theatre are those Harris kept. Working from old books kept by Drury Lane, John Philip Kemble transcribed onto his collection of playbills not only notes from the diaries of prompters Richard Cross and William Hopkins, but sometimes receipts, 'presumably as given in the treasurer's books', as Dougald MacMillan points out in the Preface to his *Drury Lane Calendar, 1747–1776* (Oxford: Clarendon Press, 1938), v.

11. See Judith Milhous and Robert D. Hume, 'A Drury Lane Account Book for 1745–46', *Theatre History Studies*, 10 (1990): 67–104.

12. See B. S. Yamey, H. C. Edey, and Hugh W. Thomson, *Accounting in England and Scotland: 1543–1800* (1963; rpt. New York: Garland, 1982); James Ole Winjum, *The Role of Accounting in the Economic Development of England: 1500–1750* (Urbana, Ill.: Center for International Education and Research in Accounting, 1972); and Richard K. Fleishman and Lee D. Parker, *What is Past is Prologue: Cost Accounting in the British Industrial Revolution, 1760–1850* (New York: Garland Publishing, 1997).

13. In *The London Stage*, Part 4, G. W. Stone misunderstands the Covent Garden accounts for both 1749–50 and 1757–58, assuming that they were intended as a very different sort of record than they actually represent.

14. The Triumvirate papers are calendared in Judith Milhous and Robert D. Hume, *A Register of English Theatrical Documents, 1660–1737*, 2 vols (Carbondale: Southern Illinois University Press, 1991), beginning from no. 2233. The Bedford Opera Papers are listed in Milhous, Dideriksen, and Hume, *The Pantheon Opera*, Appendix VIII, 764–819.

15. This process is laid out in the 'Rules and regulations for the managers of Drury Lane', National Archives LC 7/3, fols. 149–50.

16. Folger W.b. 110, no. 101.

17. Folger W.b.111, fol. 4; Folger W.b.110, no. 169.

18. Folger W.b. 110, nos. 38, 63, and 319; Folger W.b. 111, fol. 8.

19. BL Egerton MS 2159, fol. 25; Folger W.b. 111, fol. 57.

20. See Milhous, Dideriksen, and Hume, *The Pantheon Opera*, chap. 6.

21. See Milhous and Hume, 'Receipts at Drury Lane: Richard Cross's Diary for 1746–47', *Theatre Notebook*, 49 (1995): 12–26 and 69–90, at 72. Cross's estimates for 1747–48 ran about 4 per cent high overall, but were as much as £46 high and £29 low on particular nights, and there are an alarming number of £10 and £20 discrepancies.

22. Chancellor, note 6 above. Plates illustrate five openings, an extraordinary concession at this date for a magazine whose focus was art.

23. 'The Finances of an Eighteenth-Century Theatre' (note 3 above). This article has gone almost unread and uncited. It is not listed in the MLA or MHRA bibliographies and it was omitted from *Restoration and Eighteenth Century Theatre Research: a Bibliographical Guide*, ed. Carl J. Stratman et al. (Carbondale: Southern Illinois University Press, 1971).

24. At least one dresser is unknown (Hachet), and others perhaps confused with people of similar names (Day; Francis; and Elliot, who may also have served as a billsticker). Two other billstickers are misrepresented (Banks; Dymock/Dimmock).

25. The *Biographical Dictionary* contains statements such as, 'we find no contemporary bills placing [the musician] Richard Vincent [junior] as an employee of any theatre or pleasure garden' in this season (15:173), though he is on this list.

26. The following samples all concern Covent Garden. Beginning in 1749–50, John Barrington played stage Irishmen in London. In 1768–69, he accepted a cut in salary from 11s. to 6s. 8d. per diem, unnoticed in his *BD* entry, which would seem to presage the end of his career (Egerton 2274, fol. 5r). The Mrs Cable/Cabel who died before January 1767 was a washerwoman (Egerton 2272, fols. 6r, 70r). The tailor Thomas Luppino, later a major costumer, was paid for 75 nights' dressing at the end of December 1766, broadening his early acquaintance with English theatre (Egerton 2772, fol. 60r). John Quick's initial salary in 1767–68 is misreported as 5s. in both *LS* and *BD*; it was 3s. 4d. (Egerton 2273, fol. 7r). The 'first mention' of Mary Stede in the account books is not on 23 February 1768 (*BD* 14:244–45), but much earlier that season (Egerton 2273, fol. 13r).

27. See Milhous, Dideriksen, and Hume, *The Pantheon Opera*, Appendix I.

28. Projections of income and costs were made by the (inexperienced) treasurer for the Pantheon's first season, but that was a newly-created operation, not an ongoing, long-profitable company.

29. See Harvard fMS Thr 22.

30. For example, Egerton 2275 shows that in the 1769–70 season at Covent Garden, normal charges ranged between £63 and £84, depending on how close to management the beneficiary was.

31. See, for example, Elbridge Colby, 'Financial Accounts of Holcroft Plays', *Notes and Queries*, 146 (19 and 26 January 1924): 42–5 and 60–3.

32. The best available analyses of company finances now available are the 'Financial Affairs' sections in the introductions to the five parts of *The London Stage*.

33. In the seventeenth century, the constant *daily* charge.

34. In many seasons for which an account book exists, *The London Stage* will record a few advertised performances not listed in the book. Such lacunae usually indicate a dismissal for lack of audience. See, for example, the *London Stage* entry for Covent Garden on 9 November 1749.

35. As early as 1709, the management of Christopher Rich came to an abrupt end on account of extra charges he added to benefit costs, against the direct order of the Lord Chamberlain. See Judith Milhous and Robert D. Hume, 'The Silencing of Drury Lane in 1709', *Theatre Journal*, 32 (1980): 427–47.

36. On 14 March 1758, Rich paid off this loan (Egerton 2270, fol. 182r).

37. See, for example, Egerton 2270, under 2 June 1758: 'By Under Charg'd in the Stoppage Acc't for Coales 6-04-06.' But they might also give back: 'overcharge in stoppage accts for Candles and Lamps 37-14-11', under 12 June.

38. This salary allowance figure is low, since a few house servants were paid annual salaries not fully recorded in this book. The roster of performers was set before the season began, and hiring rarely occurred after mid-September. Management knew who the performers would be and what they would cost.

39. Colley Cibber, *Apology*, ed. Robert W. Lowe, 2 vols (London: Nimmo, 1889), 1:187. On the finances of such productions, see Judith Milhous, 'The Multi-Media Spectacular on the Restoration Stage', in *British Theatre and the Other Arts, 1660–1800*, ed. Shirley Strum Kenny (Washington, DC: Folger Books, 1984), 41–66.

40. See Milhous and Hume, 'David Garrick and Box-Office Receipts at Drury Lane in 1742–43', *Philological Quarterly*, 67 (1988): 323–44.

41. In a sample of four Covent Garden account books between 1746–47 and 1777–78, Scott, a copperlace man, and Stephens, a mason, recur yearly for 31 years; attorneys Forrest, father and son, for 30; the expensive embroiderers D'Almaine for 27, albeit intermittently; linen drapers Hughes, sometimes Hughes & Batten, of York St, Covent Garden, also for 27. For 20 years the theatre dealt with Charles Wilford, a house painter, and with woollen drapers trading as Smart & Hewetson, then Hewetson, then Hewetson & Lonsdale, first in Kings St, Covent Garden, then in Lombard Street. The theatre's hardware came from braziers Bedwell & Freke, then Freke alone, for 20 years. For at least

18 years they used the same glazier, Wright; silk dyer, Carpue; shoemaker, McMillen; mercers, Bellamy & Settree; and bricklayer, who rejoiced in the name Lancelot Leverton.

42. Late in his career Rich temporarily mortgaged his patent to West Indian merchant and moneylender Hutchinson Mure, who also bought a share in the oratorios (Egerton 2270, fols. 179r, 182r). Before 1796, carpenter John Mountford loaned opera manager William Taylor £425 (C13/1587/11); oil merchant Francis Glossop loaned Sheridan more than £1,000 at various times (C13/1980/52).

43. Jacob Vanderlint, *Money Answers All Things* (London: Cox and Walford, 1734), esp. 22, 75–6, 141–2, 145–6.

44. Peter Earle, *The Making of the English Middle Class* (London: Methuen, 1989), chap. 10.

45. *Boswell's Life of Johnson*, ed. George Birkbeck Hill, rev. L. F. Powell, 6 vols (Oxford: Clarendon Press, 1934–1950), I: 105.

46. For further analysis, see Robert D. Hume, 'The Economics of Culture in London, 1660–1740', *Huntington Library Quarterly*, 69 (2006): 487–533.

47. For evidence of Barry's salary at this date, see Judith Milhous and Robert D. Hume, 'Murder in Elizabeth Barry's Dressing Room', *Yale University Library Gazette*, 79 (2005): 149–74.

48. Cibber, *Apology*, 1:181 and n. 2.

49. On these cases see respectively Judith Milhous and Robert D. Hume, 'The London Theatre Cartel of the 1720s: British Library Additional Charters 9306 and 9308', *Theatre Survey*, 26 (1985): 21–37; and *Coalition, a Farce: Founded on Facts* (London: for D. Browne, 1779), vi and 16, plus commentary in *The London Stage*, Part 5, 1:191.

50. St Vincent Troubridge, *The Benefit System in the British Theatre* (London: Society for Theatre Research, 1967).

51. As an instance of what can be done in particular cases, see Matthew J. Kinservik, 'Benefit Play Selection at Drury Lane 1729–1769: the Cases of Mrs Cibber, Mrs Clive, and Mrs Pritchard', *Theatre Notebook*, 50 (1996): 15–28.

52. Egerton 2280, Covent Garden 1777–78, shows the star Mrs Spranger Barry grossing £274 from all three areas of the house, but Mrs Mattocks, who sold box tickets only, bringing in just £160. Her husband also ignored the gallery and grossed £147, whereas Quick and Dunstall, drawing on all three areas, collected £262 and £237 respectively. Exposure and personal popularity affected these totals, but sales at all levels mattered.

53. See Egerton 2273, under 23 and 29 July and 15 August 1767, when the prompter Younger was advanced a total of £42 8s.; and Egerton 2278, under 13 Jan. 1774, for a £400 bond to Clarke.

54. Egerton 2279, under 2 Nov. 1776, a loan of £300 to Mattocks, which he returned on 3 May 1777, with £6-05-00 'for 5 Months Interest'.

55. On 7 May 1714, the sempstress Mary Cuthbert asked the Drury Lane managers for an extra 7s., 'as ... my Necessety be great att present'. They paid only the face value of the bill, but a loan could have been made separately and recorded elsewhere (Theatre Museum, V&A). Over the years, no doubt various managements turned down many requests.

56. For example, Robert D. Hume, 'Drama and Theatre in the Mid- and Later Eighteenth Century', in *The Cambridge History of English Literature, 1660–1780*, ed. John Richetti (Cambridge: Cambridge University Press, 2005), 316–39, at 317.

57. See Thomas McGeary, 'Farinelli in Madrid: Opera, Politics, and the War of Jenkins' Ear', *Musical Quarterly*, 82 (1998): 383–421.

58. See Judith Milhous and Robert D. Hume, 'Construing and Misconstruing Farinelli in London', *British Journal for Eighteenth-Century Studies*, 28 (2005): 361–85.

59. See Milhous and Hume, 'David Garrick and Box-Office Receipts at Drury Lane in 1742–43', note 40 above.

60. See Milhous and Hume, 'A Drury Lane Account Book for 1745–46' (note 11 above), and 'Receipts at Drury Lane: Richard Cross's Diary for 1746–47' (note 21 above).

61. See Judith Milhous, 'The Economics of Theatrical Dance in Eighteenth-Century London', *Theatre Journal*, 55 (2003): 481–508.

62. J. W. Saunders, *The Profession of English Letters* (London: Routlege and Kegan Paul, 1964), esp. pp. 68 and 113.

63. See Judith Milhous and Robert D. Hume, 'Playwrights' Remuneration in Eighteenth-Century London', *Harvard Library Bulletin*, n.s. 10 (1999): 3–90.

64. On the ill-advised purchase and early debts, see Curtis Price, Judith Milhous, and Robert D. Hume, *Italian Opera in Late Eighteenth-Century London*, Vol. I: *The King's Theatre Haymarket, 1778–1791* (Oxford: Clarendon Press, 1995), esp. chap. 2. On later developments, see Milhous, Dideriksen, and Hume, *The Pantheon Opera*, esp. chaps. 4 and 10.

Part 2
Controlling the Theatre

5
Jeremy Collier and the Politics of Theatrical Representation

Lisa A. Freeman

As the plot of William Congreve's *The Way of the World* (1700) speeds its way towards its inevitable unravelling, Lady Wishfort hears of Mrs Fainall's affair with Mirabell and expresses her disbelief that such a thing should come to pass: 'Is it possible' she exclaims that 'you should lean aside to iniquity, who have been cast in the direct mold of virtue?'[1] Woefully beside herself and wilfully overlooking her own concupiscent tendencies, Lady Wishfort seems unable to comprehend her daughter's behaviour. Indeed, for Lady Wishfort, who keeps as choice entertainment in her closet copies of both William Prynne's *Histriomastix* (1632) and Jeremy Collier's *A Short View of the Immorality and Profaneness of the English Stage* (1698), her daughter's conduct gives rise to what can only be termed a crisis of confidence, and not just because it may cost her dearly to keep her daughter's reputation safe, but more particularly, because it would seem impossible to reconcile her daughter's practices with the principles to which she should have been exposed in the course of reading those very texts. Indeed, for all of Lady Wishfort's efforts to inculcate moral virtue in her daughter by adhering strictly to principles that might be deduced from Collier's *Short View* – shielding her from all mixed company and cultivating in her both an aversion to the playhouse and an abhorrence for its bawdy plots – Mrs Fainall still seems to have done quite well for herself in the realm of what Collier might term '*Success* in ... *Debauchery*'.[2]

With this aggressive metatheatrical thrust, Congreve offered a much more pointed response to Collier than he had previously done in his *Amendments of Mr Collier's False and Imperfect Citations* (1698).[3] Almost two years into the controversy, and working in the medium in which he felt most assured, Congreve set aside his earlier strategy of restoring to 'proper and true Signification' those passages that Collier had excerpted in his *Short View* and instead aimed his attack squarely at Collier's claims for both moral principles and moral practices.[4] The implications Congreve leaves us to draw from this representation vary in the severity of their indictment but basically boil down to two charges. Either Collier's practice violated his own supposed principles by exposing his readers to a dirty litany of bawdy passages under the veil of moral correction, producing an appetite for these diversions rather than an aversion to them. Or, Collier's method for inculcating virtue was an ineffective one, particularly insofar as it required seclusion from all social intercourse and all cultural entertainments. In the event, the counter-argument goes, comedic representations could provide better instruction in the school of virtue by reflecting the world as it is and by offering vivid illustrations of the risks and costs to be borne by those who make a sacrifice of their virtue.

Such pieces of argument take as their point of departure the neoclassical tenet which was then so widely influential and which Collier thus so cannily offered as the first sentence in his introduction to *A Short View* – that the 'business of *Plays* is to recomend [sic] Virtue, and discountenance Vice'.[5] Significantly, though most critics have recognized this introductory precept as a strategic ploy by which Collier could elude charges of having condemned the stage entirely, it has proven distracting enough for critics to take Collier at his word and to focus their attention on such questions as how well the playhouse lived up to this mandate and whether Collier's invective brought about a reformation of the stage.[6] Such concerns are surely valuable in themselves and certainly they have given rise to some very strong scholarship.[7] At the same time, however, they also have a tendency to limit our critical purview to a narrow focus on the claims of this didactic imperative and to constrict our view of the broader social, historical, and political contexts in which Collier's tract was both conceived and received.

This essay proposes to take a more expansive look at what was thought to be at stake in the Collier controversy and, in particular, at what set of historical circumstances could drive it to such a feverish pitch. Focusing on the various political arguments, rather than on the aesthetic and didactic claims, represented in the numerous pamphlets and tracts, it seeks to demonstrate how the expression of concern on both sides over history and authority as well as over the public good were symptomatic of a much larger struggle in post-Revolution England on the one side to denounce and to contain, and on the other to articulate and to validate, a new epistemology of public practice that would be driven by the more diffuse codes of civility rather than by the hierarchical dictates of religious doctrine.

It ought to be noted that this essay is part of a much larger project that takes as its subject the ways in which notions of 'the public' and the 'public good' circulate consistently, though variously, in antitheatrical and pro-theatrical discourse from Plato to the present. Focusing primarily on antitheatrical episodes in the early modern and modern periods, it seeks to situate antitheatrical incidents not merely as reactions to specific theatrical performances and texts but also as cultural performances in themselves that need to be read and interpreted. Rather than gloss the surface, then, I develop a thick, comprehensive description of the contentious discursive environment in which each episode takes place. In doing so, I seek to offer a better understanding of the instrumental and cultural significance of antitheatricality by examining when, why, and how anxieties about representation manifest themselves and by tracing the actual politics that govern these ostensibly aesthetic and moral debates. By attending to these elements in a select number of the most controversial and influential cases, I hope to demonstrate definitively, if not exhaustively, that however differently 'the public' might be defined in each epoch, what lies at the heart of antitheatrical disputes is a struggle over the character of the body politic that governs a nation and the bodies public that could be said to represent that nation. Turning in that spirit to the specific case in question, we ought to begin with a few rough brushstrokes to outline the issues before discussing some of the finer touches that were given to the debate.

By the time Jeremy Collier's *A Short View of the Immorality and Profaneness of the English Stage* (1698) triggered an avalanche of pamphlets both for and against the theatre, England had undergone a Civil War, the subsequent Restoration of the Stuart Monarchy, and the Glorious Revolution, which exiled James II and brought William and Mary to the throne. These shifts in power resulted, as many historians have argued, in the destabilization of old notions of authority and legitimacy and, amidst the financial and commercial revolutions of the late seventeenth and early eighteenth centuries, reinforced an already growing sense that social hierarchies were both fluid and fungible.[8] For Jeremy Collier, who believed in a divinely-ordained hierarchical organization of society, these transformations were not merely repugnant; rather they were intolerable both from a religious and from a political perspective. The deposition of James II represented an absolute violation of all principle for Collier, and, even more significantly, it marked a decisive turning point in his career.

As a minister in the Church of England prior to 1689, Collier had committed himself both to the principle of passive obedience and to a belief in the indefeasible right of hereditary succession, and, on this basis, he had sworn an oath of allegiance to James II. Refusing to break this oath and roused by his sense of outrage over what he termed the 'deposition' of a king, Collier became one of the most outspoken critics of the accession of William and Mary and a leading member of the non-juring church – the alternative communion organized by those who refused to take the new oaths of allegiance and who were thus deprived of office in the Anglican Church.[9] Though he had published only one minor sermon before the Revolution, as a non-juror Collier published such well-known tracts as *The Desertion Discussed* (1689), in which he disputed claims that James II had abandoned the throne and thereby left it vacant, *Animadversions upon the Modern Explanation of . . . a King de facto* (1689), in which he mounted a relentless indictment of William's claim to the throne, and *A Perswasive to Consideration Tender'd to the Royalists* (1693), in which he asserted that subjects had no right to depose a king and enjoined his audience to shun the 'unlawful Assemblies' of what he termed the 'Schismatical' Church.[10] For his actions, he spent several months in Newgate in 1688 and again in 1692. And in 1696, only two years before the publication of *A Short View*, Collier increased his notoriety by accompanying Sir William Perkins to the gallows on the day of his execution for his role in a plot to assassinate King William. Once there, Collier, along with two other non-juring clergymen, added insult to injury by administering public absolution both to Perkins and to Sir John Friend without requiring their public confession, an action that Collier characteristically defended in a series of strident pamphlets and for which he was condemned as an outlaw.[11]

When Collier published *A Short View*, then, he was still technically considered an outlaw; and, given his notoriety and his commitments, there is no question that his attack on the stage was meant to be, and was considered immediately by others, a political event as much as it was viewed as a dramatic or a literary one. From this perspective, it makes much more sense to begin an examination of the controversy with Collier's polemical preface rather than with his didactic introduction. For here we find an assertion that alerts us to the broader context in which Collier situated his attack on the stage. Setting the terms of engagement, Collier writes, '*To make sure work on't, there's nothing like* Destroying *of* Principles; Practise *must* follow *of* Course. *For to have* no good Principles, *is to have* no Reason to be Good.'[12] Echoing any number of his tracts against the accession of William and Mary, Collier maintains that what offends is not simply the representation of lewdness or immorality on the stage but, more consequentially, the kinds of principles those offences might emanate from and the influence those principles might exercise over the conduct and consciousness of an audience. Any principle that does not take its rise from authority, and in particular any principle that is not articulated and sanctioned by divine authority, is not merely a bad or a false principle, it is, quite simply, as later passages in *A Short View* make clear, no principle at all. The 'Destroying of Principles' can result, in Collier's view, in only one outcome – in his own phrase, 'a . . . Levelling in Morality'.[13]

With this allusion to 'Levelling' in the preface, Collier alerts us more particularly both to the political stakes at hand and to the historical consciousness that guides his polemic. For by associating the destruction of 'principles' with 'levelling', he recalls both the radical activities of the Levellers in the 1640s, who called for a dramatic expansion of the franchise and the elevation of the House of Commons, as well as the activities of the Whig party, which emerged during the Exclusion Crisis of the late 1670s bearing the colours of the Levellers at its Green Ribbon Club, and which, more recently, had played a crucial role in negotiating the accession of William and Mary.[14] For Collier, the Glorious Revolution distinguished those who adhered to principle from those who abandoned their principles when it became politically advantageous to do so. Those who advocated for the *de facto* government of William and Mary and who negotiated the settlements were those who respected no established forms of order – proof positive, indeed, that they had no principles at all. In this case, he implied, the Whigs, like the Levellers during the previous revolution, had sacrificed a divinely-anointed monarch to the supremacy of Parliament and ushered in a period of great uncertainty with respect to order and authority. In this manner, moreover, he purposely inserted into the discourse a sense of historical contiguity that served as the background not only for his writings but also for those of the many writers who participated in the controversy.

When we take up Collier's *Short View* and begin, then, with the preface rather than with the first chapter, it becomes possible to see that Collier's attack on the stage as a vehicle for the levelling of morality derives its force and conviction from his more fundamental concern with the levelling of authority. Collier's concern is that a loss of authority in the body politic – the realm of principle – has given rise to a concomitant loss of authority in what I term the body public – the realm of practice. What's at stake is whether that body public ought to be regulated by traditional forms of religious stricture and political authority – as Collier and his supporters would have it – or whether, given the challenge to authority – political and religious – wrought by the Revolution, that realm ought to be governed by the more secular and more pragmatic forms of stricture and authority favoured by his opponents. Either way, what becomes clear is that Collier provided the occasion for the articulation of a number of competing and often contradictory political ideologies with respect both to the accession of William and Mary and to the body public over which they were thought to preside. Indeed, the further we move away from particular responses to Collier's charges, such as Congreve's *Amendments* or John Vanbrugh's *A Short Vindication of the Relapse and the Provok'd Wife* (1698), to examine more wide-ranging and polemical works, such as *The Stage Condemned* (1698) and *The Stage Acquitted* (1699), the more clearly and explicitly pronounced are the contending political interests.

Before proceeding any further, however, it would seem prudent to inquire: why the stage? Why did Collier target the stage, and why did his attack give rise to such a fierce pamphlet exchange? What, we might ask, did the theatre or playhouse represent in late-seventeenth and early-eighteenth-century culture that made it such a volatile site of contention? And why would the stage be considered such a valuable prize on the political battlefield?

When we consider the playhouse historically not merely as a site for the performance of plays, but rather as Marvin Carlson has helped us to see, as a structured public space in which persons from a cross-section of society are brought together, we can begin to understand the unique cultural role played by the theatre in late-seventeenth-century London.[15] Indeed, as any number of prologues and epilogues from this period make clear, the theatre was recognized as a privileged space in which a heterogeneous public could be called into being, performatively constituted, as it were, through successive appeals to the pit, the boxes, and the gallery, and thus provided a conspicuous experience of affiliation across class and gender lines. Speaking of the formation of audiences in the context of the Battle between Ancient and Moderns in late-seventeenth-century France, Joan DeJean writes, 'the notion of an audience was from its origins inextricably bound up with ... anxieties – from the fear of social promiscuity, to the fear of public culture, to the fear that those not previously part of the social elite would dare to interfere in cultural matters'.[16] Though DeJean refers here to audiences for print, and indeed specifically precludes theatre audiences from consideration, I would argue that she misses something crucial even as she offers us an important insight about culture wars that we can apply to the English case at hand. For to the extent that English theatre audiences were called upon to form opinions and to play a critical role both in relation to the performance and to one another, the playhouse engendered the conditions for the production of a 'public sphere of civil society', a site, where as Jürgen Habermas defines it, private people could come together to act as a 'counterpart [to] public authority', as it was vested in the state. Locating the beginnings of these shifts in England during the period following the Glorious Revolution, Habermas explains, 'Inasmuch as culture became a commodity and thus finally evolved into "culture" in the specific sense ... it was claimed as the ready topic of a discussion through which an audience-oriented subjectivity communicated with itself.'[17] If 'for Collier', as J. Hopes explains, 'it was not simply the historical events of 1688 that were important, but their pervasive and fundamental influence on post-revolution society', then it makes a great deal of sense that in selecting his target Collier chose a cultural site of a certain public stature that functioned as a competing source of authority in the public sphere.[18] Indeed, as the responses to Collier demonstrate, the stage was viewed as a site that quite specifically sanctioned social intercourse within the body public and that encouraged audiences to exercise reason in the formation of opinion rather than rely on the judgments of hierarchical authority.

The political dimensions of the public role played by theatres are made all the more palpable when we consider a simple fact pointed out by Matthew Kinservik in a recent consideration of theatrical regulation during the Restoration period: the stage in England had long been closely associated with the patronage of the crown. Thus, in the Restoration, we have the King's Men and the Duke's Men, the two acting companies issued royal patents and named respectively for Charles II and James, the Duke of York. As Kinservik writes, 'These names were not merely honorific; rather, they signified a protective relationship between the nobler patron and the acting company.'[19] Under this dispensation, it is no wonder to find that the playhouse was construed as an agent or surrogate of the crown and engaged as a site of contention in political conflicts over the compass of sovereign power and the liberties of the body public. In this context, moreover, arguments both for and against the stage were often quite explicitly intended, and can easily be read, as both enunciations of political allegiances and commentaries on the status of power, authority, and governance in the state and in the public sphere. Collier's decision to attack the stage thus alerts us to its perceived prominence as a significant site of socio-cultural and political influence, both by virtue of its historical affiliation with the crown and by virtue of its immediate engagement and intercourse with the body public. In order to attain the most comprehensive understanding of what was at stake in the Collier controversy, then, we ought to attend to both elements – the historiographical – that is, to how the historical relationship between court and stage is rendered in each account – and the socio-political – that is, to how political principles are thought to influence the tenor of social intercourse in the body public.

Reading Collier's *A Short View* as a rhetorical occasion for the assertion of non-juring political ideology and hence as an extension of his assault both on the legitimacy of the reign of William and Mary and on the Anglican Church for acceding to their reign, we would do best to focus our attention on his chapter against the abuse of clergy on the stage. For, more than any other section of *A Short View*, it touches immediately on what were for Collier some of the most irksome aspects of the Revolution settlement and the Anglican Church's role in ensuring that settlement. In Chapter III of *A Short View*, Collier turns to what he terms 'History and Argument' in order to 'shew the Right the *Clergy* have to Regard, and fair usage', and the first reason Collier provides for this right is '*their Relation to the Deity*'.[20] Construing this relationship in terms of an absolute right, Collier asserts, 'the Holy *Order* is appropriated to the Divine Worship: And a *Priest* has the peculiar Honour to *Belong* to nothing less then God Almighty.'[21] He reiterates this position again and again in the course of his discussion and finally concludes by referring his readers to an earlier essay he had written on 'The Office of a Chaplain'. In that essay, published as part of his *Essays on Moral Subjects* (1697), Collier wrote, 'the Church is a distinct Society from the State; and independent upon it: The Constitution of the Church is founded in the Appointment of Christ, in that Commission which he gave the Apostles and their Successors, and consequently does not derive its Authority from any Earthly Power.'[22] For Collier, a clergyman could not, in principle, be compelled by the state to act against conscience, for he neither belonged to nor derived his authority from any human master. Even more to the point, the state could not abrogate the authority of a representative of the church for, as in the case of a monarch's rule, that right belonged only to God.

It would be easy to mistake such pronouncements as a general defence of the Anglican Church and its clergy rather than as an indictment of them. But Collier's status as a leading member of the non-juring church was well known, as were the positions he espoused on its behalf; and his readers, as is patently clear in any number of the responses to him, did not mistake his intent.[23] In Collier's view, as he made clear in his *Perswasive to Consideration*, the Anglican Church had violated its own principles and, for the sake of political interest and expedience, had acted against conscience to 'consecrate the Revolt'.[24] Collier's defence of the clergy in *A Short View* would have been understood, then, to bolster only those who had taken up what he termed the 'Post of Honour' and refused to subject the spiritual authority of the church to 'Secular Power'.[25] As he declaimed in his *Perswasive*, 'To suffer therefore in Defence of Authority and Government, is both a necessary and a noble Instance of Fortitude; so that 'tis no wonder Religion should expect it from us.'[26] By abandoning its own principles, the Anglican Church had cheapened its own authority and laid itself open to abuse – the effects of which Collier claims can be seen in the mistreatment of clergy on the stage. His sorrow, anger, and resentment that authority has proven so mutable and that the church and its authority should, by its own actions, be subjected so is nowhere more palpable in *A Short View* than when he bitterly spits, 'This is rare Protestant Diversion, and very much for the Credit of the *Reformation!* The Church of *England*, I mean the Men of Her, is the only Communion in the World, that will endure such Insolences as these.'[27]

These are positions he felt compelled to articulate even more emphatically in his *Defence of the Short View* (1699). Published in 1699 and composed primarily as a response to Congreve and Vanbrugh, Collier condemns Congreve's arguments about the representation of clergymen by explicitly equating them with the kinds of equivocations offered to justify the Glorious Revolution, writing, 'But Mr. *Congreve* urges, That by improper *Behaviour the Man becomes alienated from the Priest, and so the Folly is exposed, not the Function* ... This is much like the old Distinction of *Politick*, and *Personal Capacity*, applied to another Case.'[28] This other case, obviously, is that of the deposition of James II, during which many sought to justify their actions by distinguishing between the body politic and the body personal of the king. Collier thus continues:

> Though the Function and the Person are separable in Notion, they are joyn'd in Life and Business. 'Tis true, the Office and the Person are two Things; but yet 'tis the Person which executes the Office: This makes them share a disadvantage in Common; and a Censure frequently slides from the one to the other ... Upon this account Persons in Authority, whether Spiritual or Civil, ought to be privileg'd from Abuse. To make the Ministers of *Church* or *State*, the *subject of Laughter and Contempt*, disables their Authority, and renders their Commission insignificant.[29]

On this basis, Collier accuses Congreve of being engaged in a 'fit of Levelling' where all forms of distinction and authority are rendered insignificant, a charge that supports an earlier associative leap in the tract whereby the poets of the playhouse came to stand in for a revolutionary Parliament that had exceeded its proper jurisdiction.[30] Commenting on Congreve's assertion that the playhouse has the right to hold the clergy up to ridicule, he writes disdainfully, "'Tis true, the Article says, They *may be accus'd, and being found guilty, by just Judgment depos'd*. But what of all this? Are the *Poets* their Judges? And is the Stage grown *Doctors Commons*, or *Westminster-Hall?*'[31] This odd piece of rhetoric functions on any number of levels. In the simplest sense, Collier's query challenges the authority of poets to act as judges with respect to clergy, a prerogative, as we have seen, that Collier attributes only to God. In this sense, their judgement is always already insignificant, that is, it does not signify at all. In a more complicated sense, Collier insinuates that 'levelling' has penetrated so deeply into the fabric of society that poets now feel free to assume the kinds of prerogatives of judgement already illegitimately seized by Parliament in pronouncing the desertion of James II and the accession of William and Mary. A descent into anomie had been set in motion and, if not resisted, the end result, as Collier envisioned, could only be that, 'Societies must break up; and the *Foundations of the Earth be put out of Course*'.[32] Thus, we see, as J. Hopes points out, 'As the possibility of James's returning became more and more distant, Collier's opposition to the revolution took the form of an attack on the false principles which it represented and which it had helped to spread throughout society. He looked to the restoration of social and moral values to effectively undo the evil it had perpetrated.'[33] In Collier's ongoing effort to bring about a second Restoration, the stage became just one more front on which to wage the battle.

If Collier was trying to resist and perhaps even reverse the course of history, there were others, both for and against the stage, who had an interest in extending the political settlements of the last ten years. Taking the occasion of an attack on the stage to advance disparate political agendas, those who joined the fray offered their own readings of history and their own articulations of the body public. This accords with J. G. A. Pocock's characterization of the status of history in the early eighteenth century. For Pocock, history is 'public time', which is to say it is 'time experienced ... by individuals who see themselves as public beings' and who 'see society as organized into and by a number of frameworks, both institutional and conceptual, in and through which they apprehend things as happening to society and themselves, and which provide them with means of differentiating and organizing the things they apprehend as happening'.[34] As a consequence of both the failure and the abrogation of traditional forms of authority, this project was complicated in the eighteenth century by the fact that 'such orderings and their languages had drawn together to a point where it seems truer to say that time and history were ordered by consciousness of a public realm or political nation, which could itself be ordered and conceptualized in a number of different ways'.[35] In this respect, he identifies two basic modes of organization: continuity, where the emphasis is placed on 'perpetuating usages and practices, transmitting its different forms of authority and ... maintaining its legitimacy'; and contingency, where institutionality is diminished and 'is now [understood as] a continuous capacity for action rather than a continuous transmission of legitimacy'.[36]

For Collier, the Williamite accession represented a betrayal of the indefeasible right of hereditary succession, a violent break with continuity, and a dangerous movement into a form of public time marked by the contingencies of *de facto* government, where power was negotiated rather than inherited and where, as he put it disdainfully in his essay 'Of Power', 'Empire consists chiefly in the Submission of other Men's Wills; which is in a manner but reigning by Courtesy.'[37] Like Collier, as I shall demonstrate, the authors of *The Stage Condemned* and *The Stage Acquitted* are aware of themselves as public beings and as part of a public discourse, but, given their disparate and often antagonistic political commitments, their relationship to continuity and contingency in the accounts of history they provide is quite different. Indeed, not only does contingency become a source of legitimate action and transformation in their versions of history; rather the moral valences of continuity and of contingency are themselves recalibrated. Though the former condemned the stage and the latter supported it, in *both* accounts continuity comes to be understood as a form of tyranny even as contingency comes to be construed as a sign of the nation's liberty. That this was the case only begins to suggest the complexity and particularity of the various political allegiances that were brought into relief by the controversy.

Indeed, that antitheatrical moments can sometimes make for strange bedfellows is nowhere more vividly illustrated than in the troubled coupling of Jeremy Collier and George Ridpath, the apparent author of *The Stage Condemned* (1698), who was just as fierce a Puritan and a Whig, as Collier was a High Church Anglican and a Tory.[38] In his epistle dedicatory and introduction, Ridpath makes his motives for entering into the stage controversy clear. Collier, in his opinion, had done a good job up to a point; but ultimately he was hampered by his non-jurancy, which is to say, by his loyalty to the Anglican Church and the Stuart monarchy and to the Catholic tendencies of each institution. In Ridpath's sinister account, the stage was not just a site of immorality or profaneness; it was, more menacingly, one of the insidious vehicles used to 'promote the Glorious Design of Debauching the Nation, and to baffle the Evidence of the Popish Plots' and had been so since at least the 1630s when Charles I, under the influence of Archbishop Laud, had introduced the Book of Sports and blasphemed the Sabbath by entertaining at court with Sunday masques.[39] Thus, the martyr in Ridpath's history is not Charles I, as he and James II would be in Collier's account, but rather William Prynne, the author of *Histriomastix*, who lost both ears in the pillory and was branded a seditious libeller for assailing the royal prerogatives of the monarch and for challenging the authority of the archbishop. 'In those Times', Ridpath tells us:

> none were accounted Enemies to the Play-house but Puritans and Precisians, and in opposition to them it probably was that *Laud* and his Clergy became its Patrons; and it is not unlike that many of the Less-thinking Church-men continue still to favour it on that Account, as being unwilling to condemn that, for which King *Charles* I. and Arch-bishop *Laud* testified so much Passion; but these Gentlemen would do well to remember, *That the Defence of the Stage was never so much the Characteristick of their Church, as was the Doctrine of Passive Obedience; and seeing the Majority of them have relinquished that, they are infinitely the more to blame for still adhering to this.*[40]

Ridpath's commentary cuts in any number of directions, all of which are meant to point up inconsistencies and sophistries in the positions staked out by his political rivals. On the one hand, he praises Collier for coming out against the stage but upbraids him for his Jacobite affinities, that is, for supporting the papist regime that supported and maintained close ties to the playhouse. On the other hand, he mocks those clergymen who seem to have summoned the backbone to overthrow the principle of passive obedience, depose James II, and swear an oath of allegiance to William and Mary, and yet haven't found the wherewithal to root out the agent of Caroline tyranny and Jacobite popery, which is to say, the stage. Thus he caustically opines, there is 'a mighty Neglect somewhere, and the World will hardly be perswaded that our Church of *England* is unanimous in this Matter, *else it were easie for them, who shook King* James *out of his Throne, to overturn the Stage'.*[41] In Ridpath's version of history, then, the 'Incendiaries and Fomenters of the Civil War' of 1641 were not the Puritans but rather the 'Friends of the Stage, who taught Rebellion against our Constitution, set the King above all Laws, and would have trod Parliaments under foot'.[42] Shoring up his political position under the settlements of the Revolution of 1688, he thus avows that those 'very Men who were Enemies to the Stage' in '41', which is to say, those who supported the principle of rebellion against tyranny are thus 'the firmest Friends this Government [now] has'.[43] In this manner, Ridpath aligns himself politically against both the established Anglican church and the non-jurors and affiliates himself with the hard-line ideology of Puritans in the Societies for the Reformation of Manners movement, who looked to William III in the 1690s to translate the achievements of the political revolution into an equally revolutionary programme of moral reformation.[44]

While William III, as Tony Claydon has demonstrated, waged a highly effective rhetorical campaign to position himself as the 'patron of the reformation movement', this movement itself did not go unopposed.[45] Indeed, as Claydon concedes, '[t]here is, in fact, considerable evidence from the 1690s that the general run of William's subjects were highly ambivalent about having their manners reformed by statutes, and that many viewed the movement as an excuse for hypocritical interference in private lives ... poets and pamphleteers certainly attacked the movement for ... reviving the puritan terror of Cromwell's day'.[46] It is not surprising to find, then, that a rejoinder to Ridpath, *The Stage Acquitted*, was soon composed and published, presenting an argument on the side of the political base within the established Church who supported the Glorious Revolution but who sought to constrain the influence and power of the Puritan factions.

The Stage Acquitted presents us with a sceptical dialogue between two figures, Lovetruth and Fairly, who purportedly seek to cut through the reports of the town to get to the truth of the matter over the stage. The strategy of this anonymous pamphlet is to represent Collier and Ridpath as extremists who seek both to suppress individual liberty and conscience and to impose a form of tyranny, either political or moral, upon the nation, while figuring the protagonists, Fairly and Lovetruth, as paragons of rational moderation. Quite cleverly, moreover, the author often pits Collier and Ridpath against one another, not only cancelling out the supposed authority of both but also undermining the idea of authority altogether. In this manner, *The Stage Acquitted* prepares the rhetorical way for a new mode of order and governance in the body public that would be based on reason and experience.[47]

Training his sights on Collier first, Lovetruth reasons:

> it cannot be reasonably doubted but that the *Stage* is of considerable use and advantage to the *Public*; for certainly so eminent a Clergy, as that of the *Episcopal Church of England*, who have the most pure and uncorrupted Doctrine of all the *Christian* world, who are admirable for their *Piety*, and every where valued for their *Learning*, cannot be thought to encourage what would any way tend to the Corruption of the Morals of the *Age*, as Mr *Collier* would seem to affirm.[48]

Thus using Ridpath's account of Charles I's and Laud's affinity for stagecraft against Collier, Lovetruth highlights the internal inconsistency of Collier's position. For if, as a non-juror he venerated the memory of Archbishop Laud and Charles I, then it would seem strange that he would honor that legacy by attacking the institutions which they so heartily supported; he 'could not be ignorant that the *whole body* of the *Clergy* of the *Church* of *England* in the time of the Martyr, did in an *extraordinary* manner encourage Plays'.[49] Mocking Collier's self-righteousness with respect to the abuse of clergy, then, Lovetruth goes on to note that 'Mr *Collier* himself has not us'd them very kindly, when he has endeavor'd to deprive them of their hearers, with as much zeal, as he had to rob the Poets of theirs', to which Fairly replies with all due equanimity, that indeed "Tis strange that Mr *Collier* should be angry with the *Stage* for one single *Say-grace*, when he has made so severe a Satire on the *whole body* of the *Clergy* that are for the Government'.[50] Referring here to Collier's attacks on the Anglican Church and to his polemic in his *Perswasive to Consideration*, mentioned above, against attending church services under the auspices of that clerical regime, Fairly and Lovetruth conclude that the stage could hardly do more damage to the authority of clergy than Collier has already done himself.[51]

Having made their case against Collier, Lovetruth and Fairly then turn to an assessment of Ridpath. Characterizing him variously as a 'news-monger', a 'scribbler', and a 'zany', Lovetruth moves first and foremost to reconstrue Ridpath's version of antitheatrical history, remonstrating:

> Mr *Prynne* had his tryal, and was cast for acting against *Law*, in broaching ten thousand *false* and *scandalous* Reflections against both *King* and *Church,* as well as the *Stage*; and 'tis a glory to the *latter* to have suffer'd with, and on account of the *former*; and all of this is so far from a Reflection on either *King* or *Church,* as he impudently means it, that 'tis only so on himself; for he has yet shown us no *Evidence* in himself either in *Learning*, or in a Pious and Christian Spirit, that should make us believe him a *better* Judge of those matters, than the most *Pious* and *Learned Clergy* that ever flourish'd in our *English* World, and by consequence not inferiour to that of *any* Age or Nation whatever.[52]

Here Lovetruth casts Ridpath as a dangerous Puritan zealot, who defies the authority and wisdom of an Anglican establishment that favoured the stage. But he leaves it to the usually even-tempered Fairly, to express outrage over Ridpath's skewed version of history, to recall the terrifying spectre of the days of the Commonwealth, and to remind Ridpath of his place in the post-Revolutionary political order:

> How? What were the *Puritans* the only Sticklers for *properties*? Had not the Church as much to lose? And have they ever been remiss in the care of the Public Good? Have they betray'd the Trust repos'd in them by the People? Have they been false to their duty to the Publick Good? If the Church of *England* has been guilty of these Abominable Crimes, let our Author prove it, if not, how came the *Puritans* the Guardians of our Liberty? Those who invaded and disobey'd the Laws of their Country, gave not the greatest proof of their Love to, or Zeal for it; and 'tis evident enough, that even from the time of Queen *Elizabeth*, when they first appear'd, the wisdom of the Nation thought they ought to be restrain'd by *Law*, and were deny'd *Liberty* of *Conscience*, for many years before King *Charles* the First. 'Tis true, they have now the Liberty they then wanted, but they should remember to whom they owe that Benefit, *viz.* to a King of the Church of *England's perswasion*, to the very Bishops they abuse, to the Lords and Commons, all, or most of the *Church* of *England*; and that should teach them more *modestly* towards their *Benefactors*.[53]

In what appears to be a justified fury, Fairly recalls the violent upheavals of the 1640s and contrasts the radical contingencies of the unlawful usurpation of government and 'Abominable Crimes' of the Puritan regime to the wisdom, lawfulness, and continuity of the established church during the Revolution of 1688.

Although Lovetruth moves to allow that Fairly ought not to hold the entire body of dissenters responsible for the actions of one man, the pamphlet makes it clear that the new freedoms enjoyed by dissenters should be considered a matter not of right but of magnanimity. In this manner, Ridpath's authority is thoroughly undermined, and his ambitious moral and political agenda is exposed as a danger both to 'Liberty' and to the 'publick good'.

As part of its political programme, *The Stage Acquitted* makes every effort as well to debunk religious authority and inherited orthodoxies as the crutch of the weak-minded. In this respect, Collier and Ridpath are grouped together, and their appeals to Church Fathers such as Tertullian are exposed as tyrannical impositions of authority that make no rational sense. Perhaps the most damning indictment in this regard comes from Fairly when he observes:

> There is no doubt to be made, but that an industrious man of any moderate share of brains may bring *Fathers* and *Scriptures* too for a thousand *Absurdities* and *Falsities*. This is as evident as daily experience can make it. The Controversies betwixt the Church of *Rome* and *England*, betwixt the Church of *England* and *Dissenters*, betwixt the *Congregational* and *Presbyterian Divines*, betwixt the *Anabaptists* and their *Opposers*; and so on to all the *divisions*, and sub-divisions of opinions, that this Town alone affords us. Which has render'd our Common *Christianity* so obscure, that if we deny our *Reason* to be Judge of the Controversie, and tell us when the *Fathers* speak right, when the *several sides* give the true sense of *Scripture*, we must perpetually wander in the dark, and fall into the unhappy and deplorable state of *Scepticism*.[54]

The litany of schisms rehearsed here has an almost absurdist ring to it, yet Fairly's point is demonstrably supported by *The Stage Acquitted*, where we find that Ridpath and Collier, who purportedly support one another in their campaign against the stage, can actually be read to argue against one another. Thus noting how 'in the Controversy betwixt the Protestants and Papists ... both sides Charge each other with wresting or false quoting the Authorities against them', Lovetruth, like Fairly, condemns the influence of 'Faction', 'Passion and Interest', and concludes similarly, 'that the Controversie ought indeed to be reduc'd to the thing itself, without regard to the noisy pretences of Authority'.[55]

With the truth of any matter so deeply obscured by sectarian interests, the only remedy, as Lovetruth exhorts Fairly early on, is not to give in to cant but rather 'like other men, be convinc'd by your own experience; and pay the same for your knowledge that I have done. Read, read, Sir, and see.'[56] Extolling scientific discoveries and disparaging the parochial pronouncements of the Fathers, he declares:

> those *Fathers* that writ against the *Antipodes*, proceeded to actual violence, and built their opinions on several *Texts* of *Scripture*, as the opposers of *Copernicus* will shew in all their trifling Books; and yet *Galliloeus* and *Gassendus* in their defence of that *System* have evidently confuted their opinions; and Experience has evidently prov'd, that the *Scripture* was not to be understood in the same

sense the *Fathers* or the Modern *Ptolomists* wou'd have it, there being nothing now more certain, than the Orbicular form of the Earth, and by consequence that there are *Antipodes* ... which is enough to shew, that we can build no Authority on the *Fathers*, where reason is against them.[57]

If Fairly's dissection of religious history, with its emphasis on the endless waves of schism, is meant to convince us of the folly of blindly following church authorities – or, for that matter, of trying to figure out *which* church authorities to follow – then Lovetruth's dissertation on the historical triumphs of science is surely meant to convince us that the exercise of reason will prove a better foundation for judgement than the '*doctrines of Religion*' ever could be.[58] After all, as they point out, 'are not all History full of Matter of fact' that heresies and schisms and not the stage are responsible for, 'more *violent distractions, more Murders, Treasons, Assassinations, and Plots, Conspiracies, Civil Wars, Subversion of States, and the other Innumerable Evils*'?[59] Better to apply reason, it would seem, than ever to submit to a doctrine of faith again.

What impels *The Stage Acquitted*, then, is a desire to leave behind that legacy of violence and upheaval that was motivated by religious doctrine and religious faction and an interest in entering into a new era of tolerance, free exchange and dialogue regulated by reason and sociability – the two qualities exemplified, of course, in the very form chosen for this particular rejoinder. Indeed, as any number of historians have pointed out, conversation by this time was well on its way to becoming the very paradigm of politeness, probity, and civility, the privileged mode of interchange in the body public and the very sign of liberty in the body politic.[60] Thus, in the public sphere imagined by Lovetruth and Fairly in their exchange, authority would circulate much more promiscuously than it had before and principles would be formed discursively on the basis of reason. If Collier sought, then, to use the stage as a front to turn back time and to mount one last desperate assault on the new regime, he was woefully mistaken in his target. For, if anything, as this essay has demonstrated, the Collier controversy provided the occasion not only for the reiteration, looking backward, of the historical settlements in the body politic, but also for the articulation, going forward, of a new mode of governance and engagement in what was rapidly emerging as a new body public.

Notes and references

1. William Congreve, *The Way of the World* (1700), ed. Kathleen M. Lynch (Lincoln: University of Nebraska Press, 1965), V.132–3.
2. Jeremy Collier, *A Short View of the Immorality and Profaneness of the English Stage* (London, 1698), preface by Arthur Freeman (New York and London: Garland Publishing, 1972), 2.
3. This immediate rejoinder was thought to be so weak and ineffective that Samuel Johnson characterized Congreve as having 'the sword without the arm of Scanderberg'. See Samuel Johnson's 'William Congreve' in *Lives of the Poets*, ed. and introd. Edmund Fuller (New York: Avon Books, 1965), 229.

4. William Congreve, *Amendments of Mr Collier's False and Imperfect Citations* (London, 1698), 10.

5. Collier, *A Short View*, 1.

6. In *The Antitheatrical Prejudice* (Berkeley: University of California Press, 1981), for example, Jonas Barish defends Collier, writing 'It is only after affirming the educational mission of the stage that Collier moves to consider particular plays, to ask whether they serve to subvert the high cause assigned them' (224).

7. Particularly strong scholarship in this vein can be found in Joseph Wood Krutch, *Comedy and Conscience after the Restoration* (NY: Columbia University Press, 1924); Robert D. Hume, 'Jeremy Collier and the Future of the London Theater in 1698', *Studies in Philology*, 96 (Fall 1999): 480–511; and Matthew J. Kinservik, 'Theatrical Regulation during the Restoration Period', in *A Companion to Restoration Drama*, ed. Susan J. Owen (Oxford: Blackwell Publishers, 2001), 36–52, esp. 43–50.

8. In taking this view of English history, I am following the accounts of historians such as J. G. A. Pocock in his volume of essays, *Virtue, Commerce, and History* (Cambridge: Cambridge University Press, 1985). Though his overall account of the period remains influential, some of Pocock's particular arguments about the politics of virtue have been modified and revised to recognize the persistent role of religion and religious rhetoric in political discourse. See, for instance, Shelley Burtt, *Virtue Transformed: Political Argument in England, 1688–1740* (Cambridge: Cambridge University Press, 1992); and Tony Claydon, *William III and the Godly Revolution* (Cambridge: Cambridge University Press, 1996).

9. While Collier and the non-jurors were adamant in calling James II's removal from the throne a 'deposition', their political counterparts were careful to characterize his removal as an 'abdication'. For more on the terms of engagement and their significance in this political struggle, see, J. P. Kenyon, *Revolution Principles: the Politics of Party 1689–1720* (Cambridge: Cambridge University Press, 1977). For a useful history of the non-juring church, see, L. M. Hawkins, *Allegiance in Church and State: the Problem of the Nonjurors in the English Revolution* (London: George Routledge & Sons, 1928).

10. For an exhaustive account of Collier's essays, see Kathleen Ressler, 'Jeremy Collier's Essays' in *Seventeenth Century Studies*, ed. Robert Shafer, 2nd series (Princeton: Princeton University Press 1933), 179–285. I am quoting here, however, from the 3rd edition, corrected, of Collier's *A Perswasive to Consideration* (London, 1695), 22, 24.

11. Among Collier's pamphlets in the case were *A Defence of the Absolution Given to Sir William Perkins* (1696) and *A Further Vindication of the Absolution Given to Sir William Perkins* (1696). For just one response to Collier, see *An Answer to Mr Collier's Defence of His Absolution of Sir William Parkins* (London, 1696). Though much of the information in the account above can be readily gleaned from *The Dictionary of National Biography*, I am also indebted for some details to J. Hopes, 'Politics and Morality in the Writings of Jeremy Collier', *Literature and History*, 8 (1978): 159–74. No discussion of the Jeremy Collier controversy would be complete without noting the exhaustive month-to-month and year-to-year descriptions of the pamphlets and tracts provided in Sister Rose Anthony's *The Jeremy Collier Stage Controversy, 1698–1726* (1937; New York: Benjamin Blom, 1966).

12. Collier, *A Short View*, Preface, A2r-A3r.

13. Collier, *Short View*, Preface, A5r.

14. As Christopher Hill writes in *The Century of Revolution 1603–1714* (New York and London: W. W. Norton, 1982), 'The Green Ribbon Club, established in London in 1675, may be regarded as the first party headquarters. Its green colours were those of the Levellers. The ghosts of the Interregnum were walking again' (199).

15. Marvin Carlson, *Places of Performance: the Semiotics of Theatre Architecture* (Ithaca: Cornell University Press, 1989).

16. Joan DeJean, *Ancients against Moderns: Culture Wars and the Making of a Fin de Siécle* (Chicago and London: University of Chicago Press, 1997), 31–2.

17. Jürgen Habermas, *The Structural Transformation of the Public Sphere*, trans. Thomas Burger with Frederick Lawrence (Cambridge, MA: MIT Press), 29.

18. Hopes, 'Politics and Morality', 160.
19. Kinservik, 'Theatrical Regulation', 47.
20. Collier, *A Short View*, 127.
21. Collier, *A Short View*, 127.
22. Jeremy Collier, 'The Office of a Chaplain', *Essays on Moral Subjects* (1697), Sixth Edition, Corrected (London, 1709), 211–12.
23. In *Vindication of the Stage* (London, 1698), for instance, Collier and the non-jurors are berated for doing more damage to the clergy by encouraging schism than the stage could ever do: 'Nay, Mr. *Collier* himself, and all others of this Principles, are more bitter and sharp Invective against the Order, by their Refractory and Obstinate Separation from the Greatest and most Pious Part of their Brethren, than any can be writ by the most Atheistical Pen; and wound it more severely' (18–19). In the same spirit, *A Defence of Dramatick Poetry* (London, 1698) caustically refers to Collier as a 'sometimes Minister of the English Church', and explicitly casts Collier's attack on the stage as a 'second Perswasive' (48, 98).
24. *A Perswasive to Consideration*, 22.
25. *A Perswasive to Consideration*, 29, 25.
26. *A Perswasive to Consideration*, 8.
27. Collier, *A Short View*, 108.
28. Jeremy Collier, *A Defence of the Short View of the Profaneness and Immorality of the English Stage* (1699), preface by Arthur Freeman (New York and London: Garland, 1972), 70.
29. Collier, *A Defence*, 70. Collier extends this analogy to the problematically Catholic James II to an even finer point when he writes, 'even a vicious Priest represents our Saviour, since he is God's Ambassador ... These Credentials, these Benefits, one would think, might guard him from Contempt, and make his Character inviolable' (72).
30. Collier, *A Defence*, 76.
31. Collier, *A Defence*, 72.
32. Collier, *A Perswasive to Consideration*, 8.
33. Hopes, 'Politics and Morality', 161.
34. J. G. A. Pocock, 'Modes of political and historical time in early eighteenth century England', in *Virtue, Commerce, and History* (Cambridge: Cambridge University Press, 1985), 91.
35. Pocock, 'Modes of political', 92.
36. Pocock, 'Modes of political', 92.
37. As cited in Ressler, 'Jeremy Collier's Essays', 241.
38. As Joseph Wood Krutch has noted of Collier in *Comedy and Conscience after the Restoration* (NY: Columbia University Press, 1924), 'it cannot but have been a thorn in [his] side that opposition to the stage in England had been most closely connected with the Puritans' (140). In fact, Collier was mocked in any number of pamphlets for taking a position on the stage that aligned him with his Puritan enemies. The author of *The Stage Acquitted* (London, 1699) asserts sardonically, for instance, that Collier has indeed found himself a 'fit yoke-mate' in Ridpath (48).
39. [George Ridpath], *The Stage Condemned* (London, 1698), 4.
40. *The Stage Condemned*, 9.
41. *The Stage Condemned*, 8.
42. *The Stage Condemned*, 204.
43. *The Stage Condemned*, 204.
44. For an account of the Societies for the Reformation of Manners and moral reform, see Tony Claydon, *William III and the Godly Revolution* (Cambridge: Cambridge University Press, 1996), esp. 110–21.
45. Claydon, *William III*, 120.
46. Claydon, *William III*, 120.
47. In this sense, *The Stage Acquitted* follows the precedent set in *A Letter to A. H. Esq.; Concerning the Stage* (London, 1698; rpt. in The Augustan Reprint Series; Series Three:

Essays on the Stage, 1946, introd. H. T. Swedenberg, Jr.), in which the anonymous author admonished his readers that 'Men of Probity and Learning ... are not to be mov'd by the Opinions of others no longer than those Opinions are agreeable to Reason' (3).

48. *The Stage Acquitted*, 3.
49. *The Stage Acquitted*, 17.
50. *The Stage Acquitted*, 17.
51. This position echoes *A Vindication of the Stage* (London, 1698) in which the author focuses on Collier's non-juring status and writes, 'Nay, Mr. *Collier* himself, and all others of their Principles, are more bitter and sharp Invectives against the Order, by their Refractory and Obstinate Separation from the Greatest and most Pious Part of their Brethren, than any can be writ by the most Atheistical Pen; and wound it more severely' (18–19).
52. *The Stage Acquitted*, 4–5.
53. *The Stage Acquitted*, 24–5.
54. *The Stage Acquitted*, 91–2.
55. *The Stage Acquitted*, 154–5.
56. *The Stage Acquitted*, 4.
57. *The Stage Acquitted*, 92–3.
58. *The Stage Acquitted*, 146.
59. *The Stage Acquitted*, 147–8.
60. For the seminal account of the instrumentality of conversation in the rise of the public sphere, see Jürgen Habermas's *The Structural Transformation of the Public Sphere*. For a more particular and detailed account of the rise of politeness and conversation both in politics and in the regulation of the public sphere, see Lawrence E. Klein's *Shaftesbury and the Culture of Politeness* (Cambridge: Cambridge University Press, 1994).

6

Reconsidering Theatrical Regulation in the Long Eighteenth Century

Matthew J. Kinservik

When we think of theatrical regulation in eighteenth-century England, the Stage Licensing Act of 1737 looms large, and for good reason. The banning of the non-patent theatres and the establishment of pre-performance review of play texts were harsh measures meant to silence the political opposition to Sir Robert Walpole's ministry. If the primary goal was narrowly political and short-term, the actual effects were broad and of long duration. The law was qualified and tinkered with almost from the outset, but it was not formally repealed until 1968. So when considering – or reconsidering – theatrical regulation in the long eighteenth century, the significance of the Licensing Act is undeniable.

Coming, as it did, half-way between 1660 and 1800, the law has served as a convenient marker for theatre historians and literary scholars, dividing the good drama that came before it from the bad that came after. On the one side lie *The Country Wife, Venice Preserv'd*, and *Pasquin*; on the other *The Maid of the Mill, The West Indian*, and *Douglas*. The logic behind this division is that governmental censorship inhibits free expression and, consequently, diminishes the quality of new plays. In a chapter of *The Cambridge History of British Theatre*, Judith Milhous concludes that 'The fundamental mediocrity of English drama after 1737 may be attributed directly to the suppression of competition and multiple venues imposed by the Licensing Act.'[1] I am not interested in denying this causal argument; instead, my goal is to demonstrate that it is a modern judgement that (however right it may be) has led us to disregard the contrary opinions of a number of eighteenth-century commentators about how competition and freedom from governmental oversight affect the development of drama. The widely-shared view that competition is necessarily healthy has prevented us from gaining a richer understanding of the Licensing Act and its place in the larger history of theatrical regulation in the long eighteenth century.

To understand that larger history is to regard the Licensing Act not as a product of the 1730s alone, nor as the central fact of eighteenth-century theatre, nor even as merely an anti-theatrical measure. How can we possibly regard the Licensing Act as anything but an instance of anti-theatricalism? We can do so by listening to the host of writers who were deeply committed to the success of English drama and who believed that the theatre could only flourish under the careful stewardship of the state. Among these writers are names like Thomas Rymer, Charles Gildon, John Dennis, and Aaron Hill, people whose love of theatre moved them to propose regulatory measures that anticipated (and frequently exceeded) the main features of the Licensing Act. These proposals span from the late seventeenth century right up through the 1730s, and they constitute a virtually untapped source of information on regulatory designs for the London stage. In order properly to understand theatrical regulation in the eighteenth century, we need to consider the Licensing Act as part of this neglected tradition of philo-theatrical regulatory schemes.

I. Proposals from the late seventeenth century

When the Licensing Act was being debated and passed into law, proponents and opponents of the measure engaged in a vigorous newspaper debate over theatrical censorship. This debate went well beyond the usual pro- and anti-Walpole polemics and very seriously considered the historical, literary, and theoretical justifications for the law. Ministerial writers waged a more vigorous and confident campaign in favour of the law than their opponents did against it.[2] This is partly because Opposition writers were distracted by fears of press censorship as well as theatrical censorship. But the ministerial writers also had the better of the argument because they deftly (and perhaps earnestly) deployed the arguments of many philo-theatrical proposals from the previous fifty years that insisted the stage could only flourish under the direction of the state

One writer for the pro-ministerial *Gazetteer* minced no words, insisting that 'Comedy was perfected rather by the Regulations made by the Laws of the State, than by any Rules invented by Poetry.'[3] As proof of this claim, he asks 'whether there be any Comparison between the rude Farces of our last ten Years, and the Comedies that were written in the ten Years that preceded them?' It would be easy to dismiss this question with a laugh, for who would now place *The Beggar's Opera* and Fielding's plays below those of the decade before them? Another *Gazetteer* writer specifically condemns Fielding's most recent work for its monotony: all are topical rehearsal plays that lack standard plots. Instead of aspiring to the condition of lasting art, these works are designed merely to make money and score satiric hits and, in the process, they debase the stage.[4] What the English stage needs, these writers suggest, is state oversight and the curtailment of the number of venues to ensure quality control.

Perhaps these sentiments are not surprising, given that they were voiced by ministerial writers as part of a campaign to justify the Licensing Act. But genuinely surprising are the authorities these writers cite in support of their claims. There is a predictable reliance on pat histories of the Athenian and Roman stages, showing how the Ancients produced great drama as a result of state control. But the *Gazetteer* writers also rely on more recent authorities. After surveying Ancient drama, one turns to the English stage and writes:

As to the History of the *English* Stage, I do not Care to Concern myself with it, since I know that I can say nothing Satisfactory about it. If it was never under any Regulation, as the *Craftsman* suggests, till the Civil War, it certainly deserved it; for, as Mr. *Rymer* has fully shewn, some of our most admired Plays are scandalously immoral, and Mr. *Dryden* himself has confessed, that *Rymer's* Criticisms are just.[5]

The following day, another Gazetteer writer offers nearly a full column of quotations from L'Abbé d'Aubignac's *Praticque du Théâtre* (1657), which he calls 'a work excellent in its Kind, and faithful in its Deductions from Antiquity, and that gives the truest Idea *what the Stage really is*, of any Book now extant'.[6] By citing the likes of Rymer, Dryden, and the Abbé d'Aubignac, the ministerial writers distance themselves from anti-theatricalists such as Jeremy Collier, William Law, and William Prynne. The rhetorical effect is to situate the Licensing Act in a philo-theatrical tradition of comparing the modern to the Ancient stage, finding the modern inferior, and offering proposals to restore the stage to its former glory.

D'Aubignac's *Praticque du Théâtre*, published in London in 1684 as *The Whole Art of the Stage*, is anything but an anti-theatrical text.[7] However, it ends with a brief 'Project for Re-establishing the French Theater' that makes the Licensing Act look like a timid half-measure. In it, he calls for two companies to be supported by the state and for an overseer to review all stock plays and license all new ones. If the overseer finds objectionable material, he may 'reform' the play text to make it suitable for the stage. These proposals correspond to the main features of the Stage Licensing Act, but d'Aubignac's project went further. He proposes that there always be a police presence in the theatres to make audiences behave (172–3); he prohibits single women from acting, going so far as to require widowed actresses to marry after six months of mourning (173–4); and he calls for the construction of a new theatre on an Ancient model, segregating commoners from their betters (176).

For d'Aubignac, the decline of the French stage began with the death of Cardinal Richelieu, whom he regards as a statesman/patron on the ancient model. Richelieu's protective stewardship of the French stage resulted in great drama because he understood that the state needed to both subsidize the stage and censor the content of plays. Underlying both functions is the anxiety that a commercial stage must necessarily be a debased one. The Ancients knew better: they have left no bad plays to posterity 'because all their Plays were seen and examin'd by the Magistrates; and besides, their Poets were not mercenary, but wrought for glory as much as for gain, there being a solemn Prize appointed for their reward' (170). The title page says that Richelieu commanded d'Aubignac to write the treatise and the translator's preface says that Richelieu intended to make d'Aubignac the overseer of the stage, but died before he could do so. As a result, d'Aubignac was left to lament how ignorant actors are deciding the repertory without consulting learned judges. They are performing before unruly audiences for money, no one is being edified, and no drama of lasting quality is being produced. For d'Aubignac, this is a situation that can only be remedied by state intervention.

As with so much French literary theory and criticism of the era, d'Aubignac's ideas were influential in England. The anxiety about the profit motive diminishing the quality of plays and the call for pre-performance review of play texts are the hallmarks of English philo-theatrical proposals of the long eighteenth century. At the beginning of this period, both of these ideas get expressed most effectively by Thomas Rymer, especially in *A Short View of Tragedy* (1693).

Because of the attack on Shakespeare, Rymer's book has long been notorious, and few modern scholars have bothered to set Rymer's heresy aside and take a careful look at the broader argument. But when we do so, the results are surprising. Recently, Paul Cannan has argued that *A Short View* is best characterized as 'nothing less than an appeal for increased government support – and regulation – of the English stage'.[8] Collier deliberately echoes Rymer's title a few years later, but this should not make us assume that Rymer shares Collier's anti-theatricalism. Rather, by looking back to the *Praticque du Théâtre*, we see the tradition to which Rymer properly belongs. Curt Zimansky lists d'Aubignac's book as one of the four most important influences on Rymer's thought, and the debt becomes especially clear when we compare their attitudes toward the regulation of the stage.[9] Like d'Aubignac, Rymer considers the Athenian stage to be an appropriate model for modern drama. Whereas the former suggested building an Athenian-style theatre in Paris, the latter proposes the reintroduction of the chorus into English tragedies. Admiration for the Athenian state and stage leads both men to link excellence in drama to strict governmental oversight and munificent subsidy.

For Rymer, the relationship between the state and the stage was a mutually beneficial one: the stage flourished and the state was strengthened by the values inculcated by the drama. Indeed, he says that in Athens 'the Tragedies of *Æschylus, Sophocles*, and *Euripides* were enroll'd with their Laws, and made part of their Statute-Book' (170). But this happy situation is not inevitable. In a more telling passage, Rymer equates the drama not with laws, but with weaponry, insisting, 'The Theatre is a Magazine, not to be trusted, but under the special eye and direction of a Virtuous Government' (111). Rymer singles out Ancient Athens and modern France as exemplars, and his admiration for Richelieu's stewardship of the French stage is exceeded only by d'Aubignac's (116–17). Rymer has, I believe, Richelieu's example in mind when he proposes that a council be formed to police the content of plays, calling it a 'Committee of Lay-Bishops', whose job is to 'see that no Doctrine be there broached, but what tends to the Edification, as well as to the Delight of the Spectators' (110).

Following the example of the *Praticque du Théâtre*, Rymer's text contains features that subsequent English proposals regularly recycle: it venerates the Athenian stage and calls for pre-performance censorship of play texts, and state support for, and regulation of, the stage. As Cannan has noted, although Rymer has been much maligned, his regulatory suggestions were not completely singular. In the preface to *Momus Triumphans* (1688), Gerard Langbaine calls for a great man to imitate the example of Cardinal Richelieu and recommends that the nobility and gentry edify themselves by reading d'Aubignac and Rymer's *Tragedies of the Last Age*.[10] In the preface to *Prince Arthur*, Sir Richard Blackmore picks up on Rymer's martial metaphor for the stage, asserting that '*The Stage was an Outwork or Fort rais'd for the Protection and Security of the Temple, but the Poets that kept it, have revolted, and basely betray'd it, and what is worse, have turn'd all their* Force *and discharg'd all their* Artillery *against the Place their Duty was to defend.'*[11] In this case, the stage is a weapon turned against the church, not the state, but the metaphor is the same. Also like Rymer, Blackmore suggests that the content of plays, like that of sermons, should be approved and licensed before production:

> *And 'tis great Pitty that those in whose Power it is, have not yet restrain'd the* Licentiousness *of [the stage], and oblig'd the Writers to observe more* Decorum. *It were to be wish'd that Poets, as Preachers are in some Countries, were paid and licens'd by the State, and that none were suffer'd to write in Prejudice of Religion and the* Government, *but that all such Offenders as* publick Enemies *of Mankind should be silenc'd and duly punish'd.*

Blackmore differs from other philo-theatrical projectors by displaying a flash of anger and calling for the punishment of wayward playwrights. Most others consider the state of drama to be bad, but not necessarily seditious or profane, and, operating as they are in the realm of hypothesis, they assume that their systems are foolproof and hence offer no mechanism for punishment. But the obvious debts to Rymer persuade me that Blackmore's preface belongs to the philo-theatrical regulatory tradition, not the anti-theatrical one.

In establishing this tradition, I do not want to suggest that all lovers of the stage believed as Rymer did. For instance, one of the *Gazetteer* writers claims that Dryden confessed that Rymer's criticisms were just, implying that Dryden approved of the regulatory scheme offered in *A Short View*. Was this the case? Dryden was impressed by *The Tragedies of the Last Age* (1677), and in a letter to Dennis in the 1690s he confesses reverence for Rymer's learning in *A Short View*.[12] But Dryden took specific exception to Rymer's regulatory proposals. In the dedication to *Examen Poeticum* (1693), he absolutely rejects the idea of a committee of 'Lay-Bishops' to censor the content of plays. Rather than regarding it as an earnest proposal for improving the stage, Dryden sceptically characterizes the proposal as coming 'under the pretence of reforming the stage'.[13]

Certainly Dryden's opinion has more weight with us nowadays, especially because we read his words with the knowledge of the Collier controversy that followed shortly after Dryden wrote them. As Robert D. Hume has recently reminded us, Collier's *Short View of the Immorality, and Profaneness of the English Stage* (1698) never actually calls for the abolition of the stage.[14] His opponents characterized his book, as Dryden did Rymer's, as offering merely the pretence of reform. However, it is certainly worth noting that Collier was savvy enough to attempt to link his anti-theatrical screed to the tradition of philo-theatrical regulatory proposals. His title intentionally recalls Rymer's, and a sarcastic rhetorical style also links the two. But we would be wrong to place Rymer and Collier in the same tradition. Although Collier never calls for the abolition of the stage, his motives were clearly anti-theatrical, whereas Rymer cannot be seriously characterized as an enemy of the stage.

After the publication of Collier's book, it naturally became the touchstone for future proposals to regulate the stage. One of the most important early replies is Nahum Tate's 'Proposal for Regulating the Stage & Stage-Players' (1699). This manuscript proposal, written in Tate's hand, was submitted to Lambeth Palace in February, 1699, and probably received by Archbishop Tenison.[15] Coming months after the publication of Collier's book, and being handed by the Poet Laureate to the Archbishop of Canterbury, this proposal was designed as a philo-theatrical alternative to Collier's anti-theatrical assault. The proposal is very brief and unoriginal. Tate calls on the government to appoint a supervisor of plays who will review the texts of old and new plays prior to performance. Later this position silently becomes plural, so he evidently envisioned something like what happened with the Licensing Act when an Examiner and Deputy Examiners were employed by the Lord Chamberlain to do the censorial review. Some plays could be banned outright, but those 'capable of being reform'd' would be sent back to the authors for the necessary corrections. If the authors are dead, then the supervisor could appoint qualified writers to make the corrections.

A vaguely-worded section follows, proposing that 'sufficient Encouragement be for such Persons as make ye Aforesaid Alterations &c like-wise for supervisors, and Penalties upon Default in Either' (177). I take this to mean that the supervisors and correctors are to be paid for the labours, which seems reasonable enough, but the last clause threatens penalties for both if they fail to do their jobs. This is surprising because it includes the government supervisors and correctors along with living playwrights. Tate may have included this with an eye to the recent history of the Lord Chamberlain's ineffectual calls for increased scrutiny of play texts on the part of the Master of the Revels and the theatrical companies.[16] Whereas most projectors are sanguine about the efficacy of state oversight, Tate knows better and threatens the censors themselves with punishment. He adds that these penalties should be 'so adjusted as to have due Effect, as long as any Stage shall be Permitted' (177). The prospect that the theatres might be abolished seemed real to Tate and reminds us that he submitted this proposal in the context of Collier's assault. And at the end of the proposal, Tate returns to this idea, suggesting that his proposals will be a benefit to the public and to the stage itself, 'if Continued: for whether the present stages be Reform'd or Silenc'd is left to the Government, but the one or Other is Absolutely necessary' (178).

If the hint of abolition is new, the call for pre-performance censorship of play texts is not. Unlike Rymer and Blackmore, Tate does not explicitly equate the supervision of the stage with clerical oversight, but by submitting the proposals to the Archbishop of Canterbury, he implicitly suggests as much. Tate's proposal is brief, running just over 150 words, and this brevity begs many questions, not the least of which is what motivated him to offer it. Collier's book must have been a factor, and the immorality of the drama (as opposed to aesthetic deficiencies) seems to be his main target. In any event, he concludes that the theatrical status quo is intolerable and so the government must either reform 'the present stages' or abolish them, which suggests deep discontent with both the commercial stage and the official oversight of it.

II. Proposals from Dennis and Gildon

Where Tate is silent on the exact deficiencies of Drury Lane and Lincoln's Inn Fields, others are more voluble. Chief among them are John Dennis and Charles Gildon, and in their criticism one finds an abundance of suggestions about how to reform the stage. In the spurious seventh volume of Rowe's *Shakespeare*, published in 1710, Gildon revives many of the elements of philo-theatrical regulation that we've already seen. In his dedication, he encourages the Earl of Peterborough and Monmouth to follow the example of the Ancients and 'rescue the *Drama* from *private interest*, to the *public Service*'.[17] The opposition between public service and private interest suggests that a commercial stage is incapable of producing quality drama, an idea Gildon returns to repeatedly in his criticism and that virtually every eighteenth-century projector takes as axiomatic. In the prefatory 'Essay on the Art, Rise, and Progress of the Stage', Gildon judges English drama to be inferior to the work of the Ancients because England's statesmen have left the direction of the stage to commercial entrepreneurs (lix–lx). Athens, by contrast, was too wise to let the public stage be operated as private enterprise. Rome, which was tardy in imposing theatrical regulation, is inferior to Athens, but superior to England.

Gildon concludes this historical survey, and the essay itself, with a declaration that must have pleased Rymer and the ghost of d'Aubignac:

> Thus have I given my Thoughts on *Shakespear*, laid down the Rules of true Judging, and judicious Writing, and given a View of the Rise and Progress of the *Drama* in *Greece, Rome*, and *England*; from whence it is plain that the only Way to make the Stage flourish is to put it into the Hands of the Magistrate, and the Management of Men of Learning and Genius; which wou'd once again bring this admirable Art to its Old Perfection.

The insistence that good drama can only be the consequence of tight state control is anathema to modern ideas about the freedom of expression and the market-place of ideas. Indeed even suggesting that state censorship was welcomed by most eighteenth-century English men and women is contentious. But if we want to understand theatrical regulation in the long eighteenth century, we need to recognize that sentiments like Gildon's were widely shared.

Gildon's comments in the seventh volume of Rowe's *Shakespeare* serve as the outline to a much more elaborate proposal he offered nine years later in *The Post-Man Robb'd of His Mail* (1719). In a series of seven letters, Gildon offers a 'Proposal for establishing an Academy Royal for Sciences' that he promises will be more 'reasonable', 'extensive', and 'reputable ... than that propos'd to Cardinal *Richelieu*'.[18] Extensive it is; reasonable it is not. To start with, Gildon estimates that the academy will need between eight and ten thousand pounds per annum, but asserts that this money will come neither from the crown nor from a new tax. It will be composed of one hundred members. Sixty are to be honorary members, chosen from the ranks of nobility, the House of Commons, and the universities. Forty 'beneficiary' members will be selected on the basis of talent and will be divided between ten dramatists, ten historians, and twenty miscellaneous members, five of whom should be clergymen who are good at math or otherwise distinguished by polite learning (310–13). Because the academy will be charged with preserving the purity of the English language, membership is restricted to native-born Englishmen.

Gildon clearly loved this scheme for he goes into great detail about the method of electing members, their great seal and its motto, their ceremonial robes, their communal dining schedule, and so on. Obviously this is a wholly delusional plan, but it does express the ideals of a man who thought carefully about how to improve his culture. As with his other writings, in this proposal the stage is considered the most important cultural institution, and so it gets the most attention. The other elements of this 'Total Academy' aside, Gildon's elaborate plans for regulating the stage are sufficient to give us a sense of the larger proposal.[19] Academy playwrights are obligated to produce at least one new play every two years. No playwright will be admitted to the academy until he is at least twenty-eight years old, the minimum age he imagines one must be to have attained a mature judgement of life and letters. Gildon parenthetically explains that this last item is an instance of his modern leniency, playwrights in Athens having been required to have attained the age of at least thirty before having their works performed. Academy plays will be produced anonymously, in order to avoid partisan judgements, and, unlike in the patent theatres, academy playwrights will enjoy benefits on the third and sixth day, free of house charges (the daily operating costs that theatrical managers regularly deducted from the proceeds of a benefit performance). They will receive one-eighth of the house's profit every time it is performed after the sixth day, a provision that is not limited to the continuous first run, but instead extends to the life of the playwright. After the playwright's death, the profits go to the academy alone (335). Each academy playwright is to be guaranteed a minimum salary of £100 per annum (338).

Predictably, the form and content of these plays will be strictly regulated by the academy. New plays must be either comic or tragic, but not both, and with few exceptions, they must be limited to English subjects (335–6). Playwrights will be encouraged to write plays praising virtuous and illustrious English families, as determined by a censorial committee chosen from among the members. This committee will also pass judgement on the morality and aesthetic quality of plays (337–8). In rendering these judgements, the committee must be guided by 'right Reason', not public opinion, which he characterizes as 'the Fantastic Tast of some particular Enthusiasts' (338). Elsewhere, Gildon asserts that the censorial functions of the academy will make it superior to the Académie Francaise, which was too cowed by the popularity of *Le Cid* to censure it (315, n. a). The English academy will be more muscular in influencing public opinion and taste, serving as a necessary counterweight to the demands of commercial audiences. In a weekly address, the academy will explicate the moral of the plays to be acted the following week, a mechanism designed to exercise a prior restraint on the interpretive powers of the audience, just as the censorial committee exercises a prior restraint on the imaginative powers of the playwrights.

As one modern commentator has noted, 'In its power to regulate the literary output of England, Gildon's academy approaches that of the most absolute modern state.'[20] Indeed, its nationalist emphasis and bureaucratic structure do resemble Soviet-era censorhip. In *Peri Bathous* (1728), Pope offers a burlesque proposal called 'A Project for the Advancement of the Stage' that promises to be 'more ample and comprehensive' than the 'Scheme which Mr. *D-nn-s* and Mr. *Gildon*, (the two greatest Criticks and Reformers then living) made publick in the Year 1720'.[21] The proposal Pope alludes to has never been located (if it ever existed), but judging from Pope's mock proposal, he had Gildon's academy scheme in mind when writing it. The satire is richly deserved, but if Gildon is unique for the extravagance of his proposal, he was not the only one to suggest a royal academy for literature or a censorial committee to regulate the drama. In 1721, a correspondent to *Pasquin* calls for a royal academy and, in the 1730s, many writers called for a censorial committee to regulate the stage.[22] Indeed, in the years between Gildon's proposal and the passage of the Licensing Act, we begin to see, if not a flood, at least a steady stream of regulatory proposals that lie somewhere between the ambitions of the two.

John Dennis (inevitably) weighed in on the low state of drama time and again during the first decades of the eighteenth century, frequently proposing ways to regulate the stage more effectively. Dennis's most substantive proposals come in the context of his dispute with the Drury Lane management over the timing of the premiere of *The Invader of his Country* (1720) and Lord Chamberlain Newcastle's actions against Steele and Cibber in 1720. Cibber's control of the repertory and Steele's dispute with the Lord Chamberlain aroused Dennis's anger and led him to consider how the regulation of the stage had become so laissez-faire in England, and how it might be improved. Dennis's suggestions are infinitely more practical than Gildon's, but they share many of the same concerns and assumptions about the dangers of a commercial stage and the theoretical benefits of a more censored one.

In the dedication to *The Invader of his Country*, Dennis calls on the Lord Chamberlain to exercise his ancient rights and prerogatives and improve the theatrical repertory. Newcastle, as a man of rank, has the education and taste to choose plays; Cibber, an ignorant and mercenary actor, has not.[23] In *The Characters and Conduct of Sir John Edgar* (1720), Dennis elaborates on this point, arguing that actors cannot be good judges because 'they have not the Understanding and Judgment of ordinary Gentlemen; because they have not had their Education' (2. 184). To put such persons in charge of managing a theatre royal is an absurdity. Motivated by a 'sordid Love and Greediness of Gain', actor/managers are the last persons who should exercise theatrical power. Instead, power should reside only in those with 'Birth' and 'Education' (2. 185). This was once the case in England. Contrary to so many of his contemporaries, Dennis saw the late seventeenth century as a theatrical golden age when the court dictated the theatrical repertory and showed the ignorant players and audiences what to applaud: 'For Forty Years after the Restoration, it was always under the Regulation of my Lord Chamberlain. And during those Forty Years, it flourish'd exceedingly' (2. 188). Rymer would beg to differ, but Dennis was committed to this point, returning to it again at greater length in *The Causes of the Decay and Defects of Dramatick Poetry* (1725).

For Dennis, the stage can only regain its former glory if the Lord Chamberlain takes a more active role in shaping the repertory and in encouraging other noblemen to interest themselves in the welfare of the stage. In *The Causes of the Decay and Defects of Dramatick Poetry*, he makes two proposals that strike at the heart of the commercial stage. First, he suggests that the theatrical patents be made into revocable licences. Second, these licences are valid only if the theatres produce two new comedies and two new tragedies each year. If more than two of each is submitted to the theatres, the managers must submit the scripts to 'men of known understanding in these affairs, and Honour and Impartiality to make the choice' (2. 279).

Dennis's last proposal for regulating the stage comes in his philo-theatrical treatise, *The Stage Defended* (1726). In it, he strikes many of the same notes as his previous work, but adds a proposal that an annual prize of £200 be given to the authors of the best new comedy and tragedy (2. 303). He does not specify who the judges for the prize will be, except to say that they must be impartial, and he specifies that the prize money comes in addition to the benefit nights, implying that these plays will be produced at the patent houses. Coming just a year after his more ambitious proposals in *The Causes of the Decay and Defects of Dramatick Poetry*, perhaps the latter scheme is a continuation of the former.

Although not nearly as elaborate as Gildon's academy, in Dennis's piecemeal proposals we see the same distrust of the commercial stage, an insistence that men of learning need to choose the repertory, a minimum quota for new play production, a form of public subsidy for playwrights, and a firm belief that the stage can only flourish under active state regulation. But whereas Gildon would run roughshod over cherished English liberties, Dennis is more sensitive. Like all contributors to the philo-theatrical regulatory tradition, Dennis praises the examples of Greece and Rome for showing how wise and free states involved themselves in the theatre.[24] Tellingly, Richelieu and absolutist France are left out as unworthy models for British liberty and drama.[25] Their Jacobite counterparts in England, specifically Jeremy Collier, William Law, and Arthur Bedford, have exerted 'pretended Zeal' against the low and immoral state of English drama (2. 321). But they have done so on the orders of their Jacobite masters with the goal not of reforming the stage, but in order to 'divert the People of *Great Britain* from their Real Danger, by giving them Alarms in a wrong Place' (2. 321). For Dennis, political liberty is a necessary precondition for the exercise of state regulation of the theatre. But English liberty can turn into license without proper restraint. When criticizing Cibber's control over the Drury Lane repertory, Dennis characterizes him as a tyrant and calls on Lord Chamberlain Newcastle to check his absolutism in the spirit of the constitutional settlement.[26] Dennis's proposals for regulating the stage are mindful of the necessary balance between license and liberty. All are accommodated to the English legal system, and, appropriately, he never presents them as part of a unified, grand scheme. When we have trouble appreciating how English men and women could reconcile their love of liberty with state censorship, we could hardly do better than to look at the work of John Dennis.

III. Proposals of the 1730s

One of the surprising things we discover by looking at the philo-theatrical proposals for regulating the stage is that their number and ambitions intensify in the 1730s, the very decade that theatre historians point to as an ideal. But whereas modern eyes regard that decade as a happy time of vigorous competition and freedom from state oversight, many contemporary theatre lovers saw it as a time of crudely commercial and senseless drama badly in need of state intervention. In fact, the fat profits enjoyed by Drury Lane in the previous two decades and negative effect of the patent companies' cartel on the theatrical repertory have been amply documented.[27] With the benefit of hindsight, it is easy to see that the London stage was better off with multiple venues competing with the patent houses during the 1730s. But this historical fact does not mean that we should ignore the proposals for more governmental regulation in that decade. Those proposals do not depart significantly from those of the previous forty years, but coming at a time when the stage was temporarily freed from the restriction of the patent theatre duopoly and when many new plays were being performed, these proposals are all the more striking.

The anonymous *Proposal for the Better Regulation of the Stage* (1732) reads like a palimpsest of the proposals of Gildon and Dennis. Dedicated to the managers of the patent houses, it begins with a complaint that 'the Stage has been so long enslave'd under the Tyranny of Players', and singles out Colley Cibber for particular censure.[28] Like Dennis, he complains that playwrights are cheated out of the money they deserve by ignorant and mercenary players. Also like Dennis, he employs political metaphors to represent this situation as inimical to English liberty. He calls the actor/managers at Drury Lane 'Licensers' and 'magisterial Censors' (22, 27) and represents their dominion as tyrannical and illegal:

> Nothing has been more complain'd of than the Licencing of the Press, and nothing has been more contended for, by all Parties, than the Delivery of it from that Incumbrance: These Gentlemen hang the same dead Weight upon the Stage, and play the *Licencers* even without an Act of Parliament to give them Authority ... Why should Poets be the only Slaves in the Community, or why should Dramatical Entertainments be liable to the Shackles that every other Branch of Science is deliver'd from. (28–9)

The author says that players are usurpers who have seized control of the playwrights' money and the government's censorial prerogatives. Just as Dennis represented a reinvigoration of state censorship as a blow for liberty, he says that this situation 'calls aloud for Regulation; if not, let Oppression continue' (28).

Like both Gildon and Dennis, the author believes that a liberal education is necessary to produce great drama. Actors are motivated by 'Interest' and 'Business', but the stage needs arbiters with more 'generous Views, and Noble Principles' (23). As with nearly every other philo-theatrical proposal, this one looks to Greece and Rome as societies which understood this imperative and wisely prevented the stage from becoming a private enterprise. He wonders why Englishmen, who imitate the Ancients in so many other ways, have never bothered to emulate them in this (19–20).

To lead the way, he proposes the construction of a new theatre, which he estimates will cost at least ten to twelve thousand pounds, the money to be raised by subscription (30–2). Unlike the patent houses, which he would leave as they are, this new theatre will be devoted not to making a profit, but to improving learning and politeness. It will be directed only by 'Men of Quality, and Figure, Taste, and Fortune', those who possess the means to subsidize the theatre, and the learning and impartiality needed to operate it (31). He cites the example of the Royal Academy of Music and says that if Italian songs are worth the notice of English noblemen, then the British theatre surely is, too (32).

The noble subscribers would elect a governing committee every year. This committee would exercise control over every aspect of theatrical operations, and its authority would be absolute. Authors must submit play texts for pre-performance review, and any changes the committee recommends are mandatory (33). This censorial oversight is imagined as having purely aesthetic goals. The committee is called 'the Deputies of the *Muses*' and its work is characterized by words like 'Beauties', 'polish', and 'improve' (34). Rather than suffer artistic deprivations under this system, playwrights would reap benefits. In passing judgement on plays before public performance, the committee 'would habituate Men's Minds to Criticism of the noblest Kind, and give them a just, and familiar Insight into all the Beauties of such Entertainments' (37). This indoctrination is instructive and ennobling. Playwrights will glory in the committee's approbation and be more confident on opening night, knowing that they would not be subject to an audience's negative judgement because the committee's approval would act as a screen (36). For their part, audiences will be stunned by the sublime and rational entertainment they find at this theatre and will gain collective 'Decency', 'Composure', and 'Elegancy' as a result (37).

There are also more practical benefits to playwrights who submit works to this theatre. House playwrights are to receive an annual pension of £100, and there will be plenty of such authors because the theatre will be obligated to produce at least four new plays a year (one before Christmas, three after). If there are enough qualified authors clamouring to have their works produced, the theatre will accommodate up to a dozen of them, producing a dozen new plays a year and paying out £1,200 in authorial pensions alone (40). House playwrights will also be invited to places on the governing committee and be allowed to pass judgement on the play texts submitted for approval (41). The subscribers, and especially the committee, will be hailed as 'Restorers of Learning' in a motto placed over the portico on the theatre's façade.

Although not as grand as Gildon's academy, this proposal is at least as expensive and delusional. It is also similarly explicit about the goals of disciplining the behaviour and judgement of audiences and about indoctrinating playwrights into a system of shared values and aesthetics. But like Dennis, the anonymous author represents his regulatory interventions as not just consistent with, but necessary to, English liberty. By calling for a new theatre, the proposal promises not to impinge upon the property of the patentees, but the goal is clearly to render the patent theatres contemptible and unprofitable. This last goal is one shared by the decade's other major philo-theatrical projectors, Aaron Hill and William Popple.

In a number of issues of *The Prompter*, Hill and Popple advocate more vigorous regulation of the theatres in order to change them from what they are, 'schools of public effeminacy and corruption', into what they could be, 'academies of courage, good taste, and humanity'.[29] Hill and Popple were seriously unhappy with the state of the theatres in the mid-1730s, most of which they considered to be incompetently managed, resulting in a disgraceful repertory, bad acting, and poor sets and costuming. Hill started *The Prompter* in November 1734, in order to pressure the theatres to improve their practice. A few months later, when he first heard of Sir John Barnard's bill to limit the number of theatres, he urged parliament to exploit the opportunity and enlarge the ambitions of the bill. In *The Prompter* 38 (21 March 1735), he recommends that instead of reducing the number of theatres, parliament pursue the nobler goal of reforming the old ones.[30]

Hill was perfectly content to see the government assume a more active role in the regulation of the theatres and, in urging parliamentary action, he refers to the 'political use' the public stage could be put to (40). However, in the first number of the periodical, he explains that he chose to call it *The Prompter* because he considered 'censor' to be a presumptuous and arrogant title (1). The name of the journal appeals to him, he says, because he enjoys watching the careful efficiency with which theatrical prompters regulate playhouse business. For Hill, theatrical regulation always refers to efficient and enlightened management, not restraint; good stewardship, not punitive censorship. Soon after urging parliamentary action, he realized that the narrow ambitions of Barnard's bill were not likely to be expanded, and that the bill was being lauded by anti-theatricalists. In *The Prompter* 42 (4 April 1735), he says that he is 'sorry to see a return of that Puritanical moroseness of principle' that animated the likes of Prynne and Arthur Bedford. He is equally dismissive of partisan political censorship, arguing that it is counter-productive: 'Faction, and the turbulence of party division, can have no enemy more powerful than pleasure and a disposition to amusements of fancy or genius' (47). What we see in *The Prompter* 42 are the concerns of a philo-theatrical projector that an opportunity to improve the stage might become merely a reactionary, anti-theatrical measure.

In *The Prompter* 45 (15 April 1735), Popple takes up the issue and proposes that a bill to regulate the public taste should supplant Barnard's bill. This new bill should create a board of arbitration to resolve disputes between the actors and managers and to decide the repertory (51–3).[31] A contemporary pamphlet attributed to Samuel Richardson likewise calls for an independent board to dictate the repertory and improve the aesthetic and moral quality of the stage.[32] Two days later, a correspondent to *The Grub-Street Journal* of 17 April 1735 made a proposal very similar to Popple's, but stipulating that each arbitrator be given 'a handsome salary to be pay'd by the state' and that the board be given the power to censor play texts prior to performance. The previous month a more ambitious proposal was offered in *The Grub-Street Journal* of 27 March 1735. This plan curtailed the power of theatrical managers to decide the repertory, empowering the government to step in if good plays were being rejected. It also envisioned the government arbitrating disputes between authors and managers and between managers and actors. Like Barnard's bill, it proposed restricting the number of theatres, but it added a provision regulating admission prices. And a year before that, the same journal published a proposal for parliament to establish an academy that would review all new plays and distribute £2,000 annually to deserving playwrights.[33] Another proposal for a board of arbitration comes in a petition to parliament on the occasion of Barnard's bill by the actors at Drury Lane and Covent Garden. After agreeing that the stage needs to be 'put under proper *Regulation*', the actors complain that the bill would put them completely at the mercy of the patentees acting as a cartel.[34] In order to prevent arbitrary rule, the actors propose that the legislature create a board to arbitrate disputes, specifying 'That the Arbitration thereof shall be placed in the Hands of some *Men* of *Fortune, Learning,* and *Ability*' (173). All of these proposals (with, perhaps, the exception of Richardson's) are philo-theatrical, and the appearance of so many of them in the 1730s is significant. This is the decade that theatre historians praise as an all-too-brief time when the number of theatres expanded and the amount of new plays increased.

In the event, Barnard withdrew his bill precisely because he wanted it to remain a narrowly anti-theatrical law that simply restricted the number of theatres. When Walpole introduced an amendment to give the Lord Chamberlain more control over the stage, Barnard let the bill drop.[35] After this happened, Hill felt free to explain why the law was bad and what really needs to be done. In *The Prompter* 53 (13 May 1735), he says, 'I am for applying the axe to the root of the evil' of bad theatre. 'Instead of confining the royal permission to those hands in which it has already been treated so scandalously, I am for depriving, in the first step, those *licentious* as well as *licensed* incumbents of a power they have appeared so unworthy of' (61). In the following number, he archly revises this suggestion and says that parliament should amend Barnard's bill so that instead of limiting the number of theatres, it simply limits the repertories of Drury Lane and Covent Garden to farce and pantomime; the unlicenced theatres would be limited to rational, spoken-word plays. Hill explains that 'Such an act must be approved, even by the patentees, because it would leave to those Sampsons of the stage the lovely Delilahs they are so fond of and bestow nothing upon their rivals but what they have made it a choice to part with already' (61). Frustrated by the missed opportunity for real reform, Hill turned to satire in his own writing and warm praise of Fielding's late satiric drama, which, as we know, was to be cut off by the Stage Licensing Act, a law that embodied everything Hill feared.

IV. 'Regulation' versus 'censorship'

The question that confronts us as we turn to the Licensing Act is how we choose to regard the law and the justifications of it by ministerial writers. By looking at the law in the context of the philo-theatrical regulatory proposals leading up to it, we see strong rhetorical similarities between those proposals and the Licensing Act and its defences. And despite all the (quite justified) characterizations of the law as a repressive measure that had an enormous and detrimental impact on English drama, the Licensing Act is much more modest in scope than several of the regulatory schemes that preceded it. We also need to remember that the managers of the patent theatres supported the measure as a healthy corrective to a theatre system that had gone seriously awry. Charles Fleetwood's petition to the Lord Chamberlain begins by stating that he is 'sensible the audacious liberties, taken by those who consult their own private lucre, preferable to all other considerations, makes it now highly necessary, to suppress immediately this pernicious growing Evil'.[36] This support was self-serving, to be sure. The rest of Fleetwood's petition shamelessly begs protection for his '*Large Interest, & Property*' in the Drury Lane patent. But Fleetwood is able to make these claims, as the *Gazetteer* writers are theirs, because the values and assumptions that inform the philo-theatrical regulatory proposals were widely known and shared by 1737. Also worth noting is that the anti-theatrical tradition was still alive and well, as Barnard's bill and Hill's regret over the 'return of that Puritanical moroseness of principle' show. The Licensing Act was meant to be something more than Barnard's Bill and something less than the dreams of Rymer, Gildon, and the author of *A Proposal for the Better Regulation of the Stage*. And that is what it was.

Vincent J. Liesenfeld has argued that although the effects of the law on dramatic literature and theatre were great, the actual motivations for it were mainly political. Moved by a desire to suppress political satires and to show George II that he was still firmly in control of the political state, Walpole sought passage of the law for both its practical and symbolic value. Liesenfeld does not make an absolute distinction between the 'literary' and the 'political', and today scholars are even more cautious about distinguishing between the two realms. But this is not new. Many critics and artists in the eighteenth century also insisted that literature and politics were necessarily interrelated. The problem is that, for us, this knowledge leads to an absolutist support for free speech, whereas, for them, it led to the conclusion that speech must necessarily be regulated by the government. This is because we see the stage as an important site of resistance to and critique of the state, while they saw it as an important prop to the state. These are antithetical conclusions resulting from a shared premise.

Until the past few decades, scholarly work on censorship provided little help for tackling this problem. Censorship was conceived as a negative exercise of state power over writers who naturally wish to criticize the state in literary texts. These assumptions are still widely held in literary studies, even by historically-minded scholars who grant that previous eras were not theoretically opposed to some forms of state censorship. But in recent years scholarly definitions of censorship have begun to include many other models, locating the source of censorship beyond the working of the state and (following Foucault) defining censorship's effects as both productive and negative. Before, censorship could be located in legal codes and state bureaucracies, but now it potentially turns up in every speech act. In a 1994 special issue of the *PMLA* on 'Literature and Censorship', Michael Holquist asserts that 'To be for or against censorship as such is to assume a freedom no one has. Censorship *is*.'[37] Holquist writes of a 'hortatory censorship' that is interested not in silence, but in prescribing expression, a concept and a term that have obvious application to the philo-theatrical regulatory proposals I have described here.

Although this new approach has usefully expanded our conception of censorship, this expansion has itself presented some problems. Recognizing that censorship can come from the government, the market, the schools, and the prevailing aesthetics is important. But increasingly the field of censorship studies is widening so greatly that there is little consensus about how and why to label an act as 'censorship.'[38] Beate Müller captures the problem best:

> Analysis of censorship does not become simpler if censorship is identified everywhere; and I doubt whether opening up the flood-gates makes the endeavour more rewarding. The widening of the concept reminds me of the fate of intertextuality. This term, too, became all-encompassing, and we were warned at the time that a concept that is so universal that one cannot even imagine its absence or its counterpart, must needs be of little heuristic potential. I suspect that 'censorship' has become such a cheap currency because of its rhetorical value which guarantees attention.[39]

Müller's point is a good one. If we label every critical judgement or repertory decision an act of censorship, then we cheapen the term and begin to lose the ability to draw distinctions when they really need to be drawn.

In the case of the eighteenth-century London stage, it is important that we make such distinctions because few of the writers I have discussed here bothered to do so. We see the anonymous author of *A Proposal for the Better Regulation of the Stage* labelling the actor/managers at Drury Lane 'magisterial Censors'. Gildon, Dennis, and others do this as well when they bemoan the commercial nature of the stage and the educational deficiencies of the patentees. Patentees exercise market censorship in their repertory decisions when they sacrifice aesthetic merit in favour of a play's commercial potential to draw in ignorant audiences. Fielding effectively dramatizes this grievance in *The Author's Farce* (1730), especially in the scene in which Marplay (Cibber) and Sparkish (Robert Wilks) arbitrarily alter a new play that Luckless has brought them. When Fielding finally gave up on the patent theatres and focused his energies on his Haymarket company, he playfully called it the Grand Mogul's Company, casting himself as an Eastern tyrant whose rule was absolute.

Aaron Hill is almost alone in eschewing the term 'censor' for himself and in refusing to characterize repertory decisions as censorship. Instead, he carefully distinguishes his philo-theatrical calls for reform from anti-theatrical calls for restraint. In doing so, he displays a rare sensitivity to the power of the term 'censorship.' Hill calls for parliamentary action to reform the theatres, but he refrains from offering ambitious plans for an academy or a censorial committee to oversee the stage. (Popple, by contrast, proposes the board of gentlemen to arbitrate personnel matters and make repertory decisions.) Hill seems more interested in a 'softer' regulation than most of the other projectors. In contemporary censorship studies, proposals like his have been called 'constitutive' censorship because the censorial effects are produced not by bureaucratic mechanisms, but by controlling aesthetic and critical discourse. The plans offered by Rymer, Gildon, the author of *A Proposal for the Better Regulation of the Stage*, and many others are quite different. By envisioning grand academies, the construction of new theatres, or boards of 'Lay-Bishops' to censor play texts, these proposals qualify as 'structural' censorship.[40] Dennis falls somewhere between the hard 'structural' and the soft 'constitutive' camps. He hesitates to recommend ambitious new schemes, but he tends to favour the top-down dictation of aesthetic and critical standards. These texts all belong together in a tradition of philo-theatrical regulatory proposals, but they feature quite divergent definitions of censorship under the more ambiguous term 'regulation'.

One thing they all agree on, however, is the propriety of state intervention as a means of counteracting the damaging effect of market pressures on the quality of drama. If forced to choose between a theatre system dominated by the free market and one dominated by the state, the authors surveyed here would unanimously choose the latter. In this sense, they all favour the imposition of a structural state censorship over the market censorship that they felt was ruining the English stage. This seems uncomfortably antithetical to our modern devotion to freedom from governmental intervention. But if we examine modern attitudes more closely, we see that we share important common ground with the projectors of the eighteenth century.

At the beginning of the last century, Watson Nicholson's *The Struggle for a Free Stage in London* railed against the Licensing Act's protection of the patent monopoly, but Nicholson was perfectly comfortable with the censorship of play texts, regarding it as a necessary check upon the free competition of the 1730s, which he says mutated into 'avowed license for all sorts of extravagances' in the absence of governmental control.[41] He warmly praises Hill's and Popple's calls for the reformation of the stage, and, indeed, his notion of a 'free stage' is similar to theirs. It is not a stage free from governmental oversight; rather, it is a stage free from the degradations of the profit motive (67n, 84–5). At the same time that Nicholson was lamenting the historic misuse of the public commodity of theatre for private ends, the leaders of the London stage were making a similar case. In a report of 1904, William Archer and H. Granville Barker wrote that, at present, the theatre 'is being patronized and petted, hardly, many may think, to its greatest advantage. But if it is ever to become a part of our civic institutions, its working conditions must be organized as becomes a healthy and stable civil service.'[42] As much as anything written by Rymer and Gildon, the likening of the theatre to a 'civil service' seems strikingly inartistic and unromantic. Conceptualizing the theatre as a civic institution relies on much the same set of assumptions that animated the philo-theatrical projectors of the eighteenth century. Nevertheless, the report was signed by the likes of Sir Henry Irving, J. M. Barrie, and Arthur Wing Pinero, who conclude that 'Having read and carefully considered this scheme for a National Theatre, we desire to express our belief that such an institution is urgently needed.'

Why was a National Theatre urgently needed? Because its supporters felt that the commercial imperatives of the Victorian theatre produced a repertory that was popular, but not meritorious. The basic logic behind the National's inception owes much to the philo-theatrical regulatory tradition of the eighteenth century, when advocates for theatrical reform also felt the situation required urgent redress. The emphasis on the civic role of the theatre and the call for generous state subsidies are familiar enough. But even more striking is the early vision of a repertory dominated by uncontroversial classic authors like Shakespeare and Molière while 'all plays of the class which may be called disputable', such as Ibsen and Shaw, are 'purposely excluded' (4). Of course, just because the National excluded these playwrights from the repertory does not mean that their works were suppressed; they just were not invited to be part of the state-sponsored guardian of theatrical quality.

Before we dismiss the report of 1904 as being simply a quaint relic from an increasingly distant era, we should be mindful of the gloomy assessments of the contemporary American theatre. A recent *New York Times* story lamented the fact that the Broadway revival of three American classics (*Who's Afraid of Virginia Woolf, The Glass Menagerie,* and *A Streetcar Named Desire*) will all be done under British, not American, direction. Because of commercial pressures, American theatre is dominated by musicals and spoken-word plays with very small casts. As a result, American directors seldom gain extensive experience with ambitious productions involving large casts on big stages. Their British counterparts are luckier. The producer of *Who's Afraid of Virginia Woolf* explained the phenomenon by saying:

> I can give you the answer in two words: subsidized theater. London's big theater-producing entities like the National Theater and the Royal Shakespeare Company provide vastly more opportunities for directors to work with the classics. You can't compare doing a big show in the Olivier Theater with doing a three-character play at Playwrights Horizons. It's not the same thing.[43]

The founding of the National Theatre in England is commonly considered a twentieth-century saga, but in many ways it was the long-delayed culmination of the philo-theatrical regulatory schemes first proposed in the long eighteenth century. The current discontent with the American stage suggests that this tradition may extend to another continent and another century.

Notes and references

1. Judith Milhous, 'Theatre companies and regulation' in *The Cambridge History of British Theatre, Vol. 2, 1660–1895,* ed. Joseph Donohue (Cambridge: Cambridge University Press, 2004), 125.
2. For a full discussion of the debate and the establishment of the Licensing Act, see Matthew J. Kinservik, *Disciplining Satire: the Censorship of Satiric Comedy on the Eighteenth-Century London Stage* (Lewisburg: Bucknell University Press), ch. 3.

3. *Daily Gazetteer*, 10 June 1737. The essay is signed 'R. F.' for R. Freeman and has been identified as the pseudonym of Ralph Courteville. For the attribution, see Robert L. Haig, *The Gazetteer, 1735–1797: a Study in Eighteenth-Century English Newspaper* (Carbondale: University of Southern Illinois Press, 1960), 7.

4. *Daily Gazetteer*, 6 July 1737.

5. *Daily Gazetteer*, 10 June 1737.

6. *Daily Gazetteer*, 11 June 1737.

7. Francois Hédelin, Abbé d'Aubignac, *The Whole Art of the Stage* (London, 1684; rpt. New York; Benjamin Blom, 1968). All citations will be given parenthetically in the text.

8. Paul D. Cannan, '*A Short View of Tragedy* and Rymer's Proposals for Regulating the English Stage', *The Review of English Studies*, 52 (2001): 207–26. Quotation appears on p. 208.

9. *The Critical Works of Thomas Rymer*, ed. Curt A. Zimansky (New Haven: Yale University Press, 1956), xxix. Subsequent citations to Rymer will be given in the text.

10. *Momus Triumphans: Or, the Plagiaries of the English Stage* (1688; rpt. New York: AMS Press, 1970), A3v–A4r.

11. Sir Richard Blackmore, *Prince Arthur* (London, 1695), Preface.

12. For an overview of the relationship between Dryden and Rymer, see Zimansky, xxxiii–xxxix; and Earl Miner, 'Mr Dryden and Mr Rymer', *Philological Quarterly*, 54 (1975): 137–51. For the letter to Dennis, see *The Letters of John Dryden*, ed. C. E. Ward (Durham, NC, 1942; New York, 1965), 71–2.

13. *Of Dramatic Poesy and Other Critical Essays*, ed. G. Watson, 2 vols (London, 1962), 2.161.

14. Robert D. Hume, 'Jeremy Collier and the Future of the London Theater in 1698', *Studies in Philology*, 4 (1999): 480–511.

15. Lambeth Misc. 933, Art. 57. For a complete transcription of the proposal, see Joseph Wood Krutch, *Comedy and Conscience after the Restoration*, rev. edn (New York: Columbia University Press, 1949), 177–8.

16. For more on these decrees in the context of the Collier controversy, see Kinservik, *Disciplining Satire*, 25–6, and 259, n. 15.

17. *The Works of Mr William Shakespeare. Volume the Seventh* (1710; New York: AMS Press, 1967), A6v.

18. *The Post-Man Robb'd of His Mail* (1719) reproduced in *Foundations of the Novel*, ed. Michael F. Shugrue (New York: Garland, 1972), 305.

19. For an overview of the venture and its origins, see G. L. Anderson, 'Charles Gildon's Total Academy,' *Journal of the History of Ideas*, 16 (1955): 247–51.

20. Anderson, 'Charles Gildon', 249.

21. *The Art of Sinking in Poetry*, ed. Edna Leake Steeves (New York: Russell & Russell, 1952), 86

22. For *Pasquin*, 21 January 1724, see John Loftis, *The Politics of Drama in Augustan England* (Oxford: Clarendon Press, 1963), 77, n. 1.

23. *The Critical Works of John Dennis*, ed. Edward Niles Hooker, 2 vols (Baltimore: The Johns Hopkins Press, 1943), 2. 176. Subsequent citations to Dennis' work will be given parenthetically in the text.

24. See esp. *The Stage Defended* in Hooker, *The Critical Works*, 2. 319–21.

25. In this attitude, he shares common ground with Steele. In *The Theatre*, Number 3 (9 January 1720), Steele offers a facetious eleven-point proposal for reforming the stage, which is his way of jabbing at Lord Chamberlain Newcastle, whom he accuses of having French absolutist designs on the stage. See *The Theatre*, ed. John Loftis (Oxford: Clarendon Press, 1962), 10 (eleven-point plan); 5 (Newcastle's absolutist aims).

26. Dedication to *The Invader of his Country* in Hooker, *The Critical Works*, 2. 180.

27. See, for instance, Judith Milhous and Robert D. Hume, 'Profits at Drury Lane, 1713–1716', *Theatre Research International*, 14 (1989): 241–55; and Robert D. Hume, *Henry Fielding and the London Theatre, 1728–1737* (Oxford: Clarendon Press, 1988), chapter 1.

28. *A Proposal for the Better Regulation of the Stage* (London: J. Peele, 1732), 1. Subsequent citations will be given parenthetically in the text.
29. *The Prompter*, ed. William W. Appleton and Kalman A. Burnim (New York: Benjamin Blom, 1966), 40. Subsequent citations will be given parenthetically in the text.
30. Exactly which theatres Hill refers to in the phrase 'old ones' is unclear. It may mean all of the theatres operating in the spring of 1735, or it may just refer to the patent houses. His praise of Henry Giffard's theatre in Goodman's Fields two weeks later, in *The Prompter*, no. 42 (4 April 1735) suggests that he means to imply all theatres.
31. Popple returned to the idea of a board of arbitration in nos. 93 and 94, where he imagines the board not as a government-sponsored panel, but as a voluntary association of noblemen concerned for the improvement of the stage (97–100).
32. The anonymous pamphlet is called *A Seasonable Examination of the Pleas and Pretensions of the Proprietors of, and Subscribers to, Playhouses, Erected in Defiance of the Royal Licence* (London, 1735). For the attribution to Richardson, see Alan D. McKillop, 'Richardson's Early Writings – Another Pamphlet', *Journal of English and Germanic Philology*, 53 (1954): 72–5.
33. *The Grub-Street Journal* proposals are all described in Hume, *Henry Fielding and the London Theatre*, 197, n. 99. See also Vincent J. Liesenfeld, *The Stage Licensing Act of 1737* (Madison: University of Wisconsin Press, 1984), 32. A facetious proposal of this sort is offered in *The Craftsman*, no. 140 (8 March 1728/29). By contrast to these plans, the proposal by 'Dramaticus' to establish a theatrical college as a 'means of perfecting Theatrical Entertainments' seems timid. See *The Gentleman's Magazine*, 3 (1733): 338.
34. For a complete transcription of the petition, see Liesenfeld, *Stage Licensing Act*, 172–3.
35. For a discussion of Barnard's bill, see Liesenfeld, *Stage Licensing Act*, 23–59.
36. Quoted in Liesenfeld, *Stage Licensing Act*, 190.
37. Michael Holquist, 'Corrupt Originals: the Paradox of Censorship', *PMLA*, 109 (1994): 14–25; quotation appears on 16.
38. For a discussion of this problem, see Robert C. Post, 'Censorship and Silencing,' in *Censorship and Silencing: Practicalities of Cultural Regulation*, ed. Robert C. Post (Los Angeles: The Getty Research Institute, 1998), 1–12.
39. Beate Müller, 'Censorship and Cultural Regulation: Mapping the Territory,' in *Censorship & Cultural Regulation in the Modern Age*, Critical Studies, Vol. 22, ed. Myriam Diaz-Diocaretz (Amsterdam and New York: Rodopi, 2004), 1–31; quotation is on 10.
40. For a discussion of 'constitutive' and 'structural' censorship, see Sophia Rosenfeld, 'Writing the History of Censorship in the Age of Enlightenment', in *Postmodernism and the Enlightenment: New Perspectives in Eighteenth-Century French Intellectual History*, ed. Daniel Gordon (New York: Routledge, 2001), 117–45.
41. Watson Nicholson, *The Struggle for a Free Stage in London* (1906; New York: Benjamin Blom, 1966), 42.
42. Quoted in Judith Cook, *The National Theatre* (London: Harrap, 1976), 1.
43. Charles Isherwood, 'The New British Invasion,' *New York Times*, 27 February 2005, sec. 2, p. 8.

Part 3
Theatre beyond London

7
Theatre for Nothing

Michael Dobson

I begin with a quotation from Frederick Reynolds' play *The Dramatist* (1789). We are at Lady Waitfor't's house in Bath, where Marianne is trying hard to captivate the attention of the eponymous dramatist, Mr Vapid:

> *Mari.* . . . I have been reading 'All for Love.' – Pray, sir, do you know anything about plays?
> *Vapid.* Know anything about plays! – there's a question.
> *Mari.* I know so much about them, that I once acted at a private theatre.
> *Vapid.* Did you? Then you acted for your own amusement, and nobody's else: what was the play?
> *Mari.* I can't tell.
> *Vapid.* Can't tell!
> *Mari.* No, – nobody knew, – it's a way they have.[1]

What Marianne displays here is not an affectation of modish negligence but an abrupt volte-face, as she drops the subject of amateur dramatics like a hot coal on realizing that it merely irritates the professional playwright she fancies rather than identifying her as a possible soul-mate for him. From declaring herself an eager devotee of this fashionable hobby – which has already been endorsed by her friend Ennui as 'a new mode of killing time'[2] – Marianne, within two lines, disowns the practice completely ('it's a way *they* have'). So too does Reynolds, and the remainder of *The Dramatist* has nothing further to say about 'private plays' at all.[3] According to this piece of commercial theatre, performed at Covent Garden, only the professional stage really counts: outside the West End, dramatic activity is so meaningless that its practitioners may as well not even know which plays they are acting. We professionals know what matters and what doesn't, and Marianne here learns a lesson which most professional theatre historians seem to have absorbed long ago.

I am extremely flattered to find myself sharing a volume with the likes of Judith Milhous, but my own approach to the subject of eighteenth-century theatrical economics is on this occasion slightly different from hers, since my current work on this subject is making me slightly anxious that in investigating the prices of drama in the Restoration and eighteenth century, we have sometimes assumed too much about what those prices can really tell us about its value and its meanings. I am at the moment trying to supplement my own extant work on the canoniz-ation of Shakespeare within Anglophone theatre and culture, which has hitherto concentrated on the professional theatre and commercial print, by assembling a history of non-professional Shakespearean performance. This project has been taking me into corners of Georgian theatre history into which no one seems to have been peering much since Sybil Rosenfeld published *Temples of Thespis: Some Private Theatres and Theatricals in England and Wales, 1700–1820* in 1978,[4] and towards productions of *All for Love* and other works about which no stage historian to date seems to have had much more to say than did Marianne in Reynolds' play. I am interested in the boom in non-professional drama experienced in the 1770s and 1780s, and especially so in a double bill of David Mallett's *Elvira* and Macnamara Morgan's *Florizel and Perdita: or, The Sheep-Shearing* mounted by an all-female cast in 1774, in the Cathedral Close in Salisbury. (The same year, incid-entally, saw another all-female group performing Arthur Murphy's *Zenobia* and Henry Carey's *Chrononhotonthologos* in a specially-converted summer-house in a garden in Lymington, in Hampshire.)[5] I want to read the surviving traces of the Salisbury production alongside one of the period's more substantial comment-aries on non-professional theatre, Richard Cumberland's essay 'Remarks upon the Present Taste for Acting Private Plays' (1788), to consider what it is that all these apparently anomalous non-professional shows make visible about the place of drama in eighteenth-century culture more generally. I hope to suggest that some of the comments made at the time about theatre done for nothing are at least as telling about the ways in which drama was understood to work as those made about theatre done for money.

One effect of working simultaneously on Shakespeare and on the eighteenth century is an unusual level of awareness about how different the priorities of stage historians seem to be within different chronological sub-fields. It's partly, of course, a matter of how much evidence survives and from what sorts of sources, but even so the study of Renaissance drama and of Restoration and eighteenth-century drama are very different intellectual animals. Work on the emergent commer-cial theatre of the late sixteenth century has sought to understand it within a whole range of other theatrical and quasi-theatrical activities, from folk plays and jigs up through legal moots, civic pageants, aristocratic entertainments, academic plays and the court masque, all traces of which have been extensively edited and studied. Work on the commercial theatre of the late seventeenth century and thereafter, however, has been much more heavily focused on the patent houses. The great monumental reference work on English theatre down to 1642 is the series *Records of Early English Drama*, which brings together, city by city and county by county, the surviving documentary evidence of a whole culture's engagement with performance in all its forms and at all its levels. The great monumental refer-ence work on English theatre from 1660 to 1800, by contrast, is still *The London Stage*, which placed alongside *Records of Early English Drama* looks much more like an expanded official history of a single business, the duopoly of the Theatres Royal. It's as if the second instalment of a history of sexuality had dwindled into merely a history of prostitution: suddenly all the attention shifts to people in the West End doing it for money. The participation of James I and his family in dramatic activities at court, often involving theatrical personnel such as Ben Jonson, is well-nigh central to many critical interpretations of Renaissance drama: the fact that the future George III and his siblings, tutored by the actor James Quin, performed Addison's *Cato* at Leicester House in 1749 barely warrants a footnote in most accounts of the eighteenth-century theatre. This is the case even though we still have the impressive and illuminating prologue which Prince George spoke on the occasion, and even though we still have an apocryphal remark made by Quin on hearing King George's first oration from the throne which ought to affirm drama's place at the very heart of Augustan culture: 'Ah! I taught the boy to speak.'[6]

What the histories of both periods of theatre share, however, is a narrative concerned above all with commercialization, commodification and professionalization: the master-story is usually what Muriel Bradbrook called the rise of the common player.[7] In its positive variants, this is a history, like that of authorship, which celebrates how artists achieved independence and self-determination, freed from demeaning patronage into a direct, meritocratic relationship with their audiences. (In its negative variants, this is a history either of how folk-culture was privatized and sold back to the people who used to own it, or of how a class of bourgeois entrepreneurs managed to launder their avarice by professing a devotion to public culture.) Theatre historians of the Renaissance, writing about a time when even Shakespeare's troupe the King's Men were still nominally a group of royal servants, are obliged to take James I's in-house theatricals seriously as drama; but their colleagues in the eighteenth century, describing a period when Drury Lane had long been an established and profitable business, can dismiss the young George III's thespian adventure as mere amateur theatricals. In this context, especially given the increasing anxiety of theatre historians themselves to be identified as card-carrying professionals rather than dilettantes, Quin's relationship with the Hanoverians looks like an embarrassing throwback, but in fact the theatrical economy of the eighteenth century was far more mixed between what we would define as professional and as non-professional than this would imply. As performers for hire, actors throughout the period seem to have been just as willing to work for individual wealthy patrons as for the Theatres Royal, participating extensively and lucratively, for example, in country-house productions: William O'Brien, most notoriously, took advantage of his position as salaried elocution teacher and co-performer to the Fox household at Holland House by eloping in 1764 with Lady Susan Fox Strangways (reportedly a brilliant Alicia in Rowe's *Jane Shore*).

Given the publicity this scandal attracted, we should be less surprised that some contemporary critics of amateur drama, rather than dismissing it, as does Mr Vapid, as a leisure activity indulged with an embarrassing inattention to the real expertise of professionals, are much more alarmed about the contact this activity promotes between aristocrats and the commercial stage. The one full-length play inspired by the amateur theatrical boom of the 1770s and 1780s, for example, James Powell's *Private Theatricals* (1787), manages simultaneously to celebrate the elopement of an heiress with an actor and to decry amateur drama as a moral menace. In the main plot Alderman Grubb, father of the ingenue Lucy, has recently married a second and very stage-struck Lady Grubb, who has spoiled his country estate by putting a marble bust of Shakespeare in his favourite grotto and renaming his hermitage 'Prospero's Cave'. Furthermore, she has built a stage in his drawing room, and with the help of some London professionals she is busily rehearsing *Romeo and Juliet*, with Lucy as Juliet. It is at last revealed even to Alderman Grubb that the actor who has been playing Romeo is really Juliet's forbidden suitor Villars, but in the inevitable reconciliation scene, Villars, forswearing his assumed profession with contempt, assures his future father-in-law that he is neither a mere actor, nor a supporter of Lady Grubb's chosen hobby:

> Forgive, Mr Alderman, the stratagems of love, I am no player (tho' in its proper place, an enthusiast in the art). And I think the present rage for theatrical private performances, has grown to a ridiculous pitch, and is productive of much mischief to the morals of society, by admitting the loose and profligate (who are a scandal to the age) into the houses of virtue, whose reputation and honor they generally endanger.[8]

Powell, the writer of this pious speech, is careful to make a comparable social disclaimer for himself: scorning to be identified either as a professional playwright or as a corrupted dilettante, he has this play 'Printed and sold by the Author', namely 'James Powell (of the Custom House)' – neither self-styled thespian nor theatrical hack, but a civil servant and a gentleman. Appropriately, his play has never been given either a professional production or a semi-professional one, but has only been performed once, by a blamelessly disinterested local amateur group (appropriately, in that former hotbed of Augustan amateur drama, Lymington, in 2000). As Powell recognizes, proper toffs shouldn't need professional help: as the sycophantic *Salisbury Journal* remarked in 1773, praising another all-amateur cast in terms which neatly invert the assumptions of Mr Vapid, 'theatrical merit is not confined to those who make the stage their profession ... it does not so much depend on practice, as on the taste and judgement of the performers.'[9] (The performers in this instance, undeterred by Lady Susan's elopement, were the Fox family.) We might compare here the touch of snobbery with which a 1788 prologue, spoken at Mr Fecter's private theatre in Dover, compares theatres to ships: identifying this one as a pleasure-boat 'securely anchor[ed] under Shakespeare's Cliff', the prologue refers disparagingly to the

> High Admirals of the Dramatic main,
> The *Covent-Garden*, and the *Drury-Lane*;
> Ships of vast bulk and burden, those – and made
> To stand the various strokes of war – and *trade*.[10]

One factor, however, which complicates the sense we have inherited of the boundaries between properly commercial, professional theatre and the rest – whichever side of the dividing line one privileges – is the extent to which both professional and non-professional theatre were involved in the peculiar cultural economics of the charity performance. When is a commercial performance not a specimen of trade? When the profits are all to go to a good cause – even though, of course, under the benefit system, some of the objects of this disinterested charity were the performers themselves. The pervasiveness of eighteenth-century drama's professed commitment to higher social goals than economically self-sustaining entertainment should at very least blur our sense of what is professional and what is amateur: the same rhetoric informs philanthropic prologues spoken on the London stage as those written for fund-raising productions mounted by the East India Company in Madras, or those staged at Kilkenny in Ireland, where for nearly twenty years from 1802 onwards a group of local gentlemen, assisted by hired professionals, staged annual seasons of she-tragedy and Shakespeare for the benefit of the local poor. In all of these instances the charitable purpose of the entertainment is presented as redemptive: a performance of Isaac Bickerstaff's *The Padlock* in February 1788, for example, in aid of 'an Asylum for Female Orphans', promoted Madras from being at the exotic fringe of a nascent empire to somewhere able to outdo the homeland itself: 'Tonight, superior ev'n to *Britain*'s boast, / Virtue's own Drama crowns this favoured coast.'[11] A prologue to Otway's *The Orphan* spoken in Kilkenny in 1802 goes one better, claiming that the audience for this production has its virtuous motives completely undiluted by any expectation of entertainment whatsoever. This semi-professional cast are consequently able to disown most of the criticisms directed at professional and amateur theatre alike:

> 'Tis not the curious that comes here today;
> 'Tis not the lounger, idling life away;
> 'Tis not the beauty, to display her charms,
> Nor vain coquet, nor fop with folded arms;
> Not to see *us*, you've heard so oft before,
> Nor hear old Otway, you've heard o'er and o'er;
> No – 'tis benign *Compassion* brings you here,
> Swells the fond sigh, and prompts the willing tear,
> And Pity, guardian of the helpless poor,
> Leading her *vot'ries* to our grateful door.

The extent to which this prologue registers a continuing anxiety about the morality of deliberately stimulating unreal emotions is underlined by its conclusion, which does much to gloss the preference of many charitable theatrical enterprises for plays heavily invested in the power of pathos:

> *Fictitious* tears bid *genuine* cease to flow,
> And our *feign'd* sorrows lighten *real* woe.
> Thus shall our Motives justify our Means,
> And Mercy consecrate these well-meant scenes.[12]

The most intriguingly hybrid instance of theatre in a good cause, though, is probably that provided by the seasons mounted at the John Street theatre in New York towards the end of the American rebellion, when the management of the theatre was taken over by the British military authorities. (The receipt books and published accounts from this venture are now preserved at the New York Historical Society.) The management was military, as were the principal performers, and all the bouncers (on occasion, detachments of infantry served as extras in *Richard III* as well as doing police duty around the auditorium); but the actresses, wig-makers and others were civilians, and were paid at quite good civilian rates. Over and above the overheads, the profits from these shows were laid out 'in CHARITY to the Widows and Children of the . . . Regiments', as well as to 'Refugees' and 'Inhabitants of N. York and its Environs': in 1782 the theatre paid out more than a thousand pounds in this way.[13] Comments in the local press suggest that the shows themselves – stock pieces such as *Othello, Macbeth, Richard III,* and Garrick's *High Life Below Stairs* – managed quite successfully to resemble their West End avatars: but did this constitute military theatre, or civilian? Commercial, or charitable? Amateur, or professional? The categories don't quite fit, and they probably won't help us think further about what these plays meant at this time and in this place.

So how are we to approach genuinely 'private' public performances, played to audiences present by invitation only? Let me at last return to Wiltshire, and my instance of theatre for nothing, that all-female *Elvira* and *The Sheep-Shearing,* which had no charitable purpose at all and which orthodox theatre history, invested in professionalization and box-office takings, has hitherto consigned almost to oblivion. It's another point at which I am perhaps unduly conscious of the differences between studying Renaissance drama and eighteenth-century drama: if anyone had left evidence that a provincial group had staged a play based on *The Winter's Tale* before 1642, by now it would all have been minutely assembled and reproduced and indexed, and it would doubtless be the subject of several monographs, and the relevant information would now be accessible on the open shelves of most of the research libraries that count. But the surviving evidence that a provincial group actually did stage *The Sheep-Shearing* in 1774 – constituting the first recorded all-female production of a Shakespearean play – was only brought together in a single work as recently as 2002, and it is primarily a work of musicology, most interested in the occasion as a pioneering English instance of public harp-playing.[14] The nearest thing even to an attempt to gather this material before then was made in 1958, in the relevant pages of Arnold Hare's book *The Georgian Theatre in Wessex*: this volume isn't as easy to find as it might be, and it sends one off into the pages of *The Salisbury Journal* and *The Bath Journal,* the letters of the first Earl of Malmesbury,[15] and various Victorian local histories of Salisbury.

The story this evidence tells is as follows. In late 1769 one Mr James Harris of Salisbury (known as 'Hermes' Harris after his book on linguistics), whose diplomat son later became the first Earl of Malmesbury, encouraged his two daughters Louisa and Gertrude to expand the dramatic parlour-games in which they engaged with family friends into a full-scale production of William Whitehead's tragedy *Creusa* (adapted from Euripides' *Ion*), with the pastoral *Daphnis and Amaryllis* as an after-piece. Harris had almost certainly attended the performances of Dryden's *All for Love* and Aaron Hill's *Zara* given by the Fox family and their friends in a hand-somely converted barn at nearby Winterslow House in 1766 and 1768 respectively, and the series of occasional domestic productions which he sponsored in Salisbury between 1770 and 1782 must in part be seen as emulations of the Foxes' theat-rical enterprise (which itself revived in the 1770s). The Salisbury productions were different in two important respects, however: firstly, as befitted the relative status and means of the Harrises at this time, they didn't use a full-scale theatre building but only the Chapel Room, above St Anne's Gate in the Cathedral Close, fitted up with a three-foot high stage, a small orchestra pit and sufficient benches and chairs to seat about fifty people. Secondly, instead of showcasing the sons of the family as well as the daughters, and serving as part of their training in rhetoric, the Harris family performances, with the eldest son James already away on govern-ment service abroad, featured only the daughters of the house and their friends. The predominantly teenaged cast of *Creusa*, performed in January 1770, was all-female, though a number of men assisted in different capacities: Harris himself was active behind the scenes, a Cathedral canon called Dr Stevens conducted the band for the afterpiece, and the chorus for *Daphnis and Amaryllis* was swelled by one Mr Parry (bass) and two borrowed cathedral choristers (soprano). (Mrs Harris, incidentally, took the same view as Mr Fecter on the rival merits of amateurs and mere tradespeople: 'the orchestra consists of a proper band for the Pastorall of Daphnis & Amaryllis that I have heard rehear[s]'d, she wrote to her son, '& I will say they do infinitely better than it was performd at Drury Lane').[16] Male help was accepted with aspects of the design too: the dress worn by Gertrude Harris as the Priestess of Apollo, was, as her mother boasted, 'not design'd by either milleners or mantua makers but by herself assisted by Dr [Thomas] Warton and Mr Harris'.[17] As far as I know, this was Warton's only foray into costume design: the dress was 'taken from the antique ... white sattin, quite simple & elegant, only fasten'd by a row of large pearls round the wast[;] on her head she wears a white kind of veil & round it a row of Alexandrian laurel'.[18]

Costumes, indeed, feature heavily in all accounts of the Salisbury theatricals, and they must have played their part in the choice of plays. The classical setting of *Creusa* helped to keep the girls playing male roles within the bounds of modesty, saving them from the brazenness of breeches – 'all the *lady gentlemen*', explained Mrs Harris, 'act in Eastern dresses with long robes'.[19] This did not exempt the production from some mildly titillated comments: one Mr Tobin, for example, sent the family a poem 'On Miss Louisa Margaret Harris in the Character of Ilyssus', which runs:

> In her own beauteous form Louisa can
> Secure the heart of each admiring man[,]
> But anxious still fresh conquests to persue
> Lovely Ilyssus charms the women too.[20]

However interpreted by the lewdly-minded, the same considerations of modesty probably influenced the Lymington women's choice of *Zenobia* in June 1774, when, reported the *Salisbury Journal*, '[t]heir dresses, scenes and decorations were very good; those of Zenobia and Zelmira, exceedingly rich and elegant'.[21] It was a fairly radical decision, then, when the Harrises' next production, again all-female, opted not for ancient Greece but for medieval Spain, choosing as main-piece Mallett's *Elvira* – even if the afterpiece, *The Sheep-Shearing*, could remain swathed in a vague Hellenic pastoralism. This double bill attracted a good deal of attention, and in some quarters a mild *frisson* of scandal. A letter from Mrs Harris to her son, worth quoting at some length, is again usefully informative about the women's dresses, and makes it quite clear that the girls' outfits were seen primarily as clothes rather than as costumes, affording the opportunity to display jewels and possessions which weren't felt to be signifying the status of fictitious characters alone. One accessory, indeed, retained an obstinate life of its own:

> [Salisbury, 13 November 1774]. I have but little to send from hence[,] we are so tottaly taken up with our own theatrical business that nothing else is thought on. The ladies acted last night in their dresses to all their servants [:] a most crouded house they had [.] Though I was not admitted to the performance, I saw all the ladies [:] their dresses are fine and elegant[.] Miss Trenchard makes an excellent Spanish Ambassadeur, a fine figure and richly drest. She had a prodigious large sword, and not be[ing] accostom'd to wear it, she contriv'd, as she walk'd, to run it through a scene and damag'd it greatly.[22]

This is so much what a young lady ought to do when equipped to her surprise with a masculine sword and placed on a stage that one can hardly believe it; it's as if Miss Trenchard has modelled her behaviour on that of Hippolito, the naïve principal boy in the Restoration version of *The Tempest*. The family proper, however, made no such blunders, expertly deploying and displaying props which in part derived from the son's recent period as a diplomat in Madrid:

> Louisa has taken a sword you left here, and she manages it right [.] She is very fine in a purple Spanish dress, all the buttons Irish diamonds, a fine button and loop to her hatt, and your King of Spains picture hanging from her neck[.] The Queen (Miss Hussey) is blue and silver with a number of diamonds[;] Miss Wyndham [,] who is Elvira[,] white trim'd with pearls[.] Gertrude (the Princess), is a black Spanish trim'd with red and silver, and a great quantity of diamonds[;] it becomes her much.[23]

It's a pity that Mrs Harris is so comparatively vague about the costumes worn by those who played male roles, commenting only on their swords, though in all probability it was the swords as much as anything else which distinguished nominally male outfits from female. For the performers themselves, as loyal as befitted the first all-women Shakespearean cast to the traditions of the Shakespeare Ladies Club, these shows seem to have been first and foremost occasions for female solidarity and the celebration of female friendship, as the touching last-night poems by Louisa Harris and Miss Hinchman suggest:

> *Miss Louisa H——s, to Miss H——n, after their performing the characters of Florizel and Perdita*
>
> No more shall we with trembling hear that bell,
> Which shews me, Perdita; thee, Florizell.
> Thy brilliant eyes no more with looks of love
> Shall in my bosom gentle pity move.
> The curtain drops, and here we both remain,
> You without love, I free from mimic pain.
> Grant me this favor, though our drama ends,
> Lett the feign'd lovers still be real friends.[24]
>
> *Miss H——n's Answer.*
>
> No longer now the lover, but the friend,
> To you these lines with temper'd warmth I send;
> The first kind offer of a heart was thine,
> Deign to accept the poor return of mine.
> Hence may our thoughts, our wishes all conspire,
> In harmony, like thy sweet voice and lyre;
> May concord's sweetest note swell on till death,
> And leave us only with our latest breath.[25]

Innocently maidenly as this all sounds, the single-sex rehearsals properly quarantined against everything that was waiting to happen in Austen's *Mansfield Park* a generation later, the production's female-to-male cross-dressing did not escape criticism. The *Bath Journal* published two disapproving poems on the occasion, the first carefully timed to appear on 17 November, Queen Bess's Day. It looks nostalgically back to a time when single-sexed theatre was a male preserve:

> *On the Ladies of the Close of Salisbury now acting* Elvira
>
> In good Queen Elizabeth's reign,
>   In a decent and virtuous age,
> That they ne'er might give modesty pain,
>   No female appeared on the stage.
>
> But lo! what a change time affords!
>   The ladies, 'mong many strange things,
> Call for helmets, for breeches, and swords,
>   And act Senators, Heroes, and Kings.[26]

The following issue printed something even more hostile 'To the Ladies of Salisbury acting Elvira', this time signed 'An Old Maid':

> Happy dames, ye have found a plan
> To learn what outwardly belongs to man.
> Follow the lucky thought, encore, encore;
> The Fates decree ye never shall know more.[27]

(This malicious prophecy may in one case have come true, in so far as Louisa Harris, however advantageously displayed to the admiration of potential husbands with the harp she insisted on playing as Perdita, chose never to marry.) Loyal to its local gentry, however, the *Salisbury Journal* took a more supportive line, assuring readers that:

> Great judgement and elegance of fancy appeared in the choice of [costumes]; particularly the dresses of those who personated men; their habits were well-suited to their characters, and at the same time appeared so well-contrived, as to leave no room for censure, had they been viewed by the most evil eye.[28]

But the *Salisbury Journal* itself contributed further to the aura of transgression which attended this show, when early the following year it printed 'A RHAPSODY *by* W. B. E. *Esq.; addressed to Miss W-D-M* [Laetitia Wyndham, who played Elvira], *on seeing her in a late dramatic performance in the Close of* Salisbury' (a poem which ends with the words 'every smile proclaim'd thee Queen of Love').[29] More scandalously, the *Journal* printed an equally admiring poem on the subject by the Dean of the Cathedral himself, and not anonymously either: it appeared as '*To Miss* W-D-M, *by the* D-N *of* SARUM, *on her acting the Part of* ELVIRA.' (A whole manuscript collection of further unpublished verses written on the occasion, called 'Heliconian Trifles, on the ladies who performed male and female parts in the Private Theatricals, held in the Close of Sarum'[30] is now lost, and perhaps it's just as well). The Harrises, along with others in the congregation, were not at all pleased that the Dean's specimen (together with Louisa's own poem to Miss Hinchman and her reply) had been made public. 'Louisa has been most violently offended with the printers of the *Salisbury Journal*', wrote Mrs Harris, '. . . they have printed those [verses] the Dean made on Miss Wyndham. Tis not the thing for a Dean of a Cathedrale to be writing gallant verses to young ladies who act plays.'[31] There must have been some sort of reconciliation between performers and press, however, as in 1776 the *Salisbury Journal* was enthusiastically reporting another production by the young ladies of the Close, this time of *The Earl of Warwick* and *Cymon*. As late as 1843 a local historian remembered having seen manuscript playbills, prologues and epilogues which survived from these all-female performances in the Close, but they have long been lost,[32] and Mrs Harris's comment on the Dean's indiscretion, made in March 1775, is the last recorded word we have about the 1774 Salisbury double bill of *Elvira* and *Florizel and Perdita*.

What are we to make of all this? Arnold Hare, the event's only previous historian, speaks rather disparagingly of 'fashionable ladies who used drama to help to divert the tedious years between adolescence and marriage',[33] but there is surely more going on here than that. Most obviously, as the *Bath Journal's* disapproving correspondents register, these women were using Mallett's play, despite its script's advocacy of bashful modesty, as the vehicle for a spectacular piece of self-performance. The Dean's ill-advised poem registers this with both enthusiasm and anxiety, choosing to construe Miss Wyndham's performance as Elvira as a courtship display, a public exhibition of her marital eligibility – in fact he sounds a little concerned that this overpoweringly attractive tragedy queen in his canons' midst, with her 'beauteous form', had better be married off sooner rather than later:

> 'Tis not your mimic arts our praises gain,
> You are the very thing you seem to feign;
> No wonder that so well you act your part,
> Elvira only speaks Laetitia's heart,
> And shows your beauteous form contains a mind
> Fraught with each virtue of the fairest kind.
> To animate that form each virtue strove,
> Good sense, good nature, tenderness and love:
> Oh! may you soon perform, in real life,
> The tender mother, and the faithful wife.[34]

(This pious concluding wish might have been more respectable in 1774 if the rhyme had not obliged the Dean to put the projected motherhood before the imagined marriage.) In Mallett's play, as some may remember (if only from the scathing attack the young James Boswell published after its premiere in 1763), the virtuous lady-in-waiting Elvira has secretly married the heir to the Spanish throne, and has even secretly borne him children, before the King's ruthless second queen begins exerting pressure on her unfortunate stepson to get on with performing his political duty by marrying her daughter by a previous marriage, the Princess. So tender a mother and so faithful a wife is Elvira that she conveniently dies of grief and anxiety at the play's crisis, already exhausted by a dissimulation quite foreign to her nature, and she thus enables the Prince to remarry in the national interest. Her story, in fact, is almost identical to that of Whitehead's Creusa, whom Laetitia Wyndham had played four years earlier, another secretly married, self-sacrificing heroine of sensibility who dies to solve a dynastic problem. The Dean may be trying to praise Miss Wyndham for being properly self-identical despite indulging in histrionics, when he claims that Wyndham is the very thing she seems to feign and that Elvira only speaks Laetitia's heart, but in identifying her so thoroughly with this she-tragic paragon his poem risks diagnosing her as feminine to a pathologically operatic degree. As with Mrs Harris's account of the costumes, which recognizably remain fancy dress ornamented with the family jewels, Wyndham's role in the play is understood less as something into which she disappears than as a self-revelatory masquerade. It is worth recalling here that another amateur actress, Lady Stanhope, who appeared in *The Fair Penitent* in the Delaval theatricals in St James's in the previous decade, actually had herself painted in the role of Calista by Benjamin Wilson, surrounded by the mourning props from act 5 scene 1, and the resulting picture (later engraved) looks very like one of the fancy-portraits for which other fashionable women of the time would sit in their favourite masquerade outfits.[35] As voluntary performances like the Salisbury theatricals show, eighteenth-century drama, so far from remaining confined to the picture-frame stages of the metropolis, prescribed and informed attitudes struck, at least experimentally, by eighteenth-century people, whether would-be neoclassical kings like George III or clerical pin-ups like Laetitia Wyndham (otherwise known, as one local historian tells us, as 'the admired Miss Wyndham, afterwards the wife of Sir William A'Court').[36]

The most detailed and informed critical essay we have on this whole phenomenon, Richard Cumberland's 'Remarks upon the Present Taste for Acting Private Plays' (1788),[37] is, perhaps surprisingly, just as disapproving of productions in which well-bred young women displayed themselves on private stages as was the *Bath Journal*. 'Let the foolish parent, whose itching ears tingled with the plaudits that resounded through the theatre, where virgin modesty deposited its blushes', cautions its peroration, 'beware how his aching heart shall throb with sorrow, when the daughter *quae pudica ad theatrum accesserat, inde revertur impudica*'. What Cumberland's essay reveals above all is that even a playwright could be morally shocked by the artifices of the theatre, once no longer insulated from them by their being confined to a professional caste. Cumberland affects to resent what he describes as new competition from a class which ought to have other things to do: it used to be, he claims, that people admired a great professional actor as a prodigy, but now 'the nobility and gentry to their immortal honour have broken up the monopoly, and new-made players are now as plentiful as new-made peers'. The perceived rivalry between aristocratic amateur players and professionals is especially unfair when it comes to playing certain kinds of roles, which the nobs have been rehearsing all their lives:

> In all scenes of high life they are at home; noble sentiments are natural to them; love-parts they can play by instinct; and as for all the casts of rakes, gamesters and fine gentlemen, they can fill them to the life. Think only of what a violence it must be to the nerve of a humble unpretending actor to be obliged to play the gallant gay seducer, and be the cuckold maker of the comedy, when he has no other object at heart but to go quietly home, when the play is over, to his wife and children, and participate with them in the honest earnings of his vocation: can such a man compete with the Lothario of high life?

Seeing non-professionals doing it suddenly seems to remind Cumberland of how troublingly potent and transgressive drama can be. It isn't that the public stage is a sordidly mercenary trade only laundered by its dedication to the Muses; it's that the Muses are themselves dangerous, but can just about be excused if they are only being followed for money. The full-time, paid actor, paradoxically, is 'unpretending' – but he may be trumped in his unpretending and even unwilling performance by an aristocrat who really is what he pretends to be. Cumberland's essay ends with a plea that well-born amateur players should instead, effectively, reinvent the court masque – ceasing to imitate the stages and repertoire of the patent houses, commissioning site-specific occasional plays to be performed in their grand houses as parts of whole multi-media fetes, and generally staying away from his chosen profession altogether. But of course they didn't, and their activities should remind us, as well as him, that the eighteenth-century theatre was not only an economic matter but an anthropological one, continuous with a whole range of other signifying practices which might equally be classed, for better or worse, as showing off. In Salisbury in 1774, nobody got paid, but, whatever Mr Vapid might have said, Laetitia Wyndham got noticed. There's no such thing as theatre for nothing.

Notes and references

1. Frederick Reynolds, *The Dramatist; or, Stop Him Who Can* in Elizabeth Inchbald, ed., *The British Theatre* (25 vols, London, 1808), 20:25.
2. Reynolds, *The Dramatist*, 12.
3. At the denouement, it's true, after Vapid has eloped with Marianne and she has been revealed to be a wealthy heiress, she declares 'then, faith, Mr Vapid, we'll build a theatre of our own; you shall write plays, and I'll act them' (69), but it isn't clear whether what she has in mind is a private theatre or a public.
4. Sybil Rosenfeld, *Temples of Thespis: Some Private Theatres and Theatricals in England and Wales, 1700–1820* (London: Society for Theatre Research, 1978).
5. *Salisbury Journal*, 20 June 1774.
6. William Pitt, Lord Lennox, *Celebrities I Have Known*, 2 vols (London, 1876), 1:218–22
7. See Muriel C. Bradbrook, *The Rise of the Common Player* (London, 1962).
8. James Powell, *The Narcotic and Private Theatricals* (London, 1787), 35.
9. *Salisbury Journal*, 18 Jan 1773.
10. *European Magazine*, November 1788, 373–4.
11. *European Magazine*, 1788, 103–4.
12. *The Private Theatre of Kilkenny*, Anon. (n.pl., 1825), 5.
13. See *New York, Theatre, 1782. General Account of Receipts and Disbursements for the two last Seasons* (New York, 1782). On these seasons, see also Esther Cloudman Dunn, *Shakespeare in America* (New York, 1939), 114–19.
14. Donald Burrows and Rosemary Dunhill, eds, *Music and Theatre in Handel's World: the Family Papers of James Harris* (Oxford, 2002). Burrows and Dunhill, like Hare before them, misidentify *The Sheep-Shearing* as Garrick's *Florizel and Perdita*: the full title of Morgan's adaptation was *Florizel and Perdita: or, The Sheep-Shearing*, and the Harrises refer to it simply as *Florizel and Perdita*, but the cast list for their production (Burrows and Dunhill, 780), which includes neither Leontes nor Paulina, makes it clear that the script they were using was Morgan's 1754 version (still in use at Covent Garden, it confined itself to material taken from act 4 of Shakespeare's play), rather than Garrick's adaptation of 1756 (which also adds characters and dialogue from act 5). The Harrises' use of Morgan's adaptation is confirmed by references in their correspondence to its location, since Morgan, unlike Garrick, followed Hanmer in emending the name of Polixenes' kingdom to something more classical than Bohemia. Cf. Gertude's letter to her brother,

20 November 1774: 'I have of late been so engaged between the Spanish princess & the Bithynian clown, that I have had no leisure to act the part of Gertrude Harris which perhaps I should perform more naturally than either of the aforementioned.' Burrows and Dunhill, *Music and Theatre*, 778.

15. James Harris, *Letters of the 1st Earl of Malmesbury*, 2 vols (London, 1870). Most of the materials presented in this volume are now available in much better-edited, unexpurgated form in Burrows and Dunhill, *Music and Theatre*.

16. Elizabeth Harris to James Harris Jr, 6 Jan 1770: Burrows and Dunhill, *Music and Theatre*, 575.

17. Burrows and Dunhill, Ibid., 575

18. Burrows and Dunhill, Ibid., 575

19. Burrows and Dunhill, Ibid., 575

20. Burrows and Dunhill, Ibid., 579.

21. *Salisbury Journal* June 20 1774.

22. Burrows and Dunhill, *Music and Theatre*, 777–8.

23. Burrows and Dunhill, Ibid., 778.

24. Burrows and Dunhill, Ibid., 782.

25. *Salisbury Journal*, 27 March 1775.

26. *Bath Journal*, 17 November 1774.

27. *Bath Journal*, 1 December 1774. Mrs Harris, transcribing these poems and sending them to her son on 4 December, called them 'vile verses from the Bath Journal' and dismissed them as motivated by envy: 'You may easily imagin these verses were sent by some vinegar merchant in Salisbury who [could] nott get admitted to the performance.' Burrows and Dunhill, *Music and Theatre*, 783–4.

28. *Salisbury Journal*, 28 November 1774.

29. *Salisbury Journal*, 27 March 1775. This conclusion echoes that of Mr Tobin's 'On seeing Miss Wyndham in the part of Creusa' four years earlier: 'No more sweet Girl, attempt to play / Such cold ambitious parts / While you possess a milder sway / And reign the Queen of Hearts[.]' Burrows and Dunhill, *Music and Theatre*, 579.

30. See Robert Benson and Henry Hatcher, *Old and New Sarum, or Salisbury* (Salisbury, 1843), 582.

31. March 21 1775; Burrows and Dunhill, *Music and Theatre*, 817.

32. Benson and Hatcher, *Old and New Sarum*, 582.

33. Arnold Hare, *The Georgian Theatre in Wessex* (London, 1958), 122.

34. *Salisbury Journal*, 27 March 1775.

35. See Rosenfeld, *Temples of Thespis*, plate 3.

36. Benson and Hatcher, *Old and New Sarum*, 582.

37. *European Magazine*, August 1788, 115–18.

8
Mixed Marriage: Sheridan, Macklin, and the Hybrid Audience

Susan Cannon Harris

This is a story about three things that eighteenth-century British theatre couldn't do without: marriage, plagiarism and Irish men. Specifically, it is the story of how a marriage plot originally derived from a seventeenth-century French comedy was stolen and revised by two Irish actors who, in the process of trying to further their own careers, also managed to begin the transformation and eventual recuperation of the stage Irishman. By tracing the process through which Thomas Sheridan and Charles Macklin – and, along the way, a number of unnamed and unauthorized collaborators – adapted this plot so that it could align their own desires with the expectations of their Dublin and London audiences, I hope to contribute to our understanding of how careers and conventions circulated through the international theatrical marketplace. As I will argue, this particular history also suggests some of the ways in which marriage, as a foundational and nearly ubiquitous plot element and as a real social institution, facilitated Sheridan and Macklin's innovations and helped both *The Brave Irishman* and *Love à la Mode* succeed with their heterogeneous audiences. Finally, this piece will try to account for the role that the desires of women – as readers, as spectators and as agents in the world outside the theatre – played not only in the success of both of these plays and the shaping of this new stage Irishman, but in the conceptions of national identity being contested in eighteenth-century playhouses in both London and Dublin.

The plot in question originated with Molière and passed through the hands of William Congreve and Charles Shadwell before becoming the basis for Thomas Sheridan's foray into playwriting, *The Brave Irishman*. As the precursor to Charles Macklin's *Love à la Mode*, *The Brave Irishman* played a critical role in establishing what Michael Ragussis has identified as the 'comedic subgenre' of 'multiethnic spectacle'.[1] While I share Ragussis's interest in this subgenre as a means of staging the 'contradictory discourses about ethnicity' that were always 'in conflict and in process' in eighteenth-century Britain, my argument will suggest a somewhat different genealogy and somewhat different consequences for a genre whose business it was to confront the audience with – and eventually reconcile them to – the increasingly inescapable prospect of mixed marriage.[2]

As England became Britain and London transformed itself from a relatively homogeneous national capital into 'the center of an increasingly complex and culturally mixed nation and empire', marriage became one of the dominant metaphors for representing England's complicated relationships with its partners/possessions within the British isles.[3] Powerful as it was, marriage as a metaphor or as an institution was never uncomplicated and its invocation in this context typically produced unintended consequences.[4] The textual and performance history of *The Brave Irishman* shows how the marriage plot and theatre itself became involved in the relationship between England and Ireland and what that involvement meant – not just for England and Ireland but for the development of dramatic form and theatrical practice in eighteenth-century Britain.

Throughout the century, a stream of playwrights, performers and plays flowed back and forth between London and Dublin, connecting the spectators and patrons of the Theatre Royal in Dublin's Smock Alley with those who supported Drury Lane and Covent Garden. Though this exchange was bilateral, it was never equal. Dublin was fighting to establish itself as a major capital, but it was still in many ways a small world. London, with its larger theatre-going population and more robust economy, was a stronger draw – which may help explain why Ireland exported George Farquhar, Oliver Goldsmith and the Sheridan family and imported Charles Shadwell.[5] Nevertheless, for performers and playwrights, the potential audience for their work included spectators and patrons based in both capitals. Trying to play to that hybrid audience often became a challenge and investigating the transmission of dramatic texts from one British theatrical capital to the other has much to teach us about the interactions amongst playwrights, performers and audiences during this period of theatre history.

In Dublin, hoary repertory warhorses like Ambrose Philips's *The Distrest Mother*, Vanbrugh's *Aesop* and Nicholas Rowe's *The Fair Penitent* crossed the water and took on startling new meanings as they were drawn into the battle for legitimacy that was always being waged in Dublin's playhouses. No matter how bitterly the factions that fomented eighteenth-century Dublin's many fine theatre riots may have hated each other, one thing they shared was a fascination with the power of theatre and a common investment in theatrical conventions and customs. And, as I have argued elsewhere, the conventions and customs that governed gender identity and sexual behaviour both on stage and in the theatre became particularly useful to parties on all sides of these political conflicts as a means of naturalizing and justifying their own positions while demonizing the opposition.[6] *The Brave Irishman* gives us a chance to find out how gender norms and theatrical conventions interacted when this pattern was reversed and a piece originally produced in Ireland travelled to England. This kind of exchange happened much more rarely, especially in the first half of the century; most Irish playwrights who broke into the London market did so by moving to London and writing plays for production in London theatres.

Joep Leerssen's seminal analysis of the history of the 'stage Irishman' awarded a privileged position in Irish studies to *The Brave Irishman* by identifying it as the point at which Irish playwrights began the long, slow process of rehabilitating and eventually transcending the stock 'stage Irishman' character.[7] It is also generally agreed that the afterpiece's literary merits fall embarrassingly short of its historical and ideological significance; Christopher Murray practically apologizes for including something so 'slight and even contemptible' in the *Field Day Anthology of Irish Writing*.[8] But it is precisely because Sheridan built the piece almost entirely out of recycled materials that *The Brave Irishman* becomes a useful illustration of how the transculturation taking place in the 'contact zone' of legitimate theatre conditioned and was also limited by the shared vocabulary of dramatic conventions that connected English and Irish audiences.[9] In addition, the piece's textual history provides an unusually detailed record of the transformations that audience demands and desires forced the text to undergo as it circulated.

The Brave Irishman authorizes its violation of some of the conventions governing the dramatic treatment of Irish characters by exploiting the power of heterosexual marriage as the foundational structural element of period comedy. The play's shifting representation of the O'Blunder/Lucinda marriage engaged a complex of powerful desires and fears bound up in chronic uncertainty about Ireland's status in the commonwealth and embodied in the figure of the Irish fortune hunter. Through him, these concerns are attached to uneasiness about the economic and sexual independence of English women. The play's career suggests that Sheridan's intervention was allowed to succeed on stage outside Ireland only after it had been, as it were, liberated from authorial control – but that it was his intervention that ultimately made it possible for this plot, as it was reworked by Charles Macklin in *Love à la Mode*, to begin in earnest the 'legitimization' of this particular 'ethnic voice'.[10]

Christopher Wheatley's introduction to *The Brave Irishman* divides the evolution of the text into three major phases. Sheridan's original manuscript, according to Sheldon and Wheatley, was probably written around 1740–41; a revised manuscript was submitted to the censors before the afterpiece was performed at Covent Garden in 1755.[11] Before Wheatley and Donovan's anthology made the two manuscript versions accessible in 2003, critical discussion of *The Brave Irishman* was almost entirely based on a probably unauthorized text published in 1754 after Sheridan had fled Dublin in the wake of the *Mahomet* riot.[12] Thanks to its wide circulation, the published version of the play displaced the versions performed between 1743 and 1755; over the course of the next 40 years *The Brave Irishman* went through twenty printings in London, Dublin, Edinburgh (where it was also performed), Glasgow, Belfast and Newry and the printed text was the version performed in London after 1755.[13] Theatrical tradition has it that Sheridan never authorized the published version and that it was performed in spite of his objections.[14]

If the published edition was in fact pirated, it only served Sheridan right. *The Brave Irishman* was never an original text. In both manuscript versions, the intriguer Schemewell admits to having stolen his best ideas about how to bedevil an Irishman from a French playwright: 'Molière's Squire Trelooby has furnished me with something which I believe I have improved'.[15] A half-century of cross-cultural plagiarism nests inside that sentence. Molière never named anything or anyone 'Squire Trelooby'. He did write a farce called *Monsieur de Pourceaugnac* (1669), in which the daughter of a rich Parisian merchant conspires with her urbane lover and a small army of intriguing accomplices to prevent her father from forcing her to marry a dimwitted provincial bourgeois. In 1704, William Congreve teamed up with Vanbrugh and Walsh to adapt the farce for Lincoln's Inn Fields, reinventing Molière's dimwitted Limoges lawyer M. de Pourceaugnac as a dimwitted Cornish lawyer named Squire Trelooby. Charles Shadwell, an English playwright working in Dublin in 1720, magically transformed *Squire Trelooby* into an Irish play by moving the setting to Dublin and renaming it *The Plotting Lovers; or, the Dismal Squire.* Charles Macklin made a splash in the title role of yet a third incarnation, *The Cornish Squire*, in 1734 at Drury Lane; according to Esther Sheldon, Sheridan probably got the idea for *The Brave Irishman* from watching that production.[16] Sheridan cribbed from at least one of these adaptations, but by 1755 he was also familiar with either Molière's original or a translation.[17]

By the time Sheridan gets his chance to 'improve' this plot, then, it has already circulated through three theatrical capitals and the hands of several other playwrights. Like the other thieves, Sheridan disguises his stolen vehicle by repainting it, renaming the characters and replacing the title character he inherited with a different 'fish out of water' figure. Where M. de Pourceaugnac and Squire Trelooby are only ever the butt of everyone else's jokes, however, Sheridan evens the scales by making his protagonist local (relative to the original audience) and his setting foreign instead of vice versa. Also, O'Blunder is an army officer instead of a lawyer. This allows Sheridan to endow O'Blunder with a version of Irish masculinity which, stereotyped and limited as it was, also incorporated characteristics that made it possible for Sheridan's stage Irishman to assume the role of romantic hero.

The braggart soldier as a stock figure dates back to the days of Roman comedy and many elements of O'Blunder's character are ultimately founded on that model. Military prowess functions easily as a sign of sexual prowess; the soldier has been such a reliable source of low comedy throughout the ages precisely because when a man is swaggering about the stage with a sword hanging from his belt one is never very far from the next *double entendre*. But by naming this figure Captain O'Blunder and giving him a country estate, an assortment of Irish bulls and Gaelicisms and a brogue you could drown a badger in – and then sending him over to London to marry an English merchant's daughter – Sheridan is engaging a more complex construction of masculinity that had become marked as distinctively Irish. Until the surprise ending, O'Blunder, as far as the audience knows, is both an Irish soldier and an Irish fortune-hunter.[18]

Matthew Arnold famously characterized the Celtic race as 'essentially feminine'; and indeed, because passivity, compliance, silence and self-regulation are defined in Western culture as feminine traits, the feminization of the indigenous population is one of the more well-documented and widespread effects of imperial rule. However, Ann Rosalind Jones and Peter Stallybrass have recovered an older and complementary imperial construction that dates back to the Elizabethan conquest of Ireland: the hyperviolent Irish male who is *so* ungovernably masculine that he can only be controlled through the application of extreme force.[19] Both constructions emerge as a means of managing the Irish man's capacity for violent resistance to imperial rule. If the feminization of the Irish man helps foreclose the possibility of active rebellion against an established colonial regime, the hypermasculine Irish man comes in very handy when it's time to justify the use of force in order to establish – or re-establish – said colonial regime. Throughout Britain's history imperial discourse has sustained both constructions of Irish masculinity, privileging one over the other depending on the situation.

The figure of the Irish fortune hunter incorporates both constructions of masculinity without reconciling them. From one perspective, the Irish fortune hunter is a sexual predator whose exploitation of vulnerable women represents the threat of rape encoded into that sixteenth century version of the Irish rebel as hypermasculine and hyperviolent. But from a different angle, the Irish fortune hunter is just another exploitable natural resource – a consumable object who relinquishes his masculinity when he submits to being bought, used and traded. Depending on the context, one of these aspects might become dominant; but it was also always possible to read through to the other.

Because Irish anxieties about fortune hunting were focused through anxiety about forced marriage, the fortune hunter in Ireland manifested primarily as predator.[20] While forced marriage was an issue in England as well, in Ireland it had a specifically political and racial dimension: men from the downwardly mobile families that made up the dispossessed Gaelic/Old English Catholic/convert aristocracy were, at least in theory, able to recoup some of the land and status they lost under the penal laws by abducting heiresses and using rape or the threat of rape to coerce them into marrying, thereby gaining control of their estates. It is difficult to know to what extent this phenomenon was real and to what extent it was a creation of ascendancy paranoia; but in any case, propertied Dublin spectators concerned about this idea of forced marriage would have seen the fortune hunter as dangerous.[21] In London, where the Irish fortune hunter was out of his element and within the power of a more firmly established system of law and order, he was more likely to wear his meretricious aspect.

But no matter what hand the prevailing conventions dealt the fortune hunter there was always a wild card: the unfathomable mystery of female sexuality. In a patriarchal culture where marriage regulated the circulation of property, fathers, suitors and husbands had a vested interest in refusing to 'know' the real desires of the women they traded; and the resulting ambiguity regarding consent meant that even if the fortune hunter attained his prey through the use of violence, the possibility that she might have consented to her own ravishment could never be definitively banished.[22] Conversely, it was easy enough for someone like the author of *The Adventures of Shelim O'Blunder*, a 1738 pamphlet published in London and advertised as a 'friendly caution to the fair sex of Great Britain', to mock the Irish fortune hunter's ignorance, stupidity and 'effeminate' willingness to sell himself; but this inevitably raised the question of why the 'fair sex of Great Britain' were buying Irish.[23] *The Adventures of Shelim O'Blunder* claims that fortune-hunting has become a form of organized crime carried out by a 'society of *Hibernian Beaux*'.[24] We get a corroborating view of the even seamier side of this phenomenon in *The Petticoat-Pensioners*, a 'memoir' printed in London circa 1749, which suggests the number of London ladies willing and able to buy their own beefcake is large enough to support an underground sex trade.[25] *The Petticoat-Pensioners* offers us a different perspective on Ragussis's 'multi-ethnic spectacle', including in its cast of gigolos a Scottish officer, the son of an American planter and a lawyer from 'the North'; but it also suggests that the consumers who drove *this* market were partial to one particular brand. Of the ten kept men whose stories are included in *The Petticoat-Pensioners*, five are Irish; and it is easy to see why they have have the biggest market share.[26]

The Petticoat-Pensioners opens with the story of an Irish gentleman from a Jacobite family who, having converted to keep his estate, runs it into the ground and absconds to London to escape his creditors. A string of increasingly sleazy scams lands him in debtor's prison, from which he is rescued by a notoriously lecherous wealthy older woman who happens to pass through one day and catch a glimpse of him relieving himself. One sight of his 'water engine' is enough to seal the deal; she agrees to buy him out and returns home to await delivery of her new toy:

> The old Lady . . . dreamt all night of the mighty machine, recollected the broad shoulders, brawny limbs and strong muscles by which it was moved and painted to herself the luscious banquet she should have in the possession of what she had seen.[27]

On the one hand this decayed Jacobite is bought outright by a woman whose body is described as so rotten with age and overindulgence that it has literally been the death of six men.[28] All the same, he survives and thrives in her service precisely because, in terms of size, stamina and sheer appetite, he is superior to the English article – so much so that after one afternoon with her Irish prodigy, 'the lady declared she had never known the true pleasure of manhood before'.[29] Even if, economically speaking, the Irish fortune hunter is being dominated by the English woman who owns him, her obvious appreciation for his 'mighty machine' raises questions about the 'manhood' of his English competitors.

Although both of these texts claim to be documentary history, I would not advise anyone to believe them for a moment. In fact, I would argue that these English representations of the Irish fortune hunter were produced not as cautionary tales or even as xenophobic screeds but as, not to put too fine a point on it, smut. Moreover, the imagined audience for this smut appears to include women. 'Shelim O'Blunder's' supposed biographer admits in his introduction that he is writing 'purely for the Amusement and Pleasure of the *Fair Sex*'.[30] The stories collected in *The Petticoat-Pensioners*, which include vivid if strategically expurgated descriptions of these gallants' erotic encounters, are framed as a series of letters from a London beau to a male friend; but after finishing the tale of the Irish man and his 'mighty machine', the narrator opens his next letter by upbraiding his correspondent for showing the letter to his sister Arabella in mixed company. 'All women love a warm story in their hearts', says the beau – they simply cannot afford to be seen enjoying one.[31] Later, the beau complains that he's too hung over to write, but then professes himself inspired to continue for Arabella's sake.[32] Both texts thus suggest that although the Irish fortune hunter is a source of anxiety for English men, he is an object of desire for English women – and that the figure of the Irish fortune hunter is perpetuated partly by demand on the part of the 'fair sex of Great Britain'.

As compromised as it is, then, the Irish fortune hunter's ability to awaken and satisfy the desires of women who ought to be out of his league does put him in a potentially powerful position relative not just to the 'fair sex' but to English men. Sheridan's treatment of O'Blunder seeks to capitalize on this potential by assigning him to the fortune hunter's position but then rescuing him from its most disabling consequences. In Molière's original and in the adaptations to which Sheridan had access, the plot always ends with the dimwitted stranger fleeing for his life while the heroine marries his local rival. Sheridan reverses that outcome, allowing O'Blunder to defeat not one but two rivals and get the girl. Though it does not mitigate most of O'Blunder's demeaning 'stage Irish' traits – the swearing, the awkwardness, the stupidity, the brawling, the vast appetites for meat and drink – marriage to Lucinda nevertheless achieves O'Blunder's recuperation. The conventions restricting the depiction of Irish characters on the British stage were well entrenched by 1743, but they were not as well entrenched as the conventions that dictated that a farce could not end with the heroine marrying the wrong man. Since O'Blunder gets the girl, he must deserve her.

As we have seen, in Ireland the figure of the fortune hunter was implicated in many of the histories and antagonisms that divided Irish society – and which therefore divided the Irish theatre audience. Once Sheridan assumed the manage-ment of the Theatre Royal in 1745, he began to take sides, currying favour with the Protestant and English or England-identified court circle while cultivating a supreme indifference to the desires of the rival Gaelic/Catholic aristocracy.[33] But *The Brave Irishman* was first performed in 1743, less than a week after Sheridan, with much trepidation, made his acting debut as Gloucester in *Richard III*.[34] At that stage in his career, Sheridan could not afford to antagonize anyone. The original version of *The Brave Irishman* is therefore shaped by his desire to make the piece's happy ending satisfying for everyone in his radically heterogeneous audience.

Sheridan defers to the theatre's patron class, the court circle who would have seen themselves and their fortunes as the targets of the Gaelic/Catholic fortune hunter, by disguising the secret of the fortune-hunter's success. Since it is estab-lished in Lucinda's first speech that the proposed match to O'Blunder is her father's idea and 'contrary to [her] inclination', the question of her desire for him is deferred until the final scene, in which she meets O'Blunder for the first time.[35] O'Blunder establishes his dominance not by using his 'mighty machine' on her but by forcing his effeminate rival – originally the effeminate Englishman Beau Dapper, eventually the effeminate Frenchman Monsieur Ragou – to eat a potato.[36] Having demonstrated that he is, as Lucinda's servant Betty insists in the opening scene, 'worth all the beaus in Christendom', O'Blunder then proves that he is neither mercenary nor meretricious by declaring himself ready to marry Lucinda even after he believes her father has been ruined.[37]

Because he has to play to the hunters as well as the hunted, however, Sheridan tacks on a second happy ending. In Molière's play and in *Squire Trelooby*, the heroine's local lover organizes most of the title character's torments. Since the audience's sympathies were meant to be with the local lover and against the title character, Congreve and Shadwell gave Squire Trelooby's rival the typical romantic-lead name of Lovewell. Sheridan calls him Cheatwell. Sure enough, after passing as Lucinda's devoted English lover throughout the piece, Cheatwell outs himself dramatically in the final scene:

> In the first place, sir, I am by birth an Irishman . . . Like many other gentlemen of that country, I was fool enough to think I had nothing to do to make my fortune but to go to London and that the bare name of an Irishman was sufficient recommendation to any lady that I should make my addresses to. I spent all my little fortune in this vain pursuit and had no hope left but that of marrying your daughter; since that has failed me, I have nothing now to expect but a jail.[38]

Cheatwell's confession and subsequent reformation are not particularly convincing; but they make perfect sense when we consider that the play premiered in front of a divided audience in which the men of each faction saw themselves as the *real* Irish gentlemen and defined themselves against the set of *false* Irish gentlemen sitting next to them. Because Cheatwell has never been marked as Irish before this point, his position within the volatile world of Irish politics is unknown; thus, anyone in the theatre would be free to identify the play's *real* Irish fortune hunter with their political opponents – whoever they happened to be at that moment in time.

Meanwhile, O'Blunder's superficial connections to the gentlemen who made up the Gaelic/Catholic faction – his rural origins, his brogue, his Gaelicisms and his penchant for duelling – would have appealed to the Gaelic/Catholic spectators by allowing them to identify with the hero who gets the girl while associating the more urbanized and Anglicized members of the court circle with the humiliated beau. The court circle had a different pleasure available to them: the satisfaction of laughing at O'Blunder while watching him bring the rebellious Lucinda under her father's control. Molière's original continually reminds the audience that the hero's real adversary is not M. de Pourceaugnac but the heroine's father, who at the end of the play is defeated and forced to beg the hero to marry his daughter. Because Sheridan has inverted the marriage plot, however, *The Brave Irishman* instead concludes with a bracing justification of patriarchal authority. Tradewell was right to choose O'Blunder as Lucinda's husband and insist that she give him a hearing. The headstrong daughter, by refusing to accept her father's choice because it is 'contrary to [her] inclination', unknowingly put herself in the power of the *real* Irish fortune hunter.[39] Now that O'Blunder's bravery and nobility have reconciled her to her father's choice, Lucinda will be better governed; Cheatwell, exposed and married off to Lucinda's chambermaid, will be forced to abandon his pretensions; Tradewell is vindicated; and the governing elites who preferred at this point in time to see themselves as exercising a firm but compassionate paternal authority over their amusing but childlike subjects would have been mightily pleased with all of these outcomes.[40]

Because it has been so profoundly shaped by local politics, then, the version of *The Brave Irishman* that premiered in Dublin ultimately represents this ostensibly cross-cultural marriage as a family affair. Cheatwell and O'Blunder turn out to be countrymen and though convention dictates that only one can get the girl, the conclusion strains to embrace both. Sheridan also establishes that Tradewell and O'Blunder are cousins. The fact that Cheatwell has successfully passed for English sends the message that despite O'Blunder's peculiarities, which Tradewell attributes to 'his not receiving a proper Education' (II, 435), there are no insurmountable essential differences separating the English and Irish characters and therefore the marriage of O'Blunder and Lucinda is as natural as any other marriage would be.

That has to change when the play travels to London. Sheridan went to London during the winter of 1745–46 to recruit performers for Dublin and *The Brave Irishman* may have travelled with him; its first London performance (under the title *Captain O'Blunder*) was at Goodman's Fields on 31 January, 1746.[41] However, though he is credited in the notice, it is not clear what connection if any Sheridan had with this performance or with the repeat performance at Bartholomew Fair on 26 August, 1746.[42] Both venues were marginal; the play was evidently not submitted for licensing before 1755; and instead of Isaac Sparks, for whom the role had been created, or any of the Irish actors who had performed the part in Dublin, both performances featured an obscure actor named Banberry who has left no other traces.[43]

The extreme brevity of Banberry's thespian career might have had something to do with poor judgement. He picked *Captain O'Blunder* as an afterpiece for his benefit (he was to play *Hamlet* in the mainpiece), perhaps hoping to capitalize on the popularity of the similarly-named Irish actor John Barrington. Barrington was then enjoying great success at Drury Lane as the ur-Stage Irishman, Teague in Howard's *The Committee*. The notice promises to introduce into the afterpiece 'an Irish Song called *Arrah my judy*, as sung by Barrington at the Theatre-Royal in Drury Lane'.[44] Essentially, what Banberry was offering his audience was a cut-rate bootleg version of a popular Drury Lane show, incorporating the same song and probably many of the same antics into a different stage-Irishman part. However, in late January 1746, a London audience that would find Howard's comic servant Teague palatable would not necessarily embrace Sheridan's Captain O'Blunder.

The Jacobite rebellion was still going on and the English forces had recently suffered a humiliating defeat at Falkirk. The Commonwealth, at this moment, is not exactly one big happy family; and because Irish officers are now fighting on both sides of an internal conflict that the Crown is by no means certain it will win, O'Blunder is more threatening as a lover and as a fighter than he would have been a year ago. Banberry may have tried to manage some of the uneasiness he expected O'Blunder to provoke by framing the play with a new prologue which proposes O'Blunder's masculine prowess as a possible remedy for whatever is wrong with the English soldiers who can't seem to subjugate their Scottish rivals.

Before moving on to read *The Brave Irishman*'s prologue, let me give an honest assessment of the difficulties involved in establishing exactly when and where it originated and my reasons for dating it to these 1746 London performances.

O'Blunder's prologue was first printed in the earliest dated edition of the play (Dublin 1754). From the title page, which advertises the play 'as it is Acted at the Theatre-Royal in Smock-Alley', we can infer that the prologue was already in use in Dublin by 1754. Internal evidence suggests that the prologue originated some years earlier, during or just after the 1745 Jacobite rebellion. O'Blunder refers to Irish soldiers who 'lately' stood by the apostrophized English in an unspecified 'cause'. Recognizing that 'The Cause' was a common euphemism for the Jacobite agenda, Christopher Murray's edition of the play in *The Field Day Anthology of Irish Writing* glosses this as a reference to the *1715* Jacobite uprising. Murray's reason for choosing the '15 instead of the '45 was probably the assumption that since the piece first played in 1743, its prologue can't have referenced something that happened in 1745. However, since the prologue does not appear in Sheridan's manuscript versions, there is no reason to assume that it dates from the original production.

Reading the 'cause' as the 1745 rebellion makes more sense of the term 'lately'. O'Blunder's conclusion, in which he hopes that 'then we should be freed', could be an indication that the outcome of the rebellion is still in doubt; if so, timing would suggest the 31 January 1746 Goodman's Fields performance as the origin point for this prologue. The question of space is, instructively, more difficult to settle. From O'Blunder's references to his 'business here' and the 'fronts [the Irish] here receive', he seems to assume that he is delivering this prologue in London. The question is whether the space O'Blunder occupied when he first delivered this prologue was actual or theatrical. O'Blunder could simply have been using the prologue to establish London as the setting for the play; the fact that he speaks these lines already 'in' London does not necessarily mean that the actor playing him is physically standing on an English stage.

At the same time, O'Blunder is speaking both to the actual audience in the theatre and to an audience of 'English spalpeens' who mock 'us poor Irish' while depending on them as military muscle. His question 'Have we not fought your battles, bravely too?' implicates the audience and puts them in the position of these 'ungrateful' English. This move would certainly have worked in Dublin, thanks to the presence of an English clique of aristocrats and civil servants who would have been part of the 'brilliant circle' that O'Blunder addresses in his first line. It would have greater impact in London, where more of the audience occupied that position. Thus, the prologue straddles the distance between the London and Dublin audiences and could plausibly have originated in either location.

My decision to place it in London in 1746 is primarily based on topical references and protestations of loyalty which could well mark it as part of the spate of patriotic paratheatrical entertainments going on all over London around the time of the 1745 rebellion, through which performers and managers demonstrated their loyalty and pandered to nationalist sentiment. The notice for Banberry's August 1746 performance of *The Brave Irishman* promises 'A Machine showing the capture of Cape Breton' as part of the same entertainment. Cape Breton, a Canadian territory ceded to the French by the 1713 Treaty of Utrecht, was taken by the British in the summer of 1745. Since at least one of those 1746 performances took place in the context of a spectacular illustration of British military power defeating the French – with whom the Jacobites were notoriously allied – it is not improbable that O'Blunder's prologue originated in London in 1746 as an attempt to reconcile *The Brave Irishman* and O'Blunder with the surge of nationalist feeling to which Banberry and crew were trying to appeal.

The prologue is spoken by O'Blunder and his first line – '*Oagh, brilliant shircle, shease to vent your spleen*' – suggests that feelings were running so high that the actors expected the venting to begin as soon as O'Blunder walked onstage.[45] O'Blunder's appeal to the audience to wait to condemn the '*poor Irish*' until their '*faults are sheen*' speaks to the anti-Catholic and anti-Irish paranoia that accompanied the outbreak of the rebellion, reminding the audience that the nervously anticipated Irish Catholic mass uprising has not thus far materialized.[46] After announcing that his intention in coming to London is to '*wed a fair one*', O'Blunder uses the rest of the prologue to argue for intermarriage as a way of reconciling himself to this heckling audience.

His first move is to subvert the laughter by pointing out that the same spectators who hold him in fear or contempt also depend on him to preserve and protect their own dominance:

> *Well then, 'tish strange that 'fronts we here reshave,*
> *Ven tish by us the English spalpeens live.*
> *Have we not fought your battles – bravely too;*
> *And yet, ungrateful boors, all that wont do.*

This passage makes the audience uncomfortably aware of the contradictions embedded in British attitudes toward this kind of 'stage Irishman'. On the one hand, the hypermasculine Irish man's capacity for violence renders him – now more than ever – a threat to the stability of the British empire; but on the other hand, the hypermasculine Irish man's capacity for violence is also providing important support for the army charged with maintaining Protestant dominance at home and British dominance abroad. The hypermasculine Irishman, as represented by this O'Blunder, is both a domestic ally propping up the British army and the British empire *and* a foreign enemy ready to infiltrate and destroy the commonwealth.

O'Blunder then appeals to established conventions about intermarriage to banish the second perception of the fighting Irish man and cement the first. Following a tradition that began with representations of Strongbow's marriage to Eva, O'Blunder suggests intermarriage as the best way of ensuring a legitimate, intimate and loyal relationship between England and Ireland:

> *Oagh, would the heroes of Hibernia's blood,*
> *Who lately in their caush uprightly stood,*
> *But shay with me, they'll mix their noble breed*
> *With Britain's daughters! Then we should be freed.*

Even though, at this point in the text's history, Lucinda and O'Blunder are still family, the prologue has now explicitly framed the O'Blunder/Tradewell alliance as a mixed marriage between two different 'breeds'. It has also reversed the traditional gendering of the England/Ireland intermarriage metaphor, in which Ireland is supposed to be the wife and England the husband.

While acknowledging the English spectators' desire to put some essential distance between themselves and the '*poor* Irish', the prologue's reframing of O'Blunder and Lucinda's marriage as interracial introduces some unsettling possibilities into the upcoming resolution. Since marriage is represented in period drama as a containment field for the excesses of the reformed rake, O'Blunder's marriage could serve to domesticate him and his barbaric appetites, rendering him a permanently loyal and useful member of the British family. On the other hand, since period drama also acknowledges that this containment system often fails, marriage could simply be the prelude to another round of betrayal and rebellion. Perhaps the most important implications of this move are contained in '*then we should be freed*'. Who, at this point, is '*we*'? Is O'Blunder still talking about his own '*noble breed*', or has '*we*' now been extended to include '*Britain's daughters*'? Has O'Blunder become British, or has the audience that was laughing at him a minute ago become Irish? And what does he mean by '*freed*'? Is he suggesting that intermarriage will free Britain from its military woes by infusing Irish fighting blood into an anaemic England? Or is he suggesting that once English women open their gates to Irish men, England's dominance over Scotland and Ireland will be a thing of the past?

While they might have played well to a Dublin audience or to the Irish contingent of a London audience, none of these readings would be especially comforting to English men; and if the prologue was in fact an attempt to make the brave Irishman popular with London audiences, it does not seem to have worked. As far as we know, *The Brave Irishman* was performed only twice that season and Banberry was never heard from again. The piece then disappeared from the London stage for almost a decade. But even in 1746, *The Brave Irishman* does appear to have made enough of an impact to demand a response. That, at any rate, is one way to interpret the success of Moses Mendez's ballad opera *The Double Disappointment*, which premiered as an afterpiece at Drury Lane on 18 March, 1746, six weeks after *The Brave Irishman*'s London debut.[47]

The piece pits 'Phelim O'Blunder' against the Marquis de Fanfaron in a contest for the hand of Isabel, whose uncle Gripe has agreed to marry her off to one of them in return for a cut of her marriage portion. Mendez works overtime to disable all the potential that Sheridan's O'Blunder has activated. Phelim's arrogant confidence in the charms of his person proves to be ridiculously unfounded; his pretensions to aristocratic descent are destroyed when it is revealed that he is a servant who was fired from his last place for stealing a silver spoon; he is clearly motivated throughout by the prospect of getting his paws on Isabel's fortune; and by the time Phelim tells Gripe how much he is looking forward to 'all the pretty little children that I'll beget upon that pretty gentlewoman', the effect is unambiguously grotesque.[48] The 'happy ending' is achieved when Isabel slips off to marry Lovemore in secret while Gripe, O'Blunder and Fanfaron are occupied with each other.

The Double Disappointment was performed more than thirty times at Drury Lane during the 1746–7 season. In its return to the original marriage plot and its uncomplicated confirmation of all the comforting prejudices attached to all of its characters, it served as a corrective not only to Sheridan's O'Blunder but to some of the more transgressive Irish performances going on simultaneously at Drury Lane. During this season, the Irish actor Charles Macklin revived his revolutionary interpretation of Shylock in *The Merchant of Venice*, while the Irish actress Margaret Woffington repeated her sensational gender-bending performance as Sir Harry Wildair in Farquhar's *The Constant Couple*. *The Double Disappointment* called in the normalizing power of the typical comic marriage plot to resolve the ambiguities generated by Woffington's cross-dressing and Macklin's renovation of the archetypal stage Jew. Mendez reverses Sheridan's innovation and restores the more 'natural' resolution, defeating the avaricious and tyrannical father figure and revealing the hero's rival as an empty fraud while making his exposure and expulsion one of the conditions for the successful resolution of the heterosexual romance.

After 1746, O'Blunder enjoyed success on the Dublin stage for years, thanks to Isaac Sparks's popularity in the title role and thanks to the fact that Sheridan was managing the Theatre Royal. The afterpiece did not make it back to London, however, until Sheridan resigned and fled Dublin in 1754. In all the confusion he somehow remembered to pack his now revised manuscript of *The Brave Irishman*. As it went into rehearsal at Covent Garden, Sheridan's piece finally made it to print.[49] However, the version that would survive, both in print and on the stage, was very different from the one the censors read.

Thanks to the fortuitous timing of the *Mahomet* riot, *The Brave Irishman* happens to resurface in London at a time when the institution of marriage is undergoing a major transformation. The Marriage Act of 1753 was billed as an attempt to stamp out 'clandestine marriages', where one or both parties was under age and acting without the knowledge or consent of their families and communities. By voiding any marriage not conducted in accordance with the regulations of the established church (with exceptions for Quakers and Jews but not for Catholics), by requiring parental consent or publication of the banns for participants under the age of twenty-one and by mandating that all valid marriages be recorded in the parish register, the Marriage Act made it impossible to keep marriage private. To be legitimate, a marriage now had to be exposed to public scrutiny and it had to be sanctioned not just by paternal authority but by the state-sponsored religion. This development is flagged by Lucy's opening dialogue in the published text of *The Brave Irishman:* 'Well, this same barbarous Marriage-Act is a great Draw-back on the Inclinations of young People.'[50] Whereas in Sheridan's play the check on Lucinda's 'Inclinations' is her father, in the published version Lucy's 'Inclinations' have been thwarted by her government. Her marriage is no longer strictly a family affair; it has now become the subject of national policy.

In that context, O'Blunder, as the Irish fortune hunter with the heart of gold, becomes valuable for new reasons. Lucy, as an under-age heiress, is exactly the kind of person that the Marriage Act was designed to protect by preventing her from acting on her own 'inclinations', which might well lead her into the arms of some mercenary fortune-hunter. From a different perspective, this 'protection' is nothing more than control; Lucy's father's wishes are now backed up by the power of the state and she no longer has the option of subverting them by eloping with the man of her choice. A conventional comedy like *The Double Disappointment*, in which two young lovers conspire to defeat their adversaries and overcome obstacles in order to finally marry, would support the more critical view of the Act as oppressive to women who were now more firmly under the control of their male relatives.[51]

But as we have seen, Sheridan, in the process of rehabilitating his title character, also makes the father's authority and the heroine's happiness coincide – and for whoever revised the manuscript for publication, that resolution appears to be one of the play's more interesting features. Having reframed the play with Lucy's topical reference, Sheridan's 'adapter' brings the play into the debate around the marriage act by using the rehabilitated Irish fortune hunter to suggest that the conflict between the parents' arbitrary or mercenary desires and the daughter's authentic 'inclinations' is a non-issue and that female sexual desire can safely and even happily be contained within the parameters of patriarchal authority.

Lucy sums up her opposition to the 'barbarous Marriage-Act' in her opening song: *"Tis not the Marriage, but the man we hate;/ 'Tis there we reason and debate:/ For, give us but the Man we love,/ We're sure the Marriage to approve'* (FDA 532). Any resistance she may mount to her father's wishes is thus immediately depoliticized; as long as her personal desires are fulfilled, she will have no complaints to make about the institution of marriage itself. The revised *Brave Irishman* then provides her with a man that she can't help but love. For the first time, the published version gives us a physical description of O'Blunder which establishes that even for a comic soldier he is exceptionally well-endowed:

LUCY: Oh! Mr. *Cheatwell* – pray let's have a Sight of the *Creature* –
CHEATWELL: Oh! Female Curiosity – Why, Child, he'd frighten thee – he's above six Feet high –
LUCY: (*Aside*) A fine Size – I like a tall Man.
SCONCE: A great huge Back and Shoulders.
LUCY: (*Aside*) We women love Length and Breadth in Proportion.
SCONCE: Wears a great long Sword, which he calls his *Andrew Ferara* –
LUCY: I hear the *Irish* are naturally brave –
SCONCE: And carries a large Oaken Cudgel, which he calls his *Shillela*.
LUCY: (*Aside*) Which he can make Use of on Occasions, I suppose.[52]

What we have here are two conflicting readings of the Irish fortune hunter's stereotypical characteristics. Cheatwell, who has just described O'Blunder to Lucy as 'Our common Enemy', is trying to exaggerate O'Blunder's exotic aspects in order to 'frighten' Lucy away from him; but the more Lucy hears about this hulking misshapen '*Creature*' and his two symbolic phalluses the more she wants to meet him. This new dialogue thus puts *The Brave Irishman* in the company of *The Adventures of Shelim O'Blunder* and *The Petticoat-Pensioners* as a text which captures the Irish fortune-hunter as an object of desire owned and consumed by English women.

Because he now represents both the hypertrophic parasites of *The Petticoat-Pensioners* and the upstanding loyal defender described in the play's prologue, O'Blunder can be both the man Lucy's father approves of *and* the man her mother warned her about. She gets to have her cake and eat it too; she can feel the forbidden *frisson* of attraction to this uncouth, uncivilized and utterly unsuitable 'brute' of a lover – who is now no longer related to her father and therefore more clearly marked as racially different and titillatingly exotic – while at the same time acknowledging and obeying her father's right to determine who she finally marries: 'Sir, you're the best Judge in the disposing of me.'[53] Trader earns this trust by wielding his newly-enhanced patriarchal authority with a lighter touch than Sheridan's original father figure; Lucy informs Cheatwell and the audience that 'my Father's Design is to have as many Suitors as he can, in order to have a Choice of them all'.[54] Her wording makes it ambiguous whose 'choice' it will finally be, but Lucy does at least establish that Trader has made choice possible, rather than making O'Blunder her only option.

Lucy's saucy epilogue demonstrates that even after O'Blunder has proven his love and loyalty to her and received the paternal stamp of approval, he retains his more scandalous attributes:

> *The* Irish *to our Hearts have found the Way.*
> *I ne'er believ'd it till I saw the –* Key.
> *Our dearest Secret best such Youth Rewards,*
> *Who find the* Key-hole *quick, and hit so true the* Wards.[55]

The final reference to 'wards', like the byplay about keys and keyholes, resuscitates the transgressive attributes of the Irish fortune-hunter while asserting that this ward-chasing keymaster is also 'gentle as a Dove' once he has submitted to being yoked in matrimony to his English admirer.

Compared to Sheridan's manuscripts, then, the published text of *The Brave Irishman* is not particularly concerned with rehabilitating the 'stage Irishman' or reconciling the warring political factions in the Dublin audience or in the British commonwealth. Instead, part of the appeal of Sheridan's plot and his title character is that they defuse the debate around the 1753 Marriage Act by reconciling the romantic heroine's desire to pursue her transgressive 'inclinations' with the father figure's desire to determine when, whom and how his daughter marries. Accordingly, the published text eliminates Cheatwell's revelation of his Irish origins, which for the mid-century London audience would be an unnecessary complication.

This reframing of the plot thus suggests a new explanation for the emergence of the 'multi-ethnic spectacle' marriage comedy onto the British stage after 1753. While providing the English heroine with an assortment of othered suitors gives the spectators the opportunity to enjoy their variously marked bodies and stereo-typed mannerisms and accents and gives the playwright the opportunity to pit type against type in order to promote the rehabilitation of one or the demonization of another, this new representation of the ethnically and geographically diverse marriage market also retains the transgressive aspects of the comic marriage plot without directly threatening the Marriage Act's assertion of paternalistic authority. By incorporating a hero who is othered enough to pique the heroine's interest, but like enough to become a legitimate member of the British family, *The Brave Irishman* preserves the illusion of Lucy's freedom to choose.

It was, in fact, a few years after this modification that *The Brave Irishman* finally took London by storm. Unfortunately for Sheridan, it was by that point no longer his property. It had become Charles Macklin's 1759 *Love à la Mode*, in which Macklin reappropriated a plot which Sheridan had himself probably lifted from one of Macklin's early vehicles. Unlike the other thieves, Macklin knows, and has reasons to loathe, his victim. As Irish performers trying to straddle the distance between London and Dublin and as notoriously quarrelsome and litigious people, Macklin and Sheridan had, perhaps, too much in common. Macklin was hired by Sheridan for the 1748–49 season at Smock Alley but their collaboration quickly degenerated into rivalry and backbiting.[56] A decade later, in 1757, Macklin returned to Dublin and joined with Spranger Barry to establish Crow Street as a competing patent theatre – a scheme that Sheridan, who apparently believed himself entitled to a lifetime monopoly on legitimate theatre in Dublin, vocally, vehemently and persistently opposed.[57] Macklin got his revenge by swiping Sheridan's intellectual property and remaking it into a new and improved model which would soon eclipse its predecessors.

Ragussis, as part of his persuasive reading of *Love à la Mode*, identifies it as an adaptation/elaboration of a minor scene in *The Merchant of Venice* in which Portia 'satirically reviews the (ethnic) failings of her suitors'.[58] While it is certainly possible that *The Merchant of Venice* was one source of inspiration, *Love à la Mode* is much more clearly indebted, in terms of plot, to *The Brave Irishman*. Once again, the ward of a London merchant (here, Charlotte is Sir Theodore Goodchild's niece instead of his daughter) is courted by suitors representing different comic types (here, instead of a French beau, O'Brallaghan has a Jewish beau to overpower; instead of the crypto-Irish Cheatwell he has the equally manipulative and spiteful Scot Sir Archy Macsarcasm to contend with; and Macklin has thrown in a third rival, the 'Newmarket Jockey' Squire Groom). Once again, the guardian fabricates the rumour that his fortune has been destroyed in order to test the suitors' resolve; and, once again, only the Irish suitor turns out *not* to be a fortune hunter.

The play's similarity to *The Brave Irishman* is remarked upon in the postscript to *A Scotsman's Remarks on the Farce of Love à la Mode*, a pamphlet published anonymously in 1760 which has been attributed to Macklin himself.[59] Kirkman's biography notes that Macklin deliberately provoked Scottish opposition because it was good publicity; circulating this pamphlet would have kept the fires burning while conveying enough information about the piece to inspire readers to see it for themselves.[60] Throughout the pamphlet, Macklin uses his aggrieved narrator to call attention to the play's most original features, especially the ways in which O'Brallaghan fails to be a 'realistic' Irishman.[61]

Though both Ragussis and Paul Goring treat *A Scotsman's Remarks* like an example of real outrage from an actual Scotsman, its postscript makes much more sense coming from a tongue-in-cheek Macklin.[62] In the postscript, the narrator addresses the charge that *Love à la Mode* is 'a plagiarism, a vamped-up old *Irish* farce'.[63] He then provides a plot summary of *The Brave Irishman* which includes excerpts from two of O'Blunder's songs (one of which appears only in the published text, which must have been Macklin's source) and charges that *The Brave Irishman* is the pattern 'from which . . . the author *of accident* and *truly original* genius of *Love à la Mode*, hath derived his plan'.[64] He closes, however, with this zinger: 'Thus MILTON is said to have taken the hint of his *Paradise Lost* from a *puppet-show* he had seen in *Italy!*'[65]

By suggesting such a wide gulf in quality, ingenuity, sophistication and significance between the source and the work it inspired, Macklin not only clears himself of the charge of 'plagiarism' but kicks *The Brave Irishman* right out of the realm of legitimate theatre. This move is prepared by Macklin's description of how the play got to London: 'Some strollers from *Dublin*, brought over to *Edinburgh* a farce, where it was printed in the year 1755 and is called *The Brave Irishman*.'[66] Eliding the play's legitimate performance history in London, Macklin focuses on the piece's illegitimate circulation via the pirated printed edition and the strolling players who disseminated it. The insinuation that it reached London only through Edinburgh renders the piece even more suspect in the eyes of Macklin's imagined Scotophobic readers. Macklin makes the same move in the play when Sir Archy Macsarcasm vows to get revenge on Charlotte and O'Brallaghan by inciting a 'lad of honourable family', who understands the ancient classics in a 'perfection' and who is 'now composing a comedy' to 'insinuate baith their characters intil it [sic]'.[67] This in-joke reverses this plot's chain of custody, turning Sheridan into a hack paid by the despicable Scot to write a cruder, more mean-spirited version of Macklin's play – in other words, *The Brave Irishman*.

Macklin's high opinion of the merits of his adaptation is justified. As Ragussis's reading demonstrates, Macklin's use of this material is sophisticated and metatheatrical, calling attention to 'ethnic identity' as 'merely performative' by using O'Brallaghan to excite and then frustrate the expectations of a London audience already familiar with the stage-Irish soldier (Ragussis 778). Whereas O'Blunder confirmed most of those expectations – except for the critical one of being a mercenary predator – O'Brallaghan disappoints his onstage audience as he 'fails to make a fool of himself' (Ragussis 780). But if O'Brallaghan's wooing is a 'failed spectacle' (Ragussis 780) as far as his rivals are concerned, Macklin makes sure that the spectators in the theatre get their show.

In part, he does this by including other typed characters who give good spectacle. The 'beau Jew' Mordecai bears the brunt of the racist humour that would otherwise attach to the Irish character.[68] The horse-obsessed Squire Groom assumes some of the less essentialized but equally damning characteristics that originally belonged to O'Blunder, such as uncouth social behaviour, comically inappropriate dress and even his status as sexual commodity. Groom has, on a bet, come courting in his riding outfit; and as *A Scotsman's Remarks* points out, 'a jockey garb is a curtailed, abridged and tight dress' in which all of his assets would be on view.[69] *A Scotsman's Remarks* credits King's performance as Squire Groom with having 'rescued [the play] from damnation', suggesting that his performance (and perhaps his tightly encased person) 'roused a torpified, yawning audience'.[70]

At the same time, however, Macklin manages to get O'Brallaghan to provide for the paying audience much of the entertainment they expect from him. Macklin simply protects O'Brallaghan from 'theatricality' by making other characters responsible for this self-display. O'Brallaghan does fight a duel, but only after trying and failing to convince Macsarcasm that duelling 'should be done in private'.[71] During the play-within-a-play engineered by Charlotte, in which O'Brallaghan courts her while his rivals look on, O'Brallaghan does sing, but only after Charlotte insists upon it.[72] O'Brallaghan, like O'Blunder, asserts his dominance over the feminized beau, this time in verbal rather than physical combat and only after being baited.[73] And Macklin is just as interested as Sheridan was in preserving one aspect of the Irish fortune-hunter's character: the sexual prowess that makes him a source of fascination to English women and a source of anxiety for his male competition.

Cook's biography of Macklin includes an anecdote locating the genesis of *Love à la Mode* in a real encounter between Macklin, who at the time was passing as English and an Irish soldier 'who became the model for Sir Callaghan'.[74] Macklin goads the Irishman into 'self-exhibition' by 'attribut[ing the soldier's] successes with the ladies from having a *tail behind*, as common to all Irishmen'.[75] The 'tail' reference links this anecdote to the printed incarnation of *The Brave Irishman*, in which Lucy's maid Betty tells her mistress that Irish men will 'deny' other sterotypes but that 'they all confess and boast of their *tails*'.[76] The soldier in Macklin's anecdote denies having a literal tail, but at the same time strips off his coat to show his figure and rattles off 'a long list of his amours'.[77] If we look at this anecdote not as a real encounter but as a metaphorical representation of where O'Brallaghan came from, it shows Macklin stripping off the most outlandish and dehumanizing layer of O'Blunder's hypersexuality to reveal a more credible and sympathetic embodiment of it.

O'Brallaghan's dialogue and songs still suggest sexual prowess, sexual appetite and sexual dominance, but Macklin disguises the sexual subtext, emphasizing the stress laid in *The Brave Irishman*'s prologue on the Irish officer's function as protector of the realm and its women. The one moment of accord between O'Brallaghan and his Celtic foil Macsarcasm comes during a discussion of General Wolfe's death in battle at Quebec, as O'Brallaghan makes a point of reminding the audience that the British army is powered by Celtic blood and sweat: 'Sir Archy, give me your hand: I assure you, your countrymen are brave soldiers and so are mine too.'[78] O'Brallaghan's Act I song reinforces his status as one of '*honour's defenders*', using his martial prowess to justify his amorous conquests: '*The foe and the fair,/ We always take care/ To make them surrender*'.[79] When O'Brallaghan hears of Goodchild's supposed ruin, he professes that he loves Charlotte all the more because she 'has nobody to defend her'.[80]

The song O'Brallaghan composes for Charlotte shows that, unlike O'Blunder's, O'Brallaghan's raw sexual energy has been domesticated by love:

> *Ten times in a day to her chamber I come,*
> *To tell her my passion, but can't, I'm struck dumb;*
> *For Cupid he seizes my soul with surprize,*
> *And my tongue falls asleep at the sight of her eyes.*[81]

Though the Irish soldier is still coming ten times a day, in the presence of English beauty he is paralysed until she accepts his attentions. This attractive combination of power and docility makes him a more natural choice than his less manly rivals, personified in this song as Charlotte's 'little dog Pompey': '*Then pray, my dear Charlotte, debase not your charms/ But instead of your lapdog take me to your arms*'.[82]

Like *The Brave Irishman*, then, *Love à la Mode* uses the Irish fortune-hunter to allow Charlotte to satisfy her guardian's desires and her own inclinations at the same time; after her guardian and O'Brallaghan have agreed that he will 'take her', she accepts 'with unfeigned pleasure'.[83] At the same time, *Love à la Mode* makes overt *The Brave Irishman*'s prologue's argument about the necessity of the kind of mixed marriage entered into by Charlotte and O'Brallaghan. While the racially marked and emasculated Beau Mordecai represents a more threatening form of intermarriage which the play holds out as unnatural and Squire Groom as the only English suitor is manifestly ridiculous, Sir Archy Macsarcasm caricatures the audience's own attachment to racial purity. After reminding the London audience that they are already 'a strange amphibious breed, being a composition of Turks, jews, Nabobs and Refugees', Macsarcasm allows his fixation on the antiquity and nobility of his bloodline to embroil him in an ultimately humiliating conflict with O'Brallaghan, during which O'Brallaghan insists that 'the *Scots* are all *Irishmen's* bastards ... little Terence Flaherty O'Brallaghan was the man who went over from Carrickfergus and peopled all *Scotland* with his own hands'.[84]

As in Sheridan's original *Brave Irishman*, Charlotte's guardian and O'Brallaghan are related. To explain how, O'Brallaghan invokes the legend of Strongbow and Eva, putting his own spin on it: 'Sir Theodore is a bit of a relation by the mother's side only, which is a little up-start family that came in with one Strongbow t'other day, not above six or seven hundred years ago.'[85] The same mythical sexual prowess on which O'Brallaghan implicitly relies in his dealings with Charlotte underpins O'Brallaghan's mythology about his mighty progenitors and makes it possible to reunite England, Scotland and Ireland as branches of the same family.

Like its source, then, *Love à la Mode* suggests that a London audience could be persuaded to loosen its grip on a cherished ethnic stereotype as long it was given something more important in exchange. London audiences clearly preferred Macklin's version; *The Brave Irishman* had only one recorded performance in London after 1759 (a 1770 benefit for Isaac Sparks). But *The Brave Irishman* did proliferate as a printed text even while *Love à la Mode* dominated the stage; and though Macklin's piece offered theatre audiences pleasures that are absent from *The Brave Irishman* – witty dialogue, for instance – *The Brave Irishman* was less coy about offering its readers the somewhat cruder pleasures available from texts like *The Petticoat-Pensioners*. What both pieces offer and what may have contributed to the success both enjoyed, was a resolution that aligned female sexual desire with patriarchal and state authority. Like O'Blunder, Macklin's O'Brallaghan remains just exotic *enough* to be both erotically interesting and matrimonially appropriate and is embedded in a plot which reconciles the generic insistence on transgressive love with the newly 'reformed' and patriarchally-regulated version of marriage establishing itself in England in the wake of the 1753 Marriage Act. The multi-ethnic marriage comedy becomes valuable to a British audience as these Irish playwrights' desire to rehabilitate the 'stage Irishman' happens to reconcile the conflicting desires embodied in and provoked by the attempt to make not just women but marriage itself more docile. In *The Brave Irishman* as in *Love à la Mode*, the new and improved stage Irishman helps spectators all over Britain negotiate their anxieties about the 'strange mixture' that they already know they have become and about the 'inclinations' of the women whose matrimonial and sexual adventures will determine the composition of future generations of Britons.

Notes and references

1. Michael Ragussis, 'Jews and Other "Outlandish Englishmen": Ethnic Performance and the Invention of British Identity under the Georges', *Critical Inquiry*, 26 (1999–2000): 778. I would like to take this opportunity to acknowledge all the colleagues who have offered feedback and helped me revise this piece, including Peter Holland, Michael Cordner, Margot Backus, Sarah McKibben, Mary Trotter and, most especially, Helen Burke.
2. Ragussis, 'Jews and Other', 794.
3. Ragussis, 'Jews and Other', 774.
4. Helen Burke discusses some of the unintended consequences of Molyneux's and Swift's use of the marriage trope to describe the England/Ireland relationship in the first two chapters of *Riotous Performances: the Struggle for Hegemony in the Irish Theater, 1712–1784* (South Bend: University of Notre Dame Press, 2003).
5. On the relationship between the London and Dublin repetoires and the difficulties involved in producing original plays in Dublin, see the introduction to John C. Greene and Gladys L. H. Clark's *The Dublin Stage, 1720–1745: a Calendar of Plays, Entertainments and Afterpieces* (Bethlehem: Lehigh University Press, 1993).
6. See my articles 'Outside the Box: the Female Spectator, *The Fair Penitent* and the Kelly Riots of 1747', *Theatre Journal*, 57 (2005): 33–55 and 'Clearing the Stage: Gender, Class and the "Freedom of the Scenes" in Eighteenth-Century Dublin', *PMLA*, 119 (2004): 1264–78.
7. Joep Leerssen, *Mere Irish and Fior-Ghael: Studies in the Idea of Irish Nationality, its Development and Literary Expression prior to the Nineteenth Century* (South Bend: University of Notre Dame Press, 1997), 116.
8. Christopher Murray, introduction to *The Brave Irishman* in Seamus Deane et al., eds, *Field Day Anthology of Irish Writing*, 5 vols (Derry: Field Day Publications, 1991), 1: 532.
9. I borrow the phrase 'contact zone' and the concept of transculturation from Mary Louise Pratt.
10. Ragussis, 'Jews and Other', 789.
11. Christopher Wheatley and Kevin Donovan, eds, *Irish Drama of the Seventeenth and Eighteenth Centuries*, 2 vols (Thoemmes Press: Bristol, 2003), 1: 422–3.

12. The earliest dated edition was published in 1754 in Dublin. Its title page indicates that the play is 'supposed to have been written by T——s S——n and revised with several corrections and additions by J——n P——st-n'. This is an indication that the text may have appeared without its author's blessing (or knowledge). The 2 March 1754 *Mahomet* riot, discussed in depth in Burke's *Riotous Performances* (209–40), drove Sheridan out of Dublin in a hurry and Sheldon argues that in his absence 'J——n P——st-n' and/or his associates felt emboldened to bring out their pirated edition.

13. Wheatley's speculation that the published version 'dominated the stage after 1755' (1: 424) is borne out by the cast list for a 1770 London performance of *The Brave Irishman* which uses character names found only in the published text. See A. H. Scouten et al., *The London Stage, 1660–1800: a Calendar of Plays, Entertainments & Afterpieces*, 5 vols (Carbondale: Southern Illinois University Press, 1965), 4: 1477.

14. See the entry for Thomas Sheridan in *The Thespian Dictionary; or, Dramatic Biography of the Present Age* (London: J. Cundee, 1805).

15. Sheridan, *The Brave Irishman*, in Wheatley and Donovan, *Irish Drama*, 1: 428. The 1755 Huntington manuscript of *The Brave Irishman* is the copy-text Wheatley uses in Volume I, followed by a list of variants from the 1740–1 Lefanu MS. Passages from the Lefanu MS that do not have clear analogues in the Huntington MS are included as an Appendix in Volume II. Hereafter, citations to the manuscript versions of *The Brave Irishman* will be given by volume number and page numbers from Wheatley and Donovan's anthology. It should always be clear from context which MS I am discussing.

16. Esther Sheldon, *Thomas Sheridan of Smock-Alley* (Princeton: Princeton University Press, 1967), 12.

17. This is clear from his treatment of the madhouse scene in the 1755 manuscript, which incorporates much more of the dialogue that takes place between Molière's two doctors than does the original manuscript.

18. As Leerssen shows, the figure of the Irish fortune-hunter was well established on the English stage before O'Blunder's advent (103–12).

19. Ann Rosalind Jones and Peter Stallybrass, 'Dismantling Irena: the Sexualizing of Ireland in Early Modern England', *Nationalisms and Sexualities*, ed. Andrew Parker et al. (New York: Routledge, 1992), 161.

20. For a fuller discussion of how the threat of forced marriage figured into theatrical culture in Dublin, see my 'Clearing the Stage'.

21. Although J. A. Froude's history of eighteenth-century Ireland represented forced marriage as a widespread, concerted and strategic form of indigenous resistance, later historians have challenged his interpretation. Unfortunately, most of the sources Froude cited to document this practice would have been destroyed in the Four Courts fire in 1922. James Kelly's 'The Abduction of Women of Fortune in Eighteenth-Century Ireland', *Eighteenth Century Ireland*, 9 (1994), argues that the motives for forced marriage were most often economic. Surviving period sources suggest that some abductors targeted convert families or even members of their own extended families. See my 'Outside the Box', 38–41.

22. For a discussion of sixteenth century ideas about rape and the legal problems created by the perpetually unresolvable ambiguity of the victim's state of mind, see Deborah G. Burks, 'I'll Want My Will Else: *The Changeling* and Women's Complicity With Their Rapists', in *Revenge Tragedy*, ed. Stevie Simkin (New York: Palgrave, 2001), 163–90.

23. *The Adventures of Shelim O'Blunder, Esq.; or The Irish Beau. Who, Within a very few Years has passed through many surprising Vicissitudes* and *remarkable Scence of Life. The whole Founded on real Facts* and *intersperrs'd with several diverting and amusive Incidents, with a few cursory Reflections on the common Ingredients of a* Teague-land Beau, *or* Fortune Hunter, *by way of salutary Advice, or friendly Caution to the* Fair Sex *of* Great Britain (London: 1738), 17.

24. *Adventures of Shelim O'Blunder*, 11.

25. *The Petticoat-Pensioners: Being Memoirs of the Most Remarkable of those Gentlemen, in and about London and Westminster.* (London: J. Horner, n.d. [1749?]). *The Petticoat-Pensioners* is undated, though its general period can be inferred from topical references. A copy is part of the Loeber collection of Irish fiction and housed in Special Collections at the Hesburgh Library of the University of Notre Dame.

26. The frame narrator takes it for granted that his reader will assume that the Irish have the lion's share; he explicitly introduces his first non-Irish 'kept gallant', a 'Caledonian', in order to prove to his reader that there are other men working this trade *besides* the Irish (*Petticoat-Pensioners* 40).

27. *Petticoat-Pensioners,* 28.

28. *Petticoat-Pensioners,* 5.

29. *Petticoat-Pensioners,* 35.

30. *Adventures of Shelim O'Blunder,* 1.

31. *Petticoat-Pensioners,* 18.

32. *Petticoat-Pensioners,* 139.

33. Burke, *Riotous Performances*, 126–32.

34. Sheridan's debut on 29 February, 1743 in the role of Richard III was heralded by a notice in the Dublin journal in which Sheridan – identified only as 'a Gentleman' – advises the 'gentlemen' in the audience that they will be 'refused admittance behind the scenes' for anything less than a half-guinea, adding that the 'Confusion which a Person must necessarily be under on his first appearance, will be greatly heightened by having a Number of People about him and his Perplexity on his Exits and Entrances (things with which he is but little acquainted) must be greatly increased by having a Crowd to bustle thro' (Greene and Clark, *The Dublin Stage*, 335). The nervous hysteria and the use of third person to make his own case are pure Sheridan, but the apologetic tone and the carefully laid out excuse stand in marked contrast to the approach Sheridan would take as manager three years later when he cleared the 'gentlemen' out from behind the scenes at Smock Alley.

35. Wheatley and Donovan, *Irish Drama*, 2: 434.

36. In the earliest manuscript, the effeminate rival was originally written as Beau Dapper, then crossed out and rewritten as Monsieur Ragou (Wheatley and Donovan, *Irish Drama*, 1: 422). It is unclear whether these changes were made before the play was staged or after the play's first performances. Sheridan may have picked up Monsieur Ragou's name from John Lacy's comedy *The Old Troop, or Monsieur Raggou*, premiered in the 1660s though the two characters have little in common apart from comically accented/broken English, cowardice and despicability. It is equally possible that Sheridan was simply using a common name attached to what by 1740 was the stock 'effeminate Frenchman' comic type.

37. Wheatley and Donovan, *Irish Drama*, 1: 426, 442.

38. Wheatley and Donovan, *Irish Drama*, 1: 443.

39. Wheatley and Donovan, *Irish Drama*, 2: 434.

40. For a fuller discussion of paternalism and the theatre's patron class during this period of Irish history, see my article 'The Tender Mother and the Faithful Wife: Theater, Charity and Female Subjectivity in Eighteenth-Century Ireland', *Eire-Ireland*, 37 (2002): 207–30.

41. *The Brave Irishman* has gone by both titles. The notice for the January 1746 performance identifies the play as Thomas Sheridan's (Scouten et al., *The London Stage*, 2: 1215).

42. Scouten et al., *The London Stage*, 2: 1245.

43. According to Philip Highfill Jr, Kalman A. Burnim et al., *A Biographical Dictionary of Actors, Actresses, Musicians, Dancers, Managers, & Other Stage Personnel in London, 1660–1800* (Carbondale: Southern Illinois University Press, 1973), these two notices are all that remains of Banberry in the historical record (1: 245).

44. Scouten et al., *The London Stage*, 2: 1215.

45. Deane et al., *Field Day Anthology of Irish Writing*, 532. All references to the prologue are from this edition.

46. See Burke, *Riotous Performances*, 119–26.

47. Scouten et al., *The London Stage*, 2: 1226.

48. Moses Mendez, *The Double Disappointment: or, the fortune hunters. A comedy in two acts written by a gentleman* (London: 1755), 8.

49. Because some of the published editions are not dated and because there are several editions that appeared in and around 1754, it is hard to say with certainty which was the first published edition. The English Short Title Catalogue suggests that one edition appeared in 1746, but that title page references the Crow Street theatre, which did not exist in 1746. Apart from that the earliest suggested publication date for any edition is 1754. It is possible that the play's publication preceded or prompted Sheridan's attempt to get his new version performed in London. It is also possible, as suggested in the postscript to *A Scotsman's Remarks on the Farce of Love à la Mode, Scene by Scene* (London: J. Burd, 1760), that the play was first printed in Edinburgh by the 'strollers' who brought it there from Dublin (36).

50. Deane et al., *Field Day Anthology*, 532.

51. Rebecca Probert, 'The Impact of the Marriage Act of 1753: Was It Really a "Most Cruel Law For the Fair Sex?"' *Eighteenth Century Studies*, 38 (2005): 247.

52. Deane et al., *Field Day Anthology*, 533.

53. Ibid., 533, 539.

54. Ibid., 533.

55. Ibid., 541.

56. Francis Aspry Congreve, *Authentic Memoirs of the Late Mr. Charles Macklin, Comedian* (London: J. Barker, 1798), 30–1.

57. Congreve, *Authentic Memoirs*, 58. For Sheridan's arguments against the Crow Street scheme and his own sense of entitlement, see his 1758 pamphlet *An Humble Appeal to the Publick, Together with some Considerations on the Present Critical and Dangerous State of the Stage in Ireland* (Dublin: 1758).

58. Ragussis, 'Jews and Other', 778.

59. Both the English Short Title Catalogue and the Eighteenth Century Collection Online list Macklin as the author.

60. James Thomas Kirkman, *Memoirs of the life of Charles Macklin, Esq. principally compiled from his own papers and memorandums*, 2 vols (London, 1799), 1: 402.

61. See, for example, *A Scotsman's Remarks*, 9, 14.

62. See Ragussis, 'Jews and Other', 789 and Paul Goring, ' "John Bull, pit, box and gallery, said No!": Charles Macklin and the Limits of Ethnic Resistance on the Eighteenth-Century London Stage', *Representations*, 79 (2002): 71–2.

63. *A Scotsman's Remarks*, 36.

64. *A Scotsman's Remarks*, 38.

65. *A Scotsman's Remarks*, 38.

66. *A Scotsman's Remarks*, 36.

67. Charles Macklin, *Love A-La-Mode, A Comedy in Two Acts, as it is performed at the Theatre-Royal in Covent Garden* (Edinburgh: 1782), 30.

68. Ragussis, 'Jews and Other', 779.

69. *A Scotsman's Remarks*, 21–2.

70. *A Scotsman's Remarks*, 25.

71. Macklin, *Love à la Mode*, 15.

72. Macklin, *Love à la Mode*, 23–4.

73. Macklin, *Love à la Mode*, 12–13.

74. Ragussis, 'Jews and Other', 787.

75. Cook, quoted in Ragussis, 'Jews and Other', 787.

76. Deane et al., *Field Day Anthology*, 533.

77. Cook, quoted in Ragussis, 'Jews and Other', 787.

78. Macklin, *Love à la Mode*, 13.

79. Macklin, *Love à la Mode*, 17.

80. Macklin, *Love à la Mode*, 29.

81. Macklin, *Love à la Mode*, 24.
82. Macklin, *Love à la Mode*, 24.
83. Macklin, *Love à la Mode*, 29.
84. Macklin, *Love à la Mode*, 15.
85. Macklin, *Love à la Mode*, 14.

9

Country Matters: Irish 'Waggery' and the Irish and British Theatrical Traditions

Helen Burke

A new kind of theatrical historiography, as Michal Kobialka reminds us, requires not just a different way of dealing with already established research in the archive but also a questioning of how the archive itself was constituted and produced. Rather than asking what happens to and with the outcome of research, he suggests, we must ask:

> how these singular events or fragments are brought to one's attention, how they are described, how they are made meaningful, how they become worthy of record or notice by the past and present, what labor formal arguments, emplotment, and ideological paradigms perform to secure their archivable place, what tensions are revealed by disclosing the situatedness of the object and the subject in the time of now ... and, finally, how these events or fragments participate in the practices of institutions and civic life.[1]

If we ask such questions of the eighteenth-century Irish and British theatrical archives, it also becomes clear that, from the beginning, a town/country opposition served as a key structuring and delimiting concept. To ensure the manageability of their object, writers in the emerging field of British theatrical historiography defined 'theatre' as occurring only in the urban professional playhouse, thus, for instance, effectively bracketing off the scripted performances of the London 'theatre' from the popular unscripted performances that occurred in London's own rural hinterland. And as the professional theatre spread throughout Britain and Ireland, each new urban theatrical site began to accumulate its own body of historians and experts who studied the record and practices of that site in similar isolation from its larger rural context. Thus by 1749, for instance, the 'Irish theatre' was being studied as a discrete object with its own separate history but, as in the case of the British theatre, the focus in this historiography was almost exclusively on the practices and records of the playhouses in the Irish capital, Dublin.[2]

The 'customs and manners' narratives that began to be produced in Britain and Ireland in increasing numbers in the second half of the eighteenth century also helped to consolidate this town/country way of organizing the theatrical archive, while also bringing out theatre's implicit modernizing narrative of itself. Through such 'customs and manners' narratives, the types of 'theatre' that had been ignored by theatre historians – popular entertainments practices, rites, and rituals – now began to be assembled into their own separate archive where they soon began to engage a different set of experts and researchers: antiquarians, folklorists, and eventually, nationalist historians and anthropologists. And, by identifying these kinds of performance practices with the so-called primitive cultures of the Celtic fringes – popular culture was increasingly believed to find its purest expression in these remoter, non-Anglo regions – this other set of commentators also tacitly reinscribed theatre as a uniquely urban, modern formation. An example of a narrative that would have worked in this way is '*A Description of the Manners and Customs of the Native* Irish. *In a letter from an* English *Gentleman*', an essay which appeared in the *Weekly Magazine* in 1759. In this piece, the author gives an account of 'native' Irish festivities and rituals that he witnessed while on his travels to the west of Ireland and, as he does so, he also alludes briefly to the Irish custom of performing 'plays' at wakes. 'At night fall', he writes, 'the plays begin, the young folks no way terrified at the scene of death before them, toy and play tricks and have twenty pastimes suited to the occasion'. But this writer also suggests that the Irish took such wake entertainment practices from 'the Tartars', thus creating a genealogy that effectively fixes the Irish performance tradition in an archaic, pre-modern space, and he further distances this performance tradition from that of the theatre by stressing in his prefatory remarks that 'the manners' he is describing are 'entirely different from those of the English'.[3]

In this paper, however, I will argue that there were frequent crossings back and forth between the Irish popular performance tradition and the British theatrical tradition, and I will suggest, moreover, that, as this popular performance tradition was imported into urban areas, it served as a reservoir of resistance to that urban mode of thinking that sought to order people and cultures according to its own bourgeois rationality. To make the case that the country matters in this way to Irish and British theatrical culture, however, it is also necessary to bring together the archives that have been separated by the rise of the disciplines and by the rise of nationalism – in this case, the archive of Irish popular culture and the archives of the Dublin and London theatres. And it is also necessary to focus on those artists and performances that have been deemed irrational, eccentric, or in some way anomalous within these two theatrical institutions. Just like the author of '*A Description of the Manners and Customs of the Native* Irish', whom we now assume to be Oliver Goldsmith,[4] many of those who sat in the eighteenth-century urban playhouse, or who wrote or acted on the eighteenth-century urban stage were literally 'ex-centric' in that they had moved to the city from the rural backwaters of Ireland. And as I will argue from looking at two unorthodox kinds of performance – the so-called 'waggery' of the upper gallery in the Dublin theatre, and Goldsmith's equally waggish comedy, *She Stoops to Conquer* (1773) – such 'ex-centric' or out-of-place subjects became the point of transfer between the anti-bourgeois popular performance tradition of rural Ireland and the theatre proper.

Irish 'play' and the 'waggery' of the Dublin upper gallery

From the commentary of visiting English actors and playwrights, it is evident that, by the second half of the eighteenth century, the Dublin upper gallery had developed practices and behaviours that were unknown or, at least, uncommon in London playhouses. When the English actor, James Love, published the popular Dublin epilogue 'Bucks Have at Ye All' for an English readership in 1770, for instance, he felt it necessary to include two explanatory footnotes after the passage describing the behaviour of the 'Bucks' in the Dublin upper gallery. The first note concerned the upper gallery's 'Custom' of passing 'Jests ... to and fro between the Galleries and their favourite Actors during the Performance', and the second related to the upper gallery's habit of singling out, by name, particular members of the elite as they came into the theatre, and favouring these patrons with either applause or groans. On the latter practice of 'groaning', for instance, Love writes the following footnote: '*Groan* – The Spirit of the Times, in Party Matters, boiling over amongst the lower Order of People to great Excess; a rude and daring Liberty was taken by the *Upper Gallery* of calling to account the People of Fashion, and distinguishing them with Marks of Contempt or Approbation – Noblemen, Gentlemen, nay even the Ladies themselves were called upon by name, as they entered the Boxes, and saluted with a *Clap* or a *Groan*.'[5] The memoirs of Charles Dibdin the Younger, who was playwright-in-residence at Astley's Peter Street Amphitheatre in Dublin in the 1790s, also suggest that these upper gallery practices had evolved into something of a separate art form as the century progressed. By the 1790s, Dibdin's account reveals, the upper gallery patrons were not only joking with actors during the performance but they were also joking among themselves throughout the whole evening's entertainment, and they had expanded their practice of 'calling to account the People of Fashion' to encompass absent as well as present members of the ruling elite. Dibdin writes:

It is the custom with Irish audiences to express their opinions, political and otherwise, very strongly during the intervals between the acts of a piece, and while the curtain is down between any two pieces. On these occasions very whimsical and entertaining dialogues are carried on, replete with shrewd humor and acute repartee; while upon the entrance into the boxes of any popular character, some one in the Gallery vociferates, 'A clap for So-and-So,' and a general plaudit, often thrice repeated takes place. On the contrary, the appearance of any unpopular personage is succeeded by 'A Groan for So-and-so' and a universal howl takes place. Absentees are noticed in the same manner, where there is no conspicuous character present, and at this time Mr. Pitt, who was premier, was an object of pretty general dislike. I heard every night during the season, with scarcely an exception, 'A Groan for Pitt' – it was like a Red Indian whoop, 'A Clap for Pat' – that was like the clattering down of immense falling stacks of deals.[6]

The commentary on these uniquely Irish theatrical 'customs' in mainstream Dublin or London publications also tended to follow the trends in commentary on popular Irish culture at large. For much of the eighteenth century, these behaviours were read as evidence of Irish recidivism or barbarity and were condemned accordingly. In a letter to the Managers of the Dublin Theatre Royal that appeared as a pamphlet in Dublin in 1755, for example, an anonymous theatergoer argued that 'the amazing Insolence, the terrible Outrages, Scurrility, and Obscenity, which every Play-night assail our Ears from the Ruffians in the Upper Gallery are intolerable; a Scandal to the Age and Nation, as the like was never heard of before, nor could be believed of a civilized People, but for the nightly Evidence of our Senses; it revives the Charge of *Barbarism* against us; hindering many Persons of Distinction, of both Sexes, from coming to the Play.'[7] But by the early nineteenth century, the visiting English actor William Macready was celebrating the by-now legendary 'waggery' of the Dublin upper gallery – 'the anecdotes are numerous that have been current of the Dublin galleries' waggaries', he writes in his account of his first 1815 visit to Dublin – seeing it as the expression of a charmingly spontaneous (but no less primitive) 'national character'. 'The national character might be read with tolerable correctness in their theatre', Macready writes.

> Keenly sensitive to the commanding truth of the poet's or the players' passion, they [the galleries] would as often find resource in their own humour from their [the poet's or the players'] dullness or inefficiency . . . disturbing the more sedate of the spectators and utterly discomposing the player; until, checked by some touch of nature they would surrender themselves to the potent influence of the scene and beneath its charm no assembly could watch more intently with more discriminating taste, or more lavish applause, the 'dream of passion' passing before them.[8]

Matthew Arnold's sensitive and unworldly Celt, it would seem, was already present in the Dublin 'gods' in 1815.

If we look at the shifting demographics of Dublin city in the second half of the eighteenth century, however, we can find a less romanticized explanation for these customs, and one that, by contrast, does not seek to deny the 'coevalness'[9] or contemporary existence of the Irish masses and their culture. The playful upper gallery emerged as a phenomenon in the Dublin playhouse around the middle of the eighteenth century, thus around the time that the city was shifting from being a primarily Protestant city to a primarily Catholic, i.e. 'native Irish', city,[10] and this increase in Dublin's Catholic population was largely due to migration from the provinces. These migrants – who became domestic servants, clerks, teachers, petty traders – also made up an increasingly large part of the audience in Dublin playhouses[11] and, as is clear from the reactions of the countryman that Jane Francesca Wilde – Oscar Wilde's mother – recorded in the late nineteenth century, many of these migrants continued to see the theatre through a horizon of expectation shaped by Irish popular culture. After seeing a play for the first time in Dublin, this rural Irishman told Lady Wilde: 'I have now seen the great English actors and heard plays in the English tongue, but poor and dull they seemed to me after the acting of our own people at the wakes and fairs: for it is a truth, the English cannot make us weep and laugh as I have seen the crowds with us when the players played and the poets recited their stories.'[12] In the eighteenth and early nineteenth century, before the Famine had played havoc with the traditional rural way of life, Irish popular cultural practices would have even more powerfully shaped the migrant population's expectations about what constitutes good 'acting' and good entertainment, and it is the attempt to make the theatrical entertainment conform to such expectations both in its structure and ideological content, I suggest, that is registered in the so-called primitive upper gallery customs mentioned above.

In Irish rural culture, for instance, the community always asserted its right to stage itself in the interstices of organized rituals and assemblies, and this staging, which was performed by the young unmarried men of the region, generally took the form of comic plays, tricks and games. At wakes, weddings and Christmas entertainments, the area's 'prime lads' or 'hardy boys', as they were called in English, led by a trickster master of ceremony known as the *borekeen* [from the Irish *bórachán*: joker], would burst in, often disguised in straw and unannounced, and disrupt the arranged ritual or festivity with their boisterous games or plays. Wedding parties, for instance, were frequently disrupted by these impromptu entertainers' demands to kiss or dance with the bride, Christmas festivities were routinely disrupted by their mumming plays, and wakes (as noted in the Gold-smith piece above) were frequently disrupted by their trickery and little comical staged dramas.[13] The anthropologist, Henry Glassie, who studied such popular entertainment practices in a rural community in Northern Ireland in the twentieth century, also notes that this kind of disruptive play had a broader integrative social function. In his discussion of the mumming plays that were still being performed in County Fermanagh, for instance, Glassie notes that, as these plays progressed, they broke down the wall between performers and audience, so that by the end, the roles were completely reversed and the audience entertained the players with food and drink. 'This movement is an attack upon the Western tradition that separates an artist from his audience, a teacher from his class, a politician from his mob', Glassie concludes, ' . . . the mummers attacked the forces that keep people apart'.[14]

The 'wags' in the gallery who were trading jests with the players and among themselves, then, were also carrying on this socially integrative tradition of play, while displaying the native Irish entertainer's characteristic ability to move between social contexts and cultural traditions. As a number of Irish studies have noted, there were continuities between the rural entertainers who provided enter-tainment at the festivities mentioned above and such figures as the *drúth* and the *crosán*, the jesters and tricksters who provided entertainments in pre-modern Gaelic assemblies,[15] and these same Gaelic entertainers, it has also been noted, showed a remarkable ability to adjust to the changing circumstances of Irish society in the early modern period. By the early seventeenth century, for instance, as Alan Fletcher has pointed out, many of these entertainers had made their way into the houses of the country's new rulers, the great Anglo-Irish lords, and were providing dual-culture entertainments for these new patrons.[16] The repertoire of Irish wake games and mumming plays also indicates that the popular entertainers who were their successors were no less versatile. One of the earliest records of an Irish mumming play, an account of a play that was performed in Cork in 1685, for instance, reveals that Irish performers had adapted the kind of Hero-Combat play that was common throughout the British Isles to fit an Irish context by adding an Irish hero, Saint Patrick, to such traditional heroes as Saint George and Saint Dennis, and by including a particular nemesis of the seventeenth-century Catholic Irish, 'the bold usurper, Cromwell', among the play's villains.[17]

Even as these popular entertainers adopted plays and material from the broader British culture, however, as this last example shows, they continued the Gaelic tradition of using humour and satire to deal with those who threatened the community's life and values, and it is this more specifically political dimension of the Irish performance tradition, I suggest, that also explains the upper gallery's 'rude' custom of groaning for members of the elite. Mocking 'play' was regularly deployed in the Gaelic tradition to enforce a traditional, group-oriented way of life and to punish those who offended against these customary norms. The toying and trickery of the 'young folk' that Goldsmith mentions as being part of the wake ritual, for instance, were frequently directed at hosts who were considered to be insufficiently inhospitable or at old men who were considered to be anti-social or unneighbourly, and in some of their little comic mimetic plays, as Irish folklorists have noted, players at the wake would impersonate priests, police and judges and hold mock-marriages and mock trials.[18] As Gearóid Ó Crualaoich notes, such mocking practices were also a response to the new forms of civil and clerical control that were attempting to regulate and control rural community life in the early modern period; they were 'both a commentary on and a resistance to social forces threatening the continuance of old ways and old mentalities'.[19]

When the gallery 'Bucks' groaned at members of the ruling elite for their failure to act in the interest of the larger Irish community, then, they were bringing this tradition of mocking 'play' to bear on national politics, and this kind of mockery, ironically, took on an added power to disturb in this context precisely because of the Dublin theatre's imbrication in the colonial system. The viceregal court and other prominent members of the Anglo-Irish elite regularly appeared at the boxes in the Dublin playhouse throughout the eighteenth century and, as was well known, these stagings were consciously designed to elicit claps and other positive responses from the Irish public.[20] By groaning for some members of the elite, as they came into the theatre, and by applauding for other less patriotic ones, however, upper gallery theatergoers subverted this convention, while also reconstituting some of the power which the Irish community had lost when it had come into contact with the forces of colonialism and modernity.

Not all of the young penniless men who migrated into Dublin with the knowledge of Irish 'customs and practices' in their heads were of native Irish Catholic stock, however, nor were all rural Irish migrants content to remain in that city. Some, like Oliver Goldsmith, whose first experience of the theatre was most probably while he was an undergraduate in Dublin in the 1740s, subsequently made their way to London, and as we will see from *She Stoops to Conquer*, this 'ex-centric' Irishman also upset the 'People of fashion' in that city when he brought this kind of Irish 'waggery' on to the London stage.

Irish popular culture and Oliver Goldsmith's *She Stoops to Conquer*

It may seem strange to stress Oliver Goldsmith's connection to native Irish culture since in the above-mentioned '*Description*', he specifically identifies himself as 'an English *Gentleman*' and, in this essay, he described the native Irish and their customs with the cool detachment of a sophisticated English outsider. In everyday life, however, Goldsmith was anything but cool and sophisticated, as his English friends repeatedly noted. His tendency for giving away his meagre possessions to the poor earned him a reputation for reckless generosity, and his playful antics in polite company led this company to think of him as a show-off and a buffoon. Sir Joshua Reynolds, for example, said that 'to draw the attention of the company', Goldsmith would 'sing, stand upon his head, [or] dance about the room',[21] and Goldsmith himself reported that the Duke of Hamilton's circle regarded him 'more as a *jester* than a companion', dubbing him 'the facetious Irishman' for showing his 'talent' in that company.[22] In a recent essay, Terry Eagleton attributes these extravagant behaviours to the insecurities of 'the colonial blow-in' who seeks to ingratiate himself with his English metropolitan hosts by acting in stereotypically stage-Irish ways.[23] But a better explanation for these jester-like behaviours and for the so-called 'low' comedy in *She Stoops to Conquer* might be this colonial migrant's inability or unwillingness to forget the cultural values and practices that he learned during his younger days in Ireland. His generosity, as Declan Kiberd has noted, could be read as honouring the 'old Gaelic tradition of *flaithiúlacht* [hospitality or generosity; literally, feast-giving])',[24] while his comic stagings both in drawing rooms and in the theatre, could be read as a reactivation of a related Irish tradition of 'play' that he had learned – possibly painfully – during his rural upbringing in County Westmeath in the midlands of Ireland.

It has long been asserted that the central engine of humour in *She Stoops to Conquer* – the mistaking of a gentleman's house for an inn – came from an event in Goldsmith's childhood. Goldsmith's sister, for example, recounted that the playwright himself made the same kind of mistake as he was making his last journey from his father's house in Lissoy, County Westmeath to a school that he had been attending in Edgeworthstown in nearby county Longford. Finding himself in the village of Ardagh at nightfall, she explains, the young boy enquired for 'the best house in Town' and was shown the house of an old friend of his father, which he then treated, much to his later embarrassment, as an inn.[25] James Prior, one of Goldsmith's early biographers, however, throws a different light on this incident when he elaborated on it from Irish sources. In his account, the confusion was not the effect of an innocent misunderstanding on the part of an ignorant villager (as Goldsmith's sister implies) but a trick consciously designed by a local 'wag' in order to punish the young Goldsmith for 'swaggering'. Prior writes:

> Inquiring for the best house in the place, meaning the best inn, he chanced to address, as is said, a person named Cornelius Kelly, who boasted of having

taught fencing to the Marquis of Granby, and was then domesticated in the house of Mr. Featherstone, a gentleman of fortune in the town. He [Kelly] was known as a notorious wag; and willing to play off a trick upon one whom he no doubt discovered to be a swaggering school-boy, directed him to the house of his patron.[26]

This anecdote suggests, then, that *She Stoops to Conquer* has its roots in that Irish popular tradition of mocking play discussed above – a tradition that was always quick to punish those whom it considered to be upstarts – and, whether literally true or not, it also suggests that this play has its origin in Goldsmith's own tortured relationship to the place of his birth. Even as he denounced Ireland for having no conversation other than a 'smutty toast or a baudy song', in a letter to his brother-in-law in 1757, for instance, Goldsmith wrote that the memory of that former life was 'souring the pleasures' that he presently possessed: 'If I go to the opera where Signora Colomba pours out all the mazes of melody; I sit and sigh for Lishoy fireside, and Johnny armstrong's last good night from Peggy Gorden.'[27] And as he tried to appropriate the manners of an Englishman, he was also constantly measuring himself by the mores and values of the rural society back home and often finding himself wanting by that measure. 'I have passed my days away among a number of cool designing beings and have contracted all their suspicious manner, in my own behaviour', he wrote to his brother Henry in Ireland in 1759, and he went on to add: 'I should actually be unfit for the society of my friends at home as I detest that which I am obliged to partake of here. I can now neither partake of the pleasure of a revel nor contribute to raising its jollity. I can neither laugh nor drink, have contracted a hesitating disagreeable manner of speaking, and a visage that looks ill nature itself.'[28] The famously reserved Marlow, who is reluctant to spend money on his own food and drink, who is unable to talk openly to Kate, and who is disdainful of his rural surroundings, then, is a figure for this new English self, and in making this character the butt of humour in his staged play, it could be argued, Goldsmith was reenacting the trauma of a primal scene – a scene in which he was always both native to the Irish countryside but yet not a 'native' because of his English ancestry and Protestant background.

However, the comic butt in *She Stoops to Conquer* is not only Marlow, the character who stands in for the young Goldsmith, but also Mr Hardcastle, the character who stands in for the rich householder, Mr Featherstone, in the original incident, and to understand this other strand of mockery in Goldsmith's play and also this play's broader anti-bourgeois critique, it is necessary to turn to another Irish source from the scene of Goldsmith's childhood, namely, the Westmeath poet, Lawrence Whyte. In 1740, after he had moved to Dublin, Whyte published a book of poems about life in the Westmeath countryside in the early part of the eighteenth century,[29] and one of these poems, 'The Parting Cup, or the Humours of Deoch an Doruis', has long been mentioned as the possible source for Goldsmith's *The Deserted Village*.[30] Like Goldsmith's famous pastoral, 'The Parting Cup' also tracks the effect of modernity on a once-thriving rural community; it begins by describing, in three cantos, the contented life of an Irish farming family at a time when the gentry as well as their native Irish tenants practised 'Hospitality' and good neighbourliness, and it ends by showing in its fourth and final canto, the later, utter desolation of this whole rural community under the regime of a new more grasping kind of landlord.

The practice of 'Hospitality' in this poem, however, is also inextricably linked to the practice of providing, and engaging in, 'Entertainment' – in his preface, Whyte says that 'The Parting Cup' *'sets forth the great Hospitality and good Entertainment formerly met with in* Irish *Families'*[31] – and because Whyte's poem gives detailed descriptions of these 'Entertainment' practices, it provides an equally important context, I suggest, for reading Goldsmith's dramatic work. In cantos 2 and 3 of 'The Parting Cup' we are given detailed pictures of the festivities provided both by the poem's central character, the Irish tenant farmer, 'Deoch an Doruis', and by the neighbouring gentry, both Catholic and Protestant, in the Westmeath area of Goldsmith's youth. The Irish farmer, whose name literally means 'the drink at the door', kept 'open house' (68) for his landlord and all the neighbourhood at Christmas, we are told, and an ethnically mixed group of gentlemen – '*Nugents, Dillons, Daltons, Gambles, / Fitzgeralds, Kellys* and *Mangans*' (84–5) – went out 'in Squadrons' to entertain and be entertained at Christmas or whenever there was a '*Crist'ning, Feast or Wedding*' (86–7). Like the native 'hardy boys' in other parts of the country, too, Whyte's poem shows, this 'independent *Troop/* of *Squires* and *Gentlemen*' (86) meted out rewards or punishment to householders according to the way they were treated, thus serving as the enforcers of the community's unwritten and central law of 'Hospitality'. In the days after Christmas, for instance, this band went out 'a Mumming merrily', seeking food and drink as well as 'Merriment and Plays' (87), and if they were well received by the man of the house, they stayed in that house 'some Days and Nights' regaling the owner 'With various pastimes and delights'. But if they were not treated hospitably – if some 'Churl' dared 'kill a Goose or Hog,/ Sit down to eat his *Christmas* Prog/ His *Barrel* Tap, or give it *Vent*/ Without due notice to them sent' – they waged war on his household and property, making his life an utter misery:

> 'Twere better for him go to War,
> Against the *Turks*, the *Moors* or *Czar*,
> Or throughout *Europe* range and roam,
> Than think to live in Peace at *Home*. (90)

Tony Lumpkin's attack on his stepfather's house – and also possibly Cornelius Kelly's attack (via the unwitting young Goldsmith) on the house of his employer, Mr Featherstone, in the original anecdote – takes its meaning from this tradition of rough play, I suggest, and, like the rude play of the band of squires in Whyte's poem, Goldsmith's 'low'[32] play also takes aim at possessive individualism and the new bourgeois form of gentility that was undermining traditional, more community-oriented ways of living. At its core, *She Stoops to Conquer* is about an event that would have featured importantly in the cycle of festivities in the Irish countryside of Goldsmith's youth, namely, a wedding in the big house of one of the gentry. As we learn in the first act, a marriage has been arranged between Kate, the daughter of Squire Hardcastle, and Marlow, the son of Hardcastle's old friend, and the father of the bride is already preparing the big house for the reception of the prospective bridegroom and his father. After informing his daughter, Kate, about Marlow's imminent arrival, Hardcastle says he has to 'go prepare the servants for his reception' as 'we seldom see company'.[33]

This last point about not frequently seeing 'company', however, also suggests that Hardcastle is the antithesis of Deoch an Doruis, the model rural Irish gentleman who kept 'open house' in Whyte's poem, and this suggestion is reinforced both by his 'hard' name and by his subsequent behaviour in this play. In an explanatory footnote on Whyte's poetry which he includes in his Goldsmith biography, Prior writes that 'one of the greatest offences of the more opulent class in Ireland in the eyes of the peasantry at that time, was any seeming want of the duties of hospitality', and he went on to add that 'almost the first point noticed in the character of an Irish squire by a peasant of the present day is whether he is or is not a "*hard*" or close man'.[34] Hardcastle's behaviour to his inferiors in this play mark him as a 'hard' man in this peasant sense and, if the critical and staging tradition in relation to this character has generally painted him as a more benign figure, it is undoubtedly because it has accepted at face value this character's own idealized self-representations.[35] Hardcastle certainly portrays himself to his family as someone who loves 'old manners' (1.11) and old-fashioned hospitality, and as he notes himself, he behaves 'in the old style' when he goes himself to give Marlow and Hastings 'a hearty reception at the gate' of his house (2.20–1). But as the scene with his servants so clearly dramatizes, this ethic of hospitality and openness does not extend downward to his own peasantry. Diggory may have been brought in from the barn, and Roger may have been brought in from the plough for the upcoming festivities (2. 21–3) but they are to be present at this pre-nuptial feast only as servants and not as participants. 'You must hear us talk, and not think of talking; you must see us drink and not think of drinking; you must see us eat and not think of eating', Hardcastle informs them (2. 6–8), and he adds that when they hear him 'say a good thing, or tell a good story', they must not 'all burst out a-laughing, as if [they] made a part of the company' (2.20–3). The one exception to this rule – Diggory is told he may still laugh at the story of 'Ould Grouse in the gun-room' (2.24–5) – also works to reinforce rather than to undermine this separation of the social spheres. Whereas it was once taken for granted that the servant could share in the jokes and amusements of his master, it is now necessary for him to receive permission for this right of participation. In the Hardcastle house, a fourth wall has been erected, as it were, that serves to divide elite from popular culture, and this wall is being used to deny the community its customary right of joining in the festivities of the big house.

The larger economic and social implications of this kind of 'hard' behaviour are also evident from the Alehouse scene that precedes this scene. Like the above scene, this Alehouse scene also shows us a member of the big house – in this case Hardcastle's step-son, Tony Lumpkin – interacting with a group of locals but here the rituals of eating, drinking, and entertainment create a very different social and economic dynamic. In the first place Tony is shown sitting at the same table with 'several shabby fellows' (albeit 'a little higher than the rest') (1. 3–5), and, as the scene unfolds, we see that he is not only sharing his punch, tobacco, and songs with these rustics but also his money. 'But come, my boys, drink about and be merry, for you pay no reckoning', he tells his company (1.19–20). Such dispensing of largesse, as well as his willingness to engage in popular pastimes, also position Tony as the representative of an older landlord type. Indeed, one of the 'shabby fellows' says that Tony 'takes after his own father, old Squire Lumpkin' who was the 'finest gentleman' and who was unparalleled 'for winding the streight horn, or beating a thicket for a hare, or a wench' (1.11–14). But, as this scene reveals, the young Squire Lumpkin's ability to pursue the same pleasures as his father is also limited because he has not yet come into his inheritance, and this blockage in the system of intergenerational exchange has also created blockages in the sexual and material economy of the whole area. Because he has not been given his inheritance, Tony can neither pursue Bett Bouncer nor the miller's grey mare (1.18), and local businesses are suffering, as the same 'fellow' implies when he suggests that 'It would be well for all the publicans within ten miles round of him' if the squire were to 'come to his own' (1.3–6).

When Tony decides to 'be revenged on the old grumbletonian' (1. 11–12), his step-father, then, he is acting on behalf of the community as well as on behalf of himself, and like the tricksters in the Westmeath of Goldsmith's youth, this 'composition of tricks and mischief' (as Hardcastle describes his step-son) (1. 6) also relies on the assistance of a band of locals to set his vengeful play in motion. It is with the cooperation of the Landlord of the Three Pigeons that he first convinces Marlow and Hastings to go to Hardcastle's house and to mistake it for an inn (1.19–25), and it is with the help of another group of pranksters within the house – Kate and Constance (who are soon joined by the outsider, Hastings) – that he wages the kind of 'war' on the offending squire's house that was typically the punishment reserved for inhospitable 'Churls' in the countryside of Goldsmith's youth. As Hardcastle himself states in the fourth act, his whole house has been turned 'all topsey turvey' (4. 7) because of the behaviour of the deluded Marlow.

If Mrs Hardcastle is similarly turned 'topsey turvey' in this play – she ends up, of course, in the horse-pond at the bottom of the garden (5.19) – it is also because she is the moving spirit behind her husband's 'hardness' (we learn at the end of the play that she is the one who has devised the age fraud that kept Tony from receiving his inheritance [5.13–16]). In inspiring this inhospitable behaviour in her husband and household, too, she also directly contravenes the customary role of the 'woman of the house' in Irish traditional society. In Whyte's poem, for instance, it is actually the old Irish gentleman's '*good Wife*' who greets the guests 'with full *Brimmers*' at the door during the Christmas festivities, and it is also she who instructs the guests to drink heartily of her home-brewed '*Aquavitae*' so that they will 'over-flow with *Wit*', song and talk (75–6). The woman of the house thus performed a crucial role in mediating between inside and outside, thereby ensuring the flow of people and goods through the community. Mrs Hardcastle, by contrast, impedes this kind of circulation and displays contempt for the local community (she says at one point that her love of the 'town' 'serves to raise me above some of our neighbouring rustics' (2. 16–17)). And as the one who has the key to the bureau that contains Tony's money and also, as we learn, his cousin Constance's jewels, she is the most visible symbol of the hoarding that is creating all of the sexual and economic problems throughout this play. After her overthrow at the end of the play, then, the barriers that served to confine people as well as property are quickly broken down, and the way is cleared for a series of weddings and a celebration, to which, significantly, the whole community is invited. In his last speech Hardcastle announces that for 'the merry morning' the next day – that is, for the wedding celebrations – 'we shall gather all the poor of the parish around us' (5. 20–1). With the reform of the bourgeois householder, the ethic of 'Hospitality' once again prevails, this play suggests, and the big house is poised to become, once again, the open house of Goldsmith's youth,

But in Irish popular culture, as we have seen, the ethic of 'open house' was always as much about the rich and the poor sharing entertainment as it was about these classes sharing goods, and it is the high/low, town/country barriers that were erected to prevent this kind of sharing in the playhouse itself that were also undone – however temporarily – by Goldsmith's play. While the view that the London stage was awash in sentimental comedy in the second half of the eighteenth century has been properly challenged by Robert Hume and others,[36] it is nevertheless true that the reformers who had been trying to exorcize 'low' culture from the stage since the late seventeenth century were gaining new ground in the later eighteenth century, thanks to the control they were exercising over dramatic criticism in the popular press. In the 1760s and 1770s, as Frank Donoghue points out, the two most influential reviews, *The Monthly Review* and *The Critical Review*, were increasingly critical of new plays that failed to have 'sentimental strokes' or that did not meet the 'genteel' standards of sentimental comedy.[37] Goldsmith himself had been forced to withdraw the bailiff scene in the production of his first play, *The Good Natur'd Man*, (1768) 'in deference', as he himself noted, 'to the public taste, grown of late perhaps too delicate'.[38] As with the theatrical historiography discussed at the beginning of this paper, a 'customs and manners' narrative also sustained the argument for excluding 'low' entertainments matters from the theatre, and this 'customs and manners' narrative also relegated rural culture to an archaic period, this time in Britain's own past. In criticizing Goldsmith's comedy, for instance, William Woodfall, the editor of *The Monthly Review* wrote:

> Our customs and manners have undergone a gradual alternation. A general correspondence arising from trade, and the progress of the arts, has brought the nation, as it were, together, and worn off those prepossessions and habits which made every little neighbourhood a separate community and marked every community with its peculiar character ... Some of our late writers have therefore had recourse to what is called *Sentimental Comedy*, as better suited to the principles and manners of the age. A general politeness has given a sameness to our external appearances, and great degrees of knowledge are every where diffused.[39]

The enormous success of *She Stoops to Conquer* with audiences not only in London but in every part of the British mainland, however, made it difficult for these critics to sustain the narrative about the 'general politeness' of British culture or, for that matter, to sustain the related argument that the British mainland had a more evolved and refined taste than Ireland or the other colonies. If Goldsmith's play was popular in Dublin and 'our American plantations', as *The Morning Chronicle* noted in June and September, 1773, it was no less popular with audiences at home in Britain. 'There is hardly a town in England which boasts a playhouse, or a village which has a theatrical barn in it', this paper reported, 'where Tony Lumpkin's drolleries have not been ha! ha'd at this summer'.[40]

The country/town, Irish/English cycle also came full turn, it is worth noting, with John O'Keeffe's appropriation of Goldsmith's trickster character for his performances in provincial Ireland in the 1770s and early 1780s. O'Keeffe is best known today for the many successful pantomimes and pastoral comedies that he wrote for the London stage in the 1780s and 1790s. But before he emigrated in 1781, this Dublin native was one of Ireland's most famous itinerant comedians, and his first dramatic writings were to supply material for his own comic acts.[41] His most popular entertainment from this period was also a one-man, stand-up comic routine called 'Tony Lumpkin's Rambles [or Frolicks]', a piece that imaginatively followed the later adventures of Tony and Bet Bouncer (now his wife), as the comic pair encounter town-life and fashionable society for the first time.[42] The appeal of this performance for Irish provincial audiences is also not hard to understand. The town that Tony and Bet visited always just happened to be the one that O'Keeffe was performing in, so that (as in present-day pantomime) local landmarks and local lore became as much the dramatic subject matter as the adventures of this fictional character. The advertisement for O'Keeffe's benefit night performance of 'Tony Lumpkin's Frolicks in Cork' in October 1780, for instance, promised Cork theatregoers

a descriptive view of the public Edifices, Streets, Taverns, Coffee-houses, Red-house-walk, Sunday's well, Etc. Humorous and Satirical Remarks; Whimsical Adventures, Anecdotes, Etc, as they may have recently occurred, a Tavern Dinner, Dyke-house Breakfast, Bet Bouncer full dressed, complete Female Macaroni for 1780, Tony and Bet in Masks, correct pictures of a Masquerade and Fashionable Drum, Captain, Quaker, Dutchman, Patriot, and Lawyer at Cards, a Passage from England, Tony and Bet at the Play, Etc.[43]

For a Cork audience accustomed to viewing an English world on their stage, the prospect of hearing about such familiar sites – Sunday's Well and the Mardyke (as in 'Dyke-house Breakfast') are still well-known landmarks in Cork to this day – would have proved irresistible.

But for O'Keeffe, whose family had migrated from the Irish countryside to the city after they lost their lands in the Jacobite wars, the imaginary travels of Tony and his wife Bet Bouncer through the urban landscape also provided a vehicle for foregrounding an 'ex-centric native' perspective on the Anglo world and, with it, an Irish anti-bourgeois and anti-colonial kind of play. As noted above, O'Keeffe's act included a description of the 'complete Female Macaroni for 1780', and this kind of London-derived sartorial excess was apparently the principal focus of his dramatic satire in that season's Cork 'Frolicks'. A Cork newspaper from August 1780 reported that 'When the Tragedy ended, Mr. O'Keeffe made his appearance as Tony Lumpkin, in which character for near half an hour, without any auxiliary or stage assistant he amused a very brilliant audience, with a most laughable interlude on the follies of Dress', and this report went on to add that 'His principal object was the Female World'.[44] Since Swift's time, however, the fashionably-dressed English female had also been a synecdoche for the British state that tried to impose its economic and political will on Ireland,[45] and it is thus this state's 'customs and manners' (and those who try to emulate these manners in Ireland) that were also held up for his audience's mockery in O'Keeffe's act. Like the *borekeen* in the native Irish performance tradition, or the wags in the Dublin upper gallery, this joker was also using his local knowledge and wit to slyly laugh back at the imperial centre.

If a character from a popular English play could become the vehicle for this kind of subversive Irish laughter, it was also because – contrary to the emphasis of traditional theatrical historiography – eighteenth-century theatre was a 'travelling' rather than 'rooted' culture. To cite from the anthropologist James Clifford from whom these terms are borrowed, the theatre was a site that was constantly being 'traversed from outside',[46] and, as such, it was always capable of producing acts that challenged modernity's disciplinary impulses.

Notes and references

1. Michal Kobialka, 'Theatre Historiography: the Archive, the Object, and the Look', Talk given at Florida State University, spring 2005. I wish to thank Professor Kobialka for providing me with a copy of this talk.
2. See William R. Chetwood, *A General History of the Stage, From its Origin in Greece down the Present Time* (London, 1749). Other important Irish histories from the period were Benjamim Victor's *The History of the Theatres of London and Dublin*, 2 vols (London, 1761) and Robert Hitchcock's *Historical View of the Irish Stage*, 2 vols (Dublin, 1788–94).
3. '*A Description of the Manners and Customs of the Native Irish. In a letter from an English Gentleman*', in *Collected Works of Oliver Goldsmith*, ed. Arthur Friedman (Oxford: Oxford University Press, 1966), 3: 29, 25.
4. For evidence of Goldsmith's authorship, see Arthur Friedman, 'Goldsmith and the *Weekly Magazine*', *Modern Philology*, 32 (1935): 291–2. Friedman felt the evidence sufficiently strong to include this piece in Goldsmith's *Collected Works* (see note 3).
5. 'Bucks Have At Ye All', in James Love, *Cricket, an Heroic Poem: Illustrated with the critical observations of Scriblerus Maximus. To which is added an Epilogue, call'd Bucks Have at Ye All. Spoken by Mr. King at the Theatre Royal in Dublin in the character of Ranger in the Suspicious Husband* (London, 1770), 29–30.
6. From the manuscript copy of Charles Dibdin's memoirs, cited in William J. Lawrence, 'Notebooks on the History of the Dublin Stage', 99 vols, University of Cincinnati Library, 50: 163–5.
7. *A Letter to Messieurs Victor and Sowdon, Managers of the Theatre-Royal* (Dublin, 1755), 9.
8. *Macready's Reminiscences*, ed. Sir Frederick Pollock (New York: Macmillan, 1875), 76.

9. Johannes Fabian, *Time and the Other: How Anthropology Makes its Object* (New York: Columbia University Press, 1983). Fabian coined the phrase 'the denial of coevalness' to describe Western culture's tendency to locate 'primitive' cultures in a different temporal frame, one anterior to itself (31).

10. Patrick Fagan, 'The Population of Dublin in the eighteenth century with particular reference to the proportions of protestants and catholics', *Eighteenth-Century Ireland*, 6 (1991): 121–56.

11. See my *Riotous Performances: the Struggle for Hegemony in the Irish Theater, 1712–1784* (Notre Dame, Indiana: University of Notre Dame Press, 2003), particularly chapters 3, 4 and 8.

12. Jane Francesca Wilde, *Ancient Legends, Mystic Charms and Superstitions of Ireland* (London, 1888), 122.

13. See Seán Ó Súilleabháin, *Irish Wake Amusements* (Cork: Mercier Press, 1967); Alan Gailey, *Irish Folk Drama* (Cork: Mercier Press, 1969); Alan Harrison, *The Irish Trickster* (Sheffield: Sheffield Academic Press, 1989); Gearóid Ó Crualaoich, 'The "Merry Wake"' in *Irish Popular Culture*, ed. James S. Donnelly and Kerby A. Miller (Dublin: Irish Academic Press, 1998), 173–200; Georges Dennis Zimmermann, *The Irish Storyteller* (Dublin: Four Courts Press, 2001). For the 'hardy lads' and the 'borekeen', see Ó Crualaoich, 'The "Merry Wake"', 91, 193.

14. Henry Glassie, *All Silver and No Brass* (Bloomingdale and London: Indiana University Press, 1975), 93.

15. For the connection between popular entertainers and the *crosán*, see Harrison, *The Irish Trickster*, 87–101; for the connection with the *drúth*, see Alan J. Fletcher, *Drama, Performance, and Polity in Pre-Cromwellian Ireland* (Toronto: University of Toronto Press, 200), 36–46.

16. Fletcher, *Drama, Performance, and Polity in Pre-Cromwellian Ireland*, 206–60.

17. For the account of this 1685 performance, see Gailey, *Irish Folk Drama*, 8. For the prevalence of the Hero-Combat play throughout the British isles, see 68–80.

18. See Ó Súilleabháin, *Irish Wake Amusements*, 66–8, 75–101.

19. Ó Crualaoich, 'The "Merry Wake"', 193.

20. See *Riotous Performances*, chapter 2 for an account of the politics of the 'government night' and command performances in the Dublin theatre.

21. Cited in Terry Eagleton, *Crazy John and the Bishop* (Notre Dame, Indiana: University of Notre Dame and Field Day, 1998), 106.

22. *The Collected Letters of Oliver Goldsmith*, ed. Katharine C. Balderston (Cambridge: Cambridge University Press, 1928), 17, 18.

23. Eagleton, *Crazy John and the Bishop*, 106.

24. Declan Kiberd, *Irish Classics* (Cambridge, Mass.: Harvard University Press, 2001), 109.

25. 'Mrs. Hodson's Narrative' in *The Collected Letters of Oliver Goldsmith*, 167–8.

26. James Prior, *The Life of Oliver Goldsmith*, 2 vols (London: John Murray, 1837), 1: 45–6.

27. *The Collected Letters of Oliver Goldsmith*, 28, 29–30.

28. Ibid., 58.

29. Lawrence Whyte, *Poems on various subjects, serious and diverting, never before published* (Dublin, 1740). This collection was reprinted, with some new additions, as *Original Poems on Various Subjects, Serious, Moral and Diverting*, in Dublin in 1742.

30. See Prior, *The Life of Oliver Goldsmith*, 1: 39–43, 501–15.

31. Whyte, *Poems on various occasions* (Dublin, 1740), vii. Subsequent allusions to 'The Parting Glass' are to this edition and page numbers will be included in the text.

32. Some newspapers condemned *She Stoops to Conquer* as 'low' when it first appeared (see Friedman, *Collected Works*, 5:91).

33. *She Stoops to Conquer* in the *Collected Works of Oliver Goldsmith*. ed. Arthur Friedman (Oxford: Oxford University Press, 1966), 5: 113 (Act 1, lines 18–19). All subsequent references will be to this edition and will be included, with act and line number, in the text.

34. Prior, *The Life of Oliver Goldsmith*, 1: 43.

35. Marlies K. Danziger, for example, states that 'Hardcastle, like Kate, represents the ideal values of the play, especially good sense and affection' and that he is 'a plausible spokesman for Goldsmith's values' (*Oliver Goldsmith and Richard Brinsley Sheridan* [New York: Frederick Ungar, 1978], 54.)

36. See Robert Hume, *The Rakish Stage* (Carbondale and Edwardsville: Southern Illinois Press, 1983), 312–55.

37. Frank Donoghue, ' "He Never Gives us Nothing That's Low": Goldsmith's Play and the Reviewers', *ELH*, 55 (Autumn, 1988): 665–84.

38. Goldsmith, Preface to *The Good Natur'd Man* in *Collected Works*, ed. Friedman, 5: 14.

39. *Monthly Review*, 48 (March 1773): 309–10.

40. *Morning Chronicle*, 3 June 1773; 8 September 1773.

41. For an account of O'Keeffe's early career, see William Smith Clark, *The Irish Stage in the County Towns* (Oxford: Clarendon Press, 1965).

42. The *Hibernian Magazine* referred to 'Tony Lumpkin's Frolicks' as O'Keeffe's 'chef d'oeuvre in dramatic writing in Ireland' (April, 1782), 204. O'Keeffe first performed this piece in Cork in 1773 (Clark, *The Irish Stage in the County Towns*, 103).

43. *Hibernian Chronicle*, 2–5 Oct. 1780.

44. *Hibernian Chronicle*, 24–8 Aug. 1780.

45. For a discussion of this trope and also its anti-colonial thrust in the Irish context, see, for example, Laura Brown, 'Reading Race and Gender: Jonathan Swift', *Eighteenth-Century Studies*, 23 (1990): 425–43. For instances of the use of this trope on the Irish stage, see my *Riotous Performances*, chapter 2.

46. James Clifford, 'Traveling Cultures' in *Cultural Studies*, ed. Lawrence Grossberg, Cary Nelson, Paula A. Treichler (New York and London: Routledge, 1992), 101.

Part 4
Representations

10
Universality, Early Modernity, and the Contingencies of Representing Race

Mita Choudhury

> The universal announces, as it were, its 'non-place', its fundamentally temporal modality, precisely when challenges to its *existing* formulation emerge from those who are not covered by it, who have no entitlement to occupy the place of the 'who', but nevertheless demand that the universal as such ought to be inclusive of them. At stake here is the exclusionary function of certain *norms* of universality which, in a way, transcend the cultural locations from which they emerge.[1]

Thus Judith Butler introduces some of the fundamental tensions and contradictions inherent in the concept of 'universality' as it is perceived today. The relationship between universality and hegemony is central to any discussion of power relations, and especially so in the contexts of colonialism and imperialism because universality – when yoked to ideas of progress and benevolence – provides the easy logic for expansionism both then and now. In the eighteenth century, those who were either not covered by the 'universal' or about to be incorporated into it (the colonial subject) had few explicit demands; consequently, the claims of universality, for the most part, remained unchallenged.[2] Even as the empire is gradually established in reality and British hegemony comes to occupy the cultural imaginary, the performance of Otherness remained firmly rooted in universality, in principles that solidified the unacknowledged cultural specificity of the Other. As a theoretical principle, universality has a long historiography and a dominant place in Western metaphysics; as a prescriptive rule in the theatre (or any artistic endeavour), universality provides one among many mechanisms to articulate the dialectical relationship between reality and representation, between nature and art. In *An Essay on the Art of Acting*, Aaron Hill stipulates that the actor 'must follow applications of the general rule by particular references'. In his universally applicable scheme, 'there are only ten dramatic passions ... all others being relative to, and but varied degrees of, the foregoing'. These passions include joy, grief, fear, anger, pity, scorn, hatred, jealousy, wonder, and love. Hill goes on to argue that an actor's 'imagination must conceive a strong idea of the passion' – the passion which is 'undesigned and natural'.[3] The merits of Hill's pronouncements cannot be easily dismissed. After all, the performance of character on stage, generally speaking, must negotiate between *individual* predicaments as well as *universal* experiences, with the latter providing the necessary empathetic link between the character-performer and the spectator. Tendencies in the art or philosophy of acting in the eighteenth century were echoed in the world of painting portraiture where emotions and passions were conceptualized afresh. Francis Hayman, for instance, designed a detailed folding plate that depicted the twelve passions – including contempt, joy, sadness, hope, fear, and so on – on twelve separate faces, based upon Charles Le Brun's *A Method to Learn to Design the Passions*. The plate depicting *The Passions* was published in 1748 in Dodsley's *The Preceptor*.[4] Originally a scene painter and a book illustrator, Hayman went on to paint portraits and was for many years closely associated with the Royal Academy while Le Brun was the chief painter to Louis XIV and was known to have specialized in 'the psychology of expression and the beauty and utility of universals'.[5] But the new interest in anatomy and psychology in the eighteenth century, which extended into the twin domains of painting and performance, remained unthinkingly Eurocentric and universalist in scope and premise.

Moreover, if the financial success and entertainment value of a play are loosely tied to its universal appeal, an inevitable correlation at the time, then individuality or particularity (of character or action or passion) is pulled in the direction of the normative. Never ideologically neutral, universality paves the way for the normative. The purpose of this paper is to explore whether the theatre's tendency toward the normative, and its concomitant allegiance to the universal, have an impact on what I see as the insularity of the eighteenth-century British theatre. In this theatre, character and individuality are yoked to the European (which is the 'natural' extension of the British) self or some protean derivative of it. Even if in (performance) theory the split between the particular and the universal can be conceptualized, can the eighteenth-century theatre accommodate, both in terms of ideology and practice, I ask in the first part of this paper, the particularity of the Other? The most forceful evidence of this theatre's insularity lies in the fact of the infrequent appearance of the Black (and, by extension, the Jewish or the West Indian or any Other) character, who was, at best, an occasional force on the eighteenth-century stage; therefore, the impact of the Black character could only have been marginal, I propose in the second part, even though postmodern revisionist readings suggest otherwise. I examine disparate sites of performance practice and theatre history with David Garrick serving as prime example. Fully aware of the arbitrary nature of such a perspective, I am nonetheless comfortable with this methodological circumscription due to Garrick's huge impact on every facet of theatrical practice over several decades in the eighteenth century. His accommodation of the Black or the Jewish character, as I argue in the third part of this paper, perhaps unsurprisingly followed the patterns of universalist logic that tends to repress Otherness (or individuality) in order to create the broad appeal necessary for success at the box office.

From Betterton to Garrick: a paradigm shift?

The particularity of a character and its universal appeal, its innate (and thus internal) attributes and the ways in which they are manifested in performance deserve attention, particularly in discussions of race and representation. Whether he is the Southerne–Hawkesworth Oroonoko or Shakespeare's Othello on the eighteenth-century stage, the particularity of the black character is subsumed by the power of the image created by universalist notions of the Other.[6] In the play's first scene, Iago warns Brabantio of the dangers inherent in his daughter's marriage to the Moor by invoking in various ways Othello's bestiality: '[A]n old black ram is tupping your white ewe', and again, 'you'll have your daughter cover'd with a Barbary horse, you'll have your nephews neigh to you'. While the reference is specifically to Othello, the metaphors of bestiality work to elicit, among other responses, the universal resistance to miscegenation and the universal resistance to the offspring of miscegenation. In performance the universal continues to be the source and substance of the appeal; and the passions – expressed through facial expressions, gestures, and postures of the actors – are recognizable and believable.

Slavoj Žižek and Judith Butler, among others, have conceptualized the ingredients of particularity (its defining features or its specific attributes) as being fundamentally internal and *seemingly* in opposition to the external, social circumstances. Moreover, they argue, any 'effort to find the defining feature internal to the object is thwarted ... by the recognition ... that a thing is conditioned by its external circumstances'. Agreeing with Žižek's position on the matter, Butler says that 'at the same time that external and arbitrary conditions are rendered as immanent and necessary features of the thing, the thing is also grounded and unified by this performative act of definition'.[7] Useful as this internal–external split is in a homogeneous context, it becomes doubly significant *and* incommensurable when a White actor imitates the passion of a Black character. The urge to define is innate and irrepressible, but if this urge forces the external, known, and recognizable, i.e. universal, elements on to the specific formulations of a particular character, what then are the practical consequences of a Garrick playing Othello? In Aaron Hill's words (taken out of his context), 'unless the passion is first known, how is it possible it should be painted?'[8] In performance, the actor plays a critical role in transforming the nuances of the particular, mired in narcissistic self absorption, on to the realm of the universal where the attributes emerge or are manifested as both visible and believable. In Hill's theoretical framework, this process is necessary because the actor should always work towards 'the effacement of himself'.[9]

According to George Winchester Stone and George Kahrl, British acting theory and practice in the eighteenth century made the slow but sure transition from the conventional style that had defined acting technique since the Restoration – derived from the rhetorical tradition going back to Cicero and Quintilian – to the more creative expressions of emotion based upon the specific attributes of a character and demands of a situation. Following the lead of David Garrick, they claim, this new style of acting replaced the formulaic, stylized performances in tragedy, comedy, and farce with something that was far more realistic. The essential elements of this new style, in the words of Stone and Kahrl, are as follows: 'the triumph of the sympathetic imagination in preparing the role, the attention to detail in the idiosyncrasy of characterization, the particularization of the villain, rather than the generalized universal appearance of villainy'.[10] Not specific to British practice only, the conventional style was wedded to the value of presenting universals which had a long tradition in France as well as ties to the sister arts, painting and sculpture.[11] Charles Gildon, William Oldys, and other contemporary theatrical commentators point to Thomas Betterton as being the consummate actor in terms of conveying 'the expression of universals' in the previous era. The emphasis had been on the gestures, motion, and the art of declamation – all of which had to convey passion. But the universal passions of hatred, contempt, love, and horror had to be conveyed, they point out, in set styles with prescriptive acting formulas articulated in, for instance, Charles Le Brun's *A Method to Learn to Design the Passions* and Aaron Hill's *Art of Acting.*[12]

Why change something that had worked so effectively for so long? Stone and Kahrl rightly point out that the effectiveness of the 'methods' laid out by Le Brun and Hill was not universally accepted in the eighteenth century. The 'new' mid-eighteenth century preference was for what Charles Macklin did in his inter-pretation of Shylock on 14 February 1741: 'Shylock, traditionally a buffoon on stage, became with Macklin a serious, revengeful man, but *not* an example of abstract vengeance', because Macklin rejected the principles laid out in the acting manuals and introduced a whole new approach to character and interpretation. In his *Essay on Acting*, David Garrick observed that Macklin succeeded in his portrayal of 'one of Shakespeare's most inimitable and difficult characters' because of 'his great attention and observation of the manners, dress and behavior of a peculiar tribe of people'. In Stone and Kahrl's recuperative framework the actor was thus for the first time in a position to explore and express emotions tailored to unique situations and characters – with Macklin's innovative approach serving as a partic-ular example and Garrick's entire acting career symbolizing the new style.[13] But to what extent was there a paradigm shift in acting in the eighteenth century? And could there have been any perceptible difference in the ways in which the Other was conceptualized and then represented on stage?

I would first point to the necessarily speculative nature of any firm conclu-sions and go on to argue that what appears at first glance to be a movement from a universal approach to character or situation – based upon the methods of acting proposed by Hill and others – to one that caters more consciously to the particular has to be examined carefully because that is not exactly what happens specifically in the example of Macklin as Shylock and more generally in the eighteenth-century London theatre.[14] While the earlier Shylock was indeed a stock character and a straightforward abstraction representing vengeance, the 'new' Shylock was arguably more real and thus more humanized. But note that the realistic rendition was the result of 'great attention and observation', and in this endeavour the attributes of 'the tribe' had to be unified and created into a coherent formulation that was still recognizable, still readily associated with the Jew, and was universally recognized as such in performance. The postmodern instinct is to ask 'observation of whom?' For one thing, the particular cannot operate without the universal even as it resists the universal and the universal is inevitably made up of discrete particularities even though it cannot possibly contain all. It would be a mistake to think that the 'new' convention – permeating through both theories of eighteenth-century acting and the actual performances on stage – rejected the universal. The point of reference, the 'alien' construct that is being represented on the eighteenth-century stage, is still a nebulous construct; having no entitlement to occupy the place of the 'who' (to echo the words of Judith Butler), the Jew participates in his naturalization ritual without resistance. What happened gradually in the course of the eighteenth century is that the stylistic changes produced a new and distinct conception of the abstract *and* the universal. Universality came to have a radically different relation to the particular where the particular role/character was now delivered to an audience attuned to realism and to life-likeness rather than being opposed to universalist approaches toward understanding and experiencing passion, predicament, and character.

Current philosophical discourses point to the complexity of positioning universality within postmodern radical politics although there is tacit agreement about 'the paradoxical notion of the Universal as simultaneously impossible and necessary'.[15] So, for instance, Ernesto Laclau observes that *'The universal is an empty place, a void which can be filled only by the particular, but which, through its very emptiness, produces a series of crucial effects in the structuration/ destructuration of social relations. It is in this sense that [universality] is both an impossible and a necessary object'.*[16] According to Slavoj Žižek also 'the Universal is empty, yet precisely as such always-already filled in, that is, hegemonized by some contingent, particular content that acts as stand-in – in short, each Universal is the battleground on which the multitutude of particular contents fight for hegemony'.[17] In Shakespeare's *Merchant of Venice,* Venice stands in for Britain while the Christian characters fight to regain the hegemony that was never lost. Shylock before and after Macklin represents two discrete entities, each with its universalist assumptions, each uniquely 'hegemonized by some contingent, particular content', to use Žižek's words. His eighteenth-century reincarnation is just as hegemonized as his former self which was a mere caricature of the Jew. Indeed, Shylock's dehumanization would have been just as readily accepted in his new and 'natural'ized state, in the interpretation associated with Macklin, as it had been in the Renaissance.

David Garrick's strong objections to John Home's *Douglas* and his reasons for not wanting to stage it at first provide a glimpse into the ways in which the process of play selection worked but also the ways in which the considerations of universality – broadly configured – were brought into dialectical play with the demands of an audience and the conventions of contemporary dramatic action. In his letter to the Earl of Bute dated 10 July 1756, Garrick describes his objections to *Douglas* with meticulous care and some of it goes as follows:

> The Story is radically defective & most improbable in those Circumstances which produce dramatic Action. ... It is romantic for want of those probable Strokes of Art, wch ye first Poets make use of to reconcile strange Events

to ye Minds of an Audience. . . . But these and many other Defects, wch I will not trouble Y^r Lord^p with, might be palliated & alter'd perhaps; but the Unaffecting conduct of ye Whole & which will always be ye Case, when the Story is rather told, than represented; when the Characters do not talk or behave suitably to ye Passions imputed to them, & the Situation in Which they are plac'd; when the Events are such that cannot naturally be suppos'd to rise; & the Language too often below the most familiar Dialogue; these are the insurmountable Objections, which in my Opinion, will Ever make *Douglas* unfit for ye Stage.[18]

Clearly, romance and realism are set up as aesthetically antithetical. Probability, suitability, believability – all contingent factors – assumed significance and determined the parameters within which the characters and action could operate. In order to be believable, according to Garrick, events have to arise naturally from one to the next, creating an unspoken consensus between spectator and actor.[19] But that which is apparently natural at any given point in time is also necessarily the product of or subject to contingency.

Othello and Oroonoko: challenges to the formula?

Selective constructions of eighteenth-century theatrical records can be misleading when discussing representations of racial/ethnic differences as perceived and understood then. It is true that both *Othello* and *Oroonoko* were performed with regularity, over and over again, throughout the long eighteenth century. And popularity or staying power over time is an important indicator of a play's effectiveness; but this selective view is uniquely ours – a product of revisionist, postmodern ethical and aesthetic instincts – rather than an accurate indication of what might have been. Elsewhere, I have argued that the 'black' character emerges only as an occasional force on the eighteenth-century British stage.[20] I would argue once again and especially in this context that a season by season analysis of performances in the major London theatres – which coincides more closely with the perceptions of contemporary theatregoers and the concerns of managers and actors at that time – would inevitably reveal that any number of successful plays were juxtaposed against innumerable others and many of them were Renaissance or Jacobean and Caroline plays, most of them staged in the eighteenth century with some degree of revision.[21] Thus *Othello* is one among many other Renaissance tragedies and comedies that were successful on the eighteenth-century British stage. The methodology of selective narratives – that isolate the impact of *Oroonoko*, for instance – should at least be questioned if not challenged also on the grounds that the specific and immediate contexts of performances are often neglected in the face of the panoramic sweep that paradigmatically links, for instance, the eighteenth-century 'Oroonoko' to its twentieth-century reincarnation. Arguably, one can assume that Aphra Behn was not uppermost in the minds of the theatregoers who happened to catch a performance of *Oroonoko* in 1759 (roughly 70 years after Behn's death), although postmodernist revisionism demands that Behn be present and acknowledged at every twist and turn of this play's performance history. In our minds, Behn and Southerne may forever be etched as twin comrades in the cause to rehabilitate and humanize the Slave; but the impact of one character, Oroonoko, cannot be overestimated as a result.

Theatre historians are aware of the contingencies of rehearsal and production (with myriad other related issues that unfold invisibly behind the stage and before opening night and during benefit night and with each set of circumstances having some direct or indirect impact on the box office receipts). A great deal depended on the availability of actors and their preparation/ability/suitability for certain parts. All of these contingent factors had an impact on what was finally produced. What can be said with some certainty is as follows. The black character flitted in and out of the British cultural imaginary with some degree of regularity, but its impact (at least till the very end of the eighteenth century, and that too mostly in the realm of the Novel and private performances) should not be exaggerated, especially when one considers the plenitude of extant evidence related to the London theatre pointing to its theoretical framework, its elaborate operations, its celebrities, and, simultaneously, the paucity of commentary that points directly to the identity of the black character or the contingencies of representing racial and ethnic differences. A critique of eighteenth-century British culture must confront the erasures rather than creating, wittingly or not, false perceptions of a national preoccupation with Blacks or slavery.

In her essay titled 'Transnationalism and Performance in 'Biyi Bandele's *Oroonoko*', Elizabeth Kowaleski Wallace considers the circum-Atlantic and transnational force of the Oroonoko 'story' by pointing to various overlapping and remarkable tropes in the Behn, Southerne and Bandele versions. About Bandele's work, Wallace observes that it

> returns us to the diasporic underpinnings of the Oroonoko story. Despite everything that has been written about the story, for Bandele it remains a tale of violent dispersal, of trauma, and of suffering. In the play's best moments – especially in its keen attention to issues of gender politics and language – his *Oroonoko* accomplishes what is arguably the highest purpose of diasporic art: to move its audience first through and then beyond human suffering to a place that makes possible the identification and connection with those who have suffered a historical wrong.[22]

Wallace's conceptualization of 'the highest purpose of diasporic art' may, in some senses, be said to echo the kind of effect that John Ferriar was attempting to elicit in his *Prince of Angola*. But as I have pointed out elsewhere, any attempt to reconfigure the Southerne-Hawkesworth play's *functionality*,[23] diverting it from pure entertainment to one that is imbued with counter-hegemonic logics, was bound to fail – as Ferriar's did. His idealistic, impassioned, and sincere anti-slavery sentiments were squelched by a theatrical system with a long history of licensing, state-sponsored entertainment, and an unwitting propensity for evasion. Wallace goes on to say that 'Bandele counteracts a pseudouniversalism, a Eurocentric representation disguised as universal, in favor of a more precise understanding of how Africa represents itself in the face of Western representation'.[24] While Bandele's attempt is commendable, its impact is not as easy to ascertain. In the best of circumstances, the collective memory of the spectators and the collective memory of the black characters represented on stage (both in the 1759 and the 1999 productions) diverge and cannot be forcibly made to converge by any retrospective or current impulse toward 'global humanism'.[25] Both then and now, the point of empathy – if this is indeed achievable in the theatre – has to have some dialectical relationship with universality in all its psychic and social dimensions. In the absence of a common heritage and collective memory (that binds the actor to the spectator), the 'empty' universal is once again filled in by the power of the gaze that consumes at this point in time in 1999 a specifically Nigerian narrative. Describing the difference between the French and English spectator, Thomas Davies observed, 'The Frenchmen ... are taught habitually to cry at scenes of distress. The Englishman looks upon the theatre as a place of amusement; he does not expect to be alarmed with terror, or wrought upon by scenes of commiseration; but he is surprised into the feelings of these passions and sheds tears because he cannot avoid it. The theatre, to most Englishmen, becomes a piece of instruction by chance, not by choice.'[26] This stereotype may have had some basis in truth then. I would question the level of empathy (or even understanding) now primarily because this 'new' empathy in my view is always already and still tainted by an irrepressible and *simultaneously repressed* response to the exotic.

In her essay, Wallace lists some 'visual clues' in Bandele's *Oroonoko* that director Gregory Doran uses to 'deessentialize the category of "Africa"'. While some characters 'wear turbans and other accoutrements of the desert farer', the people of Cormantien are 'dressed in the coastal Yoruba style of "agbada" and "dashiki"'. In this critical formulation, Behn's novella was a 'seventeenth-century reflection of an African reality' while 'Biyi Bandele's is a 'modern, cosmopolitan reflection of a Nigerian reality'.[27] The notion that the subaltern can now speak and not only be understood fully but also have an impact on the ways in which politics intersects with the forces of global economics is a lofty one. We all readily agree with Wallace that that is how it should be. The London theatre in the late twentieth century can accommodate both black actors and, in this case, the 'agbada' and 'dashiki'. But the use of specific styles of clothing on stage does not do anything to deessentialize the purveyors of difference. The difference is marked and can be understood only superficially at best, as Gayatri Spivak and others have argued. Explaining Spivak's point, Judith Butler says '[t]here is no one "other" there, at the site of the subaltern, but an array of peoples who cannot be homogenized, or whose homogenization is the effect of the epistemic violence itself'. More importantly, Butler asks, 'Can we read for hegemony without knowing how to read for the mobility of this kind of exclusion, without assuming in advance that the translator's point will be to bring this writing into forms of agency legible to an Anglo-European audience? In this sense, the task of the postcolonial translator ... is precisely to bring into relief the non-convergence of discourses so that one might know through the very ruptures of narrativity the founding violences of an episteme.'[28] What would be the difference if Bandele's play were to be performed on a Brook-like empty stage without the accoutrements of specificity such as the agbada and dashiki and fancy strobe lights for whatever added effect they were used? The fact is, the epistemic force and meaning of these signs – be they costumes (external), names (internal and external), language (Yoruba; internal and external) and even the bare black skin (innate; internal and external) – remain elusive, distant, and still very exotic, symbolizing an 'other' whose act is perpetually displaced even when the violence of the displacement is lost in the other's memory and even if the speaker is a native who is uniquely qualified to narrate (Bandele) and to act (Monu).

Jessica Munns reads Bandele's *Oroonoko* with somewhat less optimism regarding its agenda and impact. She discussed the play with Simon Reade, who was the dramaturg at the Royal Shakespeare Company. According to Munns, Reade

> agreed that Bandele had decided for 'dramatic reasons' to make Orombo a 'baddie' and have Oroonoko as a 'goodie'. Orombo's role as a 'baddie' greatly reduces the significance of the slavers who are subordinated to roles as benefi-ciaries of political in-fighting in an African state, and it also somewhat exculp-ates them as they do not use trickery to gain slaves but merely round up those sold to them. The increase in African agency is ambiguous, for Bandele's African kingdom is a place of betrayal, brutal sexuality, violence, and exploitation.[29]

Oroonoko had been the 'goodie' and much more since the original conception; he was identified, named, and even glorified then by the steadfastness of Behn's gaze which seldom chanced upon another object. The radical change that is sought (and I believe not found) in the 1999 production is a fantastic illusion; the agency of the African hero can hardly be expected to go beyond the ambiguous to a definitive stance of resistance that can only materialize in a level-playing psycho-social field. The use of sex and violence in Bandele's *Oroonoko*, mentioned by both Wallace and Munns, is at least one way to drive home the inevitable point about the rupture that divides the ontological imperative of here and the ontological imperative of there – both distinct trajectories that seldom converge and do so mostly to collide.

The obsession with feathers, but what's the difference?[30]

On Garrick's stage, there was a new interest in costumes and the budget for wardrobes was increased. Consequently, according to one contemporary account, dresses were 'no longer heterogeneous and absurd mixtures of English and foreign and ancient modes, which formerly debased our tragedies, by representing a Roman General in a full-bottomed peruke, and a sovereign of an eastern empire in trunk hose'.[31] What was perceived as seventeenth-century absurdity is thus replaced in the eighteenth century with what I would characterize as a conscious effort to bring the costumes closer to 'reality', but realism had to contend with the weather which did not permit scant clothing in spaces that had no means of heating. Four or five distinct styles emerged nonetheless: 'Turkish or Eastern (for oriental or exotic characters, with turbans and full trousers gathered at the shoe top)' in addition to Spanish, Roman, old English and so on. Interestingly, '[f]urs and skins had been adopted by the French actor LeKain to distinguish barbarous personages – a convention speedily imitated by Garrick in England'.[32] Broad strokes rather than realistic detail prevailed.

Thomas Betterton and Barton Booth were reportedly great Othellos, but Garrick's performance in the lead role was deemed mediocre and he stopped performing the role after only four appearances. There are many speculative explanations why Garrick failed in this role, whereas he was so successful in his rendition of Richard III, Lear, and Macbeth, among others. Garrick biographers Stone and Kahrl note that he had spent a great deal of time preparing for this role and he would often recite lines from it, but the spectators did not take to him as Othello. Quin was the indisputable favourite, which some attributed, among other factors, to the advantage of his greater height. Garrick's letter to Francis Hayman, dated 18 August, 1746, is an instruction manual of sorts written for the painter who was about to represent a scene from *Othello*.[33] It provides the best and most detailed evidence of the following: (a) the specificity and attention to detail with which Garrick had created a 'story board' – from our perspective, with Brechtian or Hitch-cockian precision – of the scene that he considered to be of critical importance in *Othello*, and (b) the extent to which, according to Garrick, this climactic scene is pivotal in creating the exact tragic outcome upon which the success of the play as a whole depended. I quote from this letter at length here in order to highlight how and why universality prevails despite and even due to the excruciating specificity:

> The Scene wch in my Opinion will make the best Picture,[34] is that point of Time in the last Act, when Emilia discovers to Othello his Error about the Handkerchief.
>
> Emil – Oh thou dull Moor! That Handkerchief &c – Here at once the Whole Catastrophe of the play is unravell'd & the Groupe of Figures in this Scene, with their different Expressions will produce a finer Effect in painting, than perhaps Any other in all Shakespear, tho as yet never thought of by any of the Designers who have publish'd their Several Prints from ye same Author. The back Ground you know must be Desdemona murder'd in her bed; the Characters upon the Stage are Othello, Montano, Gratiano & Iago (ye Principal) upon ye right hand (I believe) must be thunderstruck with Horror, his Whole figure extended, wth his Eyes turn'd up to Heav'n & his Frame sinking, as it were at Emilia's Discovery. I shall better make you conceive My Notion of this Attitude & Expression when I see You; Emilia must appear in the utmost Vehemence, with a mixture of Sorrow on Account of her Mistress & I <think> should be in ye Middle: Iago on ye left hand should express the greatest perturbation of Mind, & should Shrink up his Body, at ye opening of his Villany, with his Eyes looking askance (as Milton terms it) on Othello, & gnawing his Lip in anger at his Wife; but this likewise will be describ'd better by giving you the Expression when I see You; the other less capital Characters must be affected according to ye Circumstances of the Scene, & as they are more or less concern'd in ye Catastrophe: I could say a great deal upon the Choice of this Scene, but I hate writing.[35]

Garrick clearly gave the minutest attention to bodily gestures and movements, facial expression, as well as the exact positioning of the characters in relation to each other – factors that contribute to the totality of the meaning and the intended effect, all of which are tightly scripted in his theatre. The relationship between the live performance and this painting is an organic one, at least as conceptualized by Garrick, with the logic of the live performance deeply embedded in the rhetoric of the moment captured in frame.[36] Twice Garrick defers describing the exact facial expressions of Iago and Othello till he met with Hayman – preferring the accuracy of the face-to-face performance/communication to relying upon words to convey his intention/expression. He had given a great deal of thought to every aspect of the 'discovery scene' and, as the evidence suggests, the entire play.

Notice, however, that none of the following is of concern to Garrick. The difficulties of representing what we perceive to be the racial divide so starkly revealed in this scene (with all the 'principals' lined up); or the challenges of representing, for instance, the difference between the venality of the white character and the uncontrollable passion of the black character; or the possibility of communicating in tone (performance) and texture (painting) the rage of the Moor versus the malignity of Iago. Twentieth-century interpretative strategies cannot be conflated, in other words, with the contingencies of eighteenth-century performance practice. Thus while the text is imbued with sometimes violent and at other times heightened images and metaphors of cultural and corporeal differences between the African and European principals, one assumes that in performance on the Garrick stage these elements were articulated without the ideological weight they carry for us; in other words, the actors, whether Garrick or Quin, through their individual and distinctive styles of acting, worked toward perfecting the universal themes and emotions 'by annexing at once, the *look* to the *idea*'.[37]

An equally significant letter from David Garrick addressed to John Hawkesworth (dated 14 August, 1759) reveals Garrick's take on some scenes in *Oroonoko*. Hawkesworth had sent Garrick a proof of the play for the manager's comments and corrections. In his reply to Hawkesworth, Garrick refers to 'a Small alteration or two' and the need for 'a few omissions', but then goes on to provide some additional details as follows:

The Soliloquuy of *Aboan*, in yᵉ Page where yᵉ first paper is, must be alter'd as we settled it, by wᶜʰ means, his abrupt Entrance into yᵉ Conspiracy will be a Beauty – pray Enforce the Sentiment we agreed upon – viz. *the Necessity of Striking quickly, least He shᵈ like yᵉ rest Grow acquainted wᵗʰ Slavery & be satisfy'd with it.* In Act 3ᵈ – page 44 – of yᵉ printed side, – the third Scene between *Hotman & Aboan* is introduc'd too precipatately – [sic]

The line before of yᵉ last Scene is Spoken by *Aboan*; & it is surely unnatural to immediatly begin yᵉ followˢ Scene with yᵉ Same Person, & who by his first Speech, tells yᵉ audience that he has been opening *Oroonoko's* Scheme to *Hotman* – so quick a transition will always appear unnatural, & tho it is excus'd in yᵉ Old Writers, Yet It will be thought a blemish in a Modern one; I wᵈ advise You to alter it –

Suppose that ye 3^d Scene of ye 3^d Act was to begin with the common Blacks of ye Conspiracy, & after two or three Speeches *Aboan & Hotman* may Enter to Them, and ye Scene go on Exactly as it does now – this is ye only thought that has yet occur'd to me.[38]

This letter is markedly different from the one addressed to Hayman, discussing *Othello*. Garrick refers directly here to both 'slavery' and 'Blacks' in the context of refining the stage effects of the slave rebellion. Garrick's analysis here as elsewhere reveals his persistent efforts to present scenes and characters that would 'appear' natural to the spectator. Again and again he makes a distinction between the 'Old' writers and the 'Modern' ones – and insists that the sequencing of the scenes as well as the presentation of the characters must be believable. Aboan and Hotman must stand out and be distinguished from the 'common Blacks' because they represent the dissatisfied Black while the rest of the Blacks, accustomed to slavery, must be seen here as passive background material, adding tone and texture to the subversive forces at work but lacking the agency that he sees these two characters as having.

Devoid of any political or hegemonic agenda, the consciousness of this critic is geared toward the exigencies of the dramatic situation. Within this framework, there is no antagonism between the subject and the object. The actor-manager-playwright-editor is seen here operating within a normative framework that does not accommodate the possibility of disruptions. Contained within a tightly-knit dramatic structure and performance space, there is no 'real' threat of rebellion beyond the boundaries of the stage.

In her preface to *Troping Oroonoko from Behn to Bandele*, Susan Iwanisziw points out that in Hannah More's 'The Slave Trade' (or 'Slavery', 1787), written on behalf of the Anti-Slavery Society, 'Oroonoko's noble identity and romantic heroism are subsumed by concerns with universal liberty and evangelism. More voids Behn altogether, but she also supplants Southerne's focus on Oroonoko's exceptional worth by a call to universal pity: "For millions feel what Oroonoko felt".' Iwanisziw then observes that Hannah More's egalitarian impulse 'is premised solely on the equality of souls before God and not any notion of cultural parity'.[39] The notion of cultural parity has been challenged by postcolonial discourses for a variety of reasons. If anything, the twentieth century has shown that there is no cultural and economic parity within and between nations; indeed searching for parity in the face of overwhelming evidence of its absence both then and now would be ahistorical and counterproductive. Transnational human rights activism – beginning circa 1947 – is predicated upon the belief that individual and group rights have to be protected despite and in response to the limitations of local/state jurisprudence and the imperial inclinations of superpowers and supranational forces. And the purpose of universal declarations of human rights – however limited their impact on domestic law – is both to acknowledge inequality and to fight it across the borders of nation and sovereignty in order to preserve and protect the rights of individuals and groups. Any argument that holds the eighteenth-century public intellectual – essayist, poet, playwright, or novelist – accountable for denying or promoting egalitarianism must acknowledge with specificity the limitations of such pursuits.[40] Also, the author of *Thoughts on the Education of Daughters* (1787) and *A Vindication of the Rights of Woman* (1792) need not necessarily have seen the merits of reinstating Behn and her contributions to the imperial imaginary. So Hannah More 'voids Behn' as did John Ferriar because both were consumed by the immediacy and contingencies of the anti-slavery movements, such as they were, in Manchester, Liverpool, and elsewhere toward the late eighteenth century. More's concern for the twin concepts of 'universal liberty and evangelism' are familiar markers of the far-right socio-political agendas in the early twenty-first century. Indeed notions of universality are often linked to evangelism for the precise purpose of 'spreading faith' and 'bringing hope' with the Christian working toward these goals as both catalyst and representative of Christ.

The theatre as chronicle?

Postcolonial discourse has for several decades now delved into the ways in which the discursive practices of the West have unconsciously positioned the West as the agent of meaning, representation, and action while framing the rest as the object of those meaning-producing, representational operations and strategies. In this inherently hierarchical politics of power relations, theatrical representation has a pivotal place since these relations can very literally be rehearsed on stage, 'acted out', and then framed in the context of live spectatorship. But does the extant evidence measure up to what one expects to find?

The sale of slaves was a fact in the eighteenth century – a fact authenticated by documents, diaries, memoirs, although literary critics turn most frequently to 'narratives' such as the one written by John Gabriel Stedman, which in some senses authenticates Behn's narrative. Objecting to Joseph Roach's claim that there were slave auctions in early eighteenth-century coffee houses, Robert D. Hume points to (a) lack of evidence of such activities and (b) the problems inherent in making generalizations based upon insufficient evidence. Indeed there seems to be no solid evidence of such activities, with or without the stray advertisement in one 1709–1710 issue of the *Tatler*.[41] But without slave auctions, how could slaves have been bought and sold? Does lack of evidence – written testimony – indicate that there were none? For my purposes here, the venue is less important (London, elsewhere) than the fact itself if it could be authenticated. More important, would such activities be advertised frequently in the contemporary papers? I would argue that Steele – the bone of contention in this particular debate between Robert D. Hume and Joseph Roach, two established eighteenth-century scholars – or Garrick or Hill or any prominent individual in the eighteenth-century public sphere would not consciously censor materials. I agree with Hume when he says that they were not really interested in matters of racial difference or slavery even though they must have known what was going on. And even if they were interested in what was then considered to be matters of trade and commerce, could they have known how to use such material toward creating theatrical entertainment? Clearly not, since the evidence shows that they would fall back on the few tried and tested examples over and over again.

The success of *Oroonoko* pales in comparison to the success of *The Beggar's Opera* – if one looks at eighteenth-century theatre records – although *Oroonoko* has come to assume the kind of academic stature in the twentieth century that Gay's play has not achieved despite Brecht's equally innovative intervention 200 years later (with a significant ripple effect on the New York stage even as this piece is being written). Whether this trend to magnify *Oroonoko* has anything to do with the left-leaning liberal politics that pervades most of academia (according to those in the Right at least) is a matter of opinion. I would only draw attention to the fact that there is sketchy evidence in the theatre of any sustained argument of European superiority such as it was conceptualized by social contract theorists such as Denis Diderot, David Hume, Edmund Burke, and Jean-Jacques Rousseau. Performances in private spheres – such as the ones described by Michael Dobson in this volume – instead of in public venues were more in tune with social and political realities although the 'why' can perhaps never be answered.

The realism that Garrick was so adamant on recreating had not matured to the point where it could be contaminated by the 'moment of the ethical', to use Ernesto Laclau's phrase. Laclau has explained the interdependent and the antagonistic relationship between the normative and the ethical. The normative has a huge role in the everyday functioning of individuals who make decisions and act in certain ways. As Laclau explains, '[t]he subject who takes the decision is only partially a subject; he is also a background of sedimented practices organizing a normative framework which operates as a limitation on the horizon of options'. Any decision-making is, in some senses, 'always already contaminated by normative particularity'. The subversive 'moment of the ethical', in other words, cannot just magically manifest itself.[42] John Ferriar's play was never performed and predictably so from the retrospective point of view. Ferriar's anti-slavery aesthetic cannot be sustained by *Oroonoko*, which is, from the very outset, invested in romance, fantasy, tragic heroism, and European benevolence, the creative manifestations of which can be found in the postmodern nationalist instincts toward naturalization, homogenization, and universality. The narratives of performance in the eighteenth century point to the culture's abiding interest in theatricality – but to assume that this volatile medium, this at once chimerical and very real pasttime, can rise above and beyond the 'backgound of sedimented practices' and subvert the forces of the normative would be to underestimate the eighteenth-century theatre's deeply evasive impulse.

Notes and references

1. Judith Butler, 'Restaging the Universal: Hegemony and the Limits of Formalism', in Judith Butler, Ernesto LaClau, and Slavoj Žižek, *Contingency, Hegemony, Universality: Contemporary Dialogues on the Left* (London: Verso, 2000), 39.
2. Etienne Balibar has argued that '[n]o theoretical discourse on the dignity of all cultures will really compensate for the fact that, for a "Black" in Britain or a "*Beur*" in France, the assimilation demanded of them before they can become "integrated" into the society

in which they already live ... is presented as progress, as an emancipation, a conceding of rights. And behind this situation lie barely reworked variants of the idea that the historical cultures of humanity can be divided into two main groups, the one assumed to be universalistic and progressive, the other supposed irremediably particularistic and primitive.' See Balibar, 'Is there a Neo-Racism?', in Etienne Balibar and Immanuel Wall-erstein, *Race, Nation, Class: Ambiguous Identities* (London: Verso, 1991), 25.

3. Aaron Hill, *An Essay on the Art of Acting* (London: J. Dixwell, 1779), 9–10. Hill was an amateur outsider and mostly critical of English practice, but his work has been a convenient (although not necessarily the most reliable) English source for tracing contemporary views on the theatre.

4. See Brian Allen, *Francis Hayman* (New Haven and London: Yale University Press, 1987), 19–20.

5. See George Winchester Stone, Jr. and George M. Kahrl, *David Garrick: a Critical Biography* (Carbondale: Southern Illinois University Press, 1979), 32.

6. In his preface to *Troilus and Cressida*, Dryden had observed (1679) that '[i]f Shakespeare be allowed, as I think he must, to have made his characters distinct, it will easily be inferred that he understood the nature of the passions: because it has been proved already that confused passions make undistinguishable characters'. The *reasons* for making characters distinct and the *theories* related to the necessity of clear communic-ation of distinct passions had been in circulation for almost a century before Hill and others start articulating these ideas in the eighteenth century. See *John Dryden, Selected Criticism*, ed. James Kinsley and George Parfitt (Oxford: Clarendon Press, 1970), 174.

7. Judith Butler, 'Restaging the Universal', 25.

8. Aaron Hill, *An Essay*, 12.

9. Aaron Hill, *An Essay*, 13.

10. Stone and Kahrl, *David Garrick*, 28. Stone and Kahrl, in this segment of their argument, rely upon the memoirs of Richard Cumberland and acknowledge that 'Cumberland was remembering from a boyhood glimpse of Quin and Garrick as they play together in Rowe's *The Fair Penitent* ... and he suggested that the change from the older to Garrick's newer style was wrought quickly'. See page 29.

11. In reference to William Hogarth's painting of Garrick as Richard III (1745), Stone and Kahrl observe that 'the extended right hand with five fingers spread as fending off gesture ... comes directly from the acting manuals of the rhetorical tradition, familiar to actors and audiences alike in the 1730s and 1740s', immediately prior to Garrick's impact and the prevalence of the so-called 'new' style on the London stage. See Stone and Kahrl, *David Garrick*, 28.

12. See Stone and Kahrl, *David Garrick*, 32–5.

13. Stone and Kahrl, *David Garrick*, 36.

14. Robert D. Hume has argued emphatically against any notion of a paradigm shift in acting and in theatrical practice in general in the eighteenth century. Applying the Kuhnian concept of a paradigm shift – which applies to scientific research – to theatrical practice does not work, Hume says. Regarding Garrick, Hume rightly points out that 'Garrick was not particularly theoretical; his protégés did not work closely in his image; no School of Garrick ever emerged.' My focus is on charting how the 'particular' which was of interest to Garrick – even though he does not articulate it as such – as well as to theorists like Hill diverges from what we understand as the 'individual' or, more precisely, culture-specific individuality. See Hume, 'Syncretism and Borrowing', in *Reconstructing Contexts: the Aims and Principles of Archaeo-Historicism* (Oxford: Clarendon Press, 1999), 163–74.

15. 'Questions from Slavoj Žižek', 10. This is an essay in the Butler/LaClau/Žižek volume cited in note 16.

16. Ernesto LaClau, 'Identity and Hegemony: the Role of Universality in the Constitution of Political Logics', in Judith Butler, Ernesto LaClau, and Slavoj Žižek, *Contingency, Hegemony, Universality*, 58.

17. Slavoj Žižek, *The Ticklish Subject: the Absent Centre of Political Ontology* (London: Verso, 1996), 100–01.

18. David M. Little and George M. Kahrl, eds, *The Letters of David Garrick*, 3 vols (Cambridge: Harvard University Press, 1963), I: 245–46. Henceforth *Letters*.

19. The 'strange Events' in *Robinson Crusoe* (and the blurring of the probable–improbable as well as the known–unknown divide in Defoe's novel) could be captured on stage only in a farce and in the liminal space provided by the afterpiece. See Mita Choudhury, 'Imperial Licenses, Borderless Topographies, and the Eighteenth-Century British Theatre', in Michal Kobialka, ed., *Of Borders and Thresholds: Theatre History, Practice, and Theory* (Minneapolis: University of Minnesota Press, 1999), 70–109.

20. See Mita Choudhury, 'Epilogue', *Interculturalism and Resistance in the London Theatre: Identity, Performance, Empire* (Lewisburg: Bucknell University Press, 2000).

21. For a detailed analysis of why neat and tidy parameters do not work when measuring success or trends, see Robert D. Hume, 'Theatres and Repertory', in Joseph Donohue, ed., *The Cambridge History of British Theatre* (Cambridge: Cambridge University Press, 2004), 2, 53–70.

22. Elizabeth Kowaleski Wallace, 'Transnationalism and Performance in 'Biyi Bandele's *Oroonoko*', *PMLA*, 119, 2 (March 2004): 266.

23. Aphra Behn's novella was published in 1688; Thomas Southerne's play was published in 1695; and the Hawkesworth–Garrick revision was produced in 1759.

24. Wallace, 'Transnationalism and Performance', 271.

25. Wallace, 'Transnationalism and Performance', 266.

26. Thomas Davies, *Memoirs*, I: 176, quoted in Stone and Kahrl, *David Garrick*, 565–6.

27. Wallace, 'Transnationalism and Performance', 271.

28. Judith Butler, 'Restaging the Universal', 37.

29. Jessica Munns, 'Reviving Oroonoko "in the scene": From Thomas Southerne to Biyi Bandele', in Susan B. Iwanisziw, ed., *Troping Oroonoko from Behn to Bandele* (Burlington, Vermont: Ashgate, 2004), 189.

30. I borrow this phrase 'Obsession with Feathers' from Joseph Roach's chapter on 'Feathered Peoples' in *Cities of the Dead: Circum-Atlantic Performance* (New York: Columbia University Press, 1996), title of Chapter 4.

31. *Collection of the Dresses of Different Nations*, quoted in Stone and Kahrl, *David Garrick*, 330.

32. See Stone and Kahrl, *David Garrick*, 330–1.

33. Originally a scene painter for Drury lane, Hayman was one of the founders of the Royal Academy and was tutor to Gainsborough.

34. Francis Hayman's illustrations of Lear and Othello – based upon Garrick's suggestions – appeared in Shakespeare editions of 1770 and 1773.

35. Little and Kahrl, *Letters*, I: 82–3.

36. In the eighteenth century, the relationship between painting and performance in general was frequently acknowledged and promoted. In his detailed catalogue of the works of Francis Hayman, Brian Allen points to 'a fascinating letter from the dramatist Aaron Hill to Garrick' in which Hill observes 'how much the *painters* may improve, by copying Mr. *Garrick*, and what little room there is, for *his* improving, by the painters'. In this letter, Hill urges Garrick to consider the example of the French artists who masterfully capture precise 'attitudes' in their 'history pieces' and in their 'fine statues of antiquity'. Animation is the key concept in Hill's praise of the French, and Hill suggests that Garrick learn to apply on stage the 'animation' in the attitudes and posture of their static subjects. See Brian Allen, *Francis Hayman* (New Haven and London: Yale University Press, 1987), 20.

37. Aaron Hill, *An Essay*, 15.

38. Little and Kahrl, *Letters*, I: 316–17.

39. Susan B. Iwanisziw, 'Preface', *Troping Oroonoko from Behn to Bandele* (Burlington, Vermont: Ashgate, 2004), ix.

40. In 'The Eighteenth-Century Marketing of Oroonoko: Contending Constructions of Maecenas, the Author and the Slave', Susan B. Iwanisziw says the following about

Elizabeth Griffith: '[s]he is hardly an egalitarian. Griffith assumes that Africans might be savages imbued with vices from which Europeans have learned, rather than vice versa'. See *Troping Oroonoko from Behn to Bandele*, 158.
41. Robert D. Hume, *Reconstructing Contexts*, 171–4.
42. See Ernesto Laclau, 'Identity and Hegemony', in *Contingency, Hegemony, Universality*, 82–3.

11
Hearing the Dead: the Sound of David Garrick

Peter Holland

> Could *how Betterton* spoke be as easily known as *what* he spoke; then might you see the Muse of *Shakespear* in her Triumph, with all her Beauties in their best Array, rising into real Life, and charming her Beholders. But alas! since all this is so far out of the reach of Description, how shall I shew you *Betterton?*[1]

I began with a desire not to speak with the dead in Stephen Greenblatt's fashion but simply to listen to them, to hear the voices of eighteenth-century actors. It is not a new wish. In 1775 Joshua Steele wrote with the same regretful awareness that I have been feeling throughout this project, about the sound of these voices which cannot be heard:

> We have heard of Betterton, Booth, and Wilks, and some of us have seen Quin; the portraits of their person are probably preserved, but no models of their elocution remain; ... Had some of the celebrated speeches from Shakespeare been noted and accented as they spoke them, we should now be able to judge, whether the oratory of our stage is improved or debased.[2]

Steele's wish to hear – or at least to have a visual notation for what the audiences of the past heard – was a desire to value, a Whiggish search for proof of progress or decline. My aim is to see what can be recovered, through Steele's own method and the contexts provided by many others' writings, of what David Garrick sounded like. There is no wish here to value, simply to attempt to reconstruct a way of hearing.

This article is, of course, doomed to failure. I shall assemble some fragments, make some claims, chart some details. I shall, of necessity, find myself arguing over tiny matters, for, as Richard Warner suggested, in publishing as a letter to Garrick his proposal for a Shakespeare glossary, Garrick was the deserved recipient, given '[t]he intimate acquaintance you have had with his writings, the very *minutiœ* of which you have made your study'.[3] But it is also a necessity as I resist the bland generalizations that usually characterize such analysis, the clichés that then and now too often pass for accounts of voices. To be told the following is not really to be told very much of use:

> Mr. Garrick's voice was clear, impressive, and affecting; agreeable, though not harmonious; sharp, though not dissonant; strong, tho' not extensive. In declamation uncommonly forcible, in narrative unaffectedly simple.[4]

I shall at the end explore the conflicting accounts of exactly what Garrick sounded like when as Lear he cursed Goneril. I shall, perhaps with worthwhile results, try to foreground some undervalued parts of the Garrick literature, that vast mass of pamphlets that his career generated (not least ones written by himself against himself), drawing attention to items in the Garrick bibliography that have been surprisingly ignored. But it is still going to be hopeless.

Why even try? In part, this is a conventional academic gesture of asking us to look at some materials we have not noted as strongly or as often as the article-writer believes we should have done. My delight in my discoveries of what came out of Garrick's mouth (Look on him, look, his lips) generates the 'look there, look there' gesture of the scholar. I was surprised how rarely the standard modern studies of Garrick have anything much to say about the sound of Garrick, even though his contemporaries said a good deal.[5] I shall also, inevitably, be suggesting further directions for future research for others with more finely-honed skills, particularly in historical phonology and in the history of elocution, as ways that would enhance the image I will be sketching.

But I want, too, to point to a fundamental flaw in theatre history's concerns, one that it shares with much that recounts or accounts for performance, for our discipline is apparently, at times I have come to fear irretrievably, tied to the visual rather than the aural. Visual evidence tends to survive and our exploration of the physical shape of theatres, the evidence that can be retrieved from paintings of actors or handbooks of gesture, from the accounts for costumes and sets, have become the basis for our work. A longer account of this problem would need to investigate the nature of acoustic memory, why it should be that, say, theatre reviewers always tell us what a production looks like but rarely what it sounded like, why I should find, as I leave the theatre, that I can minutely describe set, costumes, movement and gesture but cannot recall much of how an actor sounded at a particular point, how s/he inflected a line, even when I have been intrigued by the inflection at its moment. Our recall of music is strong and our recall of the speaking voice is weak. In addition, even where we do recall, we cannot describe. We have strikingly failed to develop a vocabulary to record in prose (unlike recording on audio cassette) precisely what an actor has sounded like. We can describe pauses but not tonality, volume but not inflection, other than by using complex devices of linguistic analysis beyond all except experts.

But something has changed between Garrick and now in that regard. That there was minute dissection of Garrick's way of speaking particular lines is in itself remarkable, a sign of a theatre history, specifically a history of audience response as listening, marked now by discontinuity. As early in his acting career as

16 December 1741, Garrick received a letter from one of his greatest fans, the Rev. Thomas Newton, like Garrick Lichfield-born and an heir to an alcohol merchants. Newton, while concerned for Garrick's health ('I hope in the mean time you will spare yourself as much as you can, till you are recovered from your cold, and your voice may appear in perfection'), is also unable, as Boaden puts it, to allow a 'trivial error to sully long the general merit of his performance' as Richard III:

> In the last scene between Richard and Lady Ann, there is one thing that I think you did not speak quite properly, though I am somewhat doubtful. She says
> 'What have I done? What horrid crime committed?
> *Rich.* To me the worst of crimes – outliv'd my liking.'
> In the latter part, *outliv'd my liking*, you spoke with the same voice, only exalting it; whereas I imagine it should have been with an alteration of voice, more peevishly and angrily.[6]

Did Antony Sher receive similar letters when he played Richard III? Or was Toby Stephens as Hamlet told in the summer of 2004, by an anonymous correspondent,

> something that seems to me wrong about the pronunciation of a single word ... It is tropically. That *o*, I imagine, should be pronounced short, as we pronounce the *o* in logical; and both for the same reason, because the vowel in the original words, from whence they are derived, is in both an o, not an ω – a short *o*, not a long one. I believe you will find custom to be on this side of the question ... [7]

Or was Simon Russell Beale, when he was playing Macbeth, informed, as Garrick was in January 1744, that 'I see no reason for pronouncing the speech that begins with "Blood hath been shed ere now," aside'?[8] Even more striking is the fact that Garrick seems to have kept the letters, for, while most of the correspondence Boaden included in his 1831 edition of Garrick's correspondence, still the major printed source for letters *to* Garrick, is from the 1770s, the early letters that survive in his collection are, apart from the ones to and from Garrick's family, predominantly the ones of complaint about such matters of delivery. Rather than throwing them in the bin, Garrick seems to have cared enough to answer them, when not anonymous, and keep them. His answers were often detailed and strikingly apologetic in tone. In other words, Garrick engaged with this kind of detailed analysis of delivery, more evidence of his concern with 'the very *minutiæ* of which you have made your study' when it comes to the sound (here rhythm, syntax, pronunciation and stage-focus) of Shakespeare.

There is an implicit parallel to the investigation into the sound of long-dead actors in the acoustic history of music, for the recreation of the sound of earlier performances, once only of early music, now of Berlioz, Wagner and even Elgar, has been one of the most marked meetings between historical research and performance in recent years. Bach not performed on reproductions of early instruments is beginning to sound odd. The technologies of performance, the scale of surviving evidence, and the interest of performers have made such work desirable. But the recreation of an earlier human spoken voice has been relatively unexplored. There have been attempts across the late twentieth-century to perform Shakespeare in early modern pronunciation, most recently and elaborately in the performances at Shakespeare's Globe in London in June 2004 of *Romeo and Juliet* and in the summer of 2005 of *Troilus and Cressida*, spoken in a style coached by David Crystal.[9] Reflecting on that experiment, Crystal wonders:

> Why stop with Early Modern English? ... What about Restoration dramatists? ... It has always struck me as curious that a play from the eighteenth or nineteenth centuries is faithfully presented using its dialect grammar and vocabulary, because this is reflected in the text, but its associated pronunciation is not, because it is hidden by the standard English spelling. Why not Sheridan in OP?[10]

But, even if I found the recreations of early modern pronunciation more convincing than is the case, I do not believe it to be significantly effective or desirable to perform in the vocal style of Garrick, though performances in the gestural style might well be revealing and though modern actors certainly have much to learn from the evidence for eighteenth-century actors' ability to work in a more rhetorically aware and metrically sophisticated tradition. Reconstruction of performance is a quite different aim from reconstruction for performance and the old complaint about lacking eighteenth-century eyes and ears is far more potently relevant here than for 'authentic' music performances. I do not want to hear someone pretending to be Garrick; I want to hear Garrick.

What I am centrally concerned with is our refusal or at least reluctance to be historians of sound, even in the aftermath of Bruce Smith's ground-breaking study of early modern soundscapes.[11] We have, for instance, nothing about the sound of eighteenth-century performance to set beside Dene Barnett's study of gesture.[12] Robert Hume's mapping account of our territory in this volume speaks of the state of our research in the physical conditions of costume and scenery and movement but, apart from theatre music, not of sound. The complex sensescape of theatre, the interaction of vision and hearing, has been only half explored. This chapter merely asks, by using Garrick as the inevitable example, that we might start to look at the other half more closely. I begin the enquiry at the level of the phoneme, move through speed, silence and syntax to end with a single example of interpretation and the performance of character, Lear's curse.

* * *

When Garrick was in Dublin in August 1742, he received yet another anonymous letter of complaint, this time over 'your false pronunciation of several words':

The words that I chiefly remember are these: – *matron, Israel, villain, appal, Horatio, wind*; which you pronounced, *metron, Iserel, villin, appeal, Horetio*; and the word *wind* you pronounced short. I cannot imagine what your objection can be to the letter *a*, that you should change it into an *e*, both in the English language and the Latin ... [13]

Since the correspondent suggests that *matron* is made 'Greek', Garrick may have made the *e* long in Greek style (equivalent to a Greek eta) or the writer may have made the *a* of *matron* short as in *mat* – anonymous letter-writers are not always clear. Though the correspondent was writing in Dublin it does not follow that his accent is Irish. Here, as elsewhere, the material is rebarbative and needs further analysis.

The attack on Garrick's orthoepy, his choice of pronounciation, reappeared again in 1759 when John Hill, author of *The Actor* (1750 and 1755), published *To David Garrick, Esq; The Petition of I. In behalf of herself and her Sisters*. Boaden comments that '[t]hey who have critically examined the English vowels, are not to be told that the letter *i* is sometimes allowably an usurper upon the letter *u*. Dr. Hill, however, maintained otherwise.'[14] For Hill, 'the indelicate and indeterminate sound *u*' had 'taken the place of most of the vowels and dipthongs' (9). If the choices were simply, say, 'ungrateful' over 'ingrateful', it might not be so intriguing, but Hill's complaint was over words like *virtue, Hercules, earth* and *heard*, in each of which, he complained, Garrick sounded the first vowel as a *u* (7, 15) and:

Your Petitioner does, and must conceive, the original and natural Pronunciation of the good word FIRM, to be at least as elegant, and expressive of the Sense, as the coarse boggy FURM, which you have introduced into its place, and which your many Excellencies, fixing the Stamp of Judgment upon Folly, have forced into the Throats of others. (6)

My difficulty, of course, is that I cannot pronounce the words any other way. Modern RP will not allow me to distinguish *firm* and *furm* at all; Michael Cordner could distinguish them if he switched from RP to his native Northern Irish. It is easy to hear what Hill was on about when he complains that Garrick's 'Delicacy, disgusted at the broad Roman Accent' pronounced the vowel *a* 'as others speak *ey* in *they*, a soft and civil Diphthong' so that Cleopatra became CLEOPEYTRA (11). But the rest of the complaining is a mark of a historical distance and a strikingly different soundworld. Garrick responded to the petition with an epigram:

> If 'tis true, as you say, that I've injured a letter,
> I'll change my note soon, and I hope for the better:
> May the just right of letters, as well as of men,
> Hereafter be fix'd by the tongue and the pen;
> Most devoutly I wish that they both have their due,
> And that *I* may be never mistaken for yo*U*.[15]

A link between the two men was also voiced by Garrick as Roscius in Samuel Pratt's pamphlet on his retirement: 'Not Sir JOHN HILL, so much has wrote, / As I have spoken through my throat'.[16]

None of these complaints about Garrick's speech specifically identify his accent as regional, though there are signs that he may have had some Lichfield tinges to particular words. Thomas Sheridan made some of the same points as Hill, in his elementary guide to teaching reading and pronunciation, *Elements of English*, in 1786, pointing out, as he defined the correct pronunciation of *ir* forms, that Garrick pronounced words like *gird, birth*, and *firm* with a *u* vowel plus /r/ sound where Sheridan demanded a short *e* plus /r/ sound.[17] Sheridan called this 'a very improper pronunciation' which 'has of late gained ground, owing to a provincial dialect with which Mr. Garrick's speech was infected' (note here the conceptualization of a sanitized orthodoxy that leads Sheridan to dub this an infection). Garrick made these errors 'according to Staffordshire custom': 'Nay he did the same where the vowel *e* preceded the *r*' and Sheridan gives as examples *heard, earth* and *interr'd*. But, while Garrick might be forgiven for failing to eradicate the pernicious traces of his provincial roots, Sheridan adds that 'His example was followed by many of his imitators on the stage, who would do well to correct this impropriety, as it is now easily in their power.'[18]

Though Sheridan's description definitely places the effect as a regional burr, Michael MacMahon suggests, in his outstanding account of English phonology from the late eighteenth-century to the present, 'Whether this reflected an aspect of phonological reality – not just in Staffordshire but also in London – rather than some socially induced pretence is impossible to judge.'[19] MacMahon's 'phonological reality' effectively divides the stage voice from the social voice. None of the accounts of Garrick's particularities of pronunciation have anything to do with his off-stage speaking, only the voice of the performer, and we accept that stage voices are and were necessarily distinct from others, not least through the need to project and fill the increasingly substantial acoustic volumes of theatre spaces, producing vowels often rounder and fuller than those in use off-stage.

The phonology of London English in Garrick's time was not hugely different from that of the present. Insofar as it is possible to reconstruct that sound (and MacMahon is my professional guide here), there are distinctions that would be striking. The initial letter of *humble* or *hospital* was silent, as in the current US pronunciation of *herb*. The second vowel of *oblige* was a long *e*, *obleege*. *China* was nearer to *chaynee*. And there are other examples. It is less the search for distinctions – as if we would hear Garrick's speech as belonging to another country – than the period's search for an orthodoxy that is striking. What, in turn, is most significant about the move towards the orthoepical doctrine and prescription that marks lexicography after Dr Johnson is the intimate connection between that movement and the theatre.

There are three crucial figures in the late-eighteenth century publication of books on elocution and pronunciation (dictionaries, guides, manuals, rhetorics and courses of lectures). All three were closely connected with Garrick's Drury Lane. The most combative was William Kenrick (1729/30–79), author of *Falstaff's*

Wedding (1766) and *The Widowed Wife* (1767), would-be editor of Shakespeare and the man who, angry about the distribution of the profits, accused Garrick of a homosexual relationship with Bickerstaff in the poem *Love in the Suds* (1772). Kenrick had attacked Johnson's dictionary too and published in 1773 *A New Dictionary of the English Language*, prefaced by a substantial *Rhetorical Grammar*, later published separately in 1784.

Like the others Kenrick was concerned with defining rules for pronunciation but he was far less influential than John Walker (1732–1807) who joined the Drury Lane company in 1757, rising to the rank of second-level roles in tragedy before leaving the stage in 1768 to start a school and begin the series of publications on pronunciation that defined the 'mechanical school' of elocution; rule-bound, fiercely constricting and placing all its emphasis on analysis over feeling.[20] Walker dedicated his *Dictionary of the English Language* to Garrick in 1775, announcing that if either of his works (the *Dictionary* or his proposal for it)

> have a sufficient degree of merit to recommend them to the attention of the public, it is in a great measure owing to the early opportunities I have had of observing your pronunciation on the stage ... (sig. π2r–v)

This was a reverse dictionary, alphabetized by the final letters and including a long index of rhymes, defined as 'perfect and allowable', so that it is 'allowable' imperfectly to rhyme *cab* with *babe*, *made* with *dead*, *safe* with *deaf* or *laugh* (402f). Its quotation sources are not drama but the corpus of poetry. In his *Critical Pronouncing Dictionary and Expositor of the English Language* of 1791, a work reprinted over a hundred times by 1904, Walker set out not only meanings and sounds but, as the title-page put it, 'where Words are subject to different Pronunciations, the Reasons for each are at large displayed, and the preferable Pronunciation is pointed out'.

In his *Elements of Elocution* (1781), Walker regrets that he has to rely on his own experience 'to convey such turns and inflexions of voice as accompanied the pauses and emphasis of a good speaker; and this, had that great actor and excellent citizen Mr. Garrick lived, I should have exemplified in some of his favourite speeches' (1:xii). Garrick, then, functions for Walker as a model for elocution both as outstanding thespian but also because his social status and civic pride make him a social hero. He must, then, implicitly lie somewhere behind Walker's *The Melody of Speaking Delineated* of 1787 which sets out to teach elocution 'like music' (title-page) and which prints a number of Shakespeare speeches on facing pages with the clean text confronted by one divided into feet with light, heavy and equal stresses marked and with the mood and tone defined. I do not mean that Garrick's voice is what Walker is here recording but rather that the modelling is theatrical before it is socially elocutionary. The effect is a careful encoding of the vocal effects of various stratified forms of speech (high, middle, low; plaintive, didactic, grand, and so on). John of Gaunt's set-piece speech in *Richard II*, for instance, opens on a 'High plaintive tone of voice', moving to a 'Lower tone, simple and didactic' at 'His rash fierce blaze of riot', on to a 'Low, solemn monotone' for 'This royal throne of kings', 'Rapture; higher plaintive tone' at 'This blessed plot', 'Grand description; lower and more solemn tone' at 'Renowned for their deeds', 'Lower and more familiar tone' at 'Is now leased out', and various other increasingly rapid switches, four in the last six lines alone, ending on 'Lower and reproaching tone' (50–4).

I emphasize that I am not suggesting that Walker's prescription here is a description of Garrick, not least because the whole rise of elocution at the end of the century is bound up with educational practice in schools and universities, not with stage performance. Yet elocution is profoundly performative and the pervasive presence of Shakespeare and other dramatists within these systems warrants attention.

If Walker was a minor actor, the same cannot be said for Thomas Sheridan (1719?–1788), actor and manager in Dublin and London.[21] Sheridan's lectures on elocution were given at both Oxford and Cambridge, earning him honorary MAs from both universities in 1758 and 1759. In 1762 he published his *Course of Lectures on Elocution*, following it with, among other works, a two-volume *Lectures on the Art of Reading*, one on prose and one on verse, in 1775, directed primarily at the clergy and at schoolteachers, and in 1780 his *General Dictionary of the English Language*, a work which paved the way for Walker's dictionary later. Sheridan's dictionary was, according to Robin Alston, 'the first attempt to provide for the whole vocabulary an accurate indication of the way words should be pronounced'.[22] Sheridan, incidentally, like Garrick's Dublin correspondent, opts for a long *i* in *wind*, a word he sees as in dispute, 'upon this principle, that there is no monosyllable in the English language terminating in *ind* in which the vowel *i* is not pronounced long' (58). Sheridan, as a Dubliner, was particularly concerned to help 'the Natives of Ireland' to 'attain a just Pronunciation of English' (59) and, in so doing, highlights some intriguing forms for London English with *cheerful* and *fearful* sounded as *cherful* and *ferful*, while *beard* is *berd* (60). Sheridan, like many a pioneer, was criticized by those who followed for errors in his choices, for, as Walker gleefully complained, he sounds the *t* of *creature, nature, tune* and *tumult* as *tsh* or *tch*.[23]

The work of these three has been extensively investigated by historical phonologists but not by theatre historians and the pickings would be rich. It would be possible to go through a speech and check each word against Sheridan's and Walker's prescriptions for pronunciation – and, indeed, against other accounts of mid- to late-eighteenth century forms and against the identifiable features of Garrick's diction in order to reconstruct both Garrick's and a possibly more normative form of such speech. But research in the materials on late eighteenth-century theories of elocution could go far beyond such phonological concerns. Sheridan, in particular, minutely explicates the meaning of a number of Shakespeare passages in his *Course of Lectures on Elocution* as part of his concern about where emphasis should be placed, a dissection of disagreements over rhythm and punctuation at the level of sound in intimate interconnection with the semantics of dramatic meaning. He is sure that phrasing Macbeth's line 'Making the green one, red' is 'flat nonsense', urging 'Making the green – one red':

Here is a most sublime idea conveyed, ... Nor, if we consider the disturbed state of his imagination at that time, will this thought, hyperbolical as it may seem at first view, appear at all unnatural. For it is highly probable that his fancy at that instant presented all objects about him as of that sanguine hue; nay converted the very atmosphere that surrounded him, into a sea of blood. (65)[24]

If Sheridan's recommendation to Othello to say 'Put out the light, and then put out *the* light' or 'Perdition catch my soul but I dò love thee' – 'the emphasis . . . marks the vehemence of his affection much better than any emphasis on the verb love could' (65–6) – sound distinctly odd, they are thoughtfully argued and come from someone with a profound experience of eighteenth-century theatre. They also bring an awareness of character and imagination to bear on processes of rhythm and emphasis. While these texts in elocution are not designed for the stage, they are nonetheless at a performative intersection between theatre and education, as in, for instance, *The Sentimental Spouter or Young Actor's Companion* (1774) with its 'Treatise on Oratory' or the precise evidence of the modes of speaking Thomas Sheridan and another actor and elocutionist John Henderson (1747–1785) demonstrated in a pamphlet *Sheridan's and Henderson's Practical Method of Reading and Reciting English Poetry . . . and the manner pointed out in which they were read or recited by the above Gentlemen* (1796), with numerous examples from Shakespeare. We can, for instance, carefully compare Lichtenberg's and others' accounts of Garrick's Hamlet meeting the Ghost and the speech 'As repeated by the late Mr. Sheridan' who began it 'With a *low, solemn, awful* voice, as if repeating a short prayer' for 'Angels and ministers of grace, defend us': 'Then pausing ere you proceed, you raise your voice a little, not forgetting the greatest solemnity of *tone* and *manner*' and so on and on, requiring many pages for the one speech, a bulk of evidence that is well worth considering.[25] It is striking that in 1753 Sheridan, then still an actor, was praised – at least I think it is praise – for being 'very judicious in his Delivery . . . Perhaps a truer Orator never trod the Stage'.[26] In terms of the long shadow this casts, it is worth remembering that Sheridan was the preferred private coach for Sarah Siddons.

Sheridan's preference for a natural delivery and a feeling style aligned him closely with the 'School of Garrick' against the mechanized rule-bound prescriptive elocutionary practice of Walker. Apart from the words I have explored above, Garrick seems also to have chosen '*sism*' as the pronunciation for *schism* and ' "*burial*" the *u* long, instead of the way often made use of, as if it were spelt "*berrial*." '.[27] These last two examples come from an extraordinary pamphlet called *The Manner Pointed out in which the Common Prayer was Read in Private by the Late Mr Garrick* published by J. W. Anderson in 1797 and, as far as I can see, completely ignored by Garrick scholars. Anderson describes Garrick's gesture, movement, rhythms and voice, line by line through the service, from 'Dearly beloved brethren' onwards:

> Mr. Garrick recommended a look, expressive of the utmost *suitable gravity*, to be cast slowly around the congregation, the voice rather *low*, and denoting,

together with the whole manner, that *solemn* and *reverential respect* which is due to the place of public worship ... Here make a pause much longer than the comma, or, indeed, than the time which is thought to be necessary after a semicolon. (9)

As a detailed study of Garrick's performance of a part it is unequalled, even by, say, Lichtenberg's familiar accounts of Garrick as Hamlet.[28] The only comparable text until we reach recordings would be James Hackett's detailing of Kean's performance as Richard III.[29] It appears that Garrick instructed a young clergyman in the right way of speaking divine service and Anderson compiled his pamphlet from manuscript notes. There is no reason to suspect the report as fake, even if its status as evidence needs careful evaluation. Intriguingly, it provides a precise intersection between Garrick's mode of elocution and that advocated by Thomas Sheridan who in his *Lectures on the Art of Reading* (1775) had set out his mode of speaking the service. Anderson contrasts the two methods:

In the one [i.e. Garrick's], a *suitable fervour* of *exterior devotion* on the part of the Clergyman, as well as on that of the people, appears to be the chief thing endeavoured to be inculcated; in the other, the grand objects seem to be those of finding out the word upon which the emphasis should be placed ... while the *pious energy* and *spiritual animation* ... are left almost entirely unrecommended. The one speaks more to the *heart*, the other to the *understanding* ... (7–8)

Speaking to the heart is, of course, that emphasis on the natural and the affective which has always been defined as Garrick's most characteristic mode of speaking. At the same time, Garrick was praised – and occasionally blamed – for the speed and energy of his delivery. As early as his first triumphant performances of *Richard III*, there was a speed that startled the audience who were used to the measured pace of Quin. Among the many passages in the performance that might have surprised the audience in the 1740s I would not have suspected these lines to figure: 'The North! – what do they in the North,/ When they should serve their Sovereign in the West.'[30] But Arthur Murphy, in his 1801 biography, reported that 'The rage and rapidity, with which he spoke [the lines] made a most astonishing impression on the audience.'[31] Murphy, praising Garrick waking up from the ghosts, the next passage he describes, emphasizes the realism, 'Every thing he described was almost reality', but also the variety:

He was a spectacle of horror: He called out in a manly tone,
　　Give me another horse;
He paused, and, with a countenance of dismay, advanced, crying out in a tone of distress,
　　Bind up my wounds;
and then, falling on his knees, said in the most piteous accent,
　　Have mercy Heaven;
In all this, the audience saw an exact imitation of nature ...[32]

Macklin was less inclined to admire this:

> Garrick huddled all passions into strut and quickness – bustle was his favourite. In the performance of a Lord Townly he was all bustle. In Archer, Ranger, Don John, Hamlet, Macbeth, Brute – all bustle! bustle! bustle! The whole art of acting, according to the modern practice, is compriz'd in – bustle! 'Give me a Horse!' – 'Bind up my Wounds!' – 'Have mercy Jesu!' – all bustle! –everything is turned into bustle![33]

Something of the bustling speed is apparent in the exact representation of Garrick's voice that was included in Joshua Steele's analysis of 'To be or not to be' (Figures 11.1(a) and (b)), his one attempt to recover from the past 'some of the celebrated speeches from Shakespeare ... noted and accented as [actors] spoke them'. Steele, in his attempt to define the 'melody and measure of speech', set out rhythm, metre and inflection for the speech 'as I pronounced it' but then, '[s]ince writing the foregoing treatise, I have heard Mr. Garrick in the character of Hamlet' and he marks the differences 'that I can remember' between Garrick and himself.[34] It is the most extraordinary document to have survived to demonstrate the sound of an eighteenth-century actor, even though we have no means of knowing how accurate Steele is.[35] Where Steele spoke it 'in the stile of a ranting actor, swelled with *forte* and softened with *piano*, he [Garrick] delivered with little or no distinction of piano and forte, but nearly uniform; something below the ordinary force, or, as a musician would say, *sotto voce*, or *sempre poco piano*'. But comparing Steele's version of the first line with Garrick's it is clear too that Garrick's is about speed. In every case where the quantity of the syllable is different, Garrick is shorter: 'or' is a crotchet length (US quarter-note) where Steele has a dotted minim (half-note) and Steele gives it a whole foot where Garrick gives it a light stress

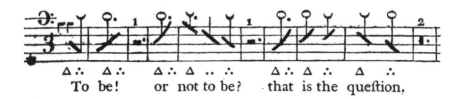

Figure 11.1(a):   Joshua Steele's version of 'To be or not to be'

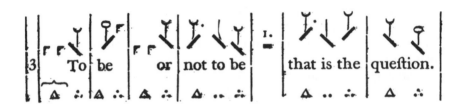

Figure 11.1(b):   David Garrick's version of 'To be or not to be' as recorded by Joshua Steele

after the pause; 'that is' is dotted crotchet and quaver (eighth-note) where Steele has a dotted minim and minim, lightening the stress on 'is' considerably from Steele's ponderous mode.[36] At the very end of the speech, Steele notes that Garrick pronounced the last word, 'orisons', with a short *i*, where Steele himself had made it 'long and heavy, by supposing the word to have been originally Norman French, *oraison*'.[37] But Garrick did without the pause after 'Nymph', just as his pauses after 'To die' and 'to sleep' were markedly shorter than Steele's. This is not just bustle but a search for the through-line of the speech, its architecture as important as its momentary effect. Steele, incidentally, particularly praises Garrick for the clarity of his diction: he and Mrs Cibber 'are distinctly heard even in the softest sounds of their voices; when others are scarcely intelligible, though offensively loud'.[38]

Steele consulted with Garrick about his complex system of notation and Garrick wondered '[s]upposing a speech was noted, according to these rules, in the manner he spoke it, whether any other person, by the help of these notes, could pronounce his words in the same tone and manner exactly as he did' (54). Steele attempted to reassure him but letters Steele received after publication and which he answered in the second edition of his work, *Prosodia Rationalis* (1779), kept returning to the point. At the core of the disagreement was the crucial difference between the notation of music and Steele's notation of speech, the former lacking the precision of gracing, inflection and stresses that Steele included.[39] Difficult and abstruse though Steele's system may be, it is the most complex and considered notation of a moment of theatre speech available and Garrick's lightness and speed are conspicuously apparent.

Aaron Hill, whose writings defined an approach to performance in the 1730s, the years just before the Garrick sonic revolution, warned against speed and encouraged the careful use of pauses. In a letter he recommends,

> The actor, who pauses judiciously, will be sure to appear in earnest, like the conceiver of what he utters; whereas, without pausing, the words, arising too fast for the thought, demonstrate him but a repeater of what he should seem to invent, before he expresses it.[40]

For Hill, language takes time to be understood:

> For, without those restings, our understanding, wanting time to receive impressions from the ear, retains, but defectively, the image of the meaning, being continually hurried forward, to a *new* idea, while the *old* is unformed and imperfect.[41]

How long is a pause? For Hill, in a wonderful phrase that any actor would relish, 'the measure of time, in a pause, should vary according to the sense. But it will, in general, be enough to rest, as long as might suffice, to pronounce such a word as *power*.'[42]

Roger Pickering put the motto 'tacere qui nescit, nescit loqui' ('whoever doesn't know how to be silent, doesn't know how to speak') on the title-page of his pamphlet *Reflections upon Theatrical Expression in Tragedy* (1755), commenting that 'the best Construction of the motto . . . is Mr. Garrick's Pause' after the first line of Richard III's speech after waking, the same passage that Murphy considered, though Murphy does not mention a decisive pause: 'A Man, awaken'd in Surprize, requires *Time* to recover himself for coherent Speech'.[43] But, more often than Pickering's praise, Garrick's pauses attracted regular criticism. The bustle was, it seems, carefully, even obsessively and certainly idiosyncratically offset and balanced by the frequent pauses in his delivery.

But it was less the frequency than the length and placing that drew sharp responses throughout Garrick's career. Even the most fervent fans were dubious about his tendency to pause too long or in the wrong place. Writing to Reverend Peter Whalley in 1748, the year Whalley published his study *On the Learning of Shakespeare*, Garrick worried whether Whalley

> have mistook me in the Prologue to Henry the 5th – surely the little Pause was made at *Fire*! And I connected the subsequent Relative, Verb, and Accusative Case (*that would ascend the brightest Heav'n*, &c.) in one Breath? I know in the general I speak it so, but may have fail'd the Night you heard me.[44]

Garrick here defends himself on syntactic grounds, the analysis of sentence structure defining the moment to pause. Whalley's criticism suggests that Garrick's pause was metrical, a pause at the line-ending. Fundamental to speaking Shakespearean verse is the tension between syntax and metrics, between the demands of the sentence and the rhythm of the verse-line. It is a contradictory pull, requiring the drawing out of an acutely discriminatory sense of the balance between the two. But the reason to pause may also be a different kind of artistic sensibility, as Garrick points out to another correspondent in 1767:

> In the speaking of Soliloquys, the great art is to give variety, & which only can be obtain'd by a strict regard to y[e] pauses – the running the different parts of a Monologue togeather, will necessarily give a Monotony & take away y[e] Spirit, & Sense of y[e] Author.[45]

John Hill, in a passage in *The Actor* in 1750, offered a further explanation for the intrusive pause:

> we observ'd in Mr. *Garrick*, a fault from his very first appearance on the stage, which is grown up with him, and now much worse than at first; it is a way of resting in the middle of a line where the sense is continued; such a pause is unnatural and hateful. We can easily see that the reason of this is, that this actor has an ambition to give a peculiar emphasis to every word of a sentence where he would be particularly great in his part; the force of voice which he uses on this occasion requires so much breath to every syllable, that he cannot pronounce more than half a line together. We first observ'd this in him in King *Richard*; where, in the heat of his fury, he calls out to the archers,

Draw, archers, draw, your arrows to the head.

It is easy to see that a line like this ought to be spoken with rapidity, and the whole force of the voice reserv'd for the last word; instead of this, Mr. *Garrick* bestows so much breath on the three first, that he is forc'd to pause to get in more to speak the rest with, and accordingly he always pronounces the line with an unnatural gap in the middle,

Draw, archers, draw – your arrows to the head.[46]

Garrick was defended in 1753 by the author of *The Present State of the Stage*:

In this Place 'tis proper to obviate an Objection made against him by some superficial Critics, of stopping falsly; which from the most minute Observation I find to be groundless: 'Tis true, that sometimes he pauses in Places, where, critically speaking, there is no Pause, in order to collect his Breath, to give additional Force to what ensues; but his Tone of Voice shews plainly the Connection uninterrupted.[47]

In *The Theatrical Review* (1763), the problem is again defined as a consequence of a more general vocal limitation:

Wanting power at the top, it sometimes sinks where the passions meet with any violent agitation. Mr. Garrick has so peculiar a method of adapting it, that we scarcely perceive it is unhappily limited; and we are almost induced to believe, that it ought to rise no farther . . . than the particular key to which he has the power of extending it. (76)

Garrick is indicted for using 'a sort of hesitating stammering, when there is no natural obstacle to occasion it, merely to strike a seeming shew of something out of nothing' (79) – this is presumably the kind of thing Foote attacked in mocking Garrick's performance of Lothario's death speech in Rowe's *The Fair Penitent*: 'Adorns my fall / And chea-chea-chea-chea-chea-chears / My heart in dy-dy-dying.'[48] Here too the pauses are seen as caused 'by the too great length of a period, where he would have rendered himself absolutely inarticulate' if he had not paused. But Garrick is also indicted for using pauses 'as a trap for applause where he could reasonably expect none'.[49]

Laurence Sterne mocked the objections to the Garrickian pause in *Tristram Shandy*:

And how did *Garrick* speak the soliloquy last night? – Oh, against all rule, my Lord, – most ungrammatically! betwixt the substantive and the adjective, which should agree together in *number*, *case* and *gender*, he made a breach thus, – stopping, as if the point wanted settling; – and betwixt the nominative case, which your lordship knows should govern the verb, he suspended his voice in the epilogue a dozen times, three seconds and three fifths by a stop-watch, my Lord, each time. – Admirable grammarian! – But in suspending his voice – was the sense suspended likewise? Did no expression of attitude or countenance fill up the chasm? – Was the eye silent? Did you narrowly look? – I look'd only at the stop-watch, my Lord. – Excellent observer![50]

Sterne may be referring to a specific moment for Garrick had had to explain at length in a letter why there appeared one night to be a false division between the substantive 'single' and the adjective 'state' in Macbeth's line 'My thought, whose murder yet is but fantastical / Shakes so my single state of man' (1.3.139–40):

> *Shakes so my single* – If I stop at ye last word, it is a glaring fault, for the Sense is imperfect – but my Idea of that passage is this – Macbeth is absorb'd in thought, & struck with ye horror of ye Murder, tho but in Idea (*fantastical*) and it naturally gives him a slow – tremulous – under tone of voice, & tho it might appear that I stop'd at Every word in ye Line, more than Usual, yet my intention, was far from dividing the Substantive from its adjective, but to paint ye horror of Macbeth's Mind, & keep ye voice suspended a little – wch it will naturally be in such a Situation.[51]

Garrick goes on at length to explain what he means by 'suspending the voice ... Which in many cases I reckon a Beauty in the Speaker, when a Stop would be a great fault', using as an example a pause after 'see' in Hamlet's line 'I think it was to see my mother's wedding', 'for Hamlet's Grief causes ye break & with a Sigh, he finishes ye Sentence ... I really could not from my feelings act it otherwise'.[52] The appeal to emotion ('my' here used intriguingly as a shorthand for 'Hamlet's', a complex marker of the sympathetic identification between the actor's emotional state and the role) is crucial here, with feeling dominating over syntax or metrical, rhythmic structures.

It was not only onstage that Garrick could misaccent. Dr Johnson accused Garrick, Giffard, manager of Goodman's Fields, and other actors of having 'a kind of rant, which they run on, without regard either to accent or emphasis'. Garrick and Giffard protested and Johnson asked them to repeat the ninth commandment, 'Thou shalt not bear false witness against thy neighbour':

> Both tried it ... and both mistook the emphasis, which should be upon *not* and *false witness*. Johnson put them right, and enjoyed his victory with great glee.[53]

The most sustained analysis of Garrick's pauses and his tendency to misaccent a line was in a series of letters to journals by Thaddaeus Fitzpatrick (possibly with others), gathered together as *An Enquiry into the Real Merit of a Certain Popular Performer* (1760), an attack to which Garrick replied in his satire *The Fribbleriad* (1761) but whose detailed charges he completely ignored.[54] Fitzpatrick's main targets included Garrick as Pierre in *Venice Preserved*, a role he had not played for six years. It was not, then, exactly news. Of course it is an exaggeration, though some of its examples had been or would be mentioned elsewhere (e.g. 'I think it was to see – my mother's wedding') and hence may well have been valid. But its lists and dissections are an extraordinary satiric demonstration of Garrick's vocal mannerisms, whether accurate or not. Here are some of the twenty examples from *Hamlet*, recorded, Fitzpatrick claimed, during a performance, for 'as our memories did not serve us to clear up the point, it was agreed that we should go to the tragedy of Hamlet this evening, each man, furnished with a printed play and a pencil, mark such improprieties, in respect of speaking, as Mr. G——might possibly fall into':

> Oh that this too too solid – flesh would melt.
> He would drown – the stage with tears.
> I'll have these players
> Play something like – the murther of my father.
> Lay not that flattering – unction to your soul.[55]

Garrick is here shown separating adjective from substantive, and another group shows a tendency to emphasize the last word in a line with a pause before the next, in a fashion of which Sir Peter Hall might now approve but which Fitzpatrick opposed:

> Or that the everlasting had not *fixt* –
> His canon 'gainst self-slaughter.
> Whether it is nobler in the mind, to *suffer* –
> The stings [*sic*] and arrows.[56]

Another twenty examples from *Richard III* distinguish between 'the words printed in Italics, [which] are those he thought fit to lay emphasis on; ... such as are in Small Capitals, I apprehend he ought to have spoken emphatically' (27), for example:

> Now *are* our brows bound with VICTORIOUS wreaths,
> Our STERN alarms are *changed* to MERRY meetings;
> Our DREADFUL *marches* to DELIGHTFUL measures ...
> I, that *am* CURTAIL'D of man's FAIR proportion,
> Deform'd unfinish'd, *sent* BEFORE my time –
> Into this breathing world, *scarce* HALF made up ... (28)

One need not of course think that Fitzpatrick is necessarily right in his suggestions to recognize that Garrick may have been wrong in his. Michael Cordner rightly suggests to me that one might want to point up 'proportion' rather than 'fair'. But, if Fitzpatrick's report is accurate, Garrick's emphasis of 'am' in the line is distinctly odd.

For many of his examples, there are detailed explanations of why Garrick's choice was mistaken, for example, for Richard's line to Lady Anne 'Then bid me *kill* MYSELF, and I will do it':

> By his former conduct, and confession, it appears, that he was sufficiently ready to kill, and therefore the verb might have escaped the emphasis; but as he seemed willing to change the object, if she ordered him, he should have marked *himself*. (32)

It is a fair note to an actor and I for one often make similar mental notes when listening to actors at the RSC and elsewhere. The intelligence of Fitzpatrick's analysis of such cases as well as its compatibility with the substance of numerous letters to and by Garrick enhances the probability that, as an account of Garrick's errors, it is not far off the mark. Garrick's silence in reply, keeping his attack to a mockery of Fitzpatrick's camp style, may also be a kind of admission of fault.

The Fitzpatrick pamphlet can in some respects be seen as part of the pamphlet culture wars that surrounded Garrick's management, a sign of the cultural invest-ment – and the profit for publishers – in such wars of words focused on the institution of the theatre. Yet its detail also suggests a quite different concern, with the drama as an act of semantic communication, for, while the complaint is about emphases and caesuras, it is not an argument about the speaking of verse and the problems of metrics. Instead it is firmly concentrated on the meaning of the lines and Garrick's apparent failure to allow the movement of thought to emerge from an accurate delivery of the syntactic forms of the language. It is not a matter of tone, of character, of interpretation, for the concerns are far more fundamentally semantic than that. It is a matter of a straightforward – or at least comparatively simple – argument about how the phrase fits the action of the play, its argument through dialogue. The investment in meaning is primary and Garrick's perceived failure is a failure not only of style but also of intelligence, a failure to understand the meaning of the lines he speaks.

Yet Garrick's performances also demonstrated a sustained critical intelligence, a concern to read a role and find a way through it. I want to pursue a single passage in this respect, the curse on Goneril in *King Lear*, the speech that in Tate's version as adapted by Garrick ended Act 1 without the brief exchange between Goneril and Albany that Tate had included:

> Hear, Nature! hear, dear goddess, hear a father!
> If thou didst intend to make this creature fruitful,
> Suspend thy purpose.
> Into her womb convey sterility!
> Dry up in her the organs of encrease,
> That from her derogate body never spring
> A babe to honour her! If she must teem,
> Create her child of spleen, that it may live,
> And be a thwart, disnatur'd torment to her!
> Let it stamp wrinkles in her brow of youth;
> With candent tears fret channels in her cheeks;
> Turn all her mother's pains and benefits,

> To laughter and contempt;
> That she may curse her crime, too late; and feel,
> How sharper than a serpent's tooth it is,
> To have a thankless child! – Away, away.[57]

After Garrick's initial lack of success as Lear, he was coached by Macklin who praised a later performance: 'the curse he particularly admired; he said it exceeded all his imagination; and had such an effect, that it seemed to electrify the audience with horror'.[58] It continued to do so for nearly thirty years. Over and over again, people commented on the effectiveness of this moment but there were also complaints. Samuel Foote argued in 1747 that the curse

> should be utter'd with a Rage almost equal to Phrenzy, quick and rapid as a Whirlwind, no Mark of Malice, no Premeditation, no Solemnity; the Provocation, the Persons against whom the Curse is denounced, *Lear*'s Character, all conspire to render such a Behaviour absurd: nor can I easily pardon the Tears shed at the Conclusion ... that strange Mixture of Anger and Grief is to me highly unnatural; this unmanly Sniveling lowers the Consequence of *Lear*; this Practice may, with Propriety, be introduced in the Imitation of a vex'd Girl, who cries because she can't (in the vulgar Tongue) gain her Ends.[59]

Foote implicitly seems to have preferred Barton Booth's performance years earlier, for Thomas Davies reports that

> Booth was more rapid than Garrick, his fire was ardent and his feelings were remarkably energetic, but they were not attended with those strugglings of parental affection, and those powerful emotions of conflicting passions, so visible in every look, action, and attitude of our great Roscius.[60]

The same assumption of the dominating emotion of energetic passion underpins Charles Gildon's recommendation in 1710, couched in the voice of Betterton, that the curse 'must be spoke with an elevated Tone and enraged Voice, and the Accents of a Man all on Fire, and in a Fury next to Madness'.[61] Davies goes on at length about this sense of conflict in Garrick's performance here:

> I have heard certain critics complain, that, in pronouncing this denunciation, Garrick was too deliberate, and not so quick in the emission of his words as he ought to have been, that he did not yield to the impetuosity which his particular situation required. But we should reflect that Lear is not agitated by one passion only, that he is not moved by rage, by grief, and indignation, singly, but by a tumultuous combination of them all together, where all claim to heard at once, and where one naturally interrupts the progress of the other ... Shakspeare [*sic*] ... wrote them for the mouth of one who was to assume the action of an old man of fourscore, for a father as well as a monarch, in whom the most bitter execrations are accompanied with extreme anguish, with deep sighs, and involuntary tears.[62]

Davies was a fan writing with a long experience of the performance. But Garrick's approach was immediately defended against Foote by an anonymous pamphleteer:

> you begin
> *Hear Nature, Dear Goddess!* –
> with a *broken, inward, eager* utterance; from thence rising every Line in Loudness and Rapidity of Voice, 'till you come to [the serpent's tooth]. Then you are struck at once with your Daughter's Ingratitude; and bursting into Tears, with an almost sorrowful Heart-breaking Tone of Voice, you say
> – *go, go, my People.*[63]

If the report is accurate, Garrick moved the final line from earlier in the scene in order to provide a totally different kind of exit, less abrupt, perhaps, than Shakespeare's and Tate's 'Away, away'. This increase in speed and volume was, for Francis Gentleman, writing notes to the published edition of Garrick's text, one of the two ways of playing the speech:

> This execration is conceived and expressed in such a nervous climax of resent-ment, that it requires great abilities to give it due force. There are two justifiable modes of delivering it: one is, beginning low, as if speech was for a moment benummed; and rising to the conclusion; the other is, commencing with a burst of passion, and repressing a swell of grief, till the two last lines; then melting into a modulated shiver of utterance, watered with tears. We prefer the latter.[64]

Theophilus Cibber agreed. In 1756 he analysed the passage and Garrick's perform-ance at length, preferring Barry for his majesty and grace:

> Can the Actor be too rapid in the Delivery? – Do not long Pauses damp the Fire of it, like cold Water dropp'd thereon? ... too long a Preparation for it, seems not consistent with *Lear*'s Character: 'Tis here unnatural. Such long Pauses give him Time to reflect, which the hasty *Lear* is not apt to do 'till 'tis too late. – This philosophic Manner would become a Man, who took Time to recollect; – which if Lear did, would not the good King, the o'er-kind Father, change this dire Curse into a fervent Prayer, for his Child's Repentance and Amendment? ... so dire is the Curse, Nature can scarce endure it, unless delivered in the rapid Manner, the wild Transport of the choleric King, with sudden and unchecked Passion, would surely give it: – when it appears premeditated, – it speaks Rancour, Spleen, and Malice; a cool Revenge; not a Burst of Passion, from an o'er-charged Heart.[65]

I am deliberately ignoring here the long descriptions of Garrick's preparation for the speech, the kneeling, the clenching of the teeth and all the other physical, non-vocal devices which Garrick used. By 1755 John Shebbeare could praise Garrick at this moment above all for that dignity Cibber felt Barry had over Garrick:

This all other Actors speak with that kind of Rage, with which a drunken shoemaker curses his daughter that has secretly taken his Money from him, and prevented his going to the ale-house; it is indeed a sheer scolding. In Mr. Garrick it is a prince in anger.[66]

The effect must have been immensely powerful and Edward Taylor in 1774 used the moment as the means of resisting Johnson's assumption that all spectators are always in their right mind:

Whoever at such a critical moment can turn aside to view any other object, or not forget his own situation, and be wholly wrapt up in that of the inimitable performer, is to be pitied, not envied, for his composure and sang froid.[67]

With more space, it would be possible to analyse these conflicting accounts but, to a very large extent, the conflict is neither surprising nor troubling. The under-standing of meaning in vocal inflection is necessarily imprecise. One thing is clear, however: Garrick's form of speaking allowed for multiple and complex emotions both to succeed each other rapidly and to co-exist within a single moment. His aim was to represent that density of emotional state that most fully accorded with the differing social, familial, political, rational and cultural dynamics of the character across the play and at the precise moment.[68] If this has the kind of complexity that, say, Strindberg famously argued for in the preface to *Miss Julie*, it is a sign of the multiplicity which Garrick saw as a consequence of that 'natural' style which he and Macklin created. John Shebbeare commented, in a standard phrase of praise, '[i]t is not possible to decide which is superior in the knowledge of nature', the poet who wrote, or the player who animates these passages'.[69] Hence Garrick's recommendation to the actors in the character of Bayes in his short play *The Meeting of the Company*:

First, gentlemen, turn nature out of door,
Then rant away 'till you can rant no more.
Walk, talk and look as none walked, talked and looked before.[70]

I have ended in a familiar place, with a sense of Garrick as a natural actor, as a stylized representation of a complex cultural formation of assumptions about behaviour, affective emotion and the mind. But I start to hear him better, not yet clearly but no longer quite so inaudible.

Notes and references

1. Colley Cibber, *An Apology for the Life of Mr. Colley Cibber, Comedian* (London, 1740), 60.
2. Joshua Steele, *An Essay Towards Establishing the Melody and Measure of Speech* (London, 1775), 14.
3. Richard Warner, *A Letter to David Garrick, Esq., concerning a Glossary to the Plays of Shakespeare* (London, 1768), 92.

4. *The Theatrical Review, or Annals of the Drama* (1763), p. 76, reprinted in *The Life and Death of David Garrick, Esq.*, Anon. (2nd edn., 1779), 11.

5. There is oddly little in the two excellent standard biographies, George Winchester Stone, Jr., and George M. Kahrl, *David Garrick: a Critical Biography* (Carbondale, Ill.: Southern Illinois University Press, 1979) and Ian McIntyre, *Garrick* (London: Allen Lane, 1999); a little more in Jean Benedetti, *David Garrick and the Birth of Modern Theatre* (London: Methuen, 2000). The best account is still probably the chapter in Bertram Joseph, *The Tragic Actor* (London: Routledge and Kegan Paul, 1959).

6. James Boaden, ed., *The Private Correspondence of David Garrick*, 2 vols (London, 1831–2), 1:3–4.

7. Boaden, *Private Correspondence*, 1:11.

8. Boaden, *Private Correspondence*, 1:20.

9. See David Crystal, *Pronouncing Shakespeare* (Cambridge: Cambridge University Press, 2005). See, or rather hear, also the material on Crystal's website, www.shakespeareswords.com.

10. Crystal, *Pronouncing Shakespeare*, 171.

11. Bruce R. Smith, *The Acoustic World of Early Modern England* (Chicago: Chicago University Press, 1999).

12. Dene Barnett, *The Art Of Gesture: the Practices and Principles of 18th Century Acting* (Heidelberg: Carl Winter, 1987).

13. Boaden, *Private Correspondence*, 1:12.

14. Boaden, *Private Correspondence*, 1:xxxv.

15. Boaden, *Private Correspondence*, 1:xxxv.

16. S. J. Pratt, *Garrick's Looking-Glass* (Dublin, 1776), 4.

17. See also Francis Gentleman's complaint: 'we have often regretted an adulteration of language, by changing the *e* and *i* into *u*; this gentleman, and several after him, have pronounced *stern, sturn, mirth, murth, birth, burth*, which is really rendering our language, already sufficiently dissonant, still more so' (Francis Gentleman, *The Dramatic Censor*, 2 vols (1770), 2:483).

18. Thomas Sheridan, *Elements of English* (1786), 28–9.

19. Michael K. C. MacMahon, 'Phonology', in Suzanne Romaine, ed., *The Cambridge History of the English Language. Vol. 4 1776–1997* (Cambridge: Cambridge University Press, 1998), 373–535 (417).

20. On Walker, in addition to the fine entry by Joan C. Beal in the *Oxford Dictionary of National Biography*, see also Bryan K. Brown, 'John Walker (1732–1807)' in Michael G. Moran, ed., *Eighteenth Century British and American Rhetorics and Rhetoricians* (Westport, Conn.: Greenwood Press, 1994), 230–4. See also Joseph R. Roach, *The Player's Passion* (Newark: University of Delaware Press, 1985), 76–87, for his thoughtful work on emotion in eighteenth century acting and the work of John Walker (especially *Elements of Elocution* (1787)), James Burgh (in *The Art of Speaking* (1761)); and Aaron Hill, *The Works*, 4 vols (London, 1753), 1:140; and on Burgh, Donald E. Hargis, 'James Burgh and *The Art of Speaking*', *Speech Monographs*, 24 (1957): 275–84.

21. Peter Thomson's *ODNB* entry has virtually nothing to say about Sheridan the orthoepist and Esther K. Sheldon's impressive biography of his theatrical career has little more (*Thomas Sheridan of Smock-Alley* (Princeton, NJ: Princeton University Press, 1967). But see Wallace A. Bacon, 'The Elocutionary Career of Thomas Sheridan (1719–88)', *Speech Monographs*, 31 (1964), 1–53; W. Benzie, *The Dublin Orator* (Menston: University of Leeds School of English, 1972); and Wilbur Samuel Howell, *Eighteenth-Century British Logic and Rhetoric* (Princeton: Princeton University Press, 1971), 214–43 as attempts to rectify the balance.

22. Robin C. Alston, prefatory note to facsimile reprint (Menston: Scolar Press, 1967), vol. 1.

23. Benzie, *The Dublin Orator*, 103.

24. The same passage, always a bone of contention in eighteenth-century Shakespeare editing, is discussed in the context of Garrick's pronunciation, in Arthur Murphy's

article in *The Gray's Inn Journal* for 27 January 1752 (see *The Gray's Inn Journal*, 2 vols (1756), 1:100–1).

25. Thomas Sheridan and John Henderson, *Sheridan's and Henderson's Practical Method*, (1796), 14–15.

26. *The Present State of the Stage in Great-Britain and Ireland* (1753), 51.

27. J. W. Anderson, *The Manner Pointed out in which the Common Prayer was Read in Private by the Late Mr Garrick* (London, 1797), 43–4. A more elaborate edition with further notes was published in 1840 as *Garrick's mode of reading the liturgy of the Church of England* (London, 1840).

28. See G. C. Lichtenberg, *Lichtenberg's Visits to England*, ed. Margaret L. Mare and W. H. Quarrell (Oxford: Clarendon Press, 1938), 1–30.

29. See Alan S. Downer, ed., *Oxberry's 1822 edition of King Richard III: with descriptive notes recording Edmund Kean's performance made by James Hackett* (London: Society for Theatre Research, 1959).

30. The first line in Cibber's adaptation reads 'The North! Why, what do they in the North' (*The Tragical History of King Richard III* (1700), 44) but Murphy may be misquoting.

31. Arthur Murphy, *The Life of David Garrick, Esq.* (Dublin, 1801), 16.

32. Murphy, *Life of David Garrick*, 16–17.

33. Quoted McIntyre, *Garrick*, 2.

34. Steele, *An Essay*, 39 and 47.

35. David Thomas's comment that it is 'impossible to interpret meaningfully' is unduly cautious. See David Thomas and Arnold Hare, eds, *Restoration and Georgian England, 1660–1788* (Theatre in Europe: A Documentary History, Cambridge: Cambridge University Press, 1989), 353.

36. Steele, *An Essay*, 40 and 47.

37. Ibid., 48.

38. Ibid.

39. Joshua Steele, *Prosodia Rationalis* (1779), 203–6.

40. Aaron Hill, *The Works*, 4 vols (London, 1753), 1:140.

41. Hill, *Works*, 1:139.

42. Hill, *Works*, 1:140.

43. Roger Pickering, *Reflections upon Theatrical Expression in Tragedy* (London, 1755), 51.

44. David M. Little and George M. Kahrl, eds, *The Letters of David Garrick*, 3 vols (London: Oxford University Press, 1963), 1:93.

45. Ibid., 2:559–60.

46. John Hill, *The Actor* (1750), 309. The passage is repeated, unacknowledged, as one of the few criticisms of Garrick allowed into the first biography, *The Life and Death of David Garrick, Esq.*, 16.

47. *The Present State of the Stage*, 20.

48. Quoted by Alan S. Downer, 'Nature to Advantage Dressed: Eighteenth-Century Acting', *PMLA*, 58 (1943): 1002–37 (1017).

49. *The Theatrical Review*, 79.

50. Quoted in Ronald Hafter's excellent article, 'Garrick and *Tristram Shandy*', SEL, 7 (1967): 475–89 (484–5).

51. Letter to Hall Harston, *The Letters of David Garrick*, 1:350.

52. *Letters*, 1:350–1.

53. James Boswell, *The Life of Samuel Johnson*, ed. George Birkbeck Hill, revised L. F. Powell, 6 vols, (Oxford: Clarendon Press, 1934–50), 1.168–9. Michael Cordner suggests to me that Johnson is not necessarily persuasive here and that a reader might not wish to emphasize 'not' every time.

54. See Stone and Kahrl, *David Garrick*, 149–50.

55. Thaddeus Fitzpatrick, *An Enquiry into the Real Merit of a Certain Popular Performer* (1760), 21.

56. Ibid. See also Boswell's account of Colonel Pennington's complaint of Garrick's failure of emphasis in *Hamlet*: 'I will speak *daggers* to her; but use *none*', instead of 'I will *speak* daggers to her; but *use* none' (Boswell, *Life of Samuel Johnson*, 5:127).

57. The principal printed text of Garrick's version of *King Lear* is the one in Bell's Shakespeare, 'as performed at the Theatre-Royal, Drury-Lane. Regulated from the prompt-book, with permission of the managers, by Mr. Hopkins, Prompter'. The speech is in *Bell's Edition of Shakespeare's Plays*, 9 vols (London, 1774), 2:20. The standard account of Garrick's production is still George Winchester Stone, Jr., 'Garrick's Production of *King Lear*: a Study in the Temper of the Eighteenth-Century Mind', *SP*, 45 (1948): 89–103. See also the edition of Garrick's adaptation in Harry W. Pedicord and Frederick L. Bergmann, eds, *The Plays of David Garrick*, 7 vols (Carbondale: Southern Illinois University Press, 1980–2), vol. 3.

58. William Cooke, *Memoirs of Charles Macklin, Comedian* (1804), 107. See also John Hill's praise: 'It is impossible to say whether Mr. Garrick expresses in this passage more fire or more feeling. Each is carried to the height, and they cast a new lustre upon one another' (*The Actor* (London, 1755), 129–30).

59. Samuel Foote, *A Treatise on the Passions* (London, 1747), p. 17; see also J. T., *A Letter of Compliment to the Ingenious Author of a Treatise on the Passions* (London, 1747), 18–21 for an elaborate description of Lear's feelings and emotional state.

60. Thomas Davies, *Dramatic Miscellanies,* 3 vols (London, 1784), 2:279.

61. Charles Gildon, *The Life of Mr.Thomas Betterton* (London, 1710), 115–16.

62. Davies, *Dramatic Miscellanies,* 2:279–80.

63. *An Examen of the New Comedy, Call'd The Suspicious Husband* (London, 1747), 31–2.

64. *Bell's Edition,* 2:20.

65. Theophilus Cibber, *Cibber's Two Dissertations of the Theatres* (London, 1756), Second Dissertation, 31.

66. John Shebbeare, *Letter to the English Nation,* 2 vols (London, 1755), 2:286–7. Joseph Pittard steals the passage in his *Observations on Mr. Garrick's Acting* (London, 1758), 10.

67. Edward Taylor, *Cursory Remarks on Tragedy* (London, 1774), 16, quoted Stone, 'Garrick's Production of *King Lear*', 102.

68. See, for his overall view of King Lear, his letter of 1770, *The Letters of David Garrick*, 2:682–3.

69. Shebbeare, *Letter to the English Nation,* 2:288.

70. Pedicord and Bergmann, *The Plays of David Garrick,* 2:247.

12
The Visuality of the Theatre

Shearer West

Art and theatre historians are blessed with a healthy quantity of portraits of actors and representations of the stage from the eighteenth century in the form of paintings, prints, sculptures, caricatures, even decorated mugs and fans. There is no doubt about the richness of this material, but there is less consensus about how representations of the theatre can be 'read' and what these readings tell us about actors and their audiences at this particular historical juncture. Like any historical evidence, there is a temptation to interpret images as documentary and revelatory, but as Christopher Balme has cautioned, 'To study pictorial evidence purely in terms of its *documentariness*, i.e., its function in reconstructing the theatrical past, is to deprive iconographical objects of much of their discursive potential.'[1] It is this 'discursive potential' that needs to be uncovered in eighteenth-century representations of actors. By considering these images as part of a burgeoning visual culture in London from the 1760s onwards, it is possible to demonstrate a fertile relationship between visual art and theatre that does not merely make one subordinate to the other. On the one hand, this visuality fed into what we now know as the modern idea of celebrity, in its manipulative, commercialized, commodified form. However, the eighteenth century was also a period of transition in which a visual culture of celebrity still functioned creatively, rather than repressively. Portraits of actors did not merely signify the unthinking desires of a nascent capitalist society; they also both reflected and affected the way the public engaged with their leisure life and social world.

It is tempting to assume that paintings and prints of performers and the stage provide insights into the physical trappings of the theatre of the past: how the stage was arranged, what settings and props were used, what actors wore and how they looked. This documentary quality has been challenged, but a developed method of interpreting such imagery has not yet replaced it. Barbara Hodgdon's consideration of photographic images of the stage as providing a kind of Derridean 'supplement' that is both integral to, yet on the margins of, our understanding of stage performance offers a tantalizing possibility for thinking about portraits of eighteenth-century actors.[2] Although the interpretations of painters lack the direct material association between referent and image that is characteristic of photography, paintings and engravings did have a relationship with the real people and events that they represented. How to understand and articulate this relationship is what is at stake when examining the rich iconography of eighteenth-century theatre. Robert Erenstein has suggested that theatre and art 'share a cultural system'.[3] It could be argued that in the eighteenth century, this cultural system was predicated on changes in the visual world, or visuality, and the way people responded to those changes.

But first, it is necessary to explain what is meant by 'visuality' and assess why this concept is crucial for both theatre and art in the latter half of the eighteenth century. Peter de Bolla has defined visuality as 'the modes of address human agents take to different objects in the visual field . . . the techniques of seeing and decoding the optical information received by the cerebral cortex'.[4] Visuality is about reception – or *how* people look at their world – and it is inextricably linked with *what* people look at, or the visual culture that is accessible to a population at a given time. Visual culture is not limited to art, but to any object that is designed to be looked at, which can include theatre and other kinds of performance.[5] De Bolla argues that we can trace a paradigm shift in visuality, and he locates this shift in the London art world of the 1760s. After the 1760s, according to de Bolla, an expansion of visual stimuli led Londoners to begin to think of themselves as viewers and to develop more sophisticated forms of visual engagement with the objects of their perusal. While the chronological reductivism of this argument is open to challenge, it is certainly true that from the 1760s, London society had a regular exposure to visual art in a way that it had never had before, and responses to this new plethora of imagery became increasingly complex and sophisticated.[6] From 1760 the annual Society of Artists exhibitions signalled the beginning of a new type of regular exhibition experience, and, with the advent of the Royal Academy and its attendant annual shows from 1768, an abundance of visual art was available to London audiences. The enhancement of the visual sphere was not confined solely to art exhibitions, which, after all, took place only sporadically. Even before annual exhibitions, the London public was exposed to the decorations of the Foundling Hospital, including works by Hogarth; to Vauxhall Gardens with its sculptures, supper box paintings and perspective views; and to scores of old master paintings on sale at auction houses. There was also a dramatic increase in the number of print shops in London in the second half of the eighteenth century, and, even for those who could not afford to purchase prints, the shop windows offered changing displays available to anyone passing on the street. Viewing continued to take place also in the theatre, of course, but equally in novel pseudo-theatrical contexts, such as demonstrations of phantasmagoria, magic lanterns, popular science and the developing technologies that eventually became the panorama and diorama.

There is no question that there was a great deal more to be looked at in London after 1760 than there had been before, but the proliferation of imagery does not explain how spectatorship changed. As Jonathan Crary put it in *Techniques of the Observer*, 'a history of vision . . . depends on far more than an account of shifts in representational practice'.[7] The presence of more works of art, more types of performance and other visual novelties does not explain how these displays were viewed. Some scholars have argued that the new viewing regimes can be understood in terms of power, and therefore this expanded range of imagery empowered the audiences who 'consumed' it.[8] That power could be economic, or sexual, as looking implies a kind of Foucauldian surveillance. There is certainly value in this argument, but spectatorship can be considered in more nuanced ways as well. One could argue that this explosion of imagery in eighteenth-century London attracted different kinds of viewing: not just looking, but scrutinizing, gazing, observing and the more circumspect glancing or peeping.[9] Each of these types of looking signals different preoccupations on the part of the observer – some, but not all, of which involve power.

However, both imagery itself and viewing experiences were not as separate as these interpretations suggest. In the wake of an increasingly visual world, different habits of looking began to merge in what is sometimes quite a complicated way. Many of the same people who went to the theatre also attended art exhibitions, stopped by print shop windows, witnessed more ephemeral types of performances and public rituals, observed the beauties of Vauxhall gardens, etc. Visual pleasure could thus be taken in a variety of ways in a short space of time. An example of this is the response of individuals who went to look at portraits of actors and actresses. Mary Hamilton in a diary entry of 1785 noted, 'Saw a picture of Mrs. Siddons in the character of Isabella in "The Fatal Marriage" very finely executed, we also went to see Mrs. Siddons' picture by Hamilton ... My cousin and self went to the Play, saw Mrs. Siddons in the character of "Calister" [*sic*] in the "Fair Penitent" '.[10] In these anecdotes both the artistic and theatrical occurrences were conveyed in terms of 'seeing'. Emotional responses to viewing art and theatre could also be difficult to distinguish. Speaking of this same portrait of Siddons by Hamilton, Thomas Campbell, Siddons's biographer, wrote,

> Her immense popularity was now shewn in the general enthusiasm to see her picture, even when it was scarcely finished. Carriages thronged the artist's door; and, if every fine lady who stept out of them did not actually weep before the painting, they had all of them, at least, their white handkerchiefs ready for that demonstration of their sensibility.[11]

Thus, going to see a painting of Siddons had the same impact as viewing a performance by Siddons – at least in its discursive retelling. Before the foundation of the Royal Academy, the expansion of the commercial print market and greater press attention devoted to London entertainments, this rapid succession of viewing experiences would not have been so possible.

The increasing visuality in eighteenth-century London moved art and theatre close together in other ways as well. When Charles Churchill published his *Rosciad* in 1761, he disparaged the idea that being a 'fine person' or having a 'beauteous face' was enough for an actor. His famous lines about Garrick's height suggest that Garrick's ability to express emotions offset his rather short frame, which ostensibly made him unsuitable to play heroes:

FIGURE, I own, at first, may give offence,
And harshly strike the eye's too curious sense:
But when the perfections of the mind break forth,
Humour's chaste sallies, Judgement's solid worth;
When the pure genuine flame, by Nature taught
Springs into Sense, and ev'ry action's Thought;
Before such merit, all objections fly;
Pritchard's genteel, and Garrick's six feet high.[12]

Although Churchill's attitude was not necessarily typical, only a few years later the recurring emphasis in theatrical criticism and biography was on the necessity of a visual fit between actors and their roles. In 1772 Charles Macklin was hissed and caricatured for playing the vigorous Macbeth when he was 'a clumsy old man, who looked more like a Scotch Piper, than a General and Prince of the Blood', according to one critique, and Mrs Abington was maligned for both impropriety and aesthetic unsavouriness in her performance as Scrub in the *Beaux' Stratagem*.[13] A dim echo of the *Rosciad*, the *Aesopiad* of 1784, affirmed that 'Acting yields to figure and to face', thus reversing Churchill's idea that a fair countenance and good body simply were not enough.[14] To Churchill, one of the greatest criticisms of an actor was that they perform 'like statues, in one posture still'.[15] During the early decades of the Royal Academy exhibitions, 'like a statue' became an encomium, rather than a criticism, as Reynolds's popular paintings of men and women posing in the attitudes of classical sculpture coloured discussions of contemporary performers. Both Mrs Yates and Mrs Siddons were compared favourably to sculpture, and fans and detractors alike judged Kemble as being a cross between ancient sculpture and a still life.[16] Indeed, in writings about Siddons and Kemble, praise was lavished on both actors for their ability to convey passions while motionless. George III allegedly complimented Siddons for her 'total repose in certain situations', while Kemble's acting style was described admiringly by James Boaden as 'dealing in *pauses* that were not before made', which Boaden interpreted as part of Kemble's 'academic' style of acting in a deliberate echo of Joshua Reynolds's third discourse on art.[17] By the early nineteenth century, the terminology of art permeated theatrical criticism, and changes in the perception of Kemble's and Siddons's performance styles were couched in terms of the Reynoldsonian Grand Manner.[18] Whether or not these actors really did stand very still for long periods of time is of less relevance than the fact that both these descriptions and representations depict performance as gradually approaching the state of sculpture or painting. Earlier in the century, Charles Macklin's 'Art and Duty of an Actor' compared the actor to a philosopher; by the 1790s, actors were regularly equated with artists.[19]

If it can be accepted that visuality brought art and theatre closer together in the last decades of the eighteenth century, and if visual qualities of actors were beginning to take on a greater value, at least in criticism and public discourse, what do these changes imply for how we understand representations of actors? If we follow the visuality argument to the conclusion most scholars now bring

it, visuality was a symptom of a growing commodification and commercialization of society and was strongly tied up with changing ideas of celebrity. In an
increasingly commercial economic climate, a proliferation of paintings, prints and
other consumer objects eventually led to what Guy Debord referred to as 'pseudo-
needs' of a 'society of spectacle'.[20] Consumerism was not instrumental behaviour.
People did not buy goods because they needed them to live, but because they
wanted them. These 'pseudo-needs' were created and fuelled by the market.[21]
Portraits of actors, as objects in this consumerism, stimulated imaginary relationships between audiences and performers, by facilitating the fantasies of admiring
fans.[22] As Chris Rojek puts it, 'star images are inflected and modified by the
mass-media and the productive assimilation of the audience'.[23] Although there is
some agreement about how widely disseminated images of celebrities function,
the beginnings of this phenomenon are the subject of debate. Leo Braudy identifies the sculpture of the ancient world and Renaissance portrait collections as early
glimmers of a modern celebrity media culture. Joseph Roach sees Debord's pseudo-
needs appearing in audience response to theatre from the seventeenth century.
Conversely, Richard Schickel firmly establishes celebrity culture as a twentieth-
century aftershock of the industrial revolution, reliant on the new technologies of
mass media production and distribution.[24] In most of these discussions, however,
the eighteenth century is seen as a turning point, when for the first time, a large
quantity of images of famous people were made and purchased at the same time
that there was a gradual distancing in the relationship between theatre audiences
and the actors they admired.

It is worth testing this proposition to see whether the idea of celebrity it perpetu-
ates is more relevant to the twenty-first century than to the eighteenth. If images
offered vicarious ways for an audience to relate to actors, presumably images
should have several qualities: legibility, iconicity and the capacity of being manip-
ulated to provide comforting messages or to answer contemporary concerns.[25]
Some examples of theatrical portraiture demonstrate these qualities thoroughly.
Joshua Reynolds's portrait of *Mrs. Siddons as the Tragic Muse* of 1784 (Figure 12.1)
is nothing if not an icon. The work notably echoes Michelangelo's prophet Joel
from the Sistine Ceiling; it contains allusions to Aristotle's *Poetics* in the figures
of Pity and Horror behind Siddons; the monumental seated frontal pose is not
unlike traditional representations of the Madonna enthroned. But what functions
did this portrait serve in the imagination of Siddons's audiences? For a start, we
could view the work as an example of the way Siddons used portraiture to enhance
her reputation. In her *Reminiscences*, she claimed: 'I was, as I have confess'd, an
ambitious candidate for fame ... As much of my time as could now be "stol'n
from imperious affairs," was employ'd in sitting for various Pictures.'[26] The implic-
ation of Siddons's reference to 'fame' is that she felt artists could provide longevity
to an actor whose stage performances were by definition ephemeral. A portrait
could thus supply a monument for posterity and a means of elevating the actor's
normally fleeting reputation. However, the iconic quality of any portrait was
unstable, once it became public property through exhibition and engraving. Thousands saw Reynolds's portrait of Siddons at the Royal Academy and many viewed

Figure 12.1 Joshua Reynolds, *Mrs Siddons as the Tragic Muse*, 1784

or acquired Valentine Green's famous mezzotint based on the work. It was thus discussed and looked at in both the social contexts of the Royal Academy and in front of print shop windows, as well as in the more private domain of people's homes. As with any representation, the meaning of Reynolds's Siddons quickly transcended both the intentions of the artist to express Siddons's performative power and the agency of the actress who used portraiture to enhance her lasting reputation.

A clue to public response lies in a no doubt apocryphal anecdote about the sitting for the painting. In this retrospective story, Reynolds tells Siddons to 'ascend your undisputed throne and graciously bestow upon me some idea of the Tragic Muse'.[27] This anecdote, with its reference to a 'throne', points to the regal aura that was seen to surround Siddons.[28] The majestic nature of this portrait was enhanced by the fact that Reynolds's portrait of Siddons was comparable in size to state portraits of King George III and Queen Charlotte, and it was undoubtedly an influence on Thomas Lawrence when he painted a seated portrait of Queen Charlotte six years after Reynolds's work was exhibited.[29] Reynolds's regal image of Siddons was complemented by frequent references to royalty in Siddons's professional and private life from the time of this portrait onwards. Siddons was known to the royal family, and she performed before Queen Charlotte who praised her for her courtly manners.[30] Siddons specialized in playing queens such as Lady Macbeth and Queen Katherine. Observers also attributed regal qualities to Siddons's private character, although the idea of what constituted her queenly authority could vary. Thomas Campbell, for example, commented on the 'strong moral resemblance' between Siddons and Queen Katharine, whereas Hester Piozzi claimed that 'At times, in private company, she gave one a notion of a wicked, unhappy Queen, rather than of a purely well-bred gentlewoman.'[31]

These visual and metaphorical associations with monarchy extended to Siddons's brother, John Philip Kemble, who was said to resemble physically his various royal roles, including King John and Charles I.[32] Kemble's use of Van Dyck's portraits of Charles I (Figure 12.2) to effect this visual mimicry elicited comparisons with the similarly beheaded King Louis XVI – a common association during the period of revolution and war with France. Such references gained in significance from the 1790s onwards, when patriotic response to the conflict with France favoured a conservative attitude towards the monarchy.[33] The visual parallels made in art and on stage between Siddons, Kemble and a range of past and present monarchs contributed to this culture of patriotism. Siddons provided the British public with a grandiloquent and assertive, yet imaginary, queen very unlike the real monarch.

Much of this argument about Siddons's portraiture and its imaginative afterlife has to do with visuality, and the way the visual expression of celebrity is interpreted by audiences anxious to fulfil their 'pseudo-needs'. British audiences experienced the horror of Marie Antoinette's execution and the struggle of Queen Charlotte to hold the country together in the midst of George III's madness and her son's public profligacy. Reynolds's portrait of Siddons provided a comforting and authoritative foil to the contemporary realities of the monarchy that had

Figure 12.2   J. P. Kemble as Charles I in William Harvard's *King Charles I*

lasting value in the public imagination. There seems to be a legibility in the iconic qualities of the Reynolds portrait that can be readily related to contemporary concerns, the same way that images of celebrities today draw upon the anxieties and desires of the 'fans' who consume them. Furthermore, Siddons's air of superior distance in the portrait was complemented by contemporary anecdotes that expressed her detachment from ordinary mortals. Stories told about Siddons by the diarist, Henry Crabb Robinson, for instance, present the author as spying on Siddons, and ruminating on her appearance and character, rather than interacting with her.[34] A range of other anecdotes indicates the awe in which Siddons was held, even in private life, and tales abound of aristocratic admirers stealing nervous peeks at her or watching her adoringly from a distance.[35] This combination of admiring viewers and a distant and desired object is a quality that characterizes modern celebrity. Reynolds's portrait of Siddons embodies her distance from ordinary mortals through its allegorical and regal trappings. In this respect, it could be argued that we see here a foreshadowing of the way celebrity works in the early twenty-first century.

However, there is more to this visuality than simple service of a modern consumer economy, which was, after all, only in its early stages of development. The distancing between audience and object of desire that is a prerequisite of modern celebrity culture dominated some stories about Siddons, but other anecdotes puncture this image of remoteness. The artist, James Northcote, for instance, turns Siddons's superiority into the brunt of a joke that reminds his readers of the actress's lowly origins. His narrative is notably presented as a third-hand report:

> Stewardson has been telling me a queer anecdote about Mrs. Siddons, and it was told him, he said, by Queen Caroline, whilst Princess of Wales, when he was painting her portrait a few years ago. Mrs. Siddons – the Princess told him – was once dining with her, and the actress sat at table in such solemn dignity, that the rest of the company were afraid of her. There was a long and awful silence, which, at length, was only broken by Mrs. Siddons herself, who, looking round at one of the servants, said, in her deep-toned manner, 'I will thank you for a glass of table beer.' Upon this, the Princess burst into a fit of laughter.[36]

Although most contemporary anecdotes give us a Siddons who is knowable only through art and public performance, like modern 'stars', this account reveals how a celebrity was not a distant figure but was directly involved in the small social world of London. Gossip about Siddons came from people who knew her personally, and the mockery of her lowly origins in the above passage reveals a genuine intimacy with a celebrity performer that is essentially different from the simulated familiarity fuelled by the media of today. Given that there was an admission charge to Royal Academy exhibitions that effectively excluded all but the elite from visiting the annual show, the majority of viewers of Siddons's portrait are likely to have met or known the actress, which punctures somewhat the remoteness of her Tragic Muse persona.

An iconic image such as *Siddons as the Tragic Muse* was rare; what is more striking is the potential for visual and verbal images of actors to relate, reinforce and sometimes change each other. This is what is usually called 'intertextuality', but which Jacky Bratton has recently rechristened as 'intertheatricality' that 'seeks to articulate the mesh of connections between all kinds of theatre texts, and between texts and their users'.[37] There is yet another recent formulation for this kind of interchange, which is Peter Wagner's term 'intermediality', or the interactions between different media, in this case, verbal, visual and performative.[38] Intermediality doesn't involve simple borrowing. We see plenty of this in theatrical portraiture, especially earlier in the century. It involves instead a range of allusions and references – some originating from the artist, others from the critic or viewer; many of them partial, teasing, paradoxical and difficult to reduce to a single meaning. This method of understanding the visual and theatrical culture of eighteenth-century London embraces both the iconic power of images of actors as well as the argument that these representations primarily serve an increasingly passive consumer economy, addicted to the repetition of vicarious emotional experiences. However, it also allows for more varied and subtle readings of the relationships between image and performer. Intermedial exchanges can be revealing, but a certain amount of excavation has to be done before they become legible. This method offers a means of engaging with the prolific visuality of late eighteenth-century London and understanding more fully the way both art and theatre fed this new visual culture.

This method can be used to analyse two portraits of actors by Gainsborough which may not, at first, appear to tell us very much at all about the history of the theatre. Following the ground-breaking studies of Edgar Wind, art historians have interpreted Gainsborough's approach to art as the opposite of Reynolds's: where Reynolds borrowed poses for theatrical effect, Gainsborough's portraits resist an iconographic analysis in favour of more 'natural' gestures and settings.[39] Gainsborough's portraiture may therefore appear to oppose the iconicity that characterizes the imagery of early celebrity culture. Certainly his portrait of Siddons of 1785 (Figure 12.3) wearing the latest fashion is at odds with Reynolds's grandiloquent Tragic Muse and with contemporary descriptions of Siddons's character as distant, queenly and other-worldly. The larger than life quality that was already beginning to be associated with Siddons by the time Gainsborough painted her portrait is nowhere to be seen here. Although there are some portraits of Siddons in street dress, Gainsborough's is the only one that represents Siddons as a woman of fashion – or 'particularly *novelle*', as Henry Bate said.[40] Unlike other actresses such as Frances Abington, Siddons was not generally thought of as a doyenne of transient fashion. Her attire in this work is in strong contrast to what she later prided herself on in her stage dress. According to Siddons, Reynolds 'approved very much of my costumes and my hair *without powder* ... My locks were generally braided into a small compass so as to ascertain the size and shape of my head ... My short waist too was to him a pleasing contrast to the long stiff stays and hoop petticoats which were then the fashion.'[41] Gainsborough's Siddons, with her teased and powdered hair and voluminous skirts, could hardly be further from this description. However, by showing her in these 'novelle' garments, Gainsborough found a means of commenting on Siddons's novelty and fashionability on the London stage. This portrait was painted in the early years of her success in London, where

Figure 12.3 Thomas Gainsborough, *Mrs Siddons*, 1785

she had a second debut in 1782 after leaving Bath. Although she retained her popularity for several decades after this, at the time Gainsborough painted this portrait there was no reason to assume that Siddonsmania would last any longer than the fashion for black beaver hats. To an extent, Siddons here is being visualized as a passing fad.

The other striking aspect of this portrait is the profile, which emphasizes, rather than disguises, Siddons's excessively large nose. Gainsborough is reported to have

Figure 12.4   Thomas Gainsborough, *The Three Eldest Princesses,* 1784

said of Siddons, 'Confound the nose, there's no end to it!'[42] Robyn Asleson has attributed this profile pose to Gainsborough's portrait of the *Three Eldest Princesses* (Figure 12.4), which he had summarily withdrawn from the Royal Academy exhibition of 1784, the year before his Siddons portrait, because of a bad hang.[43] The princess seated on the right hand side certainly does seem to be a source for Siddons's pose, but one wonders about the irony of Gainsborough re-using this pose for the actress. In the same year Gainsborough had to withdraw his portrait of the princesses from the Royal Academy, Reynolds exhibited his own portrait of *Siddons as the Tragic Muse,* to much acclaim. So the echo of the pose here may have reminded Gainsborough of a negative personal experience. Equally, he has transposed Reynolds's suggestive seated frontal pose into a side view with a chair that is distinctly not throne-like – in challenge to what might be interpreted as Reynolds's pomposity.

The profile itself is also rich in reference. The profile was commonly used in miniatures and engraved gems but, in Siddons's case, one might think of medals or coins with their classical associations. There were certainly contemporary portraits of Siddons that represented her in this profile format, where the relationship with the classical coin or medal was much more apparent. However, Gainsborough's profile portrait bears less relationship to a classical coin than it does to a satire on Siddons by James Gillray (Figure 12.5), which was well circulated the year before Gainsborough painted his portrait of Siddons. This shows Siddons as Melpomene reaching for bags of money – an attack on several noted episodes in which she

MELPOMENE.

Figure 12.5   James Gillray, *Melpomene (Mrs Siddons)*, 1784

exhibited greed and lack of generosity. Again, the visual referent comes with a negative connotation.

But perhaps an even more likely source for the profile pose is the contemporary silhouette portrait (Figure 12.6) – another fashionable item, which was

Figure 12.6 R. Schellenberg, *A Man Drawing a Silhouette of a Woman*, n.d.

intended to convey the character of the sitter's face in a profile. Silhouette portraits were popular from the 1770s, after the publication in German of Johann Caspar Lavater's *Physiognomische Fragmente*. Although this wasn't translated into English until the 1790s, it was a collector's item for the large number of engraved portraits and silhouettes that it contained.[44] Lavater's premise that the face is revelatory of the soul was still, at this point, very much open to debate: Hogarth cautiously supported the idea, but Gainsborough's friend, John Clubbe, mocked the tendency to equate specific features with character traits in the frontispiece to his book on physiognomy.[45] Physiognomy was both cod science and, via silhouettes, the stuff of street fairs, but its popularity meant a fascination with physical features became widespread.

Siddons's nose is just such a feature. Horace Walpole said rather snidely of her: 'She is a good figure, handsome enough, though neither nose nor chin according to the Greek standard.'[46] Even her admirers had to find careful ways of dealing with the unavoidable protuberance. A 1782 eulogy on Siddons states 'Her face is peculiarly happy, the features being finely formed, though strong.'[47] Here Gainsborough was having a poke at Siddons's indelicate features, and there is another satirical reference underlying the choice of the profile. Gainsborough admired Sterne's *Tristram Shandy* of 1760–67, which includes several chapters on Shandy's father's obsession with his family's flat noses. Sterne describes the Shandy collection of books on noses, including the encyclopaedic digest of 'the great and learned Hafen Slawkenbergius'.[48] And in one of Shandy senior's exhortations on noses, he refers to 'the external organ of smelling, or that part of man which stands prominent in his face, – and which painters say in jolly good noses and well-proportioned faces, should comprehend a full third, – that is, measuring downwards from a setting on of the hair'.[49] Siddons's nose appears to be much more than a third of her face, which would make her the envy of the ill-fated Shandy family but not in possession of a well-proportioned physiognomy.

In the end, then, Gainsborough's portrait of Siddons is not a celebratory kind of theatrical portrait like that of Reynolds; it does not contribute notably to her fame or reputation; it tells us nothing about her theatrical performance; it is not an example of the commodification of celebrity, as there is too much in it to undermine this. But it does give us an insight into Siddons's social role at a significant moment in her career. The same could be said of Gainsborough's earlier and more benign portrait of David Garrick leaning against a bust of Shakespeare (Figure 12.7), most likely the work exhibited publicly at the Society of Artists in 1766 – when visual culture was, according to de Bolla, just witnessing its great birth. Gainsborough chose to represent actors celebrated for their versatility of theatrical character without any direct reference to their roles. Although Garrick was known for a variety of parts in both tragedy and comedy, in this portrait Gainsborough deliberately counteracted the protean qualities associated with the actor. A much repeated story of Garrick concerned the actor sitting for his portrait and subtly changing his facial expression as a means of driving the portrait painter to distraction.[50] Gainsborough tackles the legend of Garrick's versatility rather perversely by relating the changeable actor to the status of a portrait bust of Shakespeare. The bust portrait itself is a kind of hybrid. It is possibly related to the effigy of Shakespeare by Geerart Janssen in Holy Trinity Church, Stratford, which Gainsborough called 'a silly smiling thing' in a letter to Garrick.[51] It may refer to Peter Scheemakers's monument to Shakespeare in Westminster Abbey. It bears some resemblance to John Michael Rysbrack's bust of Shakespeare of 1760, and it notably recalls Louis-François Roubiliac's statue of Shakespeare that Garrick commissioned for his estate at Hampton in 1756 (Figure 12.8).[52] In any

Figure 12.7   James Scott (after Thomas Gainsborough), *David Garrick*, 1769

Figure 12.8 Louis-François Roubiliac, *Shakespeare* (for Garrick's villa at Hampton), 1756

event, Garrick's own features bear some resemblance to those of Shakespeare, so a spiritual relationship is conveyed by physical likeness.

The equation of Garrick with Shakespeare may, on the one hand, seem to place Gainsborough on a par with many others who found ways of paying homage to Garrick's promotion of Shakespeare. This was the portrait sent or sold to the Corporation of Stratford for Garrick's ill-fated Jubilee of 1769, but despite the rich set of visual associations in it, it lacks the heavily over-determined imagery that characterized that event and its afterlife. The Jubilee itself included, for example, a transparent screen with a design of Shakespeare being led by Time to Immortality, flanked by Tragedy and Comedy, and a number of similarly ostentatious allegorical tributes to the Bard.[53] Gainsborough's avoidance of the elaborate over-determined imagery that surrounded the Shakespeare Jubilee in this portrait may also relate to his own misgivings about his friend, Garrick's, theatrical inclinations. Gainsborough chided Garrick for abandoning his earlier ideals of 'truth to nature' and pursuing the cosmetic excesses of pantomime at Drury Lane:

> It appears to me that Fashion, let it consist of false or true taste will have its run, like a run away Horse; for when Eyes & Ears are thoroughly debauch'd by Glare & noise, the returning to modest truth will seem very gloomy for a time; and I know you are cursedly puzzled how to make this retreat without putting out your lights, and losing the advantage of all our new discoveries of transparent Painting &c. &c. How to Satisfye your tawdry friends, whilst you steal back into the mild Evening gleam and quiet middle term.
>
> Now I'll tell you my sprightly Genius how this is to be done. Maintain all your light, but spare the poor abused Colors, til the Eye rests and recovers keep up your Music by Supplying the place of *Noise*, by more Sound, more Harmony & more Tune.[54]

In his portrait of Garrick, Gainsborough eschewed both laboured allegory and pantomimic excess, but nevertheless, as with the Siddons portrait, his depiction of Garrick is replete with references that build up a vision of Garrick that is more than the sum of its parts. For example, by choosing to represent Shakespeare in bust form, rather than in whole length, Gainsborough may have been alluding to the *Lecture on Heads* begun in the 1760s by the showman George Stevens, who used bust length pasteboard heads and mimicry in order to represent a wide range of social types.[55] Stevens's lecture on heads was resolutely focused on the 'middling sort' – the rung of society which could have been said to include Garrick. However, Garrick had aspirations to gentility, as seen through his purchase of a country house, hobnobbing with the aristocracy and taking the Grand Tour. The reference to garden architecture in the background of Gainsborough's portrait might be a reference to the Shakespeare Temple on Garrick's estate at Hampton or, as Walpole thought, Prior Park, near Bath. There is a compositional echo of Gainsborough's portrait of the socially aspirant Mr. and Mrs Andrews (*c.*1750); both works include sitters on the left and an expansive landscape dominating the right hand side to signal the ownership of property. Whatever the specific allusions, these qualities emphasize Garrick's own pretensions, even while his familiar pose and the Stevens-type bust equate him with his more humble origins. Gainsborough presents Garrick as friendly with Shakespeare in what might be considered a somewhat irreverent way. As the *Public Advertiser* put it, Garrick seems 'fond' of the bust.[56] Here, as with Siddons's nose, there is a physical joke at the expense of Garrick. Garrick's diminutive stature is emphasized, rather than disguised, by Gainsborough's decision to depict a full-length but undersized Garrick reaching up rather awkwardly to his taller creative ancestor. Physical proportion, or lack of it, in an actor, again becomes a theme.

These are just a few examples of how a complex web of meaning can be attached to portraits of actors that appear, at first glance, to tell us nothing about the stage. In each of these cases, the increase of accessible visual culture and a growing sophistication of response to it made such meanings available to contemporary audiences. This sort of intermedial reading is a way to tackle visuality, but it is certainly a flawed way to understand theatre history, as the evidence gives us only echoes, veiled suggestions, occasional insights, partial solutions. Furthermore, the very idea of visuality, compelling though it is, has a number of flaws. Jonathan Crary refers to the 'autonomization of sight' – the idea that by the early years of the nineteenth century, appeals to the eye involve a separation of seeing from the other senses.[57] To Crary, the world takes the form of Debord's society of spectacle shortly after this time. But too much visuality gives us a sort of disembodied eye, functioning as a scopic monster while the other senses are muted or stifled. It is perhaps more fruitful to consider W. J. T. Mitchell's proposition that different kinds of images, whether optical or perceptual, 'are not exclusively visual in any important way, but involve multisensory apprehension and interpretation'.[58] To Mitchell, even art is not a purely visual experience, and certainly when reception is at stake, the physical experience of looking at exhibitions or viewing art in private homes no doubt awakened a range of sensory experiences from sexual arousal to the smell of a crowded exhibition hall. Equally, in theatre, the aural sense is arguably as important as the visual, and many contemporary descriptions linger on the particular timbre or sonority of actors' voices.[59] Audiences also differed in their composition and response and are not easily reconcilable to monolithic models of viewing.[60] Eighteenth-century writers and artists give us audiences that are doing anything else but sitting still and watching. They are flirting, rioting, fighting, vomiting, arguing and occasionally watching the play. This is a world apart from the music hall audiences Walter Richard Sickert represented at the end of the nineteenth century who seem almost paralysed in their wholehearted concentration on looking at the stage. Arguments about visuality can provide an important starting point for engaging with representations of actors in the eighteenth century, but this evidence often leaves us with as many questions as answers. However, it is necessary to take into account the expanding field of visual experience in any interpretation of eighteenth-century representations of performers, and this intermedial methodology gives us one way in to the shared cultural sphere of the London art and theatre worlds of the time.

Notes and references

1. Christopher Balme, 'Interpreting the Pictorial Record: Theatre Iconography and the Referential Dilemma', *Theatre Research International*, 22:3 (1997): 192.

2. Barbara Hodgdon, 'Photography, Theater, Mnemonics; or Thirteen Ways of Looking at a Still', in W. B. Worthen and Peter Holland, eds, *Theorizing Practice: Redefining Theatre History* (Basingstoke: Palgrave Macmillan, 2003), 88–119. Thomas Postlewait demonstrates the way in which theatrical anecdote, although most frequently used as 'documentation' of theatre history, actually provides just the sort of supplement that Hodgdon also argues for. See Postlewait, 'The Criteria for Evidence: Anecdotes in Shakespearean Biography' 1709–2000, in *Theorizing Practice*, 47–70.
3. Robert Erenstein, 'Theatre Iconography: an Introduction', *Theatre Research International*, 22:3 (1997): 186. Erenstein and Balme are part of the European Theatre iconography network that was formed to collect and interpret representations of European theatre. This group has provided some valuable groundwork for rethinking interpretations of theatre iconography, but much of their work also has involved assimilating and cataloguing visual material. See also Christopher Balme, Robert Erenstein and Cesare Molinari, eds, *European Theatre Iconography* (Rome: Bulzoni Editori, 2002).
4. Peter de Bolla, *The Education of the Eye: Painting, Landscape and Architecture in Eighteenth-Century Britain* (Stanford: Stanford University Press, 2003), 3.
5. See John Walker and Sarah Chaplin, *Visual Culture: an Introduction* (Manchester: Manchester University Press, 1997), 1–2: 'Visual culture can be roughly defined as those material artefacts, buildings and images, plus time-based media and performances, produced by human labour and imagination, which serve aesthetic, symbolic, ritualistic, or ideological-political ends and/or practical functions, and which address the sense of sight to a significant extent.' See also Nicholas Mirzoeff, *An Introduction to Visual Culture* (London: Routledge, 1999).
6. De Bolla confines his argument largely to England and specifically London. Others have argued for a similar kind of visual paradigm shift in, for example, Renaissance Italy or the United Provinces in the seventeenth century. For the impact of the Royal Academy on art, see David Solkin, ed., *Art on the Line: the Royal Academy Exhibitions at Somerset House* (New Haven and London: Yale University Press, 2001).
7. Jonathan Crary, *Techniques of the Observer: On Vision and Modernity in the Nineteenth Century* (Cambridge, Mass.: MIT Press, 1990), 5.
8. See Kristina Straub, *Sexual Suspects: Eighteenth-Century Players and Sexual Ideology* (Princeton: Princeton University Press, 1992), 15: 'Spectacle does not just happen; it is an instrument in the struggle for power ... The spectacle of players in eighteenth-century theatrical discourse is in part about the struggle to control the politics of spectatorship.' See also Paula Backscheider, *Spectacular Politics: Theatrical Power and Mass Culture in Early Modern England* (Baltimore: Johns Hopkins University Press, 1993); and Gillian Russell, *The Theatres of War: Performance, Politics and Society 1793–1815* (Oxford: Clarendon Press, 1995).
9. See Margaret Olin, 'Gaze', in Robert Nelson and Richard Shiff, eds, *Critical Terms for Art History* (Chicago: Chicago University Press, 1996), 208–19.
10. Elizabeth Anson and Florence Anson, eds, *Mary Hamilton, afterwards Mrs. John Dickenson, at Court and at Home, from Letters and Diaries, 1756–1816* (London: John Murray, 1925), 133.
11. Thomas Campbell, *The Life of Mrs. Siddons*, 2 vols (London: Effingham Wilson, 1834), 1:191.
12. Charles Churchill, *The Rosciad* (London: the author, 1761), 13.
13. For Macklin, see [William Cooke], *Memoirs of Charles Macklin, Comedian* (London: n.p., 1804), 284–5; for Abington, see James Boaden, *Memoirs of the Life of John Philip Kemble*, 2 vols (London: Longman et. al., 1825), 1:319.
14. *The Aesopiad: a Poem*, (Dublin: n.p., 1784–5), 45.
15. Churchill, *Rosciad*, 13.
16. See, for example, *The Green Room Mirror, clearly delineating our present theatrical performers, by a genuine reflection* (London: the author, 1785), 25–6.
17. William van Lennep, ed., *The Reminiscences of Sarah Kemble Siddons* (Cambridge: Widener Library, 1942), 13; and Boaden, *Kemble*, 1:170–1.

18. I have explored this in several essays, including 'Lawrence's "Half-History" Portraits and the Politics of Theatre', *Art History*, 14: 2 (June 1991): 225–49; and 'Body Connoisseurship', in Robyn Asleson, ed., *The Notorious Muse: the Actress in British Art and Culture 1776–1812* (New Haven and London: Yale University Press 2003), 151–70. For a contemporary example of the way in which the language of Reynolds's Discourses and the Grand Manner entered theatrical criticism, see *An Authentic Narrative of Mr. Kemble's Retirement from the Stage* (London: John Miller, 1817), xxvi: 'it is the best part of nature only, which should be faithfully given; . . . stooping to represent the common defects of common life . . . degrades the character and the art'.

19. See James Thomas Kirkman, *Memoirs of the Life of Macklin esq.* (London: n.p., 1799), 1:362 for Macklin's lecture on 'The Art and Duty of an Actor', I, 362; and James Boaden, *Memoirs of Mrs. Siddons*, 2 vols (London: Henry Colburn, 1827), 2: 62 on the actress as an artist.

20. Guy Debord, *La Société du spectacle* (Paris: Gallimard, 1992), 63: 'Sans doute, le pseudo-besoin imposé dans la consommation moderne ne peut être opposé à aucun besoin ou désir authentique qui ne soit lui-même façonné par la société et son histoire. Mais la marchandise abondante est là comme la rupture absolue d'une développement organique des besoins sociaux. Son accumulation mécanique libère un *artificiel illimité*, devant lequel le désir vivant reste désarmé.' ('Without doubt, the pseudo-need imposed by modern consumption cannot oppose any authentic need or desire fashioned by a society and its history. But the abundance of merchandise is like the absolute rupture of an organic development of society's needs. Its mechanical accumulation liberates an *artificial boundlessness* before which the living desire remains disarmed.')

21. For a discussion of the psychological impact of emergent capitalism in the eighteenth century, see Colin Campbell, 'Understanding Traditional and Modern Patterns of Consumption in Eighteenth-Century England: a Character-Action Approach', in John Brewer and Roy Porter, eds, *Consumption and the World of Goods* (London: Routledge, 1995), 40–57.

22. Cheryl Wanko relates this commodification also to theatrical biography. See Wanko, *Roles of Authority: Thespian Biography and Celebrity in Eighteenth-Century Britain* (Lubbock, Texas: Texas Tech University Press, 2003).

23. Chris Rojek, *Celebrity* (London: Reaktion, 2001), 44.

24. Leo Braudy, *The Frenzy of Renown: Fame and its History* (New York: Vintage Books, 1997), 10; Joseph Roach, 'Vicarious: Theatre and the Rise of Synthetic Experience', in Worthen and Holland, *Theorizing Practice*, 120–35; Richard Schickel, *Intimate Strangers: the Culture of Celebrity in America* (New York: Doubleday, 1985).

25. For the way 'star' images relate to social anxieties and aspirations, see Richard Dyer, *Stars* (London: BFI Publishing, 1997).

26. Lennep, *Reminiscences of Siddons*, 16–17.

27. See Ibid., pp. 16–18, and for a discussion of the various myths of Siddons's sittings, see Heather McPherson, 'Picturing Tragedy: Mrs. Siddons as the Tragic Muse Revisited', *Eighteenth-Century Studies*, 33:3 (2000): 401–30.

28. I have developed the implications of this association between Siddons and queenship in 'Siddons, Celebrity and Regality: Portraiture and the Body of the Ageing Actress', in Mary Luckhurst and Jane Moody, eds, *Theatre and Celebrity in Britain, 1660–2000* (Basingstoke: Palgrave Macmillan, 2005).

29. Lawrence later paid homage to this portrait as 'a work of the highest epic character, and indisputably the finest female portrait in the world'. See Thomas Lawrence, *An Address to the Students of the Royal Academy Delivered before the General Assembly at the Annual Distribution of Prizes* (London: W. Clowes, 1824), 14.

30. Lennep, *Reminiscences of Siddons*, 22.

31. Campbell, *Siddons*, 2: 135–6; and *Piozziana, or Recollections of the Late Mrs Piozzi*, ed. Edward Mangin (London: n.p., 1833), 85–6.

32. See, for example Boaden, *Siddons*, 1:59 on Kemble's King John, and Ibid., 1: 17 on Kemble's use of Van Dyck as his source for Charles I.

33. See Linda Colley, *Britons: Forging the Nation 1707–1837* (London: Pimlico, 2003).

34. See Crabb Robinson's anecdote of Siddons being watched in the Louvre, quoted in Yvonne Ffrench, *Mrs. Siddons: Tragic Actress*, 2nd edn, (London: Derek Verschoyle, 1954), 238. For other examples of Crabb Robinson's voyeuristic looking at actresses, see Eluned Brown, ed., *The London Theatre 1811–1866: Selections from the Diary of Henry Crabb Robinson* (London: Society for Theatre Research, 1966).

35. See, for example, William Hazlitt's assessment: 'When Mrs. Siddons used to sit in parties and at drawing-rooms, the Lady Marys and Lady Dorothies of the day came and peeped into the room to get a glance of her, with more awe and wonder than if it had been a queen.' William Hazlitt, 'Mrs. Siddons', *The Examiner*, 25 May 1828; 406–10 in *Art and Dramatic Criticism*, in P. P. Howe, ed., *The Complete Works of William Hazlitt*, 25 vols (London and Toronto: JM Dent and Sons, 1933), Vol. 18: 407.

36. Ernest Fletcher, ed., *Conversations of James Northcote, RA, with James Ward on Art and Artists* (London: Methuen, 1901), 83–4. Northcote denied this story could be true and later in the same passage insisted that 'many ladies of high rank' treated Siddons with deference.

37. Jacky Bratton, *New Readings in Theatre History* (Cambridge: Cambridge University Press, 2003), 37–8.

38. Peter Wagner, ed., *Icons-Texts-Iconotexts: Essays on Ekphrasis and Intermediality* (Berlin and New York: Walter de Gruyter, 1996). See also Tracy Davis and Thomas Postlewait, eds, *Theatricality* (Cambridge: Cambridge University Press, 2003), 26–7: 'Given the visual emphasis of performance art, it would seem to be tailor-made for semiotic analysis, but it often resists any such system of coded explanation.'

39. Edgar Wind, *Hume and the Heroic Portrait*, ed. Jaynie Anderson (Oxford: Clarendon Press, 1986). Wind distinguished between Reynolds's and Gainsborough's qualities as follows: 'An exponent of the artificially elevated style will favour theatrical gesture because he sees the exceptional moment in a person's life as decisive; an exponent of the natural style will reject theatrical gesture because he does not want to estrange man from his everyday existence' (22).

40. Bate's words are quoted without attribution of the source in William Whitley, *Thomas Gainsborough* (London: John Murray, 1915), 236.

41. Lennep, *Reminiscences of Siddons*, 19.

42. See George Williams Fulcher, *The Life of Thomas Gainsborough* (London: Longman, Brown, Green & Longmans, 1856), 133.

43. Robyn Asleson, *A Passion for Performance: Mrs. Siddons and her Portraitists* (Los Angeles: J. Paul Getty Museum 1999), 80.

44. For Lavater's private collection of portraits and silhouettes, see Gerda Mraz and Uwe Schoegl, eds, *Das Kunstkabinett des Johann Caspar Lavater* (Vienna: Boehlau Verlag, 1999).

45. For Hogarth's views on physiognomy, see Ronald Paulson, ed., *Hogarth's Analysis of Beauty* (New Haven and London: Yale University Press, 1997), 95–6. See also John Clubbe, *Physiognomy* (London: R. and J. Dodsley, 1763).

46. Quoted in James Boaden, *Memoirs of Mrs. Inchbald*, 2 vols (London: Richard Bentley, 1833), 1: 2.

47. Boaden, *Siddons*, 1:287.

48. Lawrence Sterne, *The Life and Opinions of Tristram Shandy* (Harmondsworth: Penguin, 1985), 231. For Gainsborough and Sterne, see John Hayes, ed., 'Introduction' to *The Letters of Thomas Gainsborough* (New Haven and London: Yale University Press, 2001), xx.

49. Ibid., 228. See also John Kerrigan, 'A Complete History of Comic Noses', in Michael Cordner, Peter Holland, John Kerrigan, eds, *English Comedy* (Cambridge: Cambridge University Press, 1994), 241–66.

50. See, for example, Stephen Gwynn, *Memorials of an Eighteenth Century Painter (James Northcote)* (London: T. Fisher Unwin, 1898), 85.

51. Gainsborough to Garrick 22 August 1768 in Hayes, *Letters of Gainsborough*, 60. Gainsborough's correspondence with Garrick at this time related to an ideal portrait of Shakespeare that Gainsborough was preparing for the Stratford Jubilee but which was never used in that event. For the history of this painting of Shakespeare, see Martin Postle, 'Gainsborough's "lost" Picture of Shakespeare: "A little out of the simple portrait way"', *Apollo*, 124 (1991): 374–79.
52. For discussions of the sources of the Shakespeare sculpture and the pose of the painting, see Ian McIntyre, *Garrick* (London: Allen Lane, 1999), 413–14; Michael Rosenthal, *The Art of Thomas Gainsborough: 'a little business for the Eye'* (New Haven and London: Yale University Press, 1999), 39–40; and Susan Sloman, *Gainsborough in Bath* (New Haven and London: Yale University Press, 2002), 234.
53. McIntyre, *Garrick*, 430.
54. Letter from Gainsborough to Garrick of [1772] in Hayes, *Letters of Gainsborough*, 107–8. Gainsborough also gave advice to John Henderson (letter of 18 July 1773 in Ibid., 118).
55. George Alexander Stevens, *A Lecture on Heads … to which is added an Essay on Satire* (London: G. Kearsley, 1785).
56. The *Public Advertiser* article is quoted in Whitley, *Gainsborough*, 45.
57. Crary, *Techniques of the Observer*, 19.
58. W. J. T. Mitchell, *Iconology: Image, Text, Ideology,* (Chicago and London: University of Chicago Press, 1986), 13–14.
59. See Peter Holland's essay in this volume.
60. See Marvin Carlson's conception of how different viewing communities for theatre create different kinds of reception. Marvin Carlson, 'Theatre Audiences and the Reading of Performance', in Thomas Postlewait and Bruce McConachie, eds, *Interpreting the Theatrical Past: Essays in the Historiography of Performance* (Iowa City: University of Iowa Press, 1989), 82–98.

Index